BEST BOATS

to build or buy

BEST BOATS

to build or buy

FERENC MATÉ

ALBATROSS PUBLISHING HOUSE

West Vancouver BC Canada

OTHER BOOKS BY FERENC MATÉ

From a Bare Hull
The Finely Fitted Yacht
Waterhouses
Behind the Waterfall - a novel

Design and Layout - Candace Maté and Abbie Vechter

First printing 1982. Second printing 1983.
ISBN 0-920256-06-6

Published by Albatross Publishing House
West Vancouver, B.C., Canada

DISTRIBUTED IN THE UNITED STATES
BY W. W. NORTON, 500 FIFTH AVE., NEW YORK

For all those who respect and love the sea.

Contents

Introduction

Why This Book

It all began one day when I wandered down to the docks of a large yacht club, and found, to my amazement, that I could barely differentiate among the hundreds of dull boats bobbing there, as if all had been designed and built and bought by the same person; and I remembered back fifteen years when a visit to the same place brought on endless hours of looking at one masterpiece after another, and not even a dozen visits would have been enough to get my fill.

But this time it was different. There were few things to stop at and still fewer to admire, and there was little evidence that anyone with any heart or soul had ever been near any of these craft, either at their conception or during the days since.

I decided then to go and search out the builders who still built the good boats — fine boats in small yards, one boat at a time, — independent boat-builders who just build boats for a living, unlike some conglomerates whose absentee owners also build apartments and make soap.

This is not to say that all large boatyards build bad, heartless boats, for yards like Hinckley and Nautor build some of the finest in the world, but I wanted semi-custom yards where the boat owner can have some say in what he gets, or if he chooses, take a hull and deck and turn them into a fine yacht on his own.

That was how the book started out — as a survey of the best boats in the land — and that's all I expected to find during my travels, for little did I know that I would come across fine and gentle men, both builders and designers, to whom sailing was not just sets of lines and keels and shrouds, but a heartfelt feeling around which a thoughtful life was woven.

And I was reminded then just how much sailing meant to me, reminded enough to put it down in words, and for that I hope you won't think me indulgent.

For this rekindling of old feelings I thank Lyle Hess and Cecil Lange and John Letcher and Sam Morse, and Tom Morris and the whole Cherubini family, and all those others whose craftsmanship and goodwill is so great, and dedication so honest and complete, that when you have the good luck to get a boat of their creation you will get a part of their fine spirit to take with you.

Why These Boats

These boats were not chosen through surveys or sales figures or opinion polls; they are simply the prettiest, most interesting and most honestly functional I could find, and most importantly they are boats built with integrity and conscience and care.

Some of the designs are from the drawing boards of the famous, others are by virtual unknowns, and I used fame as a measuring stick only on three racers — the Peterson, the Frers and the Santa Cruz — and since these are the boats that win the silver, I thought it only fitting.

As for the cruising boats and the cruiser-racers, they were initially chosen at first sight. The less beautiful and less sincere ones fell quickly by the way, then on closer inspection a lot more bit the dust, while even more were dropped for marginal engineering or construction or both. Then there were a few that died at the final stage, when I questioned the attitude of the builders, for I just couldn't believe that someone with bad intentions could actually build a good boat.

I did try my best to contact as many semi-custom builders as I could find. Over 200 letters went out at the start, followed by phone calls and round-about queries; and when I received no reply, or, as in some cases, no returned call after numerous of my own, I dismissed the people as unreliable, for if they did not take time to respond to a modest request, I dread to think what kind of frustration the owners and especially owner-builders of their boats would undergo when they needed help. A sailboat is not sliced salami that, once out of the store, can be completely forgotten.

While on the subject of owner-builders, I should emphasize that all boats whose builders could not provide at least some parts and *all* basic plans and measurements required for completion, were also left out. As an example, when one builder was asked what advice he gave to owners about chainplate installation, his response was a shrug and a curt, "They do what they think best." I did what I thought best: I left.

So after all that, there were a few boats left, and I chose them so as to try and avoid repetition, although I still ended up with too many double-enders between 32 and 38 feet — but I just couldn't help myself. I tried to balance these with light fin-

keelers like Naja and Raider and Sceptre and the racers and Bill Lee's featherweight Santa Cruz boats. When I came across Chuck Paine's cat-ketch centreboarder, and John Letcher's twin-keel Aleutka, I fell upon them with zeal, for I think it one of the most vital parts of sailing that so many people practise such varied and intelligent ideas, and I could think of few things as intriguing as coming into a harbour where no two boats are the same.

Why Build Your Own Boat

It usually comes down to the dollars. Saving money seems the obvious reason, and it's easy to talk about, easy for all to understand, much easier than trying to describe the joy and the pride and the satisfaction, and the feeling that what you're doing day to day actually makes sense and will result in something reasonable and beautiful in the end.

So, first the money. You can, through simple figuring, get a notion of how much you'll save if you understand that any boatyard will charge you at least twenty dollars per hour of labour, and if you multiply that by the number of hours involved you will quickly come up with a total sum. Now of course you will not be able to do most jobs as fast as a boatyard can, but you will soon learn to come close, and, anyway, the hours you put in usually don't reflect a true comparison because the care you'll take will normally be greater and the quality of your work usually better than a yard's. But back to the money.

Say you save 1,000 boatyard hours on a given boat, (a rough average of hours required to nicely finish off a 30 footer from a bare hull and deck) then your saving on labour alone can be $20,000.00. If you earn money through legal means, you can tack on the 30% income tax you would have had to pay were you to just hand over the $20,000.00 to a yard, and so the total quickly jumps to nearly $27,000.00 — just for labour alone. Now, through co-ops and odd deals you can usually save a substantial sum on hardware and materials — while the builder would otherwise charge you retail — so with little effort you can save another

$3,000.00, or with a lot of effort probably another $8,000.00, and right away your savings jump to between $30,000.00 and $35,000.00.

However initially bedazzling this sum may seem, remember one thing: you are going to earn every single penny that you save, with the hardest, most frustrating, most thought-demanding damned labour you have ever done, and there will be times when you'll be begging your mate to let go of your arms because you're going to chain saw the whole son of a bitch in half right there; but there will also be times when you'll sit with a stupified smile on your face wondering in true amazement how God could have created such a skilled pair of hands and such a dazzlingly quick mind as yours.

So, sometimes it will be hell and sometimes just plain heaven, and often all the places in between, but generally you'll make it through. And if you're lucky you'll feel like the man who with his lady completed a 35 foot cutter with teak decks and an all wood interior, and looking back on it all said, "Many times we staggered from depression, and sometimes things were so bad we were in tears, but overall I have to say it was by far the best two years of my life."

BEST BOATS

to build or buy

FERENC MATÉ

1

To Soothe the Soul
Rowing Boats

We seem to have evolved into a most peculiar species. We spend much of our lives fending off, fighting and conquering nature, as if she were some wicked alien curse whose presence we should rid ourselves of — the sooner the better. We talk of her as we talk of a fierce enemy who has such threatening weapons as "deadly jungles, and savage seas, and killer mountains," all of which she might unleash on us at unexpected times and unexpected places, treacherous, cunning villain that she is; forgetting all the while that it is our own lack of respect and limitless greed that got us poor stupids into trouble in the first place.

We don't just fight her for our survival, we fight her for our pleasure. We make idols of men who defy her, and challenge her, and bring her to her knees, and when that's done we make idols of those who can defy and challenge and humiliate her even faster. Our heroes have a glazed look of victory in their eyes, and numbers that they have just conquered reeling in their minds and, on their lips, phrases like those of Edmund Hillary's, whose most unforgettable words after climbing atop Everest were, "Well, we finally knocked off the bugger."

Men like these are our heroes, for they tame and conquer the savage wilderness, which now seems a desirable deed, but I wonder if in a few years hence we won't think their conquests just as thoughtless and offensive as we now consider Pizarro's "taming" of the Incas. And while we celebrate our new *conquistadors* loudly, we forget or think eccentric those who walk gently and silently in forests, or sit on the edge of a tidal pool and ponder its mysteries, along with all the thoughtful gazers of the stars and all who sit with eyes closed and listen to the wind.

We undertake long journeys to exotic places without knowing the magic of our own seashores and streams, and we want to touch a star a million miles away when in all our years we haven't really touched a leaf.

A peculiar species indeed, to say the least.

But there are those among us who try to understand; strangely enough it's either the very young or the very old, who spend long hours at peaceful contemplation, in gardens or seashores, on footpaths or in rowboats, humbly drifting and drinking in the beauty before them.

A rowboat is one of the last true magic carpets,

that will take you to places where nothing else can, into backwaters and marshes and up long winding streams so narrow that the trees on each side lean over and touch. And it will take you into green lagoons where the sun warms the shoal waters, and into sea caves where pirates' laughter echoes from the walls, and to the shores of rocky islets where the magic is so rich it would take you a thousand years to find and see it all.

Maybe we should all just have rowboats, with a picnic basket full of all the best, and a bright umbrella for when the sun begins to blaze, and maybe a small square sail to hoist upon an oar when the wind is behind us. Maybe that's all we need for happiness and not the great floating barns that clutter up the seashore, empty our pocketbooks and fill our minds with worry. Maybe a rowboat is all we can keep with proper care, maybe the only thing that we can find time to enjoy.

And there is nothing to compare with a few hours of pulling oars to open the lungs and get the heart kicking and the blood flowing and get colour back into ghostly cheeks.

If things were as they should be, we would all be in our boatsheds or our gardens, bending frames and planing down planks for a fine small pulling boat, and varnishing her up just so, and taking her on the finest outings of our lives; but too many of us don't have gardens, much less boatsheds, and even worse, we are too disordered to ever find the time. So perhaps the next best thing is a small finished shell that would be more demanding of care than time to finely finish and take to sea or pond.

The number of good pulling boats around us is mercifully large and it would be unfair to single out some and leave others out, so the best thing to do is to undertake your own search down on the waterfront or other places where sailors and fishermen gather, and without doubt you will find a dozen boats you like and once you find the boat, finding a builder won't be hard. The boats that I put in here I stumbled on, and they looked good to my eye, but I am sure they are not unique in any peculiar way

any more than those of other dinghy builders and canoe builders and kayak builders, and you would do well to find your own in your own neck of the woods.

To try to truly discuss the best of pulling boats would take many volumes, and indeed some fine ones have been written, from J. MacGregor's, *Cruises in Rob Roy* during the middle of the last century, to the many specialized works on kayaks, canoes and sculling shells.

The Kayak

Kayaks were, as most fine things, a simple invention to fill a need, this time in cold Arctic waters. They were first made by Eskimos using materials that floated to them in the sea — driftwood from forests far away and bones of whales that they hunted for their food.

The shapes had to be simple and long with few and gentle curves, for they had no tools to steam or laminate with, and the result was a fine little craft, light in weight and easy to build. The pieces were tied together with dried gut or hide, and the framework covered over with skin and sewn in place. The opening left was but a small part of the craft, most of the top being covered by the skins, and what opening there was, was covered up by the hunter's skin coat, the bottom of which was laced to the kayak around the opening to keep out water even if a capsize should occur. The lightness of the craft made it easy to transport over land, and modern kayaks of fibreglass have been kept even lighter, some under 20 pounds, which makes them child's play to maneuver, but rather temperamental in chop, currents, or rough water. For long trips on a broad body of water, there is simply no better craft than a kayak, for it moves swiftly and easily, is simple to balance and a joy to paddle. First, it moves well, for it has a flat smooth bottom, minimal wetted surface, and most importantly, much less weight than other small craft like rowboats or canoes. This lack of weight coupled with its length enables the body of a kayak to be narrow and shallow, opening up all but the meagerest puddles for exploration. The above does create the obvious disadvantage of a lack of stability, and quite significantly, the first thing you are taught upon lowering yourself into a kayak is how to recover from a capsize; but fear not, for although capsizes will inevitably occur, in most cases a semi-experienced kayakist will be able to prevent a capsize by quick and intelligent use of the paddle, which can actually be looked upon as momentary outrigger.

The greatest advantage of a kayak over a rowing boat (that being a boat with oarlocks and oars as opposed to canoes and kayaks which have paddles) is that you will be facing forward on your voyage, not only able to perceive and avoid hazards in your path, but also to have the great pleasure of seeing the scenery unfold before you, which somehow feels much more natural than seeing someplace after you have left it. Rowing with your back to your destination adds much length to a voyage, or worse, deprives you of seeing all the wonders, for you will discover things of interest only in time to sidetrack or backtrack, or worse to shrug them off and leave them for some other day, which sadly enough, too often never comes.

The other most important advantage of a kayak is that it can be maneuvered in complete silence with the least distraction, without the clattering of oars and oarlocks, or even the shifting of hands and paddle necessary to the operation of a canoe. With a two-person kayak the perfection of this art reaches even greater heights, especially to the beholder, for there are few things as beautiful as the sight of mirrorlike water upon which glides a long, fine kayak, being propelled in perfect unison by sets of paddles that gently slice the air, with the movement of the aft one mirroring the movement of the one forward. It reminds one of the grace of pelicans in synchronized flight or a *pas de deux* in perfect harmony.

One of the most sophisticated things about some two-man kayaks is that one does not need to worry about which side to pull how hard for steering, for they are fitted with a foot operated rudder that turns the kayak splendidly without interrupting the rhythm of the paddles.

Kayaks now come in a myriad of forms, using either fibreglass or cold moulded plywood, and of course canvas, which makes for clever collapsible affairs, whose only major flaw is that they lack the positive flotation that fibreglass and cold moulded kayaks afford. Less than an hour after I wrote this a friend rowed by and we talked about kayaks and he brilliantly suggested that a canvas kayak can be made as safe as its modern counterparts by simply stuffing an inner tube under the aft and foredecks

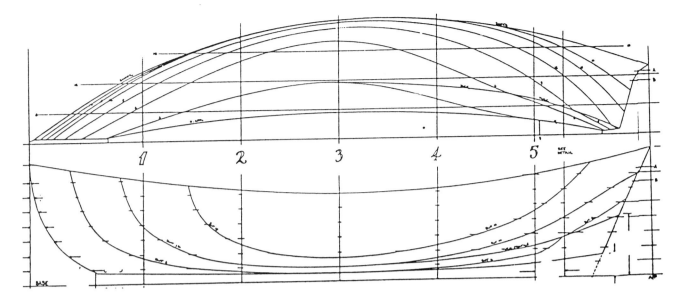

The J. R. Griffin Lincolnville Wherry.

The 14 foot Lincolnville Salmon Wherry coasting at Duck Trap. One of the few magical wood boats still being built on this continent, with oak framing, native cedar planking, oak plank keel and mahogany trim. She is a clench built rowing/sailing boat whose history goes back to the gillnetters of Penobscot Bay. Her builder, Mr. Walter J. Simmons of Lincolnville Beach, Maine, can be one very proud man. His two volume book Lapstrake Boatbuilding *should be read by all would-be wood boat builders.*

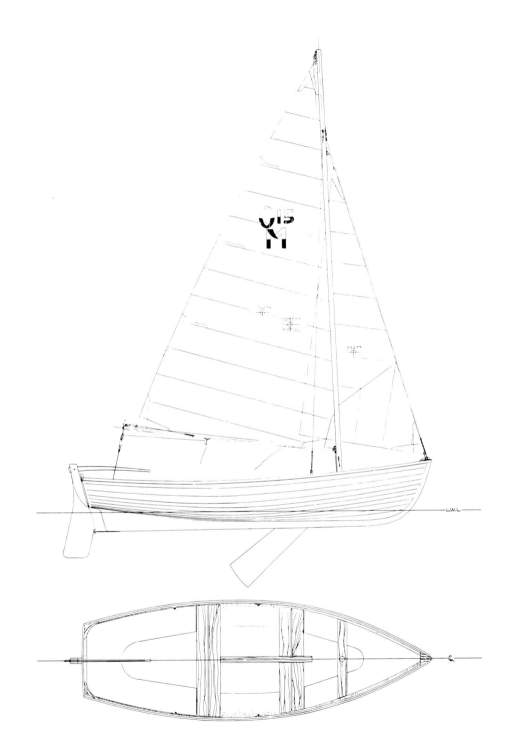

Vashon Boatworks Quarter Master 15.

The Quartermaster 8, a good tender for a large yacht, with much beam to carry a goodly load and a handy 44 square foot sail for harbour sailing.

The Quarter Master 8 footer handily carries a bunch of little people or three big ones.

and inflating it partially after the craft is assembled. That is the good news, but the news that also came to mind is that first a canvas kayak is infinitely more vulnerable to punctures than a hard one, and second it will not go through the water nearly as well as a solid bottomed one, since the canvas will be collapsed by the pressure of the water between the pieces of the framework, resulting in a waffle, which has never been considered a decent bottom surface for any yacht.

The major disadvantage of a kayak is its lack of ability to carry a sizeable payload, but if things are nicely divided up in watertight bags, then sufficient gear for camping out can easily be accommodated, even though one will have to be rather more organized when packing and stowing than one would be in an open rowboat or canoe.

Canoes

For living near the water, where objects of various sizes will often need to be hauled in a small boat without assistance of an outboard, and extended journeys requiring substantial supplies will be undertaken in same, the canoe seems to be the best choice. A canoe is normally a rugged vessel of ample beam of up to 3 feet, to give you good initial stability, and good load carrying capacity. The history of canoes is coupled tightly with the history of North America, and to begin to go into it here would be a pretension, so let us go back far enough only to mention that the development of the aluminum canoes has probably done as much for canoeing as the advent of fibreglass did for kayaking. Without doubt the aluminum canoes are the most maintenance-free and durable, but also the least pretty of the lot. For once I would opt for a not so pretty version, for if a canoe is to be used to its utmost ability, then one should not feel reluctant to venture into rocky creeks or onto gravel beaches where without doubt one will be making contact with hard objects while landing or dragging the boat ashore. To subject a lovely cedar canoe, or a shiny fibreglass one, to this fate would be a bit callous, and even though fibreglass can be easily repaired, the sensible canoeist will probably use an aluminum canoe when roughing it, and save a beautifully varnished cedar one for pleasant Sunday rides, when unfortunately he will be easily passed by the fleet-footed kayaks.

Rowboats

For those of us who think of small boats in conjunction with using them as tenders for large sailing craft, the rowboat or dinghy is still pretty much our only choice. If improperly designed, these little buggers will as soon travel sideways as ahead; but with a bit of a keel for directional stability, and finely drawn fair lines, a good little rowboat will go like a bat out of hell. It will never attain the speed, much less the grace, of a sleek kayak, but it *will* carry a decent load, and most importantly, it's the only small boat that can be stowed aboard with the least interference to the operation of the yacht. Now I know many will argue that a kayak can be lashed to the lifelines, or that a canoe can be towed astern, but both of these solutions are most unseamanly, for a kayak on deck will greatly impede traffic, while a large canoe in tow will greatly slow the boat's progress. A large dinghy can, of course, do both of these things with little effort, so one should choose his tender with utter care.

I will purposely avoid inflatables, because although they are without doubt the most ideal of any rowing craft to stow, they are not really a rowing craft, for in any chop or wind they are all over the ocean like a beach ball and even in moderate conditions become difficult to manage. All that said, I must add that for boats under about 28 feet this seems to be the lesser of two evils, the other being a stowage problem which can be so acute as to make sail handling on board a calamitous undertaking.

So we come down to minimum size for maximum capacity and come up with a few simple facts.

A pram, which has a transom type stern and bow, gives you the greatest capacity for least length and of course least weight. It will not row as well as a boat with a nicely pointed bow, but then you can't have everything. The beamier the pram the more buoyancy she will have, hence the more people she will carry and the more stable she will be. Her initial stability will be greatly enhanced by having as flat a bottom as possible, and indeed a hull form which has near vertical topsides and a totally flat bottom is the most ideal of all.

Dimensions are of course a vital factor, and consensus and experience have it that a dinghy shorter than 6 foot 6 inches will have to be almost a

The Apprenticeshop is associated with the Maine Maritime Museum of Bath, Maine. Under the eye of masterbuilder David Foster, eight apprentices work for 18 months on a no-tuition, no-wage basis, learning what it means to build a fine small boat by hand and what it means to build it well. Lance R. Lee is the director of the Apprenticeshop; the quotes under the following photographs are from him.

square box to carry three people.

If sufficient space can be found, a dinghy similar to the Quartermaster 8 would be ideal as a tender for craft over 40 feet, for her pointed bow would make her good to row, her full 4 foot beam and broad stern sections would make her safe for two in most harbour conditions, and if rigged with a centreboard and rudder and the 44 square foot sail, she could make someone very happy during afternoon harbour sails. And with a little teak trim she can look a fine little craft.

For all round non-tender use, the Q 15 encompasses good features, such as double rowing positions, 100 square feet of sail, a good sized keel, over 5 feet of beam, which gives good capacity but will still let her move through the water, and a centreboard that hinges, which obviates the need to yank it out and put it out of the way.

One major consideration with any pulling boat has to be weight. A tender for a small sailboat will

be a bear if over 60 pounds, but by the same token a good day-sailer-cum-fishing-boat, which should be looked upon as an all weather craft, should be over 200 pounds and long of waterline to be seaworthy, otherwise she will bounce around like a cork, impeding progress as well as enjoyment.

A few notes about the construction of fibreglass rowboats. First, they should be laid up by hand using fibreglass cloth only to achieve the best strength-to-weight ratio. A choppergun dinghy will be heavier than hell if it's to be strong, or if it's light it will be so weak that the first nimrod who steps into it on the beach will be wearing it around his ankles.

Second, fibreglass is mush compared to rocks or even gravel, so a sacrificial wood skid should be attached at least to the keel and preferably added along the bilges as well. Some people advocate putting half-round metal on top of the wood skid and this is fine for boats not used as tenders, but it's

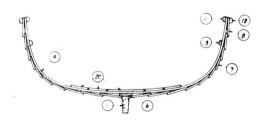

The Apprenticeshop's Washington County Peapod.

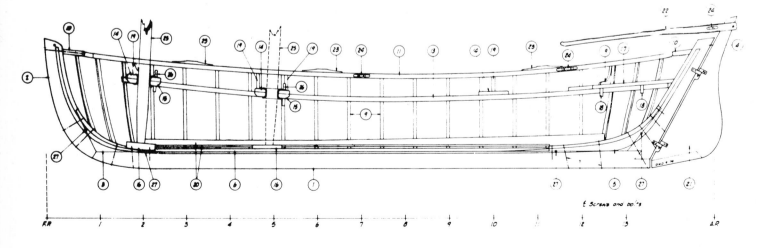

"Something has been lost—something in the inner beast of the craftsman has become perfunctory and the loss is the quality within the person rather than the building."

"Kids 50 years ago were information-poor and experience-rich. They worked on the farm, or with their fathers as fishermen, they mended nets and hauled traps. Now they're information-rich and experience-poor. As Justice Douglas put it, 'Our culture turns out doctors of philosophy but no philosophers.' It is sad."

rather daring if they are, for inevitably the metal edge or the screws that hold it, will take a neat little bite out of caprails or house tops as the dinghy is lifted aboard or shifted about.

Built-in flotation is a must. The best kind runs fore and aft either side of the bilges, thereby not taking up the most valuable stowage space in the bow and stern, where some builders unfortunately choose to put their flotation tanks.

The topsides of yachts need protection from Kamikaze oarsmen, so pad the gunwales with 1½ inch rope. And if you don't think your topsides need protection, well mine do, so pad your dinghy in case we run into each other. If you don't take this as serious advice, I should warn you that I was quite a harpooner in a previous life.

In a small dinghy a fore and aft seat is better than a thwart, for the oarsman can slide back and forth to distribute weight, depending on who happens to be his passenger, but a sailing dinghy with a thwart is a pain to use, for there is not enough room to move around come tacking time when you are sitting on the floors.

Last but not least, the oarlocks should be attached to the oars not lashed to the dinghy, for when brought aboard oarlocks in a dinghy will clatter about and handsomely gash all available pieces of woodwork, gelcoat and shin.

Even though they will not be the ideal length for rowing, the oars should be of such size as to stow inside the dinghy, otherwise you will have to find them accommodation elsewhere, and more often than not you end up having them in the way.

That's enough of that; enjoy your pulling boat and remember as you slowly drift by sea caves and islets and sparkling, glittering marshes, that you are seeing a magical piece of the earth which can teach you as much as the loftiest mountain peak or the deepest sea.

"The reason for preserving wooden boats, is the qualities that will rub off on the craftsmen and women, not simply the nature of the boats. Getting that very elusive quality back into society is much more important than having fine wood boats."

2

The Spirit of L. Francis
The Buzzards Bay 14 Footer

"I'm sorry to say Romance is a rare thing today, and some people even laugh at it, whereas it used to be incentive to carry one through fog, calm and tempest. It even seemed to make one enjoy the hardships which occur in cruising. But a modern cruiser has to have a vessel so cluttered up with mechanical gadgets and electrical devices that the cabin no longer is fit to live in and a boat has to be served by a mechanic, whereas a sailorman in the old days could take care of everything, if he had a spark of romance in him. I suppose most modern cruisers are so unromantic in looks, that all romance is killed as you board them. Those modern cruisers, particularly the motor boats, seem to be planned to be a receptacle for the insane and perverted, whereas fifty or sixty years ago the yacht was the most beautiful thing afloat."

If you are shocked at those words you will be even more shocked to know that they were written by L. Francis Herreshoff almost thirty years ago. I tremble to think what he would say if he looked around today.

I'm forever astounded by the callousness of man, for even in conceiving objects to give us pleasure, he comes up with monstrosities that spew dust and mulch the flowers of fragile deserts and shatter the precious silence for miles around; and machines that angrily plow the water as if it were in the way, stink up the sweet air of pines and wild grasses, and rattle the occupants' ears, eyeballs and brains with insufferable noises and vibrations, that send even the poor fish scurrying to another sea. And even more frightening is that the poor deceived devils call this "getting away from it all and enjoying the great outdoors in all its natural splendour."

And dare we think of the future; for how far is the day of our greatest invention yet, the one that will eliminate the need to circumvent annoying trees and thoughtlessly placed islands, the one that will conserve great scads of energy by letting us travel in absolute straight lines, the one that the whole family can enjoy sitting side by side with Cokes in hands and truckers' hats in place, and the universally envied expression of complete emptiness on their faces, as they plunder effortlessly through forests and meadows, creeks and streams and orchards, in their unstoppable, unsinkable, Amphibian Recreational Bulldozer.

Even in the sacred realm of sailing, one of the last outposts of peace and tranquillity, they intrude and offend our eyes with their mutilated versions

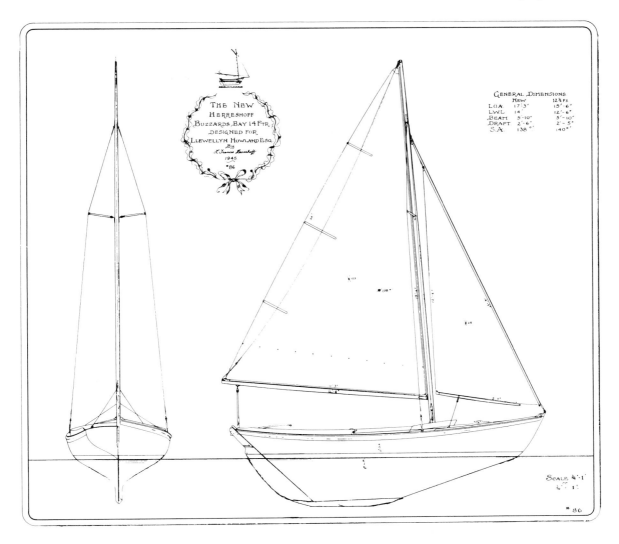

Buzzards Bay — L. Francis Herreshoff
LOA—17'3"   LWL—14'0"   Beam—5'10"   Draft—2'6"   Displ.—2,000 lbs.   Ballast—900 lbs.   Sail Area—138 sq. ft.

of beauty; with boats that are humped or slumped or tiered or deflated, boats designed by admen and hucksters and invisible investors, boats that have about as much to do with nature and the sea, as a 1957 wingtailed DeSoto. Among all that misshapen rubble, L. Francis Herreshoff's Buzzards Bay 14 Footer is a feast for the eyes.

Her bow is perky, her sheer graceful and lively, her transom refined, and her lines gentle and flowing, all are blended together in fine unity, without nervous knuckles, tucks or jags; in other words, a pure joy to behold just bobbing on her buoy. She was designed in 1945 for day sailing on Buzzards Bay, where in the words of author/publisher Roger Taylor, "The boat proved to be amazingly able in rough water, churned up by hard southwesters of the typical summer afternoon, with the steep cresting chop that inevitably results when a tide is ebbing."

If you've ever wanted a sailboat of your own — and who with even minimal sensitivity and yearning for adventure hasn't — then this would seem the proper way to begin. And for introducing young boys to the sea, teaching them not only a reverence for nature but a respect of their vessel as well, I can think of few better starting places. The boat is finished in oak, mahogany, cedar and pine and will quickly inspire any young boy to cherish and care for her. I hope you won't think me preachy for stressing this, but to me sailing in-

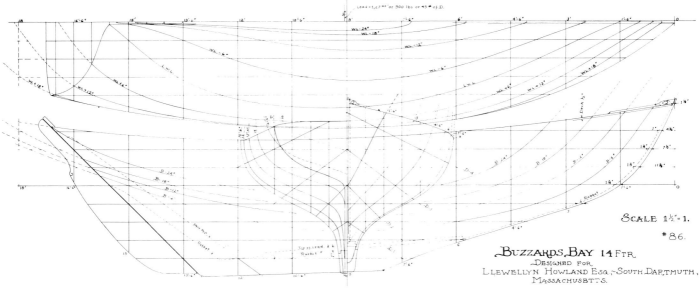

The seductively gentle lines of the Buzzards Bay 14 footer.

volves much more than just learning which line to pull, how hard and when. It is in fact one of the few true blendings of machine, nature and man, and the more complete this blending through sincerity and goodwill, the deeper and richer and truer it will be.

The Buzzards Bay is no knockabout dinghy. She's 17 feet 3 inches on deck, 14 feet even on the waterline, and she carries 900 pounds of internal lead ballast. She has been seen in good winds with a crew of six sailing in fine comfort, and with a little ingenuity and a few simple pieces, the cockpit seats can convert to a very comfortable double berth. An awning can be fabricated to fit snugly over the boom, converting the entire boat to a comfortable floating tent. If you smile, shake your head and think me naive for suggesting this, then allow me to tell you the following. Candace and I have spent time in innumerable anchorages, have seen thousands of fine sailing boats, one bigger and shinier and faster than the next, complete with cosy salons, covered cockpits, compressors that cooled, furnaces that heated, foredecks and aft-decks easily large enough for a good game of croquet, and although exposed to these creations of floating opulence I have felt truly jealous only twice. Once was in our favourite little anchorage that is surrounded by green fields and arbutus trees, when a little plywood sailboat that was only inches over 20 feet, tacked up into the cove and an-

chored a few boat-lengths from us. It was a simply built little boat, with a green hull and long cockpit, and a tiny cabin painted white, and its two hatches sparkling with varnish, and aboard her were a mother and father and two young sons who waved to us gently and spoke to each other in soft tones with deep respect for the evening silence. They set up a small camping stove in the cockpit and the boys cleaned two small cod on the deck, and in a few minutes the smell of the best fish chowder I've ever smelled drifted down toward us. After dinner the two boys went for a row and they rowed by us and even when they were alone they spoke softly. When they got back they all huddled in their cockpit as the evening darkened, and for a long time I heard only one voice; somebody aboard was telling a story.

The second time was up north in Desolation Sound when an old open 6 metre, anchored by the mouth of a creek in the inlet, and a man in his mid-twenties and a tall woman about the same, rowed out to the rocks in a little inflatable, picked oysters and barbecued them in the shell over an open fire. Later they rolled out their sleeping bags in the open boat and lay down for the night. I was down below in a big comfortable berth, protected from the dew and the night air coming down the mountain, and through the open portlight I heard them laughing and talking about the stars.

And both times I felt jealous of how close they

The Buzzards Bay 14 footer (on the waterline) was designed by L. Francis Herreshoff 37 years ago. She's an able seaboat and an extremely eye-pleasing day sailer and a worthy first project for anyone wanting to finish off a fine yacht.

were to nature, and how close nature had brought them to each other, and both times I felt like an old man shut up in a big floating barn. Cruising can and should be simple, because the simpler it is the more time you can spend looking and thinking and learning, and the less time you have to spend being a janitor to your wares.

The Buzzards Bay can be an ideal little cruiser and a source of pride, especially if one allows himself the enjoyment of finishing her off and fitting her out.

Mike Bolton, who has the eyes and the hands and the passion of a boatbuilder, and thrives on quality, builds the hull and two small deck sections in what is mostly a one-man boatyard, in Richmond, British Columbia. The hull is hand-laid-up, perfectly wetted and perfectly squeegeed. He built the plug himself, and the mould himself, and he built it so well and finished it so well that he didn't even use mould-release when he laid up the first hull, and yet it slipped out of the mould like silk. The hull is not flimsy or light. It is laid up as follows: Gelcoat, 1 ounce skin, 1½ ounce mat, 18 ounce roving, 1½ ounce mat. That is from the flange to the waterline, at which point he adds one unit of 1½ ounce mat and 18 ounce roving, plus one unit of 1½ mat and 18 ounce roving from the curve of the keel down. The two hull halves are then joined with a 2 inch wide unit, then a 4 inch wide unit, then a 6 inch, then an 8 inch, then 10 inch wide units.

The transom is then reenforced with an additional unit of mat and cloth, then ½ inch plywood then sealed with a last unit of mat and cloth.

The foredeck and aft-deck are reenforced with balsa and fitted and internally bonded to the hull. The foredeck has a 2 inch high coaming base moulded in, so that fitting to it the ½ inch oak coaming, which averages about 6 inches in height, will pose no great difficulties. The only bonding other than the decks to hull, will involve the two main bulkheads and three minor bulkheads (the latter below the sole) and small sets of knees to support the wide fore-and-aft seats. This much glassing would be an ideal first project for any novice builder, for the work is on a small scale indeed and all individual bonds can be kept small so that it would be all but impossible to create "one giant mess."

The amount and type of woodwork required for the Buzzards Bay would again serve as good introduction for the novice builder, since many little tasks will be encountered like *laminating* three layers of ½ inch plywood for the carlings, (the curved pieces that support the side-decks and to which the mahogany coaming is attached), *bonding* the ½ inch mahogany coamings into place and tapering them to fit, *shaping* the rudder out of white oak, and even a bit of *carving* on the tiller. There will also be some pattern cutting and scribing of seats, knees and bulkheads, all excellent basic training, and all small enough so as not to prove overwhelming. If Mike Bolton's plans are followed, then a builder will gain the additional benefit of working with a variety of woods, from the very hard white oak and ash, to the extremely soft red cedar. The breakdown of the woods used goes something like this: Oak — rudder, tiller, cockpit coamings. Mahogany — transom, interior, sheer strake, cockpit seats, aft side-decks, and covering boards. Red cedar — facing on bulkheads. Sugar pine — cockpit sole.

A fine feel for varnishing will be developed as well, for all the above should be coated with no fewer than six coats. The rig is left as Herreshoff first drew it, with single shrouds and no backstay, except if you choose you can have an aluminum mast, or if you're more daring you can make your own out of spruce. The sail area is 138 square feet which would make her manageable and not easily overwhelmed. The mast can be stepped by one person by attaching the shrouds, pinning the mast foot into the base, and hauling up on the forestay.

In all, I see the Buzzards Bay as a perfect little cruising sloop, that has good accessible dry stowage in lockable compartments fore and aft, is easily trailerable, and will ride well with ample ballast, giving you perfect access to quiet lakes, backwaters, or the open sea. She will be a boat that shows your pride, in craftsmanship and sailing, and best of all you'll have the spirit of L. Francis sailing along with you.

The Buzzards Bay is easily trailerable, opening up many remote lakes and distant bays.

3

Puddle Ducks
The Marshall Catboats

On the shoaling shores of Padnaram Harbour, among speckles of sunshine and rampaging lilac bushes and cherry blossoms that like the late spring so much they just refuse to go, is the sleepy town of South Dartmouth, Massachusetts, with small trim houses of weathered shakes, cared for and loved, for over a century, and still as sturdy and upright as the day they were crafted, as upright as the tombstones under the great horse chestnuts of the cemetery where farmers lie and codmen lie and boatmen lie and watch over their families from the hill.

And below on the flat waters the flat cat boats lie at their moorings much as they have done for nearly two centuries, when they awaited their crew of a man and a boy to nudge them out into the mist toward Buzzards Bay, and Martha's Vineyard, and Nantucket, in search of mackerel and cod, and bluefish, and swordfish, or scallops to be dredged up from the bottom of soft sand.

They were silent, tough and self-sufficient men, and they had to be to take what these waters dished out year round, and they worked their gear and boats with the care that they demanded, for care was what kept them alive on the cold seas.

The cat boats were built by men who eyed the curves and felt the lines, and whittled half hulls out of chunks of pine.

There was Manuel Swartz, born in Martha's Vineyard over a hundred years ago, who built two hundred cats, and G. Frank Carter, who built a hundred and fifty, and C. C. Henley, born in Maine, and Manley and Joseph Crosby, and "Stormy" John Dexter, and a man called Nat Herreshoff, who, his son L. Francis says, drew and laid out a 20 foot cat at the age of twelve in 1859, and it was built for his blind brother John in 1860, who named it *Sprite*, and *Sprite* went on a maiden voyage to New York and clipped off a hundred and seventy-five miles in twenty-eight hours. The Herreshoffs built nearly thirty cats from then to 1900 and *Sprite* is still alive in their museum, the oldest cat

What a perfect name for a 22 foot cat that draws only 24 inches with her board up. If you look closely you can see that the whole aft part of the house can be opened up to join the cockpit and belowdecks. If the large hatch were open as well, the effect would be even more interesting.

boat to hang on to her planks.

No one knows when cat boats really started, but L. Francis speculates, as he loves to do, in his book *The Compleat Cruiser*, that, "The cat boat originated at The Point (a neck of land off Newport now called Long Wharf) in colonial times . . . It seems there was a colony of boat builders there in early times, and when Newport became a summer resort these boats were much in demand for sailing parties. The Point boats were also used for fishing and shooting, for in those days there were many ducks in the bay. Most every harbour in the bay had one or two of these Point boats, so that even before 1800 there were races at Newport for this type of boat."

Howard Chapelle thought this to be conjecture, for there was no written proof of their history before 1850 when they seemed to spread all over lower New England. *Una*, a 16 foot cat built in 1852 is an exception, for she was commissioned by the Marquis of Conyngham, who, fortunately for maritime history, kept a fine record of a rather uneventful life.

The boats became famous as the racing sandbaggers for over five decades, and by the turn of the century they were great traditions, pitting local fishermen in their work boats against the holidaying dandies, until the dandies started throwing bagfuls of money at their craft, which then sailed so fast they killed the local boats, and in one fell swoop killed off the races for good.

But cat boats lived on, both as work boats and play boats and some old timers say they were still working up to the second big war.

They are a heritage in New England, an embodiment of the past when the simple things of work blended with the simple joys of leisure; so the cat boats lived on, beloved and cherished and respected by all who sailed.

Most of them were tough and stable boats with a beam that was usually half their length, and with ample sail and a boom so long that it trailed somewhere behind you like the tail of a kite, they virtually skimmed over the bays, most of them drawing less than two feet with their boards up. And with the boards up they had access to river mouths and quiet bays, grounds unattainable for longer-legged keel boats.

With their breadth they had tremendous volume for their length, both below and topsides,

where four could sit comfortably side-by-side on the high side of a tacking 18 foot cat — so they carried great payloads, then later great playloads, and were a joy to all who sailed them.

But with the large sail you must be careful and you must reef in time; as Stan Greyson wrote in the *Nautical Quarterly* a few years back, "When the word *reef* comes into the helmsman's head, it is time to take action."

One sweet, dear lady I met in Padnaram who is in her sixties now and got her first cat boat when she was ten, broadly believes that people have problems with their cats because they can't think ahead. "They can see it blowing plain as the nose on their faces, yet up goes the damned sail and the next thing they know they are out there white knuckled hanging on for dear life. Hell! You've got to reef the little buggers before you take them out and they'll be as gentle as kittens." So there you have it. One old photo shows a cat boat with four sets of reef points, so once she starts bucking, you can become one busy little fellow. But don't panic and run now, for another photo I saw with old Breck Marshall at the helm shows *Three Cheers*, an 18 foot cat beating handily in what looks like nearing 20 knots of wind, with a single reef tied in and riding as flat and pretty as you please.

Breck Marshall did a lot to keep the cat boat tradition alive, for he was the first to build a cat boat out of fibreglass and enabled many cat lovers to have one of their own. That was back in 1962 when "Pop" Arnold designed an 18 foot cat called *Sanderling*, upon whose lines all the future Marshall cats were based: the 15 foot Sandpiper, and the larger 22 and 26 footers. *Sanderling* seemed what everybody wanted, with a nifty little cuddy cabin with two berths, a table, a stove, and a counter, and over the years 540 *Sanderlings* have been let loose to prowl the eastern shores.

The Marshall boatyard is on the water's edge in South Dartmouth at the foot of a road aptly called Shipyard Lane, not far from the Concordia yard, where the beautiful Concordia yawls were born forty-four years ago and have graced the oceans ever since.

In the little South Dartmouth yard where assorted cat boats spend the winter curled up in their cradles in tidy rows, nine people now work turning out cat boats laid up to massive specifications, the same specifications Breck Marshall

Sandpiper, a lovely 15 foot day sailer, is the smallest of the Marshall Catboats. She is available with a cuddy cabin but that spoils the curve of the varnished oak coamings.

wrote down twenty years ago when "strong and heavy" was good practice, and "stronger and heavier" was even better, but more about this later in *Construction*. The Marshall boatyard is now run by John Garfield, who has been there since 1969, and he is a gentle man to whom cat boats and South Dartmouth are his life, and he works on committees and boards to keep the town the jewel that it is.

The cat boats he builds range from the little open cockpit 15 foot Sandpiper, which can bring pride to any day sailing family, right to the 26, which has a proper cat boat beam of 11 foot 9 inches, four good berths, full standing headroom, a complete galley, and even an enclosed head; and they all have spacious cockpits with wide seats and coamings nearly a foot high that keep you comfy in any blow.

All the Marshall boats have centreboards. Some of the Cape Cod cats had fixed keels but then that defeats half the purpose of the boat. The bigger boats, the 22 and the 26, can be had with sloop rigs instead of a cat rig, but to me that seems to lose the wonderful notion of simplicity by adding a bobstay and two shrouds on the 22, and a bobstay and four shrouds on the 26, plus of course a bowsprit with its assorted pains.

If you keep the cat rig, you will have but a single line to pull and you can be happy as a lark sitting back and watching the scenery or fair maidens. Winfield Thomson said it better in a 1908 *Rudder*: "Bowsprit and jib do not belong to the cat boat . . . The bowsprit is always an excrescence, a false note appended to what had been a harmonious whole."

And can you imagine the wild pleasure of racing a cat, holding but a single line while the other boys are yanking on backstays and sheets, dippoling and sail changing, and doing enough general nervous jumping around to give ulcers to a dead man.

Specifically, the 15 foot Sandpiper is a chunky little boat that displaces 1,050 pounds, has a beam of 7 foot 1 inch, and a draft with board up of a scant 1 foot 6 inches, and with the board down of 3 feet 9 inches. Her sail area is an enjoyable but ample 166 square feet with two sets of reef points. She is a joy to the eye with her tapered aluminum spar and beautifully curved oak coaming (you can't steam teak because it has too much oil in it to let the

steam in) that supports no fewer than six coats of varnish. She also comes with a cuddy cabin, if you wish, but that takes away from the simple beauty of the curved open cockpit. With her shoal draft, she has become a favourite in the Bahamas as well, and I can think of few things more beautiful than sailing in clear blue waters, going anywhere you please, watching the white sand bottom going by.

The 18 foot *Sanderling* is a cat of a different colour. She maintains the beautiful lines of the Sandpiper, including that tantalizing looking barn door rudder, but she has, as I mentioned, a proper little cabin, yet still seats eight comfortably in her cockpit. Her beam is 8 foot 6 inches, which leaves out trailering without special permits (which do nothing but nip a few more dollars from your pocket, for they certainly don't make the boat any narrower or the road wider) but her draft is still under 2 feet with the board up and 4 feet 4 inches with the board down. Her sail area is up to 253 square feet. The 2,200 pound displacement gives her enough mass to cut through waves with her fine bow. A bow this fine would have been unthinkable in a cat boat of old, because a heavy wooden mast up so far forward would have made the bow plunge with a vengeance in any kind of seaway, but with light aluminum masts this problem is a thing of the past.

The high coamings here are part of the deck mould and are trimmed in teak. The side-decks are of course narrow, as you can see, but don't forget that because of their great beam, these boats sail mostly on their bottoms where they should, so walking forward would not have the treacherous connotations that one associates with boats of the "now I lay me down to sleep" category once the wind hits 15 knots. Besides, the halyard is led aft to the cockpit, and there are no headsails to change, so except for tying in the reefs you can just stay put in the cockpit and enjoy yourself. If you want to go on a nice walk where there is lots of room, move to Texas.

The *Sanderling's* cabin has decent sitting headroom belowdeck, and for working in the galley you can open the great hatch and perch comfortably on the companionway steps and cook to your heart's delight. Where else have you seen an 18 foot boat where you can sit down in the galley?

The *Sanderling* comes with either a wheel or a tiller, but why you would want to complicate this

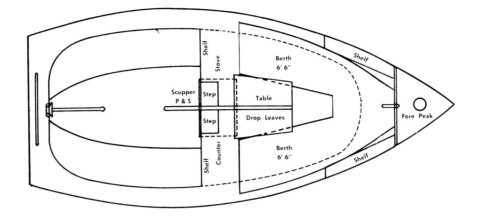

Pretty little Sanderling the 18 foot catboat with 8 foot 6 inch beam, and a cuddy cabin with a galley stove and stowage.

Sanderling 18 — "Pop" Arnold
LOA—18'2"   Beam—8'6"   Draft—19"/4'4"   Displ.—2,200 lbs.   Ballast—500 lbs.   Sail Area—253 sq. ft.

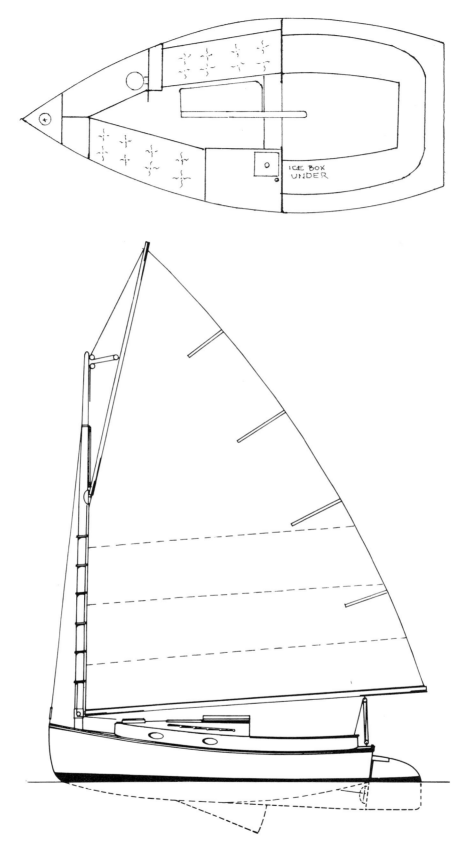

Marshall 22 — Breck Marshall

LOA—22'2"   LWL—21'4"   Beam—10'2"   Draft—2'/5'5"   Displ.—5,660 lbs.   Sail Area—388 sq. ft.

The Marshall 22 with a complete galley and head. An ideal cruiser for a couple, especially with her large cockpit.

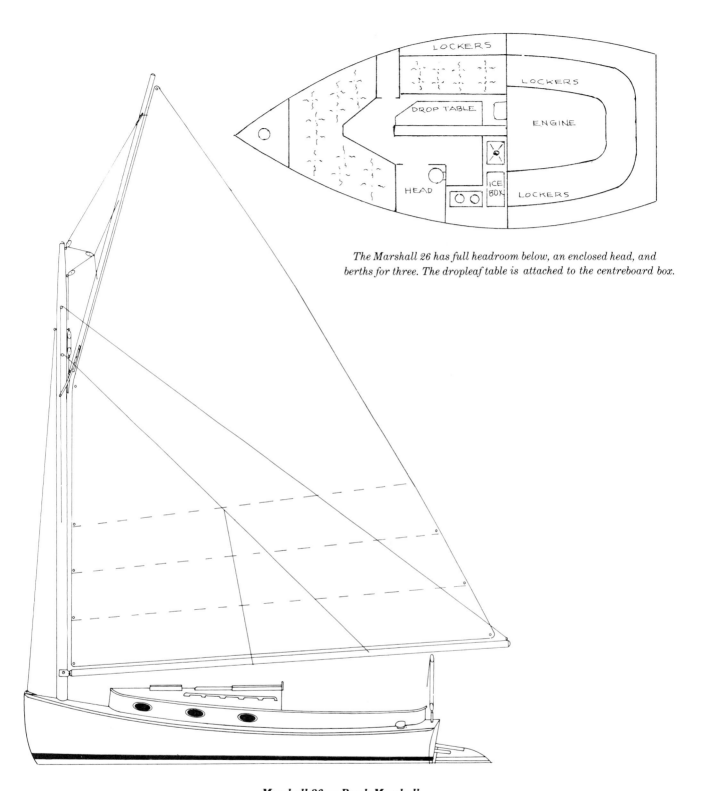

LOCKERS

LOCKERS

DROP TABLE

ENGINE

HEAD

ICE BOX

LOCKERS

The Marshall 26 has full headroom below, an enclosed head, and berths for three. The dropleaf table is attached to the centreboard box.

Marshall 26 — Breck Marshall

LOA—26'6" LWL—25'0" Beam—11'9" Draft—2'6"/5'5" Displ.—10,000 lbs. Ballast—1,200 lbs. Sail Area—540 sq. ft.

The Marshall 26 is the largest, beamiest, heaviest and roomiest of the Marshall line of catboats. With a sail her size you had better do a lot of nip-ups before you attempt to late-reef in a blow. Better yet, find a couple of Amazons and have yourself a real good time.

simple little yacht with a wheel I just don't know. The cockpit seats are open below, so there is plenty of room to hide fenders and such, and there is a good size plastic icebox, but don't forget this is wet storage, so keep rustables and soakables out of here. One *Sanderling* I saw was fitted with a single cylinder Yanmar, but this created a 12 inch high raised box in the centre of the cockpit which made the whole thing quite uncomfortable, and after all it is the spectacularly roomy cockpit that is one of the nicest points of the cat boat. But do what you like; you never listen to me anyway.

The Marshall 22 has no particular pet-name — it is simply referred to as a 22, but don't let the lack of verbal niceties fool you, for she is every bit as sweet of line as her smaller sisters. Her beam is a hefty 10 foot 2 inches, her waterline length is 21 feet 4 inches (which gives her total overhangs of 8 inches) and with a displacement of 5,660 pounds, her displacement-to-waterline-length ratio of 260, makes her a medium displacement cruiser, so she ought to move well. Her sail area of 388 square feet gives her an outstanding sail-area-to-displacement ratio of 19, so the lady was right, Elmer, if it's blowing, reef her at the dock. It will save you changing your pants later on. Her mast is nearly 30 feet long, so do forget about popping it in and

out on whim, but a couple of men can handle it fairly easily since it is only 8 inches at the base and tapers rapidly. I'll take the thin end.

The 22 has fine accommodations below, the major improvements over the 18 being the feeling of general spaciousness, a semi-private head, and enough draft below the cockpit sole to accommodate an engine without giving rise to obstructions. The cockpit sole over the engine is removable so you have good access to the engine and all sorts of light in which to tinker or repair. She has a larger cockpit than the 18, giving you two more good berths here.

Below, there is good room for a sink and a stove beside it and you can find ample galley stowage all around. There are also nifty bits of general stowage in lockers, with a sizeable water tank whose capacity remained a mystery that no one could answer after John Garfield left for the day.

Although the drawings don't show it, the starboard settee does slide out into a double, giving you a possible three and a half berths belowdeck, and the cabin is made airier than the 18 by a small opening hatch in the forward end of the house. In all, she is a truly fine little yacht.

The 26 is a fine big yacht. As I said, she has full

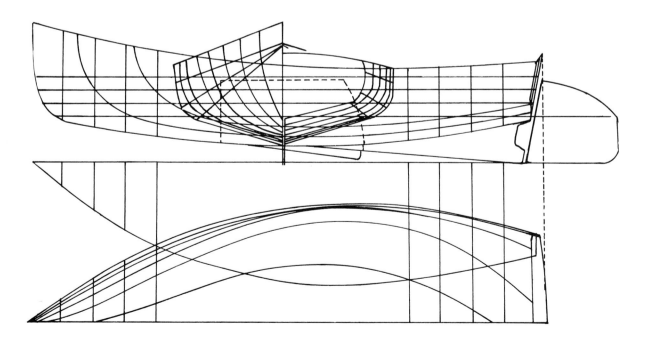

The lovely pesky lines of the Marshall catboats showing their massive beam, flat bottom and a beautiful rudder the size of a small barn door.

headroom in the galley, the enclosed head, and in the salon where there are berths for four. The galley is self-contained and includes an icebox. Her dimensions of a 25 foot waterline, 11 foot 9 inch beam, and 10,000 pound displacement, certainly lift her out of the little boat category. Her displacement-to-waterline-length ratio sneaks up to almost 300, which will give her what designer Chuck Paine calls "that comfortable, kindly motion," and her 540 square foot main is enough to make a strong man humble, maybe even humble enough to make him consider a sloop rig, which would reduce the main to 440 square feet — nothing to sneeze at but maybe just enough to avoid a hernia.

Stowage increases vastly in the 26, as does the feeling of volume, which is greatly enhanced by the opening hatch and the two large companionway doors, which in their open position can turn the entire boat, cockpit and all, into one enormous and friendly space.

The engine for this size of boat has to be substantial, at least a 2 cylinder, for which the 32 gallon tank is more than adequate, but the equal amount of water will be gone in three or four days with four people aboard.

John is totally flexible on the interiors he installs, so I won't bother trying to evaluate what is shown in the drawings. The best thing to do is to get a copy of a blueprint and play around with it until you find a layout you are really happy with.

The wheel steering in both the 22 and 26 is standard, and rightfully so, for cats can get a bit heavy on the helm and a tiller long enough to give you the power required would eliminate use of half the cockpit.

An interesting feature of all the Marshall cat boats is the ballast, which is simply laid in to the bilge in 20 pound pigs, and the explanation I was given seems acceptable enough. It was that, a)

Sanderling, the 18 foot cat, napping in the shoal end of the bay.

One look at the highly efficient interior of the Marshall 22. The centreboard box dominates the cabin but it's well used to support a hinged table, and as a base for galley counter extension.

some people prefer to trim their boats to various degrees, and b) because the boats are custom, the heavy loading of one side or the other with galley, head, equipment, as well as tankage, could necessitate retrimming. Besides, on a long tack you can shift your ballast to the high side and really surprise some of your fellow sailors.

Construction

The Marshall cat boats are built amazingly strong. Even the little 15 and 18 foot cats have two units of mat and roving in the hull, with the 18 having its bottom reenforced with another two units below the waterline. This is very good indeed and you would be hard pressed to find these kinds of specs in boats under 20 feet in length.

The 22 has three units throughout, with two more units in the bottom, while the 26 has four units throughout with the same two added in the bottom. I think that even in this book the only

specs you will find to match this in the size range is the Bristol Channel Cutter. The coring in the house tops is ⅜ inch Airex foam, but the bows (around the mast collar) are heavy solid glass. The collars around the mast actually become 2 inch thick solid glass, and don't forget that this is where the unstayed mast gets all its support.

The transom of each boat from the 18 up is re-enforced with ½ inch plywood. The deck has 1 inch high moulded bulwarks, below which the hull and deck are solidly bonded together internally with three passes of mat on the 15 and 18 footers, and four passes of mat on the 22 and 26 footers. These strips of mat are laid in as two 4 inch wide pieces, then two 8 inch wide pieces.

The centreboards are solid fibreglass, eliminating the cost and weight problems of the old bronze ones, and the rudder is likewise laid up with heavy fibreglass, and beautifully hinged on fine bronze fittings. The custom bronze hardware is truly first class in the Marshall boats, and includes portlights, chainplates, bow fitting, traveller, and even bronze steps on the rudder and the hull to serve as the simplest boarding ladder imaginable, eliminating the need to stow some cumbersome, or worse, heinous plastic abomination, in precious space. The tapered masts are very nicely extruded. The exterior teak trim is well fitted and generously heavy, especially the massive rubrail.

I almost forgot, the chainplate areas (on the sloop) are reenforced with extra layers of mat, but for some reason the washers on the chainplates are only light 1 inch diameter ones, a most unfortunate place to save money after so much fine work.

All bulkheads and shelves are well bonded in to help rigidify the hull, but I was disappointed to see exterior grade plywood used for the cabinetry. This plywood is good one side only and has knot holes on the inside, and the grain is rather coarse, so if it is painted it looks rather rough and unfriendly; perfectly fine for a work boat, but a bit lean for a yacht. What is even worse is that this grade of plywood is not marine and hence will have voids, which causes the cabinetry to end up looking messy, because as the router guide wheel runs along the edges of holes for drawers and doors as it is bullnosing, the wheel runs into the little ruts and takes a mean little bite. The end result is an opening that looks as if it were cut by a nouveau drunk. None of these boats have enough plywood in them to bring about financial devastation were a better grade of plywood used; even decent mahogany will have no knots, hence very few voids, and the improvement this would make to the boat's appearance would be very appreciable. Even if the difference of a couple of hundred dollars were passed on to the customer, I seriously doubt if anyone would mind. But again remember that these are semi-custom boats, so how you have them finished off is entirely up to you.

The exposed hull surfaces are painted over. A marked improvement could be made by using a thin malleable layer of very dense, and very elegant looking cork sheeting. Sam Morse uses this on his little Falmouth Cutter and the result is very fine indeed, and the improvement in the sound and heat insulation is substantial. The stuff is ³⁄₁₆ inch thick, comes in manageable sheets and is quite inexpensive, very easy to cut, and child's play to apply, since it bends so much that it can be fitted into place, then trimmed around with a knife, much like a rug.

The mechanical installations on the Marshall boats are very good, with full 2 inch mahogany bedlogs bonded thoroughly to the hull to act as engine supports. The engine mounts are lag bolted in place, which is good, for if the hole ever widens from vibration to the extent where the lag bolts become loose, all you have to do is pull out the bolt, fill the hole with epoxy and a dowel, then redrill and away you go. The regulation bronze seacocks are backed up with massive plates of solid ¾ inch mahogany; all hoses and wires are well led and clamped, and the centreboard box has an overflow system that drains into the cockpit for when big seas force their way up the box.

In all, the Marshall cats are wonderful little yachts that will make any owner proud, and if you think they may take a bit of learning to handle, listen to what William Lambert wrote in *Boating* in 1907:

"Every type of boat, every rig, has its peculiarities. This is particularly true of the cat boat. Her skipper needs to be her master, in fact as well as name, for she has to be managed in every sense of the word. One who receives his training in this type of craft may confidently step from her helm to that of any other fore and aft rigged boat and speedily find himself at home. But one born and bred in a sloop or schooner often finds himself at the mercy of a cat boat."

4

A Boat for Every Pocket
Flicka

I have always wondered about the kind of boats designers would design if they were told to do one for themselves. It is interesting to see that in this book three designers did just that, and what is even better, they built the boats as well — some to a greater degree than others — but the most astounding thing of all is the sizes they came up with, for Chuck Paine's *Frances,* and John Letcher's Aleutka were 25 feet long overall, and Bruce Bingham's Flicka is all of 20 feet.

You have to admire someone who practices what he preaches and Bruce Bingham did just that, for after getting Flicka he and friend Katie Burke proceeded to homestead and cruise in her for two years, including a five month winter stint. Now that's practicing.

She is a pretty boat with a 3 foot 3 inch draft that will go anywhere and she is light enough to be pushed off by hand if she goes aground, and her sails are so small that handling her is a dream, and best of all, you don't have to save for twenty years to own her. The hull of the Flicka is based on a proven old-world workboat — much as Lyle Hess' Bristol Channel Cutter was based on the Itchen ferry boats and Bill Crealock's Westsail 32 on a

Colin Archer and North Sea Pilots. Bruce Bingham's hull was drawn after the Newport boats used on Block Island Sound to tend lobster nets at the turn of the century. Now Block Island Sound is known to be the home of instant gales that come up with little warning, so the Newport boats had to be seaworthy and able to serve the lobsterman's year-round open water needs. Bruce Bingham described Flicka's (a Swedish word meaning vivacious little girl) development and his experience with her in a letter to the *Small Boat Journal*:

"I had in mind applying the Newport hull to an enclosed small cruising boat. I wanted to keep the new design within the minimum budget of an amateur builder so the hull length was reduced to 20 feet.

I thought from the first sketches that full headroom might be possible. The solution was to locate the cabin sole directly on top of the inboard ballast, and to employ a high maindeck crown, as well as an extremely high cabin crown. The latter two elements helped to keep the appearance of the cabin side height to a minimum. In practice we found both the deck and the cabin top quite comfortable to walk around on, particularly when the

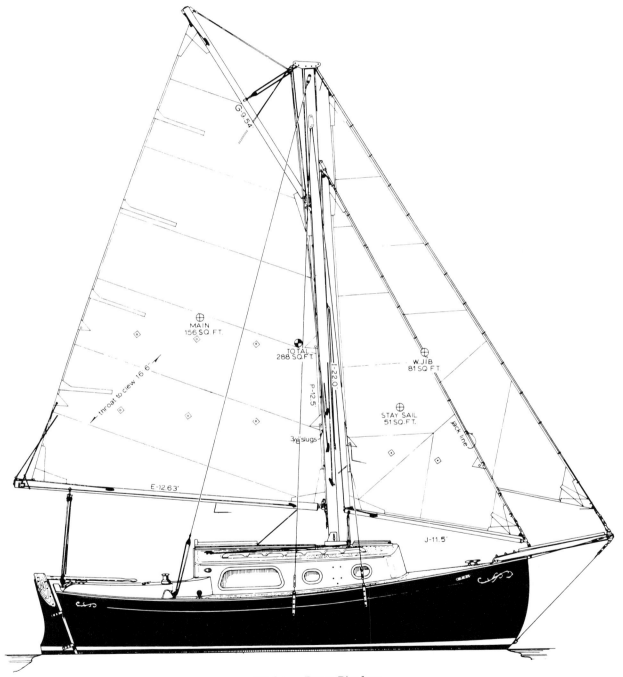

Flicka — Bruce Bingham

LOA—20'0" LWL—18'2" Beam—8'0" Draft—3'3" Displ.—6,000 lbs. Ballast—1750 lbs. Sail Area—Std: 250/Gaff: 288

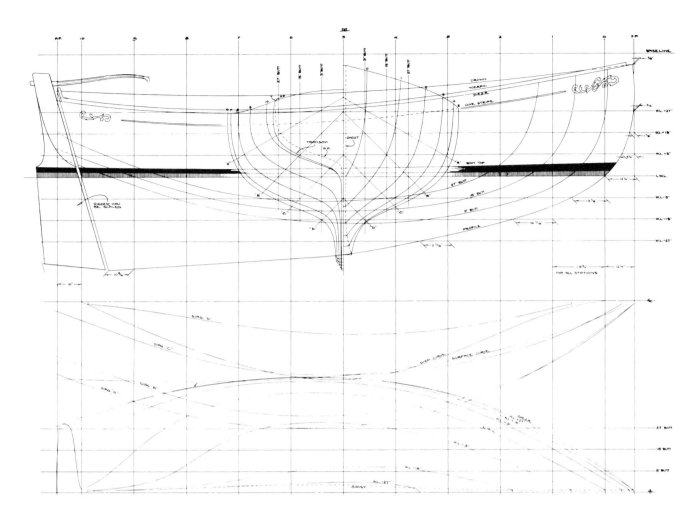

The lines of the pesky-bowed Flicka. Her powerful quarters may be a reason for her excellent sailing performance.

boat is heeled.

While I personally favoured the cat ketch or cat schooner rig, I felt that it would be too difficult to sell to the general sailing public, so I opted for a more modern masthead rig, giving the boat large headsails that she is able to handle easily.

Over a five year period more than four hundred Flicka plan packages were sold. Most of the backyard-built Flickas were of fibreglass construction although quite a number of photographs came to me depicting Flickas of strip planked and carvel planked wood. They ranged from absolute spartans to the uttermost in elegance . . . As Flickas were finished and commissioned I began receiving letters from owners describing remarkable passages of thousands of miles . . .

Both Kate and I had always wanted a Flicka of our own and decided to build one in 1974. We con-

structed a superb hull of fibreglass. I spent many days just on the carving of the bow and quarter scroll works. Kate drew up an authentic planking plan, including butt and end seams. Business pressures kept us from finishing the work, however, so the plug was sold to a group of builders. In 1978 our long time dream of owning our own Flicka came true. I became the proud owner of Pacific Seacraft's hull number 25, the *Sabrina*.

The Flicka was never intended to be a high performance boat; the prime criteria were seaworthiness and a comfortable, livable interior for long distance coastal and offshore cruising. Even though I had heard of pretty remarkable stories of better than 5 knot averages, it was only when I began to sail the *Sabrina* that I became a true believer.

Flicka's lines are so well balanced that she looks like a big ship and you have to keep looking back at the size of the helmsman to remind yourself that she's only 20 feet long. Designer Bruce Bingham has done quite a job disguising full headroom with the high crown in the house.

Within four days of her delivery in Oyster Bay, New York, with an unfamiliar crew and an unfamiliar boat, we managed to pull off an astonishing fourth in cruising class on a 200 mile Round Long Island Race. After 125 miles, we were sailing neck and neck with such reputable boats as a Cal 25, a Seafarer 33 and Tanzier 22. . .

Her light air performance is truly phenomenal, she is able to outghost boats that are as much as 15 feet longer. What she seems to like best though is the heavy stuff. With a double reefed main and a jib or a storm staysail, she is an absolute thrill to sail. When the going really gets tough and other boats are running for shelter, the Flicka seems to be in her original element. She is not a particularly dry boat when going to weather in these conditions but she is weatherly, responsive and surprisingly comfortable.

Our first opportunity to really put the Flicka to the test was a trip between the Stamford and Newport boat shows, a distance of 108 miles. We left Stamford on a leading edge of a cold front with a steady 20 knot breeze and higher gusts. We ticked off the miles in 19 hours — a 5.68 knot average.

5¼ knot passages have become almost routine aboard the *Sabrina*. At 5½ knots the quarterwave is fully five or six feet aft of the transom, yet the boat never seems to squat.

Whatever the reason, she is extremely fast. The design has stood the test of time and it has surpassed my highest expectations. Of all my designs the Flicka remains as my greatest source of pride.''

If Mr. Bingham sounds a bit like a proud poppa, well the pride is justified. Independents who sail-tested the Flicka agreed that she sails well in spite of her displacement to waterline ratio that is well over 400, but then those ratios begin to break down once you get boats with waterline lengths below 20 feet, and Flicka's is 18 feet 2 inches. The Flicka's lines are most pleasant to the eye, and Bruce Bingham has succeeded admirably in keeping the mass of the trunk cabin visually acceptable, a feat only infrequently accomplished by many designers, most of whom face much less demanding challenges than attempting to create full headroom in a 20 foot boat. The eyebrow certainly helps, as does the grabrail, to hide the great amount of crown, and the peppy sheer flows so nicely that the eye is forever busy playing back and forth along it. The bowsprit and pulpit help elongate her lines, and her plumb stem gives her a look of intrepidness. A thing of interest perhaps — from most angles she looks better in real life than she does in the drawings and that is certainly the opposite to the norm. But for a boat that may be taken offshore, the cockpit is extremely voluminous and what makes the matter even worse is the depth of the companionway opening. The single most conclusive finding that came out of the extensive investigation into the 1979 Fastnet disaster, where fifteen yachtsmen lost their lives, was that many of the boats were abandoned when their crews believed them to be taking on water through damaged hulls, when indeed much of the water was finding its way belowdecks through companionways which were, a) too large and deep, and b) left exposed when their hatchboards lifted the slight amount necessary to pop out, and floated away. The most secure hatch system is the type used on some Swans, like the 371, where the hatch is but a hole in the coach roof. With such a hatch, if the whole cockpit fills, what of it? You chuck your stepins and have a bath. Although such an extreme hatch design is not the most comfortable in many aspects, making for a very long companionway ladder, affording no view into the cockpit, and causing a rather closed-off feeling below, it is by far the safest, and the closer other hatches are designed to it the better. This does not mean that a single dropboard, or even two dropboards, will inevitably result in disaster, or that they cannot by some simple means like quick-release pins or even barrel bolts, be made irremovable for heavy weather sailing, but I cannot, no matter how hard I try, find any good reason for the existence of companionway openings that venture near *4 feet* in height. Not only is it a poor idea just because it increases the chance of a deluge belowdecks, but it also weakens the structure of the house by literally sawing it in half, and creates a need for three or four dropboards, whose handling and storage is infinitely too complex a puzzle for simple-minded sailors such as yours truly, who are still in a tizzy trying to determine whether the rabbit comes up the hole and down the tree or down the tree and around the hole.

Now that we have yanked out that little thorn, let's go back to the rest of the good things. The cockpit does have two 1¼ inch drains; a good location for the bilge pump that a single-hander can operate without leaving the helm; a very good-sized seat locker to starboard and a smaller one aft, both providing some important and handy storage space for fenders, lines and other gear, and even a propane bottle if you are a fan of big bangs — but we won't go into that. What the cockpit does lack is a few cutouts in the coaming that could very nicely house small items like winch handles, suntan lotion, binoculars, etc. Before I forget I should mention that more than half of all Flickas sailing, do so with an outboard motor secured to a bracket on the transom (all of which is reenforced by ½ inch plywood in the style of sandwiched decks) and I could not have come up with a handier place to stow a portable gas tank than under the hinged "L" lid in the aft end of the cockpit well. Here the tank is as close to the engine as possible, as isolated and secure as possible, and in as ideal a spot as can be for spills, since it is located in the low end of the cockpit floor right next to the drainholes. You just better be sure that your drain hoses are impervious to gasoline. Onward.

Winches and cleats (sensible and pretty bronze jam cleats for sheets) are well located for single handing, but wisely out of the way of spines and kidneys when you are leaning back to relax.

Some owners find the side-decks a little narrow, but if navigated with care they are quite sufficient, especially in conjunction with the double lifelines. Good old-fashioned grabrails run almost the full length of the house for safe passage. The

Flicka's amazing interior with full headroom in the main area. If I had a photo looking aft you'd see a sizable quarterberth with a large hanging locker opposite.

foredeck is small but clear, the bow platform is thoughtfully drawn with an anchor roller where the anchor can be stowed, although on long voyages the anchor should be taken belowdecks to take weight out of the bow and cut down on hobby-horsing. If you are amazed that all these things are located on the deck of a 20 footer, just wait 'til we go down below.

The 1 by 19 rigging is straightforward with a split backstay to accommodate the outboard rudder. The mainsheet has a camcleat block attached to a reenforced stern pulpit. The aluminum toerail obviates the need for genoa and spinnaker tracks. If one is desirous of leading the halyards aft to the cockpit, one will need turning blocks to get around the corner of the main hatch.

Flicka comes as a gaff cutter or a masthead sloop and although a gaff cutter is by far the prettier, it is of course by far the most complicated rig as well. The sloop carries 33 square feet less sail than the gaff cutter, but no matter, for Flicka should carry a cruising spinnaker anyway, for a little spinnaker of this size would be a joy to handle and splendid to look at. The size of the sails in general is very small. The main is 113 square feet and the jib 137 square feet, all of which makes you want to run and sail her right now, and just think how relatively inexpensive it could be to get a variety of sails for such a little ship, especially because almost any used sail would have enough good material in it to be salvaged and cut down into small Flicka sails.

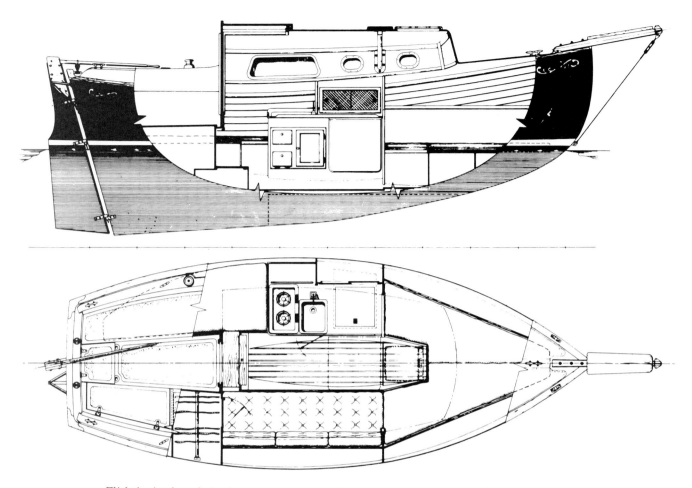

Flicka's simple and simply amazing interior with full headroom and two good seaberths and a big double forward. Possibly she is the most spacious 20 foot cruiser in captivity.

One last note before we go belowdecks. With her graceful sheer, pesky bow, bowsprit, aft hung rudder, exposed chainplates and moulded-in planklines, the Flicka has to be classified as a boat with character, but what is most important, her character is consistent — that is to say, Mr. Bingham is an honest designer of well formed convictions who does not just simply tack on a clipper bow and scrollboards on an otherwise indifferent bore-of-a-design to give it "warmth" and "charm." That kind of decoration shows about as much good taste as plastic pink flamingos and black velvet paintings of big-eyed dogs.

Belowdecks

Down below Flicka is truly impressive. The visual volume that Bruce Bingham has achieved by cutting back bulkheads to their essential minimum, eliminating the need for a vertical cabin dividing

mast support, and severely crowning the cabin top, certainly shows daring as well as a good understanding of the physical needs of cruising sailors of limited means.

There is good standing headroom in the main area, with a galley to port and a settee to starboard. A very spacious quarterberth is just aft of the galley, while to starboard is a good size hanging locker. The quarterberth is 6 foot 4 inches and airy, but for more light and good air circulation for tropical waters an opening port should be installed in the cockpit side. This would also provide precious light if the bilge pump (mounted in the cockpit side) required emergency cleaning; although we all know that the emergency will occur, as most ill-mannered emergencies do, on a dark and rainy night when even a picture window of immeasurable dimensions would be of zero use.

The galley shows cleverness in that the stove is

turned athwartships to save counter space, thereby allowing space for the quarterberth, and the stove is directly below the opening of the hatch to create quick exhaust of heat and fumes. Sink size, galley stowage, and icebox are good for a boat her size, and you must keep remembering that we are talking about a 20 foot hull. Although the stove is not gimballed it can be made to be by cutting away the countertop and doing as Mr. Bingham did on his own boat, attaching a piece of aluminum angle to either side of the stove top, drilling a hole in each and letting them swing on a pair of dinghy pintles attached to the countertop. A piece of lead would have to be added as dead weight to the stove's bottom, of course, to prevent it from doing a somersault every time you put a pot on one burner and not the other.

The table is hinged on the front of the icebox, held flush against it in down position, and held up in the open position by a mahogany leg that fits into a hole in the sole and a hole in the table leaf. Now that is simple. The settee to starboard is wide with storage outboard of it. With a filler in place, the forward V-berth can be made to be an enormous double that should satisfy the need of even the most imaginative among us. As an added plus, there is no bulkhead between the two bunks on the starboard side, so that the berths in effect run together, making this an ideal sleeping place for one very long basketball player or three average, but friendly, jockeys. Ventilation is fair with a hatch forward and four opening ports, but it can be made perfect with the installation of a Dorade vent on the foredeck, an opening port in the cockpit, and the replacement of the two fixed windows in the deck house with large 12 inch bronze ports, as found on some of the newer Flickas.

The Flicka has a liner that comes about a foot above the waterline and you may or may not want to order this with the boat. If you get the boat with the liner in place, the finishing will be extremely simple and very quick. But you are paying a bundle for it; it is very limiting in what you do with the interior, and it does restrict access to the hull for repairs, although the worst parts (the large flat pieces that fit flush against the hull) are only above the waterline. If you choose to use an outboard you will also end up with a heavy, costly and space-wasting engine pan, which Mr. Bingham chose to expel by means of a hacksaw and some muscle. To

realize the frustrations a liner can bring about, read the list of changes Mr. Bingham made to maximize the use of his own factory finished Flicka in the September, 1980 *Small Boat Journal.*

Construction

Pacific Seacraft, the boatyard that builds the Crealock 37, also builds Flicka. They have built over 200 to date, and are doing very good work on their boats. The partners who own the yard are also the main working force behind it. Henry Mohrschladt looks after design and paper work and Mike Haworth looks after production. They started in 1975 with a 25 foot cruising boat designed by Henry. Mike had been building boats for almost ten years before that, with broad experience in tooling. He has done most of the tooling at the yard, and has done a fine job indeed. He is a serious man who defends his work with passion and justifiable pride, attributing most of the success of the yard, both in quality and longevity, to what he calls the good luck of having a crew that has basically stayed with them for the last four years. This of course involves less luck than good internal relations, which must be nurtured by everyone involved. Henry has been involved in engineering as far back as 1971 with Westsail, working his way through the engineering departments of Columbia, Pacific Trawler, and Down Easter, where he designed a Down Easter 38 in its entirety. They are now working with a crew of 24.

The Flicka is structurally sound. She is hand laminated (both hull and deck) using mat and roving, resulting in a hull that is ⅜ at the sheer and ⅝ at the waterline and ¾ inches in the keel. The hull laminations are: mat, cloth, two units of mat and roving plus two more units of mat and roving down the centerline; one 36 inches wide and one 60 inches wide. The deck is reenforced with plywood, and the coachroof, because of its extreme crown, with end grain balsa, which adds a nice bit of insulation as well. The hull has the standard flange to which the deck is bolted, using ¼ inch stainless steel machine screws through the aluminum toerail. The bedding compound is polyurethane. The liner is bonded in place with a layer of mat sandwiched between the flat parts and the hull, then about 3 inches of the gelcoat is ground off the face of the liner and it is then bonded to the hull with six ounce mat and roving. Deck fittings, stanchions, and chainplates have large backup plates instead of washers and this, of course, is the ideal way of construction, for the loading is distributed more evenly and over a much larger surface.

The most interesting tidbit on the Flicka is of course, her lack of vertical support for the mast. To transfer the loading to the cabin sides then to the bulkheads, the coachroof is reenforced with a 10 inch wide beam laminated up of six layers of ¼ inch marine ply, then glassed over with three units of mat and roving. This takes the place of the more frequently seen aluminum I-beam and side pads bolted through the cabinside. The laminate procedure is infinitely cheaper and more manageable for the owner-builder, and up to now there have been no reported failures. The ballast is an internal solid casting, bonded into the fibreglass hull and bonded over with mat and woven roving. The rudder is hand-laid-up fibreglass with heavy oak cheeks and cap, and the gudgeons and pintles are bronze and through-bolted and have very nice castings. The standing rigging is 1 by 19 wire, with open body bronze turnbuckles and integral toggles.

For the home builder there are no complicated pieces required in finishing the boat either with or without the liner. I very much like the boat for both its simplicity and thoughtful design, for she has been thoroughly conceived as an ideal cruiser for sailors with little money and big hearts.

Flicka with a sloop rig is much easier to handle than the gaff-cutter but you lose about 40 square feet in the main which will hurt downwind performance unless you get a little spinnaker.

5

The Boat According to John
Aleutka

I think we have gone mad. We rave about our unquenchable thirst for peace and tranquility, and sail for days to reach secluded coves, and yet the anchor barely hits the bottom before we are off in a dinghy with the outboard screaming and the hull slap, slapping on the water, as we race up and down the shoreline "discovering nature". Madness. What can you discover with everything a blur and on top of that with your eyes rattling and your ears thundering and your nose filled with the smoke of half-burned gas and oil? To discover anything at all you have to watch and listen and to do that you have to move very slowly. You have to move slowly to see how a hawk spreads its pinfeathers as it circles over the trees, or how the rock crab moves among the crabgrass as it hunts, and you have to listen carefully to hear the wild goose cackle as it leads its young, and the oyster catcher cry "whee, whee, whee", as its orange beak flashes among the rocks. And to see and understand it all deeply, you have to think — think about the flooding of the tide, the ebbing of your years. To rob yourself of these joys is to rob yourself of understanding the world around you, and if you don't care about the world around you

then you don't belong in it. Go away.

Some people care, and it reflects in what they do and what they say and in the boats they design and the way they use them.

John Letcher cares. He has designed and built himself a lovely little boat with no engine and then sailed it 22,000 miles in tropical seas and Alaskan inlets and quiet estuaries, and when there was no wind he sat and watched and when he absolutely had to move he rowed. And John Letcher is no eccentric fool, he is a thorough thinker and a practical man, as practical as the Pardeys who sailed around the world in *Seraffyn* with no engine, and if you say, "Sure, but it took them seven years," then I say, "That's right, and therein lay their joy."

John Letcher's *Aleutka* is not the kind of vision that comes to you when your eyes are shut and someone shouts, "Sailboat!" but then *Aleutka* wasn't built along the lines of a daydream. John knew about airfoils and laminar flow and induced drag, because he did graduate work in aeronautical engineering, and a Ph.D. thesis in hydrodynamics, so he knew — as the saying goes — which way was up.

And to him *up* was a small, graceful, double-

54

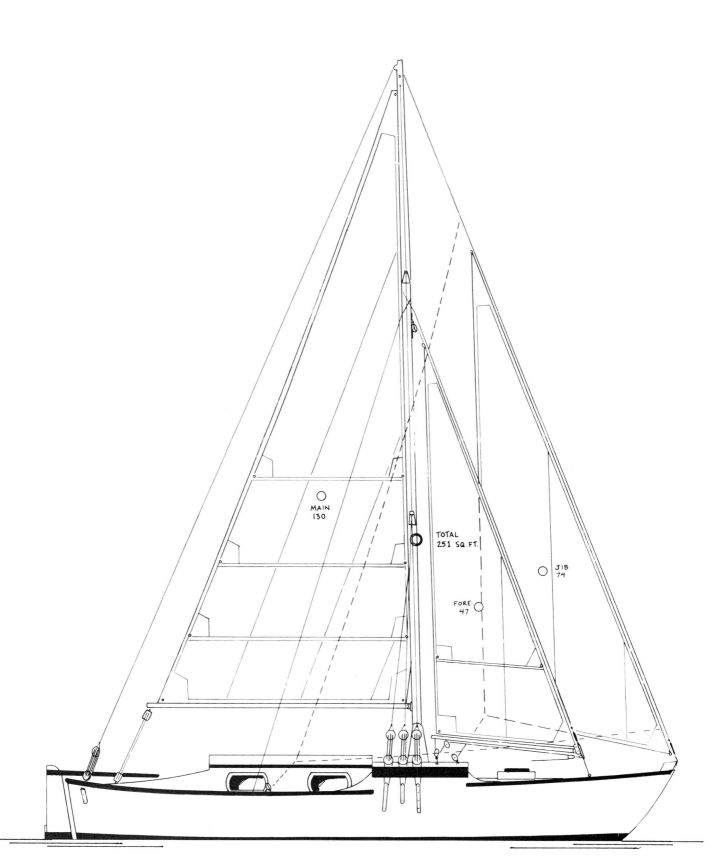

MAIN
130

TOTAL
251 SQ. FT.

FORE
47

JIB
74

Aleutka 26 — John Letcher

LOA—25′5″   LWL—22′6″   Beam—7′2″   Draft—2′9″   Displ.—5,500 lbs.   Ballast—1,500 lbs.   Sail Area—251 sq. ft.

ended hull, with twin keels and a cutter rig, and a funny little raised midship section, all of which work together well as even a blind man can see from the pictures, and John wrote me a letter and told me how it happened and here it is:

"I had just returned from a solo cruise to Hawaii and Alaska in *Island Girl*, a 20 foot wooden cruiser; the experiences of that voyage were fresh in my mind and strongly influenced many of *Aleutka's* features. She was conceived from the beginning to be easily and quickly built, cheaply maintained, and to carry safely her crew of two on long voyages, including ocean crossings and exploration of remote coasts.

I started the design from an enclosed volume (350 cubic feet, double *Island Girl's*) and a displacement of 5,000 pounds, which I thought would provide enough space and carrying capacity for two people. These volumes were shaped into a hull that's a bit on the long, narrow side (displacement-length ratio around 210) to be easily driven by a modest sail plan in the off wind sailing that dominates a passage planned to take advantage of prevailing winds. The canoe stern is to part overtaking seas while running before a gale, a reaction to *Island Girl's* broad transom which had absorbed some heavy wave impacts under these conditions. My principal reason for choosing twin keels was to avoid as much as possible the yard hauling, cradle construction and storage costs which had been my largest category of expenses during all the time I had owned *Island Girl*. A twin keeled boat can be beached anywhere for bottom painting, stowed anywhere without a cradle, and hauled anywhere on a rented truck or a simple trailer. Of course I was also interested in saving a foot or so of draft compared with a fin keel, but I am sure I didn't appreciate at the time all the other twin keel advantages we would come to enjoy. The self-maintenance aspect was enough for me.

I chose a cutter rig very similar to *Island Girl's*, which I had found versatile, efficient and easy to handle. But this time it would be all inboard, and good riddance to the bowsprit. Dispensing with an auxiliary engine was an important key to saving on initial costs and maintenance. To some extent it is her small size and shoal draft that makes this a practical alternative, for she can be safely maneuvered in many places where a bigger boat couldn't venture under sail, and can be happily rowed at 1½ to 2 knots with little effort. By making the cockpit small and the companionway off-centre we made space on deck to carry a rigid dinghy; and by having a section of raised deck in way of the mast we got comfortable sitting space below — both luxuries which I had been without on *Island Girl*.

The whole boat came together in a way which from my viewpoint is very successful. She was outward bound on a voyage to Hawaii less than sixteen months after we started construction (and I had a full time job and Patty was a full time student during nine of those months). She has since carried us a total of 22,000 miles. We have lived aboard her for a total of four years, and always felt she had just the right amount of room for two people. I don't think she has cost us more than $100.00 a year to own throughout the sixteen years. I believe the most serious damage she has ever suffered from the sea was the loss overboard in 1970, of a piece of old genoa sheet about 6 feet long, which I had employed as a sailstop. Throughout this time she has given us tremendous satisfaction, sailing both on the open ocean and through narrow coastal waters. What I have come reluctantly to recognize is that *Aleutka* is at a substantial disadvantage in sailing to windward with more conventional racer-cruisers of her size. With their deep fin keels, taller sails and greater stability they seem to get three miles to windward for every two of ours, so after an hour they are pretty far ahead. I expect the production Aleutkas to be significantly faster because of an improved keel design and the fine surface finish achieved in these hulls (infinitely better than our hasty one-off job). Nevertheless we found with some planning, and some extemporaneous changes of plans, much windward work can be avoided, and I for one am prepared to forgive a weakness in this department for all her other virtues. If Patty and I had to do it over again, after all our experience with her and all I've learned, I think we would make darn few changes. What more can I say?"

But he can say more, and does, in some other thoughts written down about *Aleutka*. Usually I shy away from taking the words of a designer or builder verbatim, because usually they are blinded by their prejudices, but when I read one of John's letters to a prospective builder, my doubts about his openmindedness disappeared. (I later spent a

John Letcher sailed his 25 foot Aleutka *from California to Hawaii, Alaska, back down the coast, and finally up the inland waterway and on to Southwest Harbor, Maine. Here she's exploring the far reaches of Glacier Bay, Alaska.*

day with him in Southwest Harbour, Maine, and got to be ashamed for my initial doubt.) Part of the letter went like this:

"A person who is building Aleutka must carefully consider his intended cruising and consciously accept her limitations in return for her advantages. As a day sailer she will be a disappointment; as a weekend cruiser in popular waters she will be an embarrassment, for every other boat will show her up."

That was good enough for me. If a man can say that about a boat he designed, built and sailed, then his comments on the boat will be worth ten times more than mine. To be fair I will give you the rest of the above paragraph first:

"All by herself on the deep ocean, running or reaching in a trade wind toward some distant island landfall, she will be a delight, for that is what she is built to do. And then she will have left ninety-nine per cent of all those lovely tall, long-legged racing boats far, far behind.

What has been compromised, plainly stated, is windward and light air performance. We generally keep up with all gaff-rigged Friendship sloops, schooners, and the heavy ketch rigged Norwegian lifeboat types."

John had some fine ideas, mostly on the conservative side, on cruising in an Aleutka, all justly reflecting her advantages and disadvantages and since many of the ideas are applicable to much of small boat cruising, here they are:

On sailing: "I think of any of the light sails — genoa, spinnaker, big twin running sails — as explicitly light weather sails, for settled, steady conditions, with less than 10 to 12 knots of *apparent* wind. When running downwind in the open, light sails are fine up to about 18 knots of true wind, but would be too much if you had to come on the wind. I tend to take the genoa off as soon as I see any whitecaps.

In heavy weather *Aleutka* runs beautifully downwind in big seas. With her weight forward and her keels relatively shallow and far aft, she tends to turn down the face of the wave instead of broaching to, and the balanced rudder keeps the steering light. We have spent all day (daylight hours) taking turns steering this way under foresail alone for better pull and doing a good deal of surfing. At night it will be a good deal harder to judge the waves. I never felt she should be slowed

down by drogues or sea anchors under these conditions . . .

Without an engine we have had to sail through a lot of narrow and ticklish places. For me that accomplishment has been an important source of satisfaction that compensates amply for the occasional inconvenience of doing without an engine. You have to learn to judge distance and current and the capabilities and responses of the boat. *Aleutka* is not quite as handy as most production boats of her size, but she does well enough. There are two reasons for this disadvantage. One, the same high directional stability that makes her good at self-steering and easy to steer, makes her slower turning than the more lively racer-cruisers, and two, in tight corners the wind is usually light and fluky; she really needs a genoa then, but unless you have an alert crew member to help the sails past the forestay on every tack, there is too much chance of a hangup to carry the genoa in tight places.

My rule is to go in with working sails, not try to keep the boat hard on the wind, but instead be satisfied with 60 degree tacks, the sheets a little free. Keep the boat moving well so she will carry through the stays and have good steerage control at all times. If there is any question about being able to get past an obstruction on its weather side, I bear off and pass it to lee rather than pinch up and lose speed. If the wind is light, I have the oars all shipped in their sockets ready for a few strokes at any time. All this is a lot of fun and gives the folks on shore a good show."

On rowing: "8 foot oars stow conveniently alongside the coamings on the side-decks. The basic rowing position is sitting on the bridgedeck facing aft. There really isn't room enough here to get your back into it, so you are pulling mostly with your arms. This is okay because you are never needing to pull very hard. Once the boat gets moving at 1½ knots or so, it's very easy to keep her gliding along at that speed. It hardly pays to pull any harder; to go from 1½ to 2 knots requires 2.4 times the power.

In any kind of tight quarters, it helps to have someone stand aft and steer. The tiller can swing almost vertically for this purpose. It has to be pivoted up at least 20 degrees to keep it clear of your hands.

An alternative rowing position is sitting on the

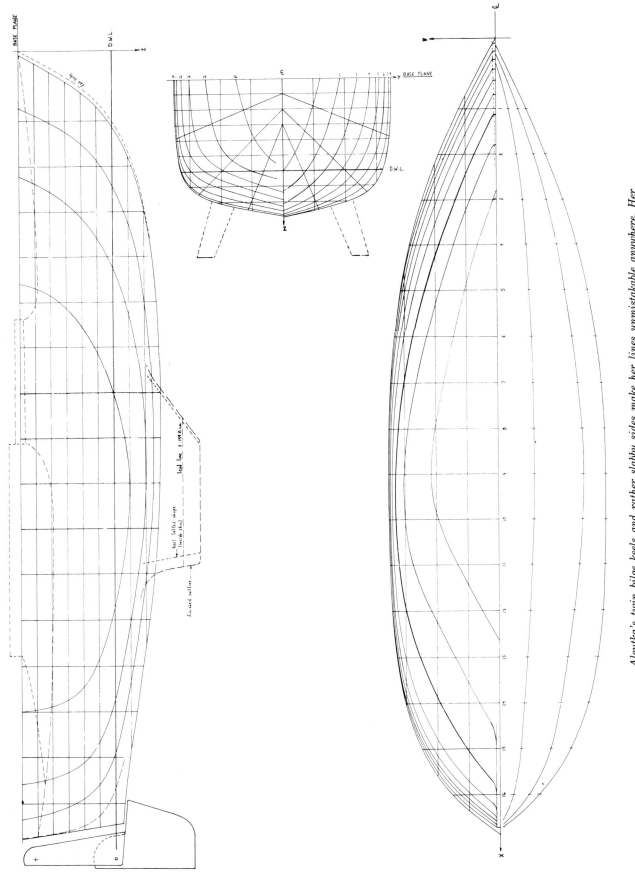

Aleutka's twin bilge keels and rather slabby sides make her lines unmistakable anywhere. Her designer, John Letcher, was working on his degree in aerodynamics when he designed her.

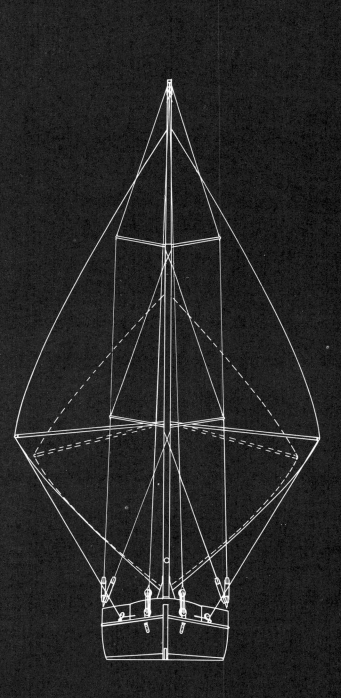

Aleutka's twin downwind rig looking so airy and magical you'd think she could fly to the stars.

lazarette hatch facing forward and *pushing* on the handles. This makes it easier to see where you are going and also to trim the sails when you come to a patch of wind. You can steer with the back of your head. However, pushing is more tiring than pulling, so I usually take this position only when riding a fair current and taking it very easy — a nice state of affairs.''

On anchoring: "My favourite anchor is a 20 pound plow. I have grown very distrustful of Danforths after a number of unpleasant experiences where the anchor failed to reset itself after the pull came from a new direction.

I very much prefer chain over rope. We have 200 feet of ¼ inch chain on board; 120 feet is on the 20 pound plow, followed by 120 feet of ½ inch nylon. The other 80 feet of chain is on the second anchor, an 8 pound Danforth, followed by 100 feet of ⅜ inch nylon.

The anchor locker under the forehatch is divided longitudinally into port and starboard bins, so these two anchors and rodes have separate stowage.

Anchoring under sail with more than 6 to 8 knots of true wind, we anchor the conventional way: round up into the wind, lower the anchor and sails as we come to a stop, snub the anchor to set it as we drift downwind; then pay out more scope. Windage of the hull and rig is enough to dig in the anchor and stretch out the chain. In light winds we have a much less conventional approach. We approach the anchorage downwind under reduced sail — often just a jib or genoa — sailing at about 2 knots. Dropping the anchor as we pass over the place we want it to be, we pay out chain and continue to sail until enough chain is out; then belay the chain, and the sail force and momentum of the boat will stretch the anchor chain out, dig in the anchor *and* give us a convincing demonstration that the anchor *is* dug in as the boat comes to a rather sudden stop.''

Beaching, shallow anchorages: "Take advantage of your twin keels. One of the big advantages is being able to anchor where no one else can — even where you will be high and dry at low tide, if that suits your schedule. Often you can go up a little creek in the evening and have an overnight berth aground on the mud that is even quieter than at anchor. One warning: don't deliberately ground the boat on a hard bottom in a place where you are

likely to have wakes from passing motor boats. During the time when you are barely afloat, a wake will bounce your keels very hard on the bottom.

It is worth learning how to interpolate between high and low water so that you can figure out the height of the tide at any time. The 'rule of twelves' is useful: the tide drops (or rises) about one-twelfth of the range in the first hour, two-twelfths in the second hour, three-twelfths in each of the third and fourth hours, two-twelfths in the fifth hour, and one-twelfth in the sixth hour.''

On navigation: "The steering compass is mounted inside the deadlight in the after end of the cabin. Here it is well protected from cockpit activity and out of the way. It can be lighted then with a

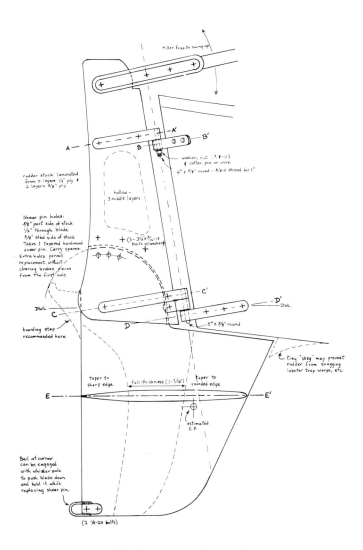

Aleutka's flip-up rudder is necessary because her twin bilge keels offer no protection to the centre of the hull.

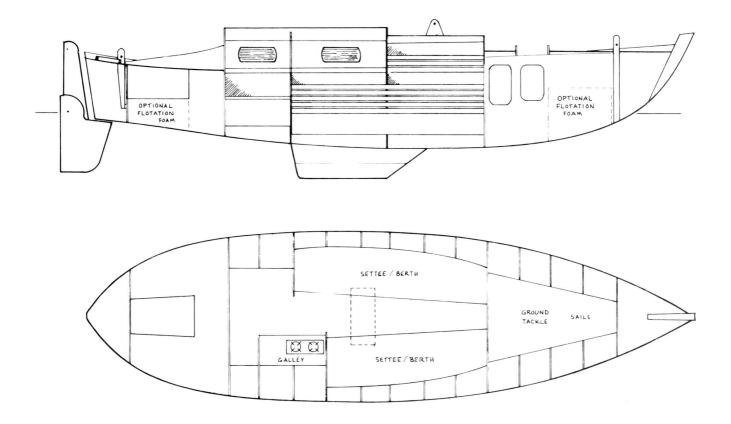

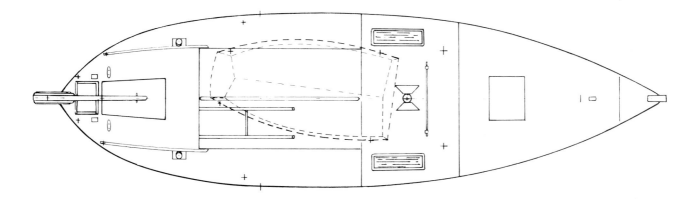

The portside berth is as long as it is because the designer/builder/sailor John Letcher is over 6 feet 6 inches tall. You can sit at the aft end of this berth and work the galley stove; that's decadence.

Aleutka's full-width raised house amidships has two large skylights to provide light to the seats below. The cockpit is that of a true ocean sailer with a small footwell to hold but a few buckets of water.

The spartan interior of the original Aleutka, *a pure long-distance cruiser without any frills or decoration.*

small lamp inside the cabin (we use a neat little spring-loaded gimballed candlestick). I have never provided much of a place for plotting in *Aleutka*. I callously fold the charts and use a large crib board in my lap to hold the required part of it flat."

On haul out: "A clean sand or fine gravel beach is best for doing bottom work. You need a range of tide of at least five to six feet to get six hours of drying time on the keels; however, if you are using a fast drying paint, a three foot range would do. You can drop an anchor and pay out rode as you sail in toward the beach; however, I find it is hard to judge the distance and depth and I am likely to drop the anchor too far out, so I usually just walk the anchor out when the tide is low and bury it at the edge of the water. This anchor will help in getting off in case an on-shore breeze should come up before she floats.

We prefer to get a timber (maybe 2 inches by 8 inches) under the toe of the keels, close to the balance point, before going on the beach. Loop two ropes on each end of this timber; then, with one person on each side pushing down with an oar, the thing can be maneuvered under the keels and tied off fore and aft. This keeps the keels from burying and allows you to paint everything but the small areas where the keels rest on the timber. The weight of one or two people on the bow will tip the boat forward on her toes so you can reach the rest of the keel bottoms."

On trailering: "A trailer for a twin-keeled boat can be a pretty simple affair. *Aleutka* is big enough to require two axles; she should be in a position so the centre of gravity is about one-third of the way from the front axle to the rear. The axles and wheels made for moving mobile homes are cheap and widely available." So there you have it, everything you wanted to know about the Aleutka and how to cruise a small boat.

Construction

The boat is built in Costa Mesa by Parker and Mendosa in the tiny, sunny yard where Westsail first started. Ed Parker is a soft-spoken but passionate man in his thirties, who wants to build boats for serious offshore cruisers, so he has assembled, aside from the Aleutka, the moulds for the Westsail 32, Westsail 38, as well as a 36 foot design by Bruce King and the moulds for the very graceful Columbia 50. There should be something in here for everyone. Mr. Mendosa is full of Latin charm and integrity, and he looks after the laminating of the hulls with his tiny crew, all of whom have over eight years experience in fibreglass work. The hulls and decks are well laid-up. Aleutka has three units of mat and roving in her hull, plus a 12 inch reenforced layer at the hull flange. Her deck is reenforced with ¾ inch end-grain balsa coring, which is lighter than plywood and has less of a tendency to delaminate, because the end grain is readily saturated by resin. The hull to deck joint is done with the use of a flange that is screwed to first, then bonded with four layers of mat and cloth on the inside. The ballast is lead.

At writing, Parker and Mendosa are offering only structural kits, hull, deck, ballast, bulkheads, sole and engine, but a complete set of working plans does come with each boat, and if you want a more finished boat, a very able Southwest Marine or a very reputable and well experienced Westerly Marine, both of whom adjoin the yard, can accommodate you.

All in all John Letcher is a very fine gentleman who has designed a very fine ship with every one of her eccentric details worked out with much thought and knowledge and—as important—care.

John Letcher at the sweeps of the original Aleutka. *She'll skim along nicely at 1½ knots under oar-power without at all straining the oarsman.*

6

When Boats Had Hearts
The Friendship Sloops

There was something magical and alive in an old wooden boat. She had a soul that came from the live trees that became her timbers, a heart from the man who hewed and shaped her frames, and a beauty and simplicity from the nature that surrounded her. She was born much like a child, out of passion and love and great hopes and endless dreams, and she passed her life being thought of and cared for, and in turn looking after those who loved her most. And she passed from sprightly youth into dignified old age, whose last years she spent quietly in sunny fields or down on the shore with the tide washing her peacefully away; and even in those last, last days she stirred the hearts of those who looked her way. And something of her passed on into the toolshed her planks mended, or she seeped respectfully away into the earth from where she came.

But wooden boats are gone now, maybe because they required too much love to build and too much thought to look after, and where all this extra love and thought have gone is hard to say because if it's still around it doesn't seem to show. So the wooden boats are mostly gone; the beautiful and the plain, the sleek and the stout, all gone to their graves, and now we have armadas of sparkl-ing shiny stuff, that came quickly and heartlessly and will float hard and indestructible until the end of time.

It is for this reason above all that we must choose and build our boats with care, because a new eyesore today will be an old eyesore tomorrow, for something ugly or thoughtlessly built will not improve with age, it will just continue its cold and ugly life without the common decency to die. So if you are about to choose a boat, please choose a beautiful one, and if you are about to build, build well and from the heart, or all you'll end up doing is passing your sad misery to others.

The sloops named after Friendship, Maine have been built by down east boatbuilders for near-ly a hundred years, built for fishermen and lobstermen whose lives depended on their stur-diness and sea kindliness, and whose bread and butter depended on their ability as work boats. Hundreds of Friendship sloops were launched in down east waters, and their elegant graceful lines were a sight to behold on the North Atlantic coast.

Who built the first one no one seems to know, the names of A. K. Carter and Wilbur A. Morse and Robert E. MacLain are argued over by the scholars of maritime history, but whoever it was

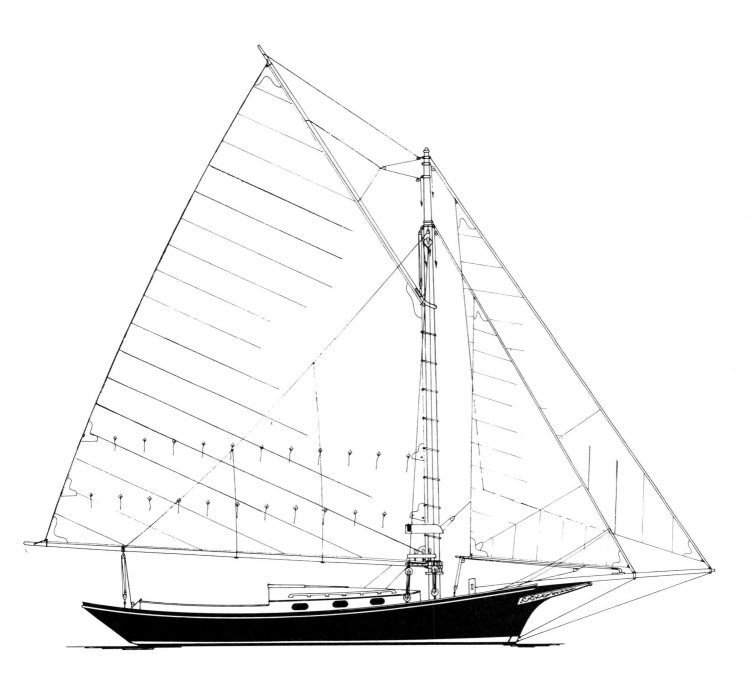

31' Friendship Sloop (Dictator)
LOA—30'10'' LWL—26'0'' Beam—10'8½'' Draft—5'0'' Displ.—17,500 lbs. Sail Area—761 sq. ft.

had the true eye of an artist and the heart of a gentle man.

Jarvis Newman, of Manset, Maine, believed it was Robert E. MacLain, and when he found a derelict 31 foot Friendship *Dictator* in a boatyard on Deer Isle, badly holed and rotting, with some planks gone to build trellises and cradles, his heart leapt, for he recognized "MacLain's sure hand in her uncommonly beautiful sheer line, in her huge rounded cockpit, in her small shallow cabin, which helped grace the elegant profile of the little sloop."

But *Dictator's* condition was desperate. Her iron fastenings had turned to powder with the years, her sturdy oak frames had softened from the rain, her beautifully hewn cut-water had vanished. Jarvis Newman didn't despair. He purchased what was left of the body of *Dictator* but he must have gotten all of her soul, for he found it in himself to spend nearly 3,000 hours and ten times that in dollars, restoring the little sloop to her once gallant state. And lucky for us that he did, for once rebuilt and refitted to a fineness that would do old Robert E. proud, Jarvis Newman took a mould off the perfect hull and assured the continuation of a craft of great beauty for a long time.

Dictator was 31 feet overall, not including her pesky sprit of course, and with her long waterline of 27 feet and fine entry, she had a good turn of speed. Her massive beam of 10 foot 8½ inches gave her lots of stability and lots of space, both of which were a must for a work boat. With her long flat keel she could settle on the mud if need be, and her great open cockpit had lots of room for a fisherman to do his work. Jarvis Newman's new sloops draw 5 feet even, displace a hefty 17,500 pounds and are ballasted either internally or externally, depending on your desires, with 5,300 pounds of lead that is spread almost from the rudder post to just below the mast, which not only gives you much space in the bilge, but also gives her the finest, gentlest motion possible in a seaway.

Her rig is short, with her mast — which is set just 6 feet from her bow — barely over 30 feet from the deck, but her boom, believe it or not, is longer than her waterline, so her gaff main becomes a monstrous 522 square feet. Her jib and staysail are small by comparison at 145 and 95 square feet, for a total of 761, but she can handily be shortened down to about 400 square feet by dropping the jib and double reefing the main. She will not be a

demon to windward as any gaff sailor knows, and Mr. Joe Richards, who has owned a smaller Friendship for going on forty years, converted his to a Marconi, to the dismay of traditionalists, but to his own delight, for he estimated that his *Princess* easily doubled her speed and literally sailed circles around a gaff rigged cousin. Aside from the gain in windward ability, he gained much security, for he cut the length of his boom to nearly half and shortened his "widowmaker" to a less perilous length, and his potential widow and his insurance man breathed a sigh of relief. Be that as it may, the original is still by far the more beautiful, and that's easy for me to say because I don't have to sail her.

On deck, the *Dictator's* offsprings are a dream. The cockpit coamings are rounded and continue forward blending perfectly into the cabinsides, and end up by making the identical curve in the forward part of the house, so in plan-view the house and cockpit form a meticulously balanced oval. Her cockpit, over 8 feet in length, is regally commodious and should in decent climes be the centre of life aboard. The seats are broad and comfortable, the bridgedeck 2 feet wide for walking or sleeping, and the coamings are high enough to support the small of your back. The decks are broad and protected by low bulwarks, and the foredecks are spacious for handling sails and groundtackle.

Belowdecks she will sleep four in comfort, including two in a true double berth starboard of the companionway, and I say 'true' because it is broad at 4 feet, and almost untapering, since it is located amidships at the maximum beam. The forepeak berths have plenty of footspace but forget about a filler, because there is a big mast in the way. The head is tucked aft to port of the companionway, and through it there is good access to the vast storage area below the deck and cockpit.

The galley is laid out in these drawings along the port side, and as you can see there is good storage in both versions, although counter space is at the minimum. Of the two layouts I should think the dinette version to be preferable, for even though it is somewhat more convoluted what with the raised floor and all, it does at least allow for some conversation "around" the table, whereas the straight settee is about as conducive to socializing as a church pew. I must confess I have no great love for arrangements without at least a semblance of a salon, but with this large a cockpit, squeezing a

The Friendship sloop Dictator *in her full glory. The sight of her under sail should touch even the coldest heart.*

salon in here is a bit difficult, although not impossible. I spent some time scaling off a plan and found an alternative that I, at least, prefer. This would involve an athwartships galley, in other words half the galley on one side, half on the other. To see what I mean look at the settee plan (not the dinette) and, leaving the stove where it is, move the galley sink directly across from it, on the starboard side. Now put the icebox directly outboard of it, also on the starboard side. This would cut the settee down to 4 feet in length, but it would make room for another settee facing it on the port side so you would have an extremely cozy but totally workable eating and drinking and chatting place for four in comfort, and up to seven in a squeeze, with three on each settee and one on the little seat just aft of the mast. You would have to chop a few inches off the aft end of the centre table, but that would be no great loss. Actually the more I think of this plan the better I like it. There is a sense of much volume below since both bulkheads are trimmed back and down, so visually the whole belowdecks is one large space.

Stowage on the boat is ample, especially of the outside variety, for there are acres of space below the cockpit seats and aft deck, with three decent-sized hatches to get at the things below. In all, *Dictator's* descendants are complete yachts, perfect for holiday cruising and they belong in a very rare and precious family that can actually add its own beauty to the sea's.

Jarvis Newman found a little sister for *Dictator* in a smaller Friendship sloop with an equally glorious heritage. This time an in-between stop was added to the continuance of history, for the mould was taken off *Old Baldy*, a sloop owned by James Rockefeller. *Old Baldy* was a replica of the original *Pemaquid*, a little 25 footer built by Mr. A. K. Carter at Bremen, Maine, around 1914.

Her lines are every bit as graceful as her bigger sister's but with a displacement of well below half she will show a much better turn of speed. Her sail area is a more manageable 432 square feet, although her boom is still longer than her waterline, and if that little sweety gets angry at you in a blow you'd better have your rosary beads smoking through your fingers. Her ballast is minimal, but don't fear for her broad beam carried amply aft and forward will give her ample stiffness.

Everything on deck has much the same proportion as *Dictator*, with a very comfortable cockpit for five, and a good deck space all around. The cockpit stowage is again voluminous, with plenty of space below for the Volvo MD6A, although more than a few of these yachts are in use down East with a pair of fine bronze oarlocks and two lovely sweeps about 10 feet in length. With the bridgedeck being as broad as it is, there should be very good room for two people side-by-side pulling on a sweep each, and you can get some very fine pulls indeed, especially if you mount your oarlocks well aft so that you can bend and reach and pull, otherwise you will forever have the sweeps' handles tucked away in the rolls of your belly, with the sweeps doing little else than slapping the water. With two good pullers pulling steadily and easily, *Pemaquid* can reach a speed of nearly 2 knots and what a lovely way it would be to see the sights and stay in shape.

Her cockpit is 7 feet in length, and with a little padding will handily sleep two kids, while below there are good accommodations for four.

The galley is split in somewhat the fashion I suggested for *Dictator*, with a couple of good quarterberths to port and starboard. Galley space is of course limited, but what can you expect on a 25 foot boat, half of which is cockpit. The area forward of the galley has two excellent berths of tremendous length, which if desired, can be filled in for use as a half acre double berth. Whatever is done, a nice size table should be fitted in between (with a high and low setting so that it can double as a filler) converting this area into a first class salon with good seating for four.

The head is hidden below a berth, and if you find this inadequate because you want privacy, just tell everybody to close their eyes, or if you are even too shy to talk about it then just close your own.

In many ways I prefer *Pemaquid* over *Dictator*, most of my preference having to do with compactness and usefulness of space, and some of it having to do with the more manageable sail area, plus of course the fact that she is about two-thirds the cost, although certainly more than two-thirds the boat. For coastal cruising for a couple or a small family *Pemaquid* would be a source of pride forever.

Perhaps, however, a word of caution is due here. Neither of these boats is for the jump-in-and-

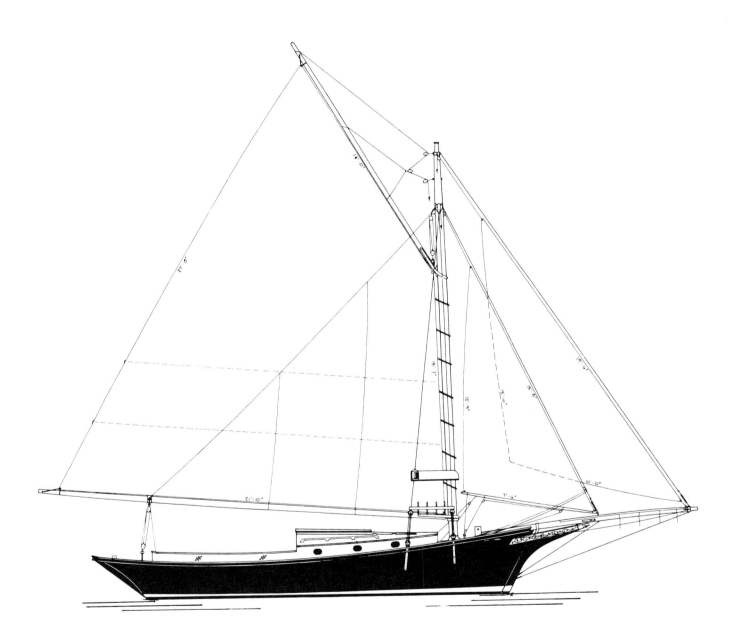

25' Friendship Sloop (Pemaquid)

LOA—25'0''   LWL—21'0''   Beam—8'8''   Draft—4'3''   Displ.—7,000 lbs.   Ballast—2,000 lbs.   Sail Area—432 sq. ft.

go sailor. They both require love and care, from their dead-eye and lanyard rigging to their varnished mast, boom and gaff, and if you are fortunate enough to be the proud owner of wood decks, you should allocate a couple of days a year for maintenance. With *Warm Rain*, a full day is required for a thorough cleaning of the decks with a very light solution of TSP, then sealing with two coats of clear (no resin, a little oil) waterproofing sealer. This should be done twice a year for best results, as should all the varnishing of caprails, hatches, coamings and trim. The varnishing is not nearly as bad as it sounds, and believe me it's a lot less work than trying to keep oiled teak looking good, or bleached teak looking bleached, especially near a city where both attempts will result in black and dead looking wood from all the flying death in the air. *Warm Rain* has varnished areas totalling the size of a tennis court: caprails, rubrails, bowsprit, boomkin, forehatches, skylight, drawboards, grabrails, eyebrows, Dorade boxes, tiller cheeks, boom gallows and covering boards and king planks for the deck, yet none of this has been stripped of varnish in her seven years since launching, for if a good varnish is used it can be lightly sanded and retouched from time to time. If done twice a year, the whole boat can be sanded down with 220 paper (using a vibrator sander on the larger surfaces) in about four hours by the two of us, which means that after a thorough sweeping and wiping down with a damp cloth, we can start varnishing by noon and be finished by two, with plenty of time left to lie in the sun. If you are neglectful and don't do this twice a year, look out, for you will get what Candace calls "deadlies," which are nasty little spots where the varnish has gone from the wood and the wood has turned black. This means removal by spot-sanding of layer after layer of old varnish, and building the whole thing back up to five or six layers which should be the basic cover from the start. I am not a varnish expert, having tried fewer than a dozen varnishes, but nothing I've found even comes close to Man of War, straight old varnish with such a rich glow and lustre that it will knock your eyes out, and solicit choruses of "oohs" and "ahs" from onlookers.

I elaborated on varnishing here, for it is a major part of owning *Dictator* or *Pemaquid* and should be done regularly, for nothing looks truly as sad as a beautiful yacht gone to neglect. Ugly boats aren't sad, they are just disgusting. "So anyway," as my favourite sea-cook injects into every third phrase of his yarns, both yachts are for the stout of heart and strong of limb, and for the sailor who understands that the sea is not just so much water, but a silent history of many who have been there before him.

Construction

Jarvis Newman is gone, but the boatyard still has his name and Lewis Moore, a stocky intense man, builds the hulls and decks of *Dictator* and *Pemaquid* in the same yard on the hill, just down the road from the Hinckley yard in Southwest Harbour, Maine. According to Peach, an independent shipwright who has worked on hundreds of boats down east, and whose tool box is built better than most yachts, Lewis Moore does the best glass work around, and that's a lot to say when Hank Hinckley's place is nearby and Tom Morris builds boats just across the harbour. But Peach says they're the best, and he spent three years at Hinckley and he says the Moore boats never have any voids or bubbles or dry spots, and Peach ought to know. And if Lewis works his laminates out well the boats ought to be strong, for his lay-up schedule is certainly as heavy as any in this book, and this book has some of the best lay-up schedules around. The 25 foot *Pemaquid* has a minimum of eight layers of glass in her in the thinnest parts, and that's two layers of mat against a gel followed by three units of 24 ounce roving and mat in alternate layers, and he adds three extra units 12 inches wide, to the area of the hull flange. *Dictator* has a minimum of four units of mat and roving in her, with four units for a flange that is 4 inches wide. Through the stem she gets to be over 1½ inches thick, where you get as many as nine units down the centre, 30 inches either side of *Dictator's* centerline and 18 inches either side of *Pemaquid's* centerline. The ballast on *Pemaquid* is a ton of external casting, while *Dictator* can have either external or internal lead. The internal lead is made up of lead pigs set in concrete and glassed over with twelve layers of glass (mat and roving counted separately).

The fibreglass deck is one piece heavily laid up with ½ inch balsa coring, that's left out in areas of stress where solid fibreglass is used. The partners around the mast are raised 1¼ inch and here the core is kept back over an inch so that solid partners

The graceful Friendship sloop decorates historical down east shores.

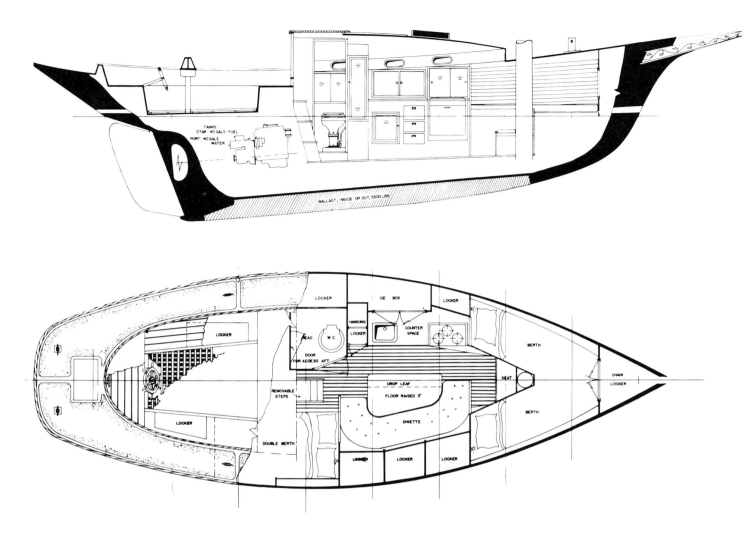

The beautiful 31 foot Friendship sloop is a replica of the famous Dictator *rebuilt to perfection by Jarvis Newman. Her accommodations would be greatly improved were a plan similar to her smaller sister* Pemaquid *followed.*

are formed. This is laid-up tapered for wedges. Other areas of stress, like cleats and travellers, also get solid glass.

The hull-to-deck joint is one of the best anywhere, with the wide hull flanges being covered with three layers of well-resined mat, and while this is all wet the deck is laid over and through-bolted on 3 inch centres with ¼ inch stainless steel bolts. Lewis believes strongly in this system, especially in the use of the layers of mat instead of just filler or caulking, for the fibres of the mat add strength and the fact that there are three layers at once will help to fill any hollows.

The mast is stepped on a base of cement bonded over, (see drawing for location) which

distributes the loading well over the hull. Don't forget at this point the hull is over 1½ inch thick. The rudder is a very fine plate of solid glass, with no coring to separate and fill with water, and the rudder shaft on *Dictator* is solid bronze with a hefty 1¾ inch diameter, and *Pemaquid's* is solid bronze with a 1 inch diameter.

From this stage on Lewis usually washes his hands of the boats, although he does install engines and provide some magnificent bits of custom bronze castings for both boats. The finishing of the yachts is all done on a custom basis, using the layouts and the wishes of individual owners. The yards that have been doing this are too numerous to count; just in Southwest Harbour there is Tom

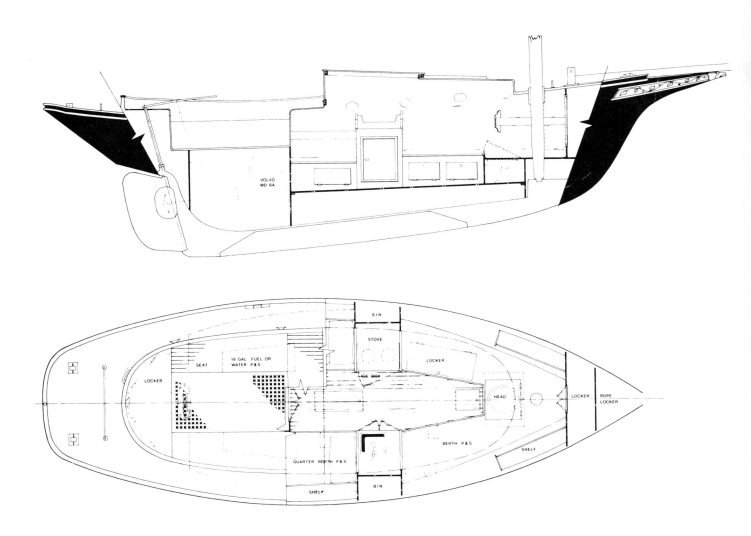

Pemaquid's *profile highlights her lovely counter and classic wedge-shaped house, while her plan-view shows how the curve of the cockpit coaming is balanced by a perfectly matching curve at the forward end of the house. For a 25 foot boat that is half cockpit she has good room below with two nice quarter-berths, a split galley and a U-shaped salon forward.*

Morris (see *The Little Yachts of Tom Morris*) and Malcolm L. Pettigrow, and of course Peach, and the work they do is in the first-class style of the best of Maine's proud tradition.

For those who care about such things, let me tell you how Peach was finishing off a Friendship when I was there. This boat was getting a wooden deck and house because the owner wanted teak cabinsides and teak decks. The deck was laid out with 1½ inch by 2¼ inch oak beams on 12 inch centres. They were doubled at the partners. The first sheer clamp was bolted with 5/16 inch stainless steel bolts. Over the deck beams came a layer of ¼ inch mahogany (varnished below for overhead) which

was sealed with two layers of mat and roving. The ⅝ inch thick teak deck was then laid over this. The bulkheads used were all ½ inch and everything; every last knee or shelf was bonded to the already massive hull, making it stiffer and stronger. The detailing and finishing of the yacht is first class, and with neighbours like Hinckley and Tom Morris it has to be.

In short, *Dictator* and *Pemaquid* have everything you can ask for in a yacht: beauty, grace, character and fine craftsmanship, and in the words of L. Francis Herreshoff, a Friendship sloop has only two disadvantages: "People will constantly want to borrow her, and she is apt to be stolen."

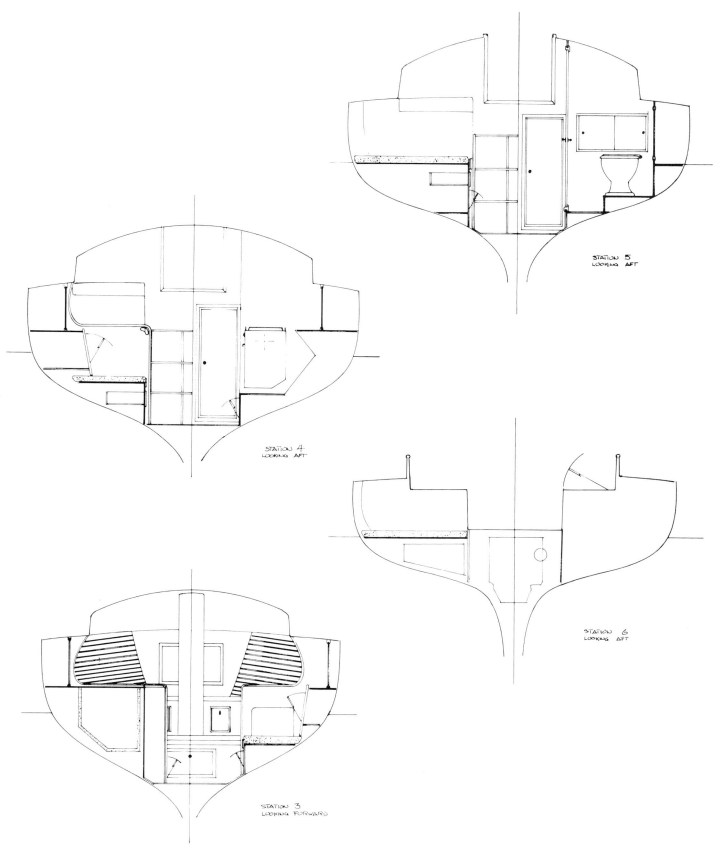

STATION 5
LOOKING AFT

STATION 4
LOOKING AFT

STATION 6
LOOKING AFT

STATION 3
LOOKING FORWARD

The 31 foot Dictator's sections show off her powerful bilges.

Pemaquid's trim interior with split galley. The two berths forward would make an ideal eating place were a small table installed.

Few things in boat design can come close to the graceful and thoughtful house and cockpit lines of the Friendship sloops.

7

One For the Eyes
Bristol Channel Cutter

It's a waste of time to try to update a duck. A duck is naturally beautiful with simple lines and serene colours, and if you bleach its feathers and dress it in satin jogging shorts, and teach it to say "awright" and "go for it" and the other thirteen phrases that make up the unabridged dictionary of modern communication, then you will only have proven to the world that you were blind to its simple beauty in the first place.

Mr. Lyle Hess has made very few major changes, except for refining the lines, to the original concept of Bristol Cutters and Itchen work boats which were designed to handle nasty steep seas and handle them in fast and seakindly fashion. His design embodies all those things that give rise to accelerated heart beats and visions of green lagoons and long-limbed ladies, unless you're a long-limbed lady yourself, or a man with a run-down pacemaker. Exaltations aside, the boat is strong, stiff, beamy and heavy, and considering its wetted surface, fast. To put it simply, it's really a 34 foot boat without the overhangs, having a total of 1 foot 10 inches of them fore-and-aft combined. The displacement of 13,800 pounds on a 26 foot 3 inch waterline gives her a ratio of 340 which is high

(a Morgan 38 has 268, a Westsail 32, 415) but her sail-area-to-displacement ratio puts her pretty close to Ted Brewer's Morgan 38 at 16.4 and Robert Perry's Valiant 40 at 16.8 and both of these are respectable movers indeed.

Generally the BCC at 28 feet is a somewhat larger version of Seraffyn, whose eight years of cruising adventures have been well recorded by the Pardeys, and their opinion of the design is such that they are now building a boat of almost identical lines with a 30 foot overall length.

The BCC profile is very pleasing with a lively sheer, classic split deck house and a stubborn-looking bow which, with its long bowsprit is reminiscent of *Sea Bird*, a design that Captain Henry Pidgeon used in his two and a half circumnavigations during the '20's and '30's.

Free-standing bulwarks (not an integral part of the hull and deck) help to visually reduce the cabin height, and accentuate the graceful sheer. The keel is as full as they come but a relatively fine entry is carried well aft, which means that she should maintain her windward speed even in the steepest chop. The draft is under 5 feet, which gives her access to most cruising grounds, and in

Bristol Channel Cutter — Lyle Hess

LOA—28'1"   LWL—26'3"   Beam—10'0"   Draft—4'7"   Displ.—13,800 lbs.   Ballast—4,600 lbs.   Sail Area—584 sq. ft.

spite of the great wetted surface, the BCC was first overall on corrected time, out of 350 monohulls, in the 1978 Newport to Ensenada Race; first in class in '79 in Ensenada; and first overall in the 1980 Panama Canal Yacht Club Race. As well, *Xyphtas*, a BCC, made the Dana Point, California to Nuku Hiva, Marquesas run of 3,150 nautical miles in 22 days, 10 hours, for an average daily run of 140 N.M. for an average speed of 5.8 knots, with best day's run of 180 N.M. or 7.5 knots average. Well now, so much for the big underbody.

The rudder is a monster with almost 9 square feet underwater, and I found it a little hard to get used to its force when backing down under power, but underway the boat balances readily and seems to love hands-off sailing. I sailed the boat off Newport, California in moderate Santa Ana winds and in the 12 knot blow she readily hit 6 knots on a reach and later went to weather better than two large double-enders alongside. This was of course done with a small genoa, and here we should perhaps digress for a moment.

Too many people with moderate and heavy-displacement cruising boats settle for slogging along in light and medium airs under small working sails or worse yet, under power, all for want of a decent sized headsail. This is absurd, especially when coupled with the fact that almost all of these same yachts are equipped with optional teak deadle-holders and varnished ironwood limper-nickels, so that lack of funds cannot be used as an excuse. A *misdirection* of funds is more like it. A sailboat is a sailboat first and foremost, and sails are its most precious and fundamental equipment, and to forget that and bob resolutely in slop like a dead slug, sporting a cast-iron jib the size of a lady's hankie is an insult to the craft, the designer and seamanship. For most coastal cruising, a genoa should be *the* standard headsail with a jib packed away for big blows. In cruising the west coast from Baja, California to the gusty fjords of British Columbia, Candace and I have used our genoa and drifter about 95% of the time and have consequently managed to do respectably against most racer-cruisers, and exceedingly well against most cruisers, and all that in a boat whose

displacement-to-length ratio is just this side of the Rock of Gibraltar's.

Back to the Bristol Channel Cutter. The deck layout is generally very fine, with a small cockpit (3 feet by 3 feet by 16 inches) that's ideal for offshore work, holding only about 700 pounds of ocean when filled to the brim. Even that will drain out in less than two minutes through a pair of 1½ inch scuppers. With as much buoyancy aft as the cutter has, even a full cockpit should drop the stern but a couple of inches. The cockpit has no seats *per se,* but coamings of triple laminated ⅜ inch teak are sloped a little, and give comfortable back support. The aft ends of the coamings are free-standing, with the jib-sheet winch-pads supporting their middle. This is a very good solution and pleasant to the eye, and can be a very good addition to many craft whose cockpit "seats" are nothing more than a vacant aft deck.

With the narrow parallel-sided trunk-cabin, the resulting side-decks (an astounding 2½ feet wide in one spot) are extremely comfortable for sleeping or sun bathing, and combined with the 8 inch high bulwarks, make for a very safe walking platform in rough seas. Since the bulwarks stand free of the deck (supported by wood block uprights on 18 inch centres in the U. S. version, and bronze castings on 36 inch centres in the Canadian version) they act as open scuppers for about 16 feet of their midship run. If that doesn't drain your decks fast, then nothing will. Another advantage of this bulwark system is that an endless-strop can be used with a snatch block, obviating the need for genoa tracks, and facilitating ready re-location of the block anywhere along the mentioned 16 open feet. The staysail has two 18 inch tracks of its own at the forward corners of the cabin trunk, with winches for the staysail sheet on the aft corners of the cabintop. To my mind this system is much to be preferred over a self-tending club-footed staysail, for although it involves a bit more work come tacking time, it can hardly be compared to an 8 foot long deranged billy club on the foredeck whose main staples are knee-caps and shins.

Although the split-trunk-cabin may cause head shaking among many for the lost volume it causes

The Bristol Channel Cutter going to windward, with her beam and full bilges holding her up. She bears much resemblance to Seraffyn, *the boat the Pardeys used to sail around the world.*

belowdeck, it does have the advantage topsides, of creating a safe, deck-level working platform where halyards and reef lines can be comfortably handled in the roughest seas. The forward hatch-house also leaves ample space around it for foredeck activities. One drawback of the rig is its lengthy bowsprit. If one is planning to use the boat primarily for cruising from a home base, meaning paying moorage at a permanent slip, then the 6 foot long sprit, which at '82 West Coast rates costs an extra $300.00 per annum, has to be viewed as a costly luxury. On the positive side, much to everyone's surprise, the bowsprit can be "reefed" by slacking off the head, bob, and whisker stays, and knocking out the wood pin that's wedged against the samson posts. Then the sprit can slide about 3 feet aft. To support the mast, the staysail stay can be left taut, for it is footed on a bronze casting that fits *around* the bowsprit.

If this method of saving rent is used, another problem surfaces, for then no permanent platform can be installed. Sail changes on a bare sprit are harrowing to say the least, often resulting in a wait-till-the-wind-changes philosophy. The obvious solution is the use of a furling jib, which many sailors view as the greatest invention since mermaids, while others would rather marry their mother-in-law than have one. I've had both good and bad experiences with the critters. Most of the time they are marvels, saving labour and fuss, but on one occasion in the Caribbean I was laid on my back for two days, because, as I was unassumingly hauling in the furling line with admirable gusto, the casing casting snapped, the line jammed, and the bottom half of my spine kept going backwards while the top half stood still, since it was indirectly attached to my arms which were hanging directly and resolutely onto the jammed line. So use a furler to your heart's content, but learn to chiropracticate yourself. Oh yes, the lazarette is so large you can supplement your income by subletting it as a small flat, to a jockey.

Two complaints before we go belowdecks. The mainsail is set up as a trackless sheeting system, robbing the boat of some versatility and causing a lot of messing around with cleating the sheet. A track could be readily affixed to the generously reenforced taffrail with very little detraction from the boat's character. My other misgiving is about the cleats specified by Mr. Hess. Although there is

little question that the bronze Herreshoffs are the most complimentary to the boat, their use with jib and staysail sheets, instead of jam and/or clam cleats respectively, seems too demanding, especially when tacking intight quarters with short crew.

Oh yes, the rig. The main is old-fashioned low-aspect ratio with slab reefing, and the headsails are generously drawn with a full jib and a low cut staysail. The slot between the forestay and the staysail stay is almost 6 feet, which is generous compared to many cutters, and should allow the genny to come through with little problem, especially if the staysail is used as well and kept taut until the genoa has come through. This will help enormously in feeding the genoa through the slot. There are no running backstays but the mast is supported against the pull of the staysail by an intermediate stay that uses the same chainplate as the aft lower shroud. Enough said.

Belowdecks

Belowdecks the boat is a wonder. In spite of the narrow deck house there is much volume, and Mr. Hess' original layout is one of the most sensible I've seen for an offshore cruising boat designed for two people. The galley is of good size, although the chart table doubles as ice-box lid which can cause inconvenience underway. Yet, many very able craft have used this solution, including the Sparkman and Stephen's Nevin's 40 line of which a great number have cruised very extensively. The galley has good storage, although much of it is a bit hard to get at due to the breadth of the side-decks. The stove is located entirely under a side-deck, so the ceiling over it must be lined with steel to prevent overheating and fire.

The quarterberth is spacious and can be made very airy for tropical cruising by installing an opening porthole in the cockpit side.

The chart table is a little narrow for my spoiled taste, but there is good space outboard of it for books and navigational instruments. There is very little space, however, for chart storage unless one installs a suspendible-type over the quarterberth (see *The Finely Fitted Yacht*).

The salon is exactly as prescribed in the eleventh commandment; with a drop-leaf table, two good settees, and a pilot berth. The last slides out into a double, although nothing overly acrobatic should be contemplated for it, because great disappointment will be incurred due to the low 18 inch high ceiling under the side-decks. The wet locker is, as in far too many cases, too tight.

The area forward of the main bulkhead reflects very thoughtful consideration for offshore needs. The head is located forward with an independent hinged lid over it, so it can be knelt or stepped on for access to the sail bin forward of it. To port is a good sized work bench, and to starboard is a very generous hanging locker and more storage. The sail bin is of adequate size, especially if a little care is taken in folding the sails instead of stuffing them. Folding can easily reduce the volume re-quired by up two two-thirds, especially by stiff heavy-clothed sails. The chain locker is kept back out of the bow, although if a solution could be found to have the chain fed even farther aft, so much the better. The weight of chain needed for such a heavy boat is great (almost 200 pounds for 200 feet) and with the entry being moderately fine, hobby-horsing, which will noticeably damage the boat's windward performance, will be a problem. Thus, every effort should be made to keep the boat's ends light to keep them from plunging. The motion may then not be as smooth and pleasant but you'll get there a hell of a lot sooner.

The Bristol Channel Cutter jumping with glee. At 28 feet she is without doubt one of the most beautiful small yachts in the world, and she's fast and extremely seakindly to boot.

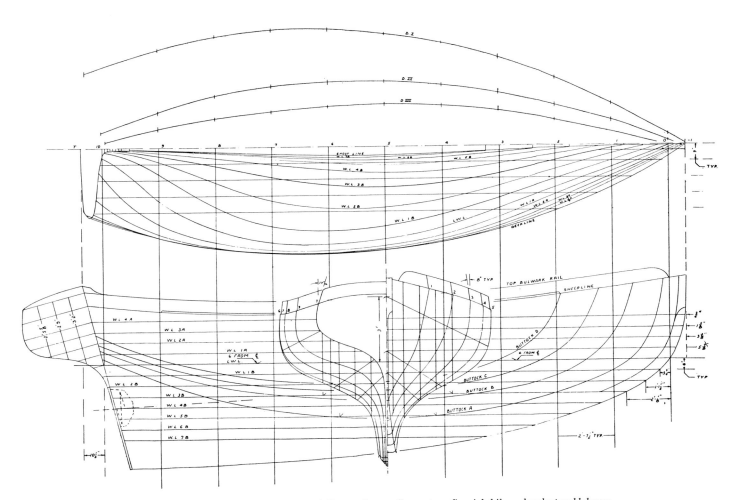

The lines of Lyle Hess' Bristol Channel Cutter show a fine entry, firmish bilges, lovely tumblehome and good buoyancy aft for power. No wonder she's such a fast sailer. Note the almost total absence of overhangs, yet she's still a very graceful little yacht.

The hatch over the forepeak area is large, enabling easy in-and-out passage of sails. A shallow ladder could be affixed to the port side main bulkhead, to eliminate the need for going aft when sail or line-handling will be required on the foredeck.

The engine is a two cylinder Volvo, although a single cylinder might suffice if you're willing to wait out tides. The fuel tankage is adequate, but for long voyages the 49 gallon water tank should be supplemented with a few collapsible jugs. This is a good idea anyway, just so one will not be obliged to perish of thirst if a water container gets contaminated. Engine noise at 1,400 RPM is not uncomfortable, but it is loud at 2,100. By applying some absorptive lining to four bulkhead areas and the cockpit sole, the noise could be greatly reduced.

A note on the accommodation layout. The BCC has no limiting fibreglass liners for the interior, so many changes are possible. Some owners have put a V-berth forward and built an enclosed head starboard of the companionway. Others have replaced the galley with a quarterberth and chart table, and moved the galley to the starboard side of the salon. The possibilities are almost infinite, but my choice is still the original layout.

Construction

The Bristol Channel Cutter is built like the proverbial brick relief station. The hull is hand-laid-up with minimum thickness of ⅜ inch at the sheer, ⅝ inch at waterline, and 1 inch in the keel area. The thickness, of course, is not an indicator of strength, for if it is achieved through sloppy squeegeeing of resin without a sufficient amount of glass fibres, then the exercise is futile, because

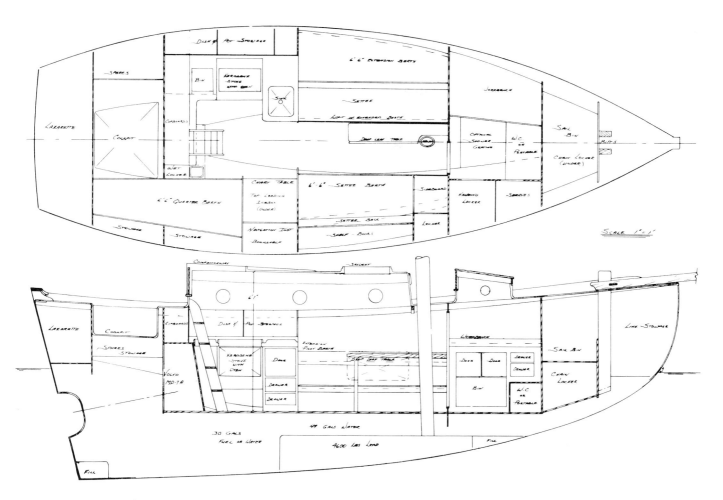

The wholesome profile of the Bristol Channel Cutter sans rudder. Lyle Hess must have run out of ink. Note intelligent use of forepeak for workbench, hanging locker, shelves and the head hidden below a hinged step, which helps to reach into the ample sail bin. A true little cruiser with two first class sea-berths (quarter and pilot) and thoughtfully great amounts of stowage.

resin itself has little strength and is almost as brittle as hard candy. The key with the BCC is the amount of fibreglass used. If we count each set of alternate layers of 1½ ounce mat and 24 ounce roving or twill, (flat roving) as one unit, then the lay-up goes something like this: Gelcoat; 1½ ounce mat; 1½ ounce mat and 10 ounce cloth; 1½ ounce mat and 18 ounce roving; 5 units (one unit at a time) up to gunwales; 5 more units underwater with 2 extra units in keel area. No wonder the boat weighs over 8,000 pounds without ballast. The Vancouver boat is built by Steveston Fibreglass, a small operation run by Béla Vigh, who, in spite of his youth has sixteen years of experience with fibreglassing, having apprenticed with a racing canoe and kayak manufacturer in Europe. With racing kayaks, every ounce counts, so if anybody knows how to get the most strength out of the

material used it should be a racing kayak builder. They are second only to sailplane builders in meticulousness. I saw a team of two laminators at Steveston laying up a hull and I can only say that the workmanship I saw performed was excellent. They also install all the plywood floors, bulkheads, and cabinetry in the BCC, and the bonding I saw was thorough and clean, well finished and ground, and what's just as important the bulkheads were square and true, and if you don't think that to be of consequence, then you have obviously not had the inimitable pleasure of building cabinetry out of trapezoids and parallelograms. Oh, the joy!

The Vancouver boat is finished off by G. & B. (Brian Gitting and Al Brunt) Woodworks, in their one-boat-at-a-time shop. They will do anything any way you like as long as it's done the way they want, which is very well indeed. Their work is precise and

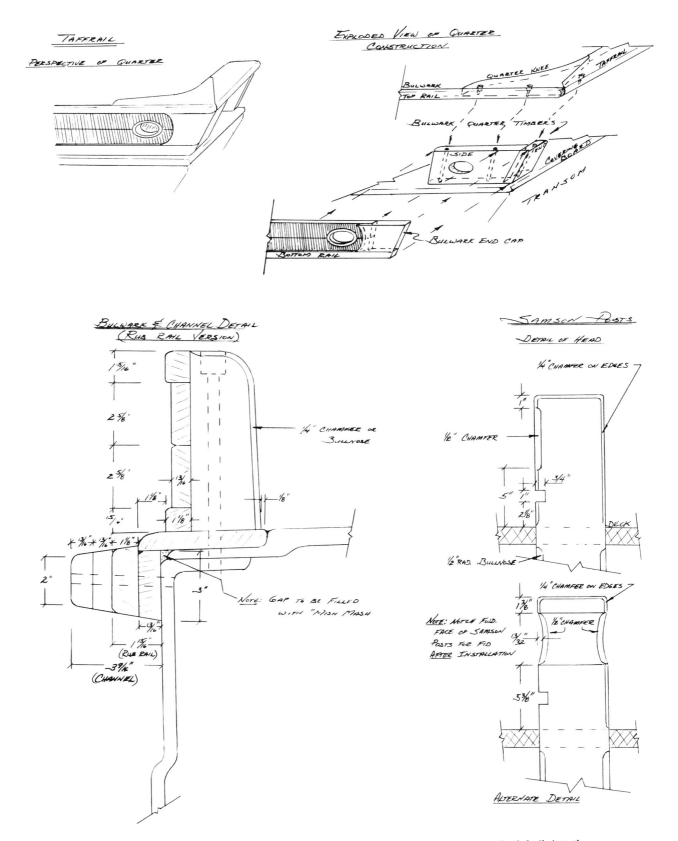

A few details of the Bristol Channel Cutter reveal the painstaking quality and care that's built into the boats. The completion of the B.C.C. is definitely for those who love woodworking, for anyone else will find the work endless and frustrating.

their attitude is that of a traditional craftsman whose work oozes pride. They'll never get rich but they sure sleep well at night.

The California hulls and decks are laid up by Crystaliner in Costa Mesa, where the brothers Jerry and Dave have been doing exactly that work almost since the invention of fibreglass. Among other things, they laid-up the first few hundred Westsail hulls and most readers know how well those were built. Enough said.

The deck is done with a similarly heavy lay-up — the Canadian version uses ¾ inch balsa core while the California version uses ½ inch plywood. The balsa has the advantage of being light and insulative, but has the disadvantage of requiring plywood inserts or large backup plates where deck hardware is being installed. We could discuss the finer pros and cons until the cows come home, but

The shippy interior of the Bristol Channel Cutter showing the elegant craftsmanship of Sam Morse's little yard in Costa Mesa, California. If you look inside the footwell you can see the bulkhead held in with giant 12 inch wide bond—half on the hull, half on the bulkhead—with a fillet of foam in between. Sam Morse doesn't fool around.

all in all it's about six of one and half dozen of the other. The hull to deck joint is achieved by what now seems to be the industry standard, that is, turning the hull laminates back at the gunwales to create a flange, in this case about 3½ inches wide. The California boat then uses ¼ inch stainless bolts on 5 inch centres with a 5,200 series polyurethane bedding compound (which sticks like Crazy Glue but remains flexible). The Vancouver boat has ⅜ inch bolts on 12 inch centres with a resin/fibre mixture between, *plus* three units of mat and roving bonding inside, of 8 inch, then 10 inch, then 12 inch wide strips. The procedure actually involves: a) fitting and screwing the deck on (with resin filler on the flange), b) bonding with the three units. c) removing screws and redrilling and   d) inserting bolts with caulking in bolt holes to stop leaks. Both yards have built over twenty boats and none has leaked at the hull/deck joint, and if all the steps are done as well as the other things they do, then none ever will.

The bulkheads are ¾ inch ply with three units of mat and cloth tapering from 6 inches to 12 inches in overall width. The Vancouver version lays in

¾ inch bevelled foam between the hull and bulkhead, and I feel this to be the preferred way for two reasons. One, I have never seen a bulkhead that is cut to absolute perfection, therefore one or two spots will sit hard against the hull, and although this would not affect a hull of such thickness, it may "read" through on a thinner hull as an unpleasant bump. In the marina next door to our house, a 30 foot instant-boat got slammed against the dock by an infrequent southwesterly swell for all of ten minutes (with fenders in place) and the main bulkhead not only *read* through but *came* right through the hull. Two, in the spaces where the bulkhead does not touch the hull, the bond can collapse as it is set in by hands and fingers. This concavity will not have the strength of a nicely radiussed laminate that can be achieved with the foam insert. Sam Morse, the delightful man who worries and frets over every detail in his California boatyard, is now worried about the bonds delaminating from the bulkheads, so he's experimenting with drilling through the laminates and the bulkhead every few inches, running through a short bit of fibreglass rope, then fraying

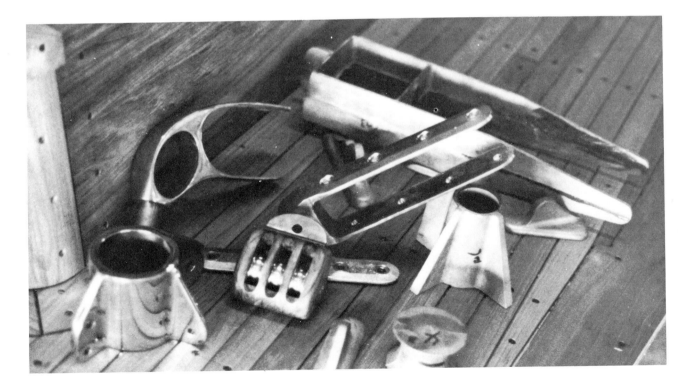

A sampling of the beautiful custom-bronze hardware the B.C.C. sports. The boats are heavily laid-up and meticulously built—one of the few times when a heartfelt design has been blended with first class craftsmanship. Why it can't happen all the time heaven only knows.

and folding back the ends and bonding them in place. This is an excellent idea. Through-bolts in a few spots would probably have much the same result although they would require good-sized washers to be as effective.

Both companies use traditional floor timbers with plywood soles and *no liners* so any alteration is possible. The bonding of the furniture to hull is very thorough in both versions, and if you're contemplating the purchase of a complete boat, I can say that the quality of finish is of the best I have seen anywhere. If I sound like I'm raving about all the wonderfulness of these boats, remember the title of this book. The chaff has fallen by the wayside long ago.

If one wants to make the BCC look as if she were all wood, it can be done. Teak decks can be laid without springing (bending) — an infrequent occurrence among fibreglass boats—since straight decks look good only with deck houses that have

parallel sides. Nibbing into the covering boards will still be a toughie but then remember, you're doing it only because you want to. The 'wale strakes and bulwarks will be a demanding task, because, for a reason that I cannot comprehend, the narrow boards that make up the strakes have to be tapered. Now *that* is cruel. The simple solution is to leave the damned things off in the first place, because even if you manage through some miraculous whittling to have the boards look right, their upkeep will be pure torture because the lower board is a full 8 inches below the deck level, hence it will spend much of its windward life submerged. So leave them off, and if your heart still yearns for the effect, then have the surface they would occupy gelcoated at the yard, or tape it off and paint it yourself, or do anything you want, except for gluing on astroturf or woodgrain-patterned wallpaper.

The forepeak with large workbench to port and much storage to starboard also doubles as the head, and what an intelligent notion that is. There is good headroom here (vertical) under the forward deck house, to work at the bench or have a shower. With the hatch open above you, the ventilation will be good indeed.

8

The Little Yachts of Tom Morris
Frances, Leigh, Annie

As you leave the town of Camden, Maine, on a sunny Sunday morning and wind along the coastal road, what will strike you most as you pass through whitewashed towns is that the only things that stick above the green of the forest are the white church steeples. And that is probably the way it should be, for if anything is to overshadow nature it may as well be the symbol of our spirit and our kindness, and not the smokestacks of our drudgery or the glass towers of our connivances.

And as you go northward you keep thinking that up here things make sense — the villages and the lobster boats, and the piles of firewood, and the small fields that run to the forest's edge and the pace of those who live here — it all seems to work so well with nature, blending and respecting instead of trying to go against her and bring her to her knees.

That is why Tom Morris lives here and builds his boats and raises his family here and not in Philadelphia. He had spent his boyhood summers here and loved the wilderness and the peace, but he started his career in Philadelphia as a bright-eyed banker full of eagerness and drive. But in a few months the eyes dulled and the eagerness ebbed, and his mind kept drifting off to Maine and sailing

boats, and one day his boss, who was a friend, called him in and said, "Tom, I'm going to do you the biggest favour of your life — I'm going to fire you." And he did. And Tom Morris packed up and came down east to Maine, back to the boats he loved, and he worked in the boatyards of Southwest Harbour until he started his own place at the bay's end at the bottom of a wide green field, that now has a small marine-ways to launch his Leighs and Annies and Franceses that come gleaming out of his meticulous boatshop, and his pine-lined office is up in the attic and his house is at the top of the green field, and his children are growing up in a town where doors are never locked, and you would have to look pretty hard to find a happier man.

Tom Morris is tall and gaunt and articulate and his only ambition is to build good boats and to give his children the good schooling that he was lucky to get, because he is determined that they should have at least the same opportunities as their father did. He is working towards the latter and doing just fine with the former, building some of the finest yachts on the continent. They are simple and honest and unpretentious in both design and construction, and maybe that comes from both builder

90

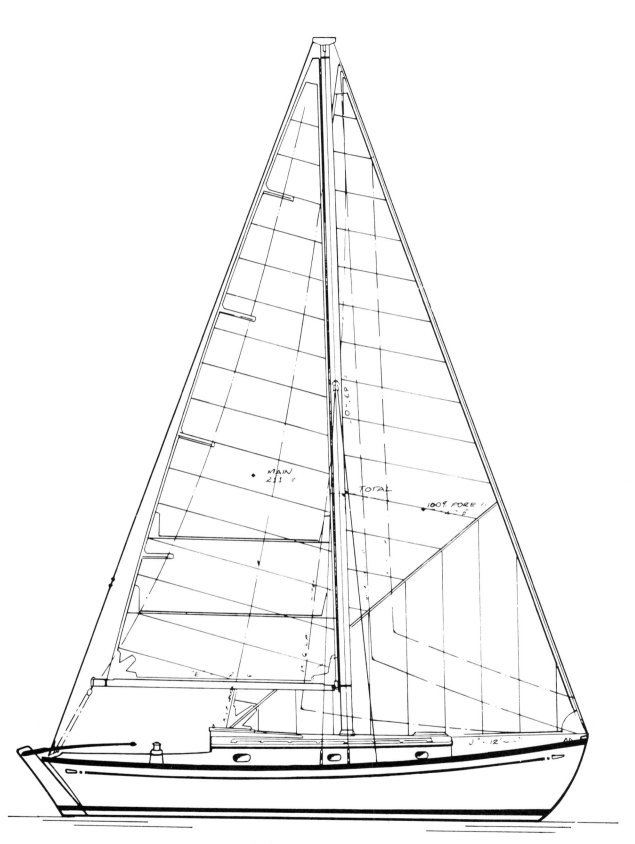

Annie — Chuck Paine

LOA—29'5"   LWL—24'6"   Beam—9'5½"   Draft—4'6"   Displ.—11,027 lbs.   Ballast—4,400 lbs.   Sail Area—456 sq. ft.

and designer living in Maine.

The designer is Chuck Paine, who lives near Camden, who draws timeless yachts after studying classic ones and deciphering their secrets. His excellent eye for grace and simple elegance is combined with a knowledge of what makes good boats fast and seakindly, and that gives Tom Morris one hell of a good start.

In Annie, a transom-sterned thirty-footer, Chuck Paine used some basic notions from J. Laurent Giles' Venture class boats, Herreshoff's H28's and Ralph Winslow Four-sum, and the Annie turned out every bit as pretty as these classics, but she has had major improvements made to hull and rig which make her a superior performer to her forefathers, especially in working to windward and ghosting in light airs. Her accommodations are, or course, much greater with a large house and full headroom (the H28 had 4 foot 8 inches), the entry is much finer and the keel is finer, both of which help her cut through the water. The bilges are fuller and stiffer and the draft is deeper at 4 foot 6 inches instead of 3 foot 6 inches, both of which help the boat enormously in carrying sail longer, and the rig is inboard so the genoa can be sheeted flatter and hence the boat can point higher.

The sail area is way up at 465 instead of 343 and the beam is greater, and all in all, those are some major improvements.

The sheer is as springy and playful as any classic, and the rudder is sensibly aft hung for simplicity of construction, repair and safety. The safety of the aft hung rudder concerns primarily the seal around the rudder shaft as it enters the hull. This perhaps has been a bit overstressed by purists, for although waterproofing of the system is not as simple as the caulking and bolting of the standard gudgeon and pintle arrangement, it is certainly not as vulnerable as the cutlass bearing stuffing box of a propeller shaft to which it has been compared, for that undergoes much beating from vibration of the engine.

Annie's tracking characteristics should be flawless with her length of keel, but she will not come about quite as quickly nor will she be as maneuverable in tight quarters as her sister Leigh, whose forefoot has been cut well back.

The rig has been kept to a simple sloop and with a relatively small headsail — her genoa is only slightly over 300 square feet — so a sail change to reduce sail should not be all that difficult even if one leaves it a little late through irrepressible enthusiasm. Her sail-area-to-displacement ratio is 14.73, which is a bit under magical numbers like 15.5 or 16 — and some people swear they wouldn't be caught dead in anything less than these — but then sail reduction can be left a little later on a boat like Annie, so all in all anything around 15 will be no Tahiti ketch in light airs — with greatest respects to Mr. Hannah.

Her decks are broad and safe and her cockpit large and comfortable, but to me therein lies the boat's greatest weakness. The cockpit is about 8 feet long, which is great if you want to have topside sleeping accommodation for basketball players, but this makes the house shorter and although this results in fine visual balance, it cuts drastically into the accommodations to the point where there is no chart table and very little counter space in the galley. The cockpit seats are about 4 inches lower than the decks and this, of course, results in very high (16 inches) and very comfortable backrests, but it does make for a rather cramped quarterberth.

The rest of the interior is well thought out, especially the less conventional aft head arrangement. As most of you know, this was a much used layout in older designs and I certainly like what it does for the interior here, for with the great part of the main bulkhead cut away, it opens the whole boat into one large space. For extended living aboard this is certainly a plus, although someone seriously contemplating offshore voyaging should keep the quarterberth instead, for not only does it offer the best seaberth, but it does create room for a sort of chart table. Still, the aft-head arrangement intrigues me, and those with much gear will like the extra storage in lockers and drawers that this creates forward of the mast, and those with many sails will like the extra sail locker under the cockpit seat to port. I do find the symmetricality of

Solutides, a Tom Morris-built Annie, with her main reefed, sinks her teeth into a quick summer storm.

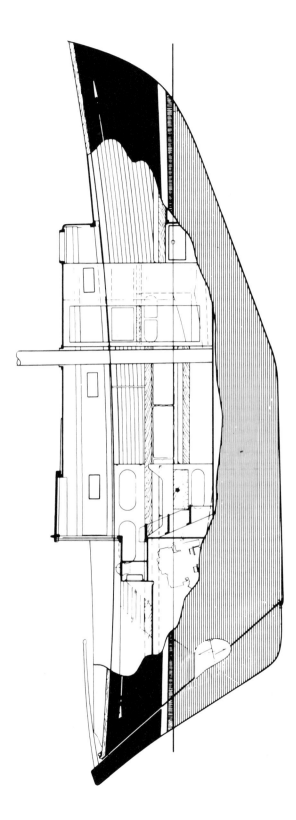

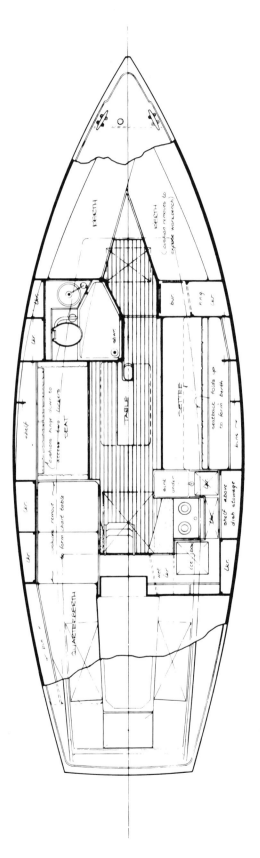

Annie's interior illustrates the problem with the off-centre companionway, for it does not allow for a fixed chart table. Were the chart table fixed, getting in and out of the quarterberth would be virtually impossible. I prefer the plan that sticks the head back here and opens up the whole interior.

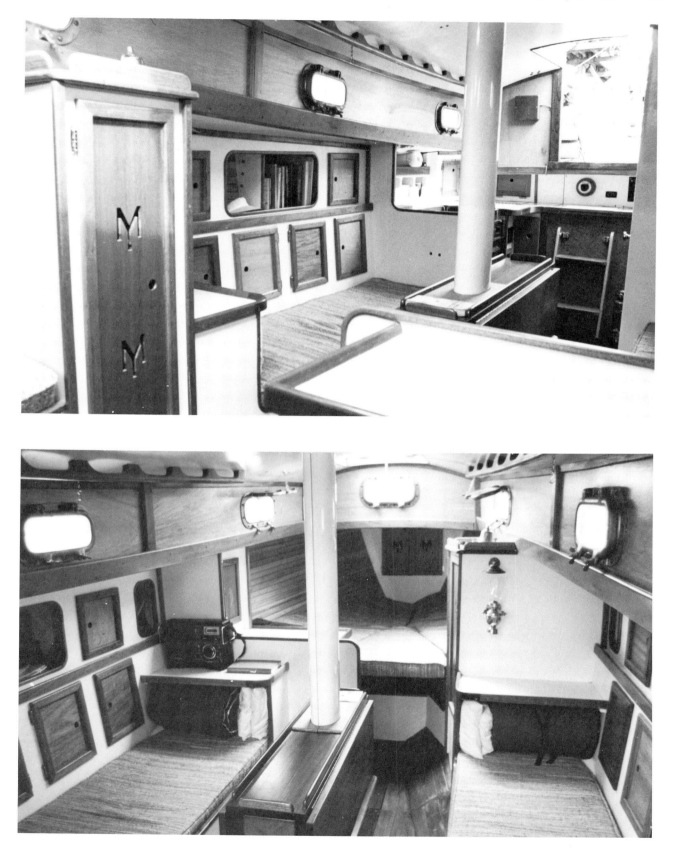

Annie's shipshape interior shows off her wide open spaces, making for a very nice feeling in a small boat. All this has been made possible by moving the head aft to port of the companionway. Note some nice touches, like footwells at the ends of the settee berths and a drawer inside the centre table.

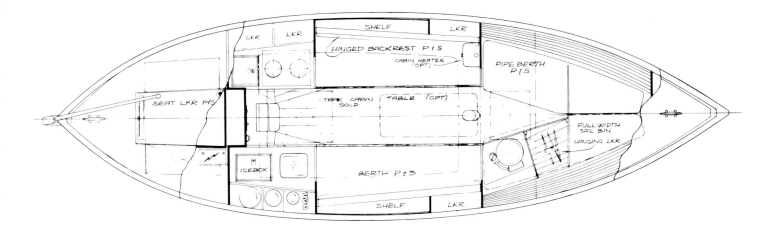

The interior of Frances in its glorious simplicity. One look at her and you say to yourself, "What more do I really need?"

the salon of the aft-head arrangement more pleasing, plus the two full length berths make for two fine places to sit back with your feet up and partake in one of life's great pleasures — reading. That two such places exist in a boat I think mandatory for all but devoted single handers and illiterates.

All of Chuck Paine's boats are moderate of beam and therefore require organized stowage, although Tom Morris has certainly built enough nooks and crannies to accommodate even the most acutely retentive.

Water tankage of 37 gallons under the port settee is too low for a long cruise, but it can be doubled by putting another tank under the starboard settee at the sacrifice of stowage. With the aft head arrangement there would be more space for potential tankage under the cockpit, but to keep hobbyhorsing to a minimum, one would do well to have as much weight as possible amidships. Access to the engine is good through a removable counter top and drop front.

Annie's little sister, the 26 foot Frances, is a completely irresistible little boat and your first reaction after looking around topsides and belowdecks is, "What more do I really need?" Chuck Paine designed and built the original Frances for himself. He likes the seakeeping abilities of traditional double-enders, but he drastically fined down the ends for Frances, making her a very weatherly boat. With 3,500 pounds of ballast on a 6,800 pound displacement boat (51% ballast-to-displacement ratio, which is very high in-

deed) Chuck was able to keep the draft down to 3 feet 10 inches, which opens up some magical places inaccessible to the usual 5 foot draft cruisers. He designed Frances during the winter of 1975 and said about her:

"She was to embody everything I knew about the design of efficient cruising vessels of fibreglass construction, to be capable of yearly cruises to and among the Caribbean Islands, to be small enough to fit my limited budget, but large enough to safely survive a gale at sea. She had to be as beautiful as her namesake, for some day I would part with her and I know well that beautiful yachts reward their owners' good taste with profit upon resale. Yet she is small enough for me to handle the little maintenance required, capable of being laid-up alongside a local lobsterman's wharf on an outgoing tide for periodic attention to the bottom, or even towed behind a good Maine Peapod if the engine and wind should choose to crap out simultaneously. Then there is always the dream of circumnavigation, and well, some year I might just find the time and have saved up the Panama Canal fee and a few cans of ravioli.

Frances is a small boat, the flush deck version does not have full headroom (the trunk cabin does) but she does have yards of sitting room. A great deal of attention has been paid to stowage space and of course any experienced seaman knows that space is no damned good if the displacement and freeboard of the yacht are so small that, should that space be occupied by usable supplies, she would float halfway up her sides. Load Frances

A pair of beautiful 25 foot Franceses work upwind in Southwest Harbor.

Frances 26 — Chuck Paine

LOA—26'0"   LWL—21'3"   Beam—8'0"   Draft—3'10"   Displ.—6,800 lbs.   Ballast—3,500 lbs.   Sail Area—337 sq. ft.

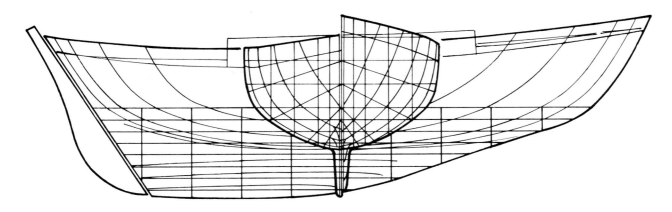

FRANCES

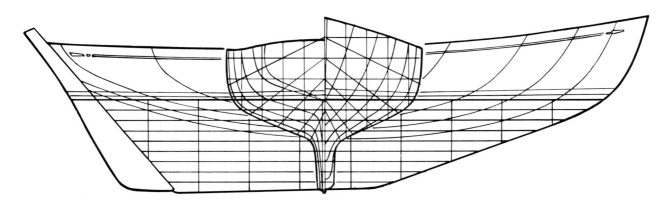

ANNIE

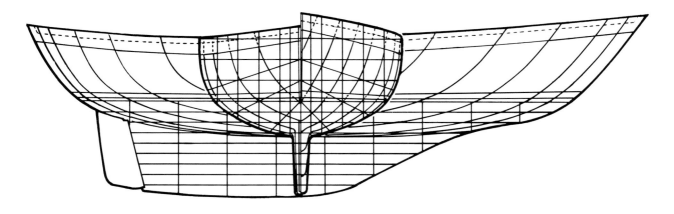

LEIGH

The lines of Chuck Paine's Frances, Annie and Leigh show refinements in firm concepts with Leigh having the most cut-back forefoot and tallest and thinnest keel, all of which should make her the most weatherly of the three. All three boats show slack bilges which will give them an easy rolling motion, and balanced ends for an even pitching motion.

with your cruising gear and she won't show it in appearance or performance."

And he goes on to talk about the hull: "The entry is quite sharp (25% half angle forward, which is sharp indeed for most racers have around 20 to 23). The keel extension is carried right up to the canoe body of the hull with a very tight fairing radius."

In other words, the hull is very modern with the keel figuratively added onto the body and not faired in, in that traditional flowing wineglass shape. This is hard to explain, but once you look at an old hull and a new hull side by side, you will know what I mean. As I write this I am looking at an old racer in the boatyard next door, built in 1940, and her keel does not become vertical until well below half way down her underbody. In contrast, if you look at the lines of Chuck's Leigh, you will see that right at the one-third mark (three out of nine lines down) the keel becomes a full wing causing lift and preventing leeway, thereby achieving a much more efficient hull than those of old.

The sharp entry, tall keel and tall rig, make her a weatherly boat and a stiff one, for as one owner, Jake Van Veedom explained, "The boat is so stiff I just haven't been able to bury the rail," and judging by a photo, Jake Van Veedom is no wilting pansy.

For those interested in what designers consider when drawing the lines of a boat, a few more comments from Chuck should clarify it:

"I wanted to end up with a boat that could carry her sail well (an essential conflict between cruising and racing yachts, the stability being penalized in the latter for rating purposes). On the other hand I wanted the desirable wave performance of a tender boat. That is, one which is an easy roller. There is only one solution to this seeming conflict. I get the sail carrying ability from the moderately heavy displacement (directly proportional to the riding moment). I achieve the easy motion by shaping the hull sections with a high angle of deadrise and very easy bilges, or more technically, designing the shape with a low metacentre. The result is a hull which is driven easily and has relatively less wetted surface for her length than many yachts of her size range." There you go.

The fractional ⅞ rig Chuck drew for Frances is rather tall, but Chuck drew the smaller headsail area with a proportionally larger main because he feels that "it's a damned sight easier to reef a main on a blustery night than go forward and change down to smaller jib." Almost as easy of course, is a split headstay rig which is also available, where half the headsails can be dropped and bagged and onward she would sail.

Below, the trunk cabin version is spacious and airy with much perfectly painted white plywood and varnished teak trim, and a layout so simple that any explanation or clarification by me would only confound it. Look at the drawings.

The rig that Tom Morris has devised has some noteworthy ideas, and you will have to look at the photo inset of the sail plan to see them. The need for a boomkin or even a split backstay, which is common with aft hung rudders to give the tiller free movement, has been nicely eliminated by offsetting the backstay to starboard. My first impression was that this would put an undue twist into the fitting at the masthead, but I was assured by a designer friend that as long as a toggle is used allowing the wire end to swivel off centre, the couple of degrees of offset will not really affect anything.

The shrouds too have been doubled up to cut down the number of penetrations through the deck from three to two. As you can see on the sail plan, the intermediate shares a chainplate with one lower shroud, while the upper shares the other chainplate with the other lower shroud. Of course the load bearing capacity of the plates had to be slightly increased, but whatever had to be done was worth it, to eliminate a major potential deck leak.

I have only one criticism of the boat, which is a general criticism. Tom and I went for a turn in Southwest Harbour, and the racket and vibration of the beastly little single cylinder diesel was just damned unearthly. If you have to have a motor on such a small, well sailing boat, then perhaps it should be a gas — wash my mouth with soap — outboard, namely a Seagull with an extended shaft. Fabrication of a bracket would not be the easiest thing on such a pointed double-ender, but whatever it would take, the price difference between a diesel and a Seagull would pay for it ten times over, not to mention the money you would save on dentist bills for replacing the fillings shaken from your teeth. The whole problem of gas storage could be solved with a tank isolated in the lazarette com-

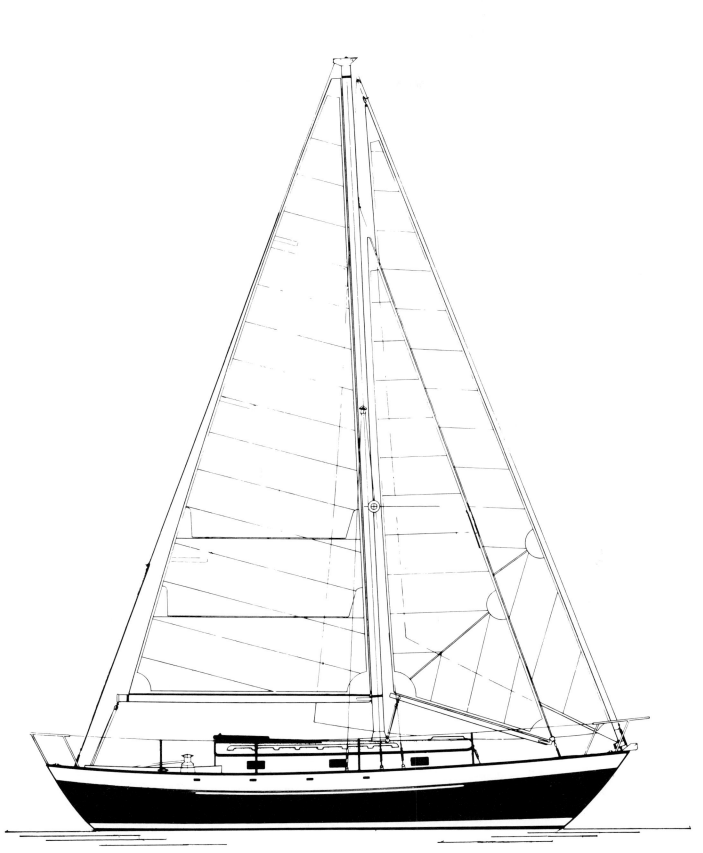

Leigh 30 — Chuck Paine

LOA—29'8"   LWL—23'4"   Beam—9'7"   Draft—4'7"   Displ.—9,100 lbs.   Ballast—4,400 lbs.   Sail Area—420 sq. ft.

partment, and by isolated I mean baffled and sealed off like one would a propane tank with an overboard drain for spillage in case of ruptured tank or fuel line. It is true that a gas outboard could be a bloody nuisance most of the time, but then that's the whole idea, you see, because you will hate it so much that you will become totally reliant on your skill with the sails and to hell with the engine except in case of absolute need. Amen.

I suppose it is of interest to no one, but the last Tom Morris boat is my favourite. Her name is Leigh and she is a very pretty double-ender, with a fine entry and a fine but buoyant stern and again, with the overall simple and elegant lines of a Chuck Paine yacht. As I mentioned, her forefoot is cut away to a much greater degree than Annie's, making her easier to bring about. Her sail-area-to-displacement ratio is 16, which makes her a bit better sailer in light airs, and her house is slightly longer, increasing accommodation without detracting from the beauty of her lines. Her keel is fined down and her sheerline is beautiful and for how she sails, I will let Chuck tell you:

"Sea trials for *Monette,* the first yacht completed to my Leigh 30 design, consisted of a brisk beat from Southwest Harbour to the Cape Cod Canal, a bit less than 200 miles. The weather varied enough to get conclusive ideas about her performance.

Most of our sail was dead to windward well offshore, and she was a natural at sea. The high freeboard with the bulwarks make for a very dry boat for her size, and the motion in a seaway was extremely comfortable, but then you would expect that from a conservative double-ender, but her best trait was her great stability. Again this should be no great surprise, since she is heavily ballasted and her moderately long keel enables the ballast to be deep down, so we were able to drive her to the breaking point — ours, not hers — and didn't have to reef, and that was reassuring on a cold starless night with gusts over 25 knots and no one volunteering to leave the cockpit. Her speed, quite honestly, was beyond my expectations. I estimated that we averaged 5½ knots on the wind against respectable ocean seas and she had very long legs once we cracked off onto a reach. We had her surf-

ing around 8 knots once the wind had faired to a beam reach and freshened to Force 6. Steering was as docile as one would expect from a full-keeled double-ender. We used a simple tiller lock and she went windward hour after hour with no human intervention. I think she will adapt well to most any of the medium expense, self-steering devices."

The deck plan is so clean and simple and the drawings so complete that I won't waste my breath repeating what is there, except that it all works well and looks very pretty. But there is one problem; if you look closely at the drawings you will see the rudder post coming through the aft portion of the cockpit sole, hence the tiller takes up all the rest of the cockpit. This is bad news for anyone but single handers, for the crew will have to sit behind the helmsman and how on earth the crew will get at the sheet winches without going over or through the helmsman I'll never know. To accomplish a tack you would have to do so much shifting and climbing and twisting and scrambling that it would make a Chinese fire drill look like midnight at the morgue. For this very reason almost all of the Leighs to date have been built with wheel steering, which is okay, but disparaging to sailors like yours truly who swear by the tiller for boats under 35 feet. The other change for the better since the drawings were made, was the relocation of the mainsheet traveller from the aft-deck to the bridgedeck and later over the main hatch, giving infinitely better control over boom and sail shape.

Down Below

Belowdecks Leigh is a work of art, not so much because of Chuck Paine's design, but because of Tom Morris' excellent taste and craftsmanship, but more about this later in *Construction.* As you can see there are two suggested layouts — although Tom will be happy to try any new intelligent ideas — and indeed the newer boats are now built with a third interior (see photo). Interior 1, with pilot berth and asymmetrical settees, looks very chopped, and Interior 2 sacrifices the quarterberth without any significant gain, i.e., still no chart table or jacuzzi. Interior 3, on the other hand, seems ideal and since there is no drawing we will have to piece it together from the old drawings

Viajero II, a Leigh of Chuck Paine's design shows off her crisp clean house and decks as she works smartly to windward.

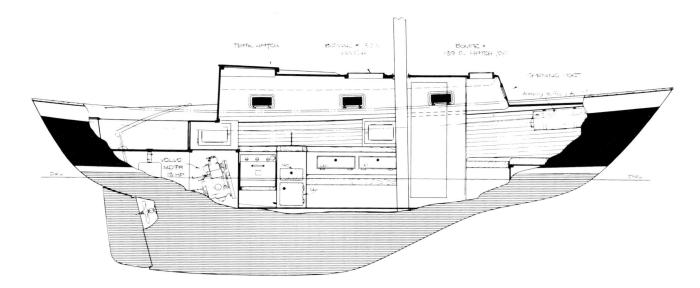

The profile drawing of the Leigh demonstrates the problem with the tiller, for it interferes with anyone and everyone in the cockpit. Almost all Leighs have gone out with a wheel.

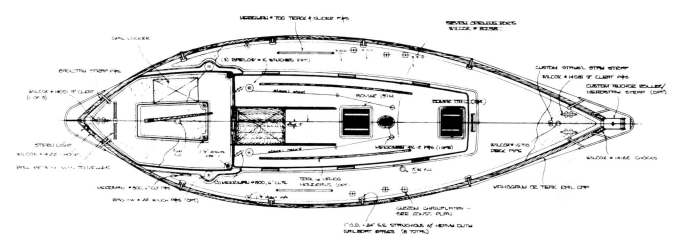

Leigh's wide decks and hardware layout are visible on the deckplan.

and a photo and my ramblings.

Take the quarterberth from Plan 1 and put a hinged-down chart table over it. Now, take the galley from Plan 2 and put the sink to port beside the companionway. Then take the salon from Plan 2 and shift the centre table to starboard, and the opening to the forepeak to the port side of the mast; don't ask me why, just do it. The head and hanging locker switch places as well, otherwise they are the same as in Plan 2 with the slide-out sink. An addition has been the installation of two vertical lockers at the foot (the forward end) of each salon berth, which greatly helps stowage.

Everything that is in the boat is all of good size: berths, settees, lockers, work spaces, and the cookie can be out of everyone's way because the main hatch has been shifted slightly starboard of centre. Engine access is good with the countertop off, and with the hatch/skylight in the salon and the eight opening bronze ports, the ventilation is plentiful and the lighting below — with all those beautifully painted white surfaces — is better than in any other boat I have seen. As you can see in the photo, there are grabrails overhead and the dripboards below the ports also serve as grabrails, so you can get as roaring drunk as you like. The rounded passageways in the bulkhead leave more strength in the bulkheads and show the elegant style of Tom Morris.

The tankage aboard is a problem as it is with

most modern boats with canoe-shaped underbodies, for they have very little bilge space, so the water tanks have to go under the settees in the salon, cutting down stowage there. Tom can get about 37 gallons per settee and one settee full would be quite enough for local cruising, where dependable refilling is available, but two settees full will be needed for long distance cruising where it is not.

Now for some general comments I dug out of my notebook: The vertical companionway opening is 24 inches high, a bit on the unsafe side for serious offshore work, but it does make companionway traffic easier. The cockpit seats four comfortably with a wheel; exterior teak trim is very heavy, should last forever; broad decks have 3 inch high bulwarks; house is 14 inches high; forward hatch is a little small for sails; very fine rudder section; lead ballast external but wedged between fore and aft keel pieces, so upon grounding, any damage, such as bending of keel bolts, is minimized; the boatshop has usually a crew of six, most of whom have been there over three years; deck has 1¼ inch drains plus the hawse pipes as drains; and lastly, very fine varnished cockpit coamings have aft ends secured to a raised moulding in the deck. And now for the best part.

Construction

Tom Morris doesn't know when to stop. His basic lay-up, installation of bulkheads, and especially his thorough double bonding (on each side) of every bulkhead and knee — and believe me, there are plenty of them — make his boats some of the strongest honeycomb structures around. Now you will probably say, "What a waste of time, who needs all that reenforcement?" and you will probably be right for most average cruisers, but heaven

The meticulously finished (except some doors are out for varnishing) interior of Tom Morris' own Leigh. A true down east yacht.

help you (because your boat sure won't) if you encounter anything terribly demanding. Let me tell you one of many stories told me by a most reliable delivery skipper.

In a heavy storm off Acapulco, a brand new 35 foot very popular production boat began to make funny noises all around the liner — crackling noises, Ed called them; they were so loud they sounded like a fire of dry cedar. When he was thrown into a bunk, the bunk felt loose, but on they sailed. Then he thought he was losing his mind because the sides of the hull kept moving in and out as if they were breathing, but very soon he got the good news that his mind was okay; unfortunately it came at the same instant as the bad news, which was that the port main bulkhead had popped out and was hanging in mid-air. Well now, when your bulkhead goes and your interior supports go, you then have a 40 foot tall stick trying to tear apart a ping-pong ball. And it did. Not completely, but enough to loosen hull and deck joints and the engine shaft-log, and the boat began to fill with water and the bilge pumps failed because they were full of bits of wood and fibreglass chips, and still the mad mast kept tearing at those seams and it looked like the deck would come off any moment when, thank God, the mast broke. To make a long story short, when the brand new boat arrived at its destination, the crew took off what little hardware was left, unbolted the keel and gave it to the locals, who then towed the dead hull inland and buried it with a bulldozer. Now let's hear all those comments about overbuilding.

Yet Tom Morris' boats are not wallowing heavy behemoths, as is obvious from Chuck's comments, and indeed the boat is light, under 4,000 pounds without ballast, engine and gear, and that is not bad, putting her in line and even under the likes of mass-produced racer-cruisers of her size, such as the Ranger 30 and the Catalina 30. So the boat is kept to a moderate weight but she is very thoroughly built and what is in her will stay in her for a long, long time.

Now for the nitty-gritty. The hulls come out beautifully and smoothly finished, because Tom uses three layers of mat next to the gelcoat, so the roving doesn't read through. Next come three units of mat and roving, then another layer of mat and roving is added below the waterline on Leigh and Annie, but not Frances. The centre is triple bonded with staggered layers of mat and roving. Tom does something interesting here. He fills the first few inches of the bottom of each keel section with a mixture of resin and powdered fibreglass and then he lays in the centre bonds. This way, if extended grounding occurs on rock or coral, and the outside skin wears through, then the centre bond or second bottom will still be intact, being some inches inside of the outer skin. This job of centre bonding is done so painstakingly that it takes three people one whole day.

The ballast is bolted on with seven Everdure-bronze bolts ¾ inch in diameter and the hull is bolted to the deck with ¼ inch stainless steel screws on 8 inch centres. This should be reduced to 4 or 6 inches in most instances, but on Tom's boats a teak caprail comes next, screwed down with #14 stainless steel self-tapping screws and these have so much bite that they add fairly good reenforcement. Somehow though, in my heart of hearts, I would still feel better if the bolts were on 4 or 6 inch centres.

There are no liners used for the interior except for a single slightly textured overhead liner, which is bonded to the deck adding structural strength, not that it really needs it because it is made up of three units of mat and roving on either side of ½ inch balsa core (with plywood in side-decks and where tracks and fittings go) and solid fibreglass putty is built up in areas like hatch coamings.

Tom prebuilds the interior cabinetry in small sections and installs them in the hull with the deck off. The major bulkheads are installed first to locate everything perfectly, and this method reaps the added benefit that some areas are reenforced with double layers of plywood since all prebuilt cabinetry is built with two complete sides, so that when they are attached to a bulkhead the plywood is then actually doubled up. Then of course, comes all the bonding I mentioned, with *two mats* and a roving on every knee and every piece both sides, and all this is done very well, uncommonly well in fact, because with the deck off there is plenty of light and air to work with.

I almost forgot. One of Tom's neat tricks is to pigment the last two layers of the resin used to laminate the hull, with a grey pigment. He also pigments the resin that bonds in the furniture as well, and this gives a completely finished look to interiors of cabinets, saving many hours of painstak-

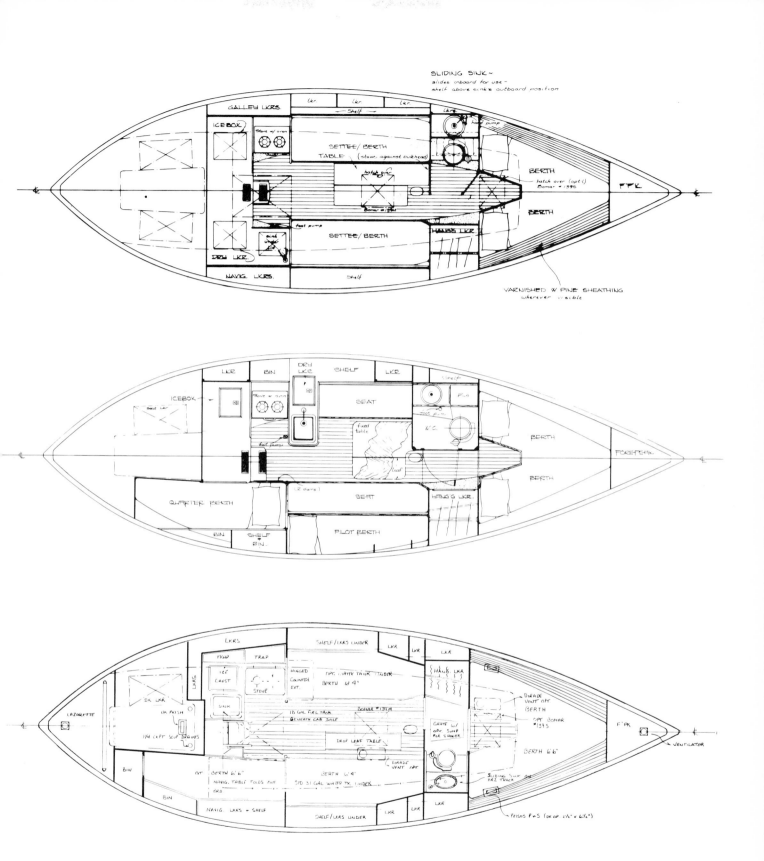

Well, you can't say Tom Morris doesn't give you enough choice for his 30 foot Leigh. The split galley may prove a bit inconvenient at sea, and the large head in the other plan seems a bit wasteful, whereas the third plan with the nifty little lockers at the forward end of the salon berth seems to be the best balanced layout of all.

ing inside cabinet painting. Besides, if any additional bonding to hull is to be done, it can be laid right over the pigment since it is an integral part of the resin. Were the hull painted, it would have to be ground down for proper adhesion and then repainted. What a pain. This pigmenting of the hull has one drawback in that it requires some very careful work when laying up, for the dryness of the fibres and air bubbles will not be seen through the pigment, so much experience and care is required for a proper job.

Anyway, everything is bonded to everything, and as proof of the strength of construction, a Frances passed a road test with flying colours when she was gracelessly dumped from a truck at 55 miles an hour and dragged about 500 feet along the road. Where she skidded she wore through the exterior mats and the first roving, leaving two units of mat and roving intact. No interior delamination or bulkhead separation occurred. The total repair bill was $1,200.00. Boats of her size built with chopper gun only would have been swept into a dust bin.

The ten floor timbers are 1 inch thick fir and all athwartship bulkheads are ½ inch marine mahogany ply. All others are ⅜ inch. The interior of the house sides is not covered over with plywood or liner, but is filled with a light paste and sanded and painted — as are all seams and joints — so one sees a perfectly finished interior without a million little bits of wood as covering trim. Now for the leftovers.

The deck is painted and seeded with nonskid, and this is much better than any moulded in nonskid, and even though it has to be repainted every few years for good looks, don't forget that it can also be repaired and repainted easily if damaged. How you repair a moulded nonskid, heaven only knows. The chainplates are ¼ inch by 1½ inch stainless straps bolted to heavily reenforced knees and major bulkheads; there is a brass protective strip over the rubrails; there are brass channels for the dropboard to slide in (and this is important as I have seen many teak slides crack away). The electrical panel is hinged for access to its rear; Tobin bronze rudder shaft is 1¼ inch solid, and the rudder is reenforced with two 6 inch by 24 inch bronze plates ³⁄₁₆ inch thick and holed to cut weight.

A closing note. When we sat aboard Tom's own Leigh discussing the ills of the world, one of the owners came back from his first weekend on his brand new Frances and gave Tom a short list of items that he felt needed attention. He sounded somewhat defensive reciting his list, as if expecting an argument or at best some belittling, but Tom listened with patient care and assured the man that all would be taken care of before his return for next weekend's sail. The man went away pleased and there was no flicker of doubt in his eyes. I didn't say anything, and Tom read over the list, folded it, and put it in his pocket. Then he looked up and saw me waiting for a comment, and said very simply, "I'm happy when they're happy."

Annie, with a reef in her, displays her moderate proportions as she clips along merrily on a perfect summer day in Maine.

9

If I Were King of Bjazarstan
Naja

Even though your chest swells with family pride because your great-great-uncle Humphrey discovered aluminum, and added to that your sweet Auntie Maud was the first to recognize the strength of hardened plastics when she broke a tooth biting into a petrified Host-less Twinkie, you still have to admit that your heart jumps upon the sighting of a real wood boat. And even if the outsides don't quite take your breath away, when you go below and see wood beams and wood frames and wood carlings, you must admit that you feel something fine inside. And what I have found most astounding after years of crawling through boats and boatyards, is that a wood boat is not only really beautiful when she is completed and impeccably detailed, but indeed she is equally elegant at nearly every stage of her construction, and certainly in her full glory just before being planked over, with her keel and frames and stringers glowing.

As for working with wood — shaping and planing and sanding — creating new forms without offending the beauty of the original, there are few comparable undertakings nearly as rewarding.

Immeasurable satisfaction will of course be gained when finishing out a fibreglass boat with wood, but I don't think one can deny that there is much added magic in starting with a pile of lumber and an empty shed, and building within it a thing of beauty with which to pay homage to the seas.

Perhaps if the world was unfolding as it should, then any family would be able to put aside a year during which they would have no other concerns than the building of a fine sailing yacht, for few things bring people closer together than sharing a project upon which they can look with pride for years to come. But then if the world were unfolding as it should, then I would be the king of Bjazarstan with a hundred long-limbed maidens at my beck, bringing laden trays of grapes and wine and camembert and marzipan. Maybe next year.

As a stopgap until the world gets itself organized, the celebrated French naval architect Sylvester Langevin, who designed the magically fast trimaran *Elf Aquitaine* (which, among other things, holds the transatlantic sail speed record) and the Whistocks Boat Yard of Woodbridge, Suffolk, England, have collaborated and come up with a beautiful thing called Naja. Now the boatyard which George Whistocks runs as his father had before him, has turned out fine classics like Francis

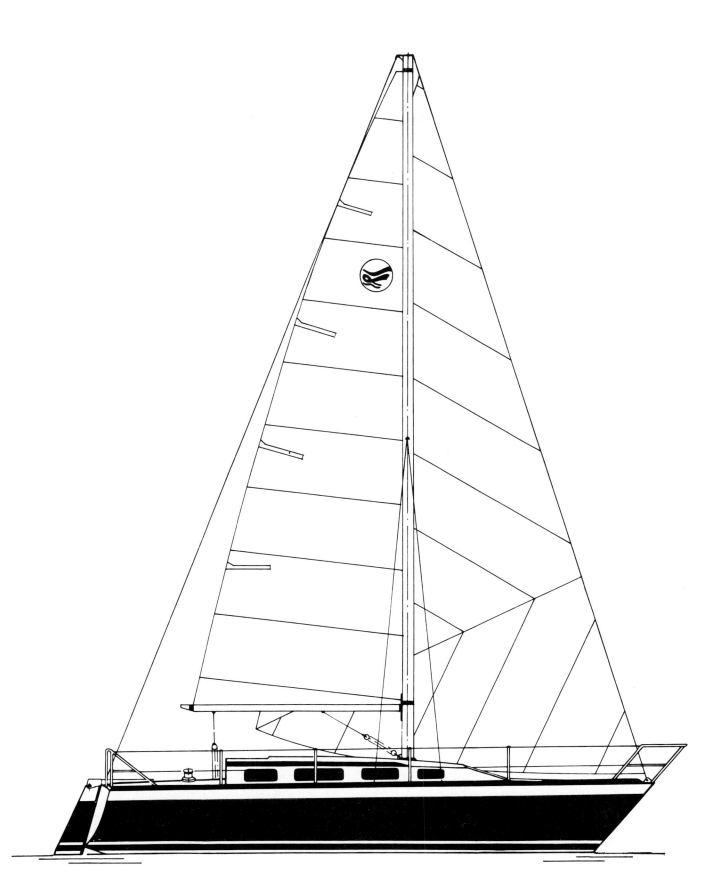

Naja 30 — S. Langevin
LOA—29'8'' LWL—27'2'' Beam—10'6'' Draft—5'9''/4'3'' Displ.—6,240 lbs. Sail Area—355 sq. ft.

Chichester's *Gypsy Moth IV* and the ocean racer *Barlovento*, and they have been doing that sort of thing regularly for fifty years, so if anyone can be trusted from long distance it should be them. They have certainly come up with a fine concept — an elegant light boat built in the WEST system of the Gougeon brothers; and what is even better is that the boat comes either complete or as a completely, absolutely and totally precut package that includes everything from keel to door handles, and all glues, fasteners and even sandpaper. So theoretically you can get a few tools, lock yourself in your shed with your crate full of parts, and come out only when your boat is ready for the water. And what will be ready for the water will be a gleaming varnished mahogany hull (or painted if you wish) and a fine little racer-cruiser of very pretty lines. What you will need to undertake this task is some working knowledge of a few decent tools, like a small table-saw, router, drill motor, and saber saw, and assorted hand tools, the most important of which

will be a good sharp plane.

Candace and I spent a few hours with Ken House who was finishing off a Naja, and he said that all the parts he has used fit together well and are perfectly marked or usually recognizable by shape anyway. The adjustments he had to make included bevelling and dressing edges and doing some trimming. What you need a lot of with this project is confidence and the patience to see it through, and not an unthinkable amount of the latter either, for Ken feels that the hours estimated by Whistocks are realistic. They estimate that to get as far as Stage 1, which means the hull assembled with all bulkheads and structural members in, takes about 250 hours or about a month and a half full time for the average decently experienced Joe. Now before you run off to get in line, read the next little bit for it will tell you that the deck house and cockpit will take another 300 hours, and last and most certainly not least, all the interior work and all the hardware installation will

Naja's aggressive good looks are highlighted by her teak decks. With her fine entry and shrouds well inboard she should be an excellent windward sailer and with her light displacement of only 6,200 pounds on a 27 foot waterline she ought to fly downwind.

take you another 625 hours. The more mentally nimble will by now have figured out that this totals 1,200 hours — give or take a few family squabbles which average about twenty-five minutes plus afterglow, but have been known to run as long as four hours to a lifetime.

The thing to do is to pinpoint how much you like woodworking, and how much your spouse likes you, then you can decide to do the whole erector set yourself or just go and buy the finished boat and crochet the doilies only. If you're not sure, get something in between, for the boat comes in three stages, broken down roughly as above.

Before we go on more about construction, a few notes on the boat.

She has extremely simple, crisp lines with a perfectly straight stem, a sheer as flat as a pancake, a low house with a faired-in forward end — all of which I would normally describe as a boat plainer than Jane; yet somehow the elements all blend together into a pesky looking little beastie with a lot of character, and I am not sure why, but maybe the aft hung rudder and the lovely teak decks have a lot to do with it. She has a short and deep (5 foot 9 inch, or longer and shallower 4 foot 3 inch) keel, one for the racer and the other for the cruiser who likes to go to shallow places. Now I notice in some older blueprints that there was a partial skeg of a rather strange shape in front of the rudder, but the newest blueprint from Monsieur Langevin, drawn in February of 1982, has no hint of one. What the new drawing called Naja Mark II does have, is a long melancholy stripe along the side of the house, and how this can be a substitute for the skeg I'm sure I don't know.

Naja is 29 feet 8 inches overall with a very healthy 27 feet 2 inches in the waterline, which, combined with her very moderate displacement of 6,240 pounds gives her a displacement-to-waterline-length ratio of 142, putting her very close to a Santa Cruz 40 which has a ratio of 100. In other words she is a very light boat indeed that will be very easily driven. She will be helped along by her fine entry, and her goodly beam of 10 feet 6 inches and full quarters will give her power to carry her sails well. The masthead rig carries 355 square feet of sail, giving her a very manageable sail-area-to-displacement ratio of 16.9, and when things start to blow she will be no problem, for her mainsail is only 144 square feet and her small

genoa only 211 square feet, so you can leave the deck-apes at home. There is a more powerful ⅞ rig available for racers and Southern Californians and people in general who live in areas tormented by light airs.

Her rudder is laminated up of solid Douglas fir, using the WEST epoxy system, and it is of the high-profile, high-efficiency variety. The first boats did have problems with rudder and rudder hardware failure, but the system has been beefed up and now seems good and solid.

This is probably as good a time as any to talk about the boat's chined hull, and clear the air. Chined hulls were invented for their ease of construction and that is the very reason why the hull of Naja is chined; but her chines are not as severely slabby as those of boats of old, many of which had topsides dropping vertically to the waterline and beams carried well forward with some resultant flat sections in the bow, with *much* resultant pounding when working to windward. This should not occur with Naja for she has multiple chines that are moderate, bow sections that are very fine and rounded, and midsections that are rounded as well, so that even the slamming of beam seas should not be nearly as thudding as on old single-chined boats.

On deck Naja is at her best. The cockpit is straightforward with freestanding teak-slab seats, which unfortunately affords no cockpit stowage, but the cockpit sole has hatches in it so there is access to a kind of lazarette space below. Through the forward part of this hatch excellent access can be gained to the stuffing box for quick adjustment or repair.

The engine, interestingly enough, is a Renault diesel of which even the stronger 16 horsepower version weighs only 209 pounds. I am not sure how available spare parts are for Renaults but they would be worth checking into. They use very little fuel, and they had better, because the boat carries only 8 gallons of it.

The standing rigging is 5⁄16 wire and it is well inboard so Naja should be able to point as high as anybody. The mainsheet traveller is a bridge in the cockpit making Naja a joy to single-hand, and there are simple inexpensive racing touches like a mechanical boom vang and a mechanical backstay-adjuster. The cockpit has good bracing room and what is even nicer, the coaming is very low so you won't forever trip over it, but it is high enough to stop the water running along the decks from coming into the seats. The bad news with this is that the back of the seats are rather low, just enough to keep you from sliding into the ocean and that is all. The side-decks are broad enough so that even with the inboard shrouds you will have lots of room to get by.

I do have a couple of quibbles about the deck layout, so I might as well get them off my chest. The toerail is less than 2 inches high, which by itself is not bad but combined with the fact that there are no grabrails on the house, passage forward could get treacherous on a heel. If the side coamings of the main hatch were to become handrails once they pass the hatch, the problem would be solved without taking away from the boat's plain good looks. My second objection is the way in which the halyards, etc., are led aft using a series of blocks in the coach roof. In a wood boat any holes that can be left out should be, for they can

leak and rot out the house, so the blocks should be replaced by a stainless steel mast-base like that of the Crealock 37, into which the blocks can be snapped. Such a base upon which the mast actually sits, transfers all the loading back to the mast itself instead of wanting to tear off the cabin top as individual blocks are wont to do. Other than that I can find no fault in the topsides layout, for everything has been nicely thought out and elegantly executed.

Belowdecks

Naja's beam gives her good accommodations below, although the layout looks as if Monsieur Langevin had a sultan's harem in mind, for there are berths as far as the eye can see, with the usual result that there is precious little stowage anywhere. How his prescribed seven people would ever spend a night on a 30 foot boat is beyond me, for the logistics of dressing, feeding, cleaning up after and providing oxygen for a herd of this size

The clean cockpit of Naja has no seat lockers but she does have stowage space below the cockpit sole.

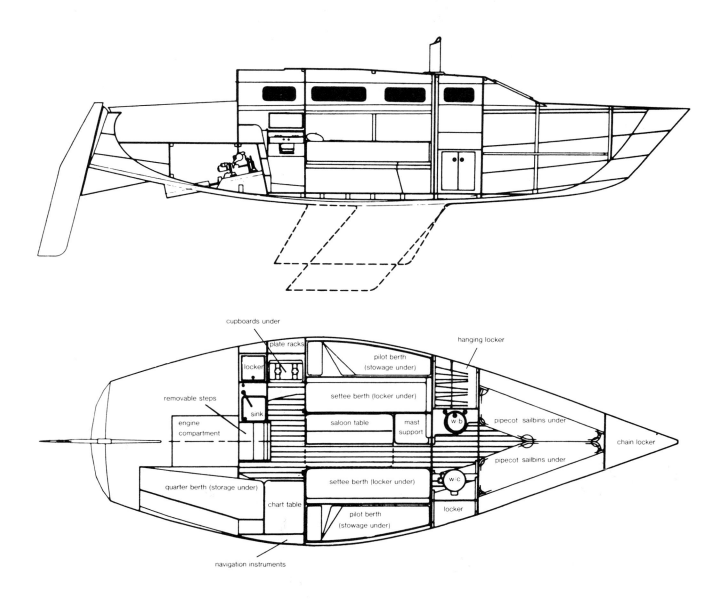

Little Naja's crisply elegant interior with good seaberths, a decent chart table, small galley and pipe berths that can be flipped up when the forepeak is to be used for stowage of numerous racing sails. Note the split head, with basin across the centreline from the head itself.

would be enough to drive a ringmaster of a flea circus to drink. Simple modifications could, however, turn Naja into a very fine boat for four, or even six on occasion. This involves simply converting the two pilot berths into bookshelves and lockers, and making the settee berth to port so it converts into a double if the table is lowered. No difficulty should be encountered here since Langevin's design is so classically pure that everything fits together snug and perfect like children's building blocks. So now you will have good stowage with a double to port, a single to starboard and a quarterberth aft, with two pipe berths left over forward for when the stampede hits town.

The galley is small, which is typical of most European boats, and I wonder if that is so because most people sailing there tend to frequent the endless array of exquisite little restaurants found in every port, whereas most of us North Americans are doomed to fend for ourselves, or pull a paper bag over our heads and crawl into the nearest hamburger haven for some chopped gristle. Anyway, the galley is minimal but workable, with room for a small icebox, sink and a two-burner ovenless stove. The salon we have talked enough about, and the head looks very straightforward, intelligently split as it is, and the forepeak with its folding pipe berths is as simple as can be. The hanging locker is rather small; those who are poor detectives should start looking in the head sink area.

One thing that I like very much in this design is that the chart table has not been compromised, but has been made a good size with a very usable quarterberth aft of it.

So that's it for the interior, short and sweet, because the boat is so plain and simple. Now let us get back to the most interesting part.

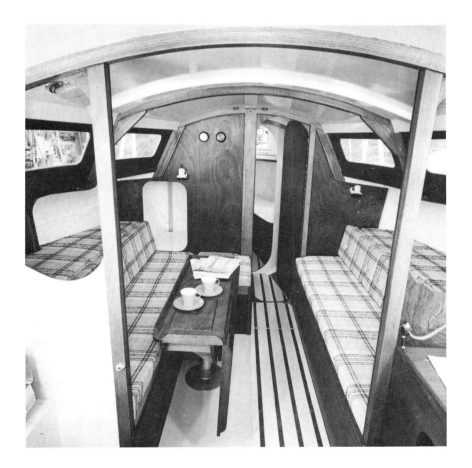

Naja's bright and simple interior. She is a dream come true for the home builder for all her pieces come pre-cut (and very well cut at that) and can be fitted with minor trimming and dressing.

Construction

Naja is built with the WEST system, meaning all her plywood is epoxy saturated, and all bonding and laminating is done with epoxy. All plywood used in her is Dutch Bruynzeel, the best marine plywood available. Her planks are Bruynzeel plywood as well, but they are not installed in normal sized sheet form, rather they come from Whistocks as full length planks running the entire length of the boat, having been properly scarfed and WESTed in their yard. Properly scarfed means cutting a scarf that has a scarf to wood-thickness ratio of 7 to 1, or in Naja's case, with her ½ inch plywood planking, a scarf that is 3½ inches wide. Now that kind of scarf you are not going to cut with your Big Johnny Toothpick and Match Carving set, so when a joint like this is well done by a yard, it should be enough to calm one's "plywood boat" anxiety.

To further pacify us worriers, Jack Van Ommen, a native Dutchman who handles Naja in North America, quite rightly points out that the massive fleet of Thunderbirds (originally developed as a promotion by a plywood company) has sailed North American waters for many years, and that ocean racers, such as *Ragtime*, were also built of plywood and certainly fared well. Besides, Naja *is* built to Lloyd's specifications. I am, however, unsure about one thing, and that is whether the dread of wood boat owners regarding toredo worms is applicable here. We all know how strong epoxy treated wood can be, and we all know that epoxy is as hard as a rock, but then so is candy, and billions of kids crave the stuff and they haven't even been trained on wood like toredos have, so I just don't know. The best thing to do is to trot down to the pet shop, get yourself a healthy plump toredo worm and plunk it into a bowl of water along with a block of wood that has been thoroughly WESTed, and go back in the morning and check the results. If the toredo has shriveled up and died of starvation you're okay; if it looks like a boa that has swallowed a cottage, start running.

To give you a rough idea of how Naja is built and what you get if you order her in pieces here are a few facts.

Hull and bulkheads — Stem and mainframe come in one continuous lamination, approximately 31 feet in length. The section at stem is 4 inches by 4 inches, at the keel 2½ inches by 12 inches, and it comes to you all planed and bevelled. There are six marine plywood bulkheads, WEST epoxy coated and sanded, with all the openings cut, ready to set on the main frame. The hull framework, deck beams, cabin roof beams, floors, etc., are all fastened, glued and bevelled. The transom is ½ inch marine ply, cut to size, bevelled and finished, complete with stern post and kneeing. The interior is WESTed and why the exterior isn't, is because it will be WESTed along with the whole hull once it is all assembled. The transom beam and other pieces are all glued and fastened on, with notches cut for structural members so everything fits together like a jigsaw puzzle. There are also two laminated belt frames (see photo showing planked hull with bulkheads) laminated to shape, cleaned up, bevelled and WESTed. The floors are solid Iroko cut to size, plus a laminated half frame. The planking as mentioned is eight strakes of ½ inch hardwood marine ply, each supplied in one full length, factory scarfed ready to fit, WESTed. The six chines are 1¼ inch by 3 inch Douglas fir, the two beam shelves are 1¼ inch by 3½ inch Douglas fir and the eight stringers are ¾ inch by 1½ inch Douglas fir, all cleaned up and ready to fit. If you don't know what all these things are, look at the caption of the photo showing the upside down unplanked hull. The ballast keel deadwood is solid Iroko cut to shape, left slightly oversize for fairing after installation. The mast support is made up of two solid mahogany posts 1½ inches by 4 inches and the package has one already glued to the bulkhead, with the other ready for fitting.

That is what you get to finish your hull, along with a couple of gallons of epoxy resin, hardener, some microfibres, twelve foam rollers, three brushes, and a critter called a "super mini-pump" for mixing resin and hardener in the proper proportions. Oh yes, you also get a WEST manual and all the fasteners thrown in for good luck.

I read through the first 20 pages of the construction book, written and well illustrated by the Whistocks yard, and I must say to my great surprise, that I followed *and* understood it all on first reading, and to fathom the significance of that you have to realize that I am a World Champion idiot when it comes to following instructions and directions, and perhaps that is why people find my boatbuilding books simple and easy to follow — they have to be or else I wouldn't be able to understand them myself. I must say though I did come to a shuddering halt on page 4 when the instructions say to do a "temporary cramp," then five lines later say "to check that the cramps are tight."

Now I know that there are lots of rituals and self-denials involved with sailing, but I can't see why you have to start hurting yourself so early in the game.

One slight initial inconvenience you will find is that everything is metric, but you can buy metric

Naja waiting for her planks. The main frame and stem are one continuous lamination, the chines (wide longitudinals) are 1¼ inch by 3 inch Douglas Fir, and the hull stringers (the narrow strips between the chines) are of ¾ inch by 1½ inch Douglas Fir.

The three stages of Naja are roughly as shown in the three photos above. She is a beautiful 30 foot racer-cruiser designed by Langevin, the French naval architect, and she is built (or pre-built if you'd rather) by the Whistock's yard in England. She is built using the WEST epoxy method.

tape measures and get accustomed in no time.

There are a couple of touchy things up to the point of finishing the hull, so I will mention them, more to give you examples of how undifficult the whole process is, rather than to actually tell you how to do it. The first and toughest example illustrates just how well Naja has been thought out. One of the most sensitive points in designing a chined boat is to figure out a good way to butt the planks, a way that is not only simple and workable but also aesthetically pleasing when finished. To try to plane and do a perfect butt is virtually impossible, for the angles compound and vary drastically as you bend on the planks, and even if you managed a rough fit, there would be no way to fair in the outsides of the planks without sanding and planing through the outside veneers, leaving a scar which could not be patched well enough to bright finish the hull. So Langevin and Whistocks have a nice system whereby the planks are butted together so that the inside edges touch and the outside edges can be left open. Next comes a bit of attentive routing. Now there is no need here to go all tight in the belly like you do when the dentist pulls out his jackhammer-size drill, for routing here will be simple if you do as the instructions say. Gather up some confidence and use a little care. For practice, get a scrap piece of wood and rout "Elmer loves Brenda" on it a few times before you go and turn the surface of your hull into a maze for earthworms. You will need a good, powerful router, with a ⅜ inch or ½ inch shank, putting out about 20,000 R.P.M., and a router bit that cuts a half round groove. Next, you measure the half width of the router base — that is, from the very centre point to the outer edge — and you fasten (tack on) a fairing batten at that distance below the centreline of the chine. This line is where the inside edges of the plywood butt. Next, you set your router bit depth so that ³⁄₁₆ inch is exposed, and using the fairing batten as a guide, and keeping the router base *firmly pressed flat* against the plank onto which the batten is fastened, proceed with routing. Try to move steadily. Switch off the machine and allow the cutter to stop before lifting off from work. Repeat using cut depths of ⅜ inch and finally ½ inch — the thickness of your plywood planks.

I took the above almost verbatim from the instructions, to show you how lucid they are. Now you will have a perfectly even, half-round groove along the joints, and into this you will epoxy and screw the half-round fir sections they provide. You will have to predrill the half-round so it doesn't split. So that is the trickiest part done. Nothing to it, right?

The second toughy can be illustrated at the very next step, which involves planing off the little excess half-round which sticks out, and you will have to do this *without* nicking the plywood with the plane blade. This is what will take true concentration and patience, but you had better develop both, for the same trimming will be encountered when you trim back the overhanging deck planking flush to the hull. Once you have blown this and gouged out the last layer of veneer, a good cosmetic repair is nearly impossible and you will have to paint the hull. This probably is a good idea anyway in areas where there is a lot of sun, for some makers of transparent coatings claim that it is *not* their product which breaks down with the years, but that the actual surface layer of the wood deteriorates from excessive ultraviolet light. How true this is is hard to say, but it's certainly worth checking into.

The last important tidbit which will be even more incorrectable than the others is the setting in place of the cabin top carlings — the framing pieces that run on the outside edge of the house top. The run of the carlings is almost dead straight in the forward section of the house, and you must eye these up when installing them, and make sure they remain so, for if you trim back the sides of the bulkhead just forward of the main bulkhead even a bit too much, and set your carlings tight to it, you will end up with a noticeable "pinch" in the house which will look like hell. So use your eyes here and during all the construction and you won't go too far wrong.

I think the photos are fairly thorough so you can readily discern how most things fit together, and I won't bore you with more details except that you will need a covered space about 32 feet by 14 feet by 7½ feet in height, if you intend to build a Naja, and I must say that after looking at the pictures and seeing the boat, it sure is hard to resist going out and building one. And if you are already smitten I must warn you that she looks even prettier in real life.

Come on world, get organized.

10

Chuck Paine Lives Near Camden, Maine
Whistler

If you are in luck you'll get into Camden, Maine when the night is cool and the spring fog thick, and you'll walk down to the harbour among silent houses, down to where the water clacks against the pilings and the great masts of ancient schooners loom into the greyness, and if you close your eyes and let your thoughts drift away you'll hear old footsteps falling on the decks, and old voices talking softly at the wheel, and you'll smell dripping tallow candles burning down below, and your blood will rush with the expectation of the great whales sounding or the first winds of a hard gale rattling in the sails, and you will fill your lungs with the air of simpler days when joy was simple, and pain was simple, and love was simple, like childhood.

Chuck Paine lives near Camden, Maine, and he designs yachts that are simple and graceful and full of respect for things past, like the town he lives near. His boat Whistler is all these things as anyone can see, and we can all put our hands together and thank the Lord that here is a designer who doesn't bore us blind with mundanity after mundanity as so very many consistently and insistently do.

Whistler is striking, not only with her unconventional rig but with her pesky sheer and good proportions, and looks generally like a boat that is dying to go for a cruise. For the stick-in-the-mud who shudders at the prospect of such a "novel" rig, let me assure him that it has been tested many a century, and lest he smiles in disbelief, allow me to enlighten his Dimness by quoting L. Francis from his *Compleat Cruiser*:

"The name of the rig which has two masts of about the same height and no headsail, is sometimes called a 'periauger.' It is a very ancient rig that was much used in Holland some three hundred years ago. It was also a rig used around the mouth of the Hudson from Dutch times until perhaps 1830. They were used for ferry boats running to Staten Island and towns on the Jersey shore, and were sometimes called "piroque" ferries. It might interest you to know that the original Cornelius Vanderbilt started the family's fortune in a periauger that he sailed out of Staten Island around 1810."

So much for one group of skeptics and now on to the next — those who think that a boat with such a rig can't possibly be handled and can't possibly

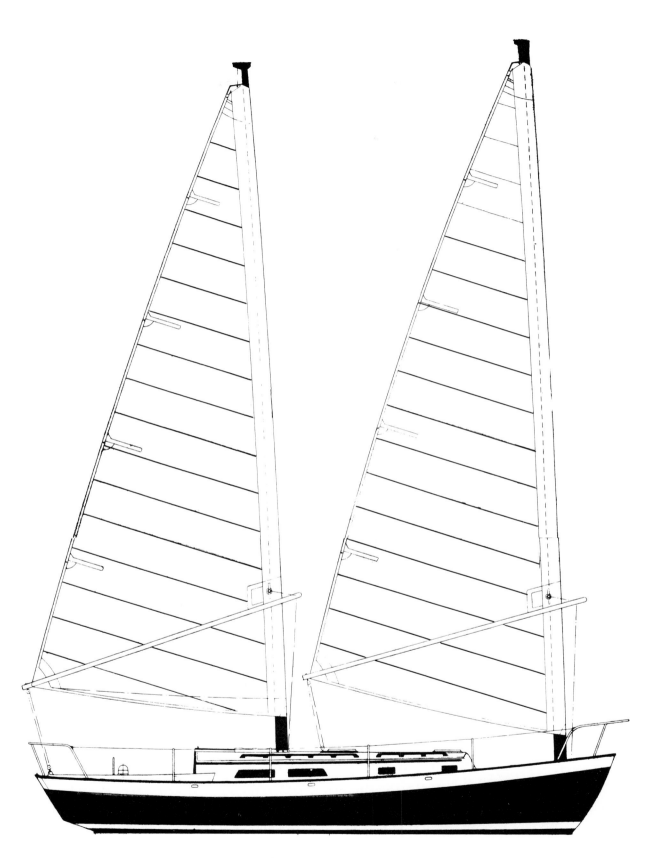

Whistler — Chuck Paine

LOA—32'½'' LWL—25'10'' Beam—10'6'' Draft—3'7''/7'6'' Displ.—11,986 lbs. Ballast—5,000 lbs. Sail Area—520 sq. ft.

sail. I give you the words of Donald Street (*The Ocean Sailing Yacht*), who has spent some time sailing and racing a Freedom 40, which has an identical rig:

"Once the sails are up they are dead easy to handle — this is a real cruising man's rig — and the boat is extremely fast. Once the sails are set one has literally nothing to do — just two sheets to trim, a board to adjust, and a boat to steer. To tack, one just puts the helm down and the vessel is off on the other tack with nothing else to be done . . . Tacking to windward while all the other crews are killing themselves cranking genoas, the hardest work for the Freedom's crew is opening beer cans for the skipper. Going downwind they do have to work once in a while, setting and trimming a mizzen staysail or occasionally playing the sheets a little. Many people insist that these boats cannot possibly go to windward, because they have no jib or genoa but her performance proves otherwise. The sails wrapping around the completely unstayed masts function as beautiful airfoils undisturbed by spreaders or rigging. [Or a mast in front of them to spoil the airflow—F.M.] The wishbone sets down on an angle so that it acts much like a boom vang. When the sheets are eased the sail swings out on a flat plane, there being very little tendency for the clew to rise or the sail to twist. Thus the sail develops unbelievable forward drive on a reach or run. When the Freedom 40 sailed in a 1976 and 1977 Antigua sailing weeks on closed courses, to windward she kept up with a Pearson 41 while off the wind she hung tight onto the Swan 44's."

So there you have it. She worked well for hundreds of years and now in modern application is putting contemporary boats to shame. Her advantages are many: there are no shrouds, turnbuckles, or swedges to fail, or pins to fall out, or tracks to jam or slides to break or hanks to snap or chainplates to leak. That from a safety point of view. Also with a great amount of weight removed aloft, the boat's stability is increased. A bare mast for a Whistler has been trimmed as low as a hundred pounds, although the standard mast is about a hundred and forty pounds, but most of that weight is down in the fat end where the mast measures 8 inches across and not at the top where it is less than 4 inches. If the weight of the 44 foot mast shocks you, remember that a goodly portion of it is made of ultra-light and ultrastrong carbon fibre.

Along with the weight, windage is reduced, which not only helps performance but eliminates one of the most disconcerting and unnerving aspects of heavy gales, which is the eternal howling and vibrating of the rigging, which on one trip I found so bad on a medium displacement, poorly tuned rig, that the whole boat vibrated like a musical saw.

The main drawback with this rig is sailsetting in general and reefing in particular, which can take longer than a normal boat, but then you won't have to set reaching poles or make sail changes in light airs.

As you may or may not know, the sail is actually a double sail wrapped around the mast and doubled back over itself. The actual sail setting can be done from one or two starting positions; the first method makes setting a little slower but certainly looks more tidy in stowed position. The sail can be stowed with the clew set in place right between the wishbones, but then a sail cover of ungodly proportions would be required to cover the whole massive apparatus. The other stowage method involves releasing the clew and rolling the downed sail forward to the mast and wrapping it with a headsail type bag there. The first method has the advantage of the sail having only to be hoisted without unrolling and clew setting, but then you have to spend untold eons wrestling the sail cover to the deck and folding it up and then you have to stow it somewhere. The second method means shackling the clew in place, but then the sail bag is considerably smaller and more manageable. The second method has the added advantage of allowing the wishbone to be lowered to the deck at anchor, out of the way of bodies and of wind which can raise havoc and cause lots of chafe with the large winglike bagged sail.

For times when the weather gets really mean the sail can be lowered, left with tack and clew in place, wrapped with a single line to prevent unnecessary flapping, and the storm tri-sail can be set right above it.

So now that we have exhausted sail stowage and sail setting, let's look at reefing and shortening sail. There are two schools of thought regarding this. The first school simply lowers the aft sail and goes on, and apparently the boat handles all points of sail and all maneuvering perfectly well

Whistler sailing in her full glory. The carbon fibre cored masts bend but hold well. There are no stays or fittings that can fail and bring the mast down on your head. The sails are actually a double layer that wrap around the mast.

under the front sail alone. The advantage of this system is that you simply drop one sail and leave everything else alone, but the disadvantage is that much force is now exerted on a single mast and that force is high up to boot. If one would want to worry about the failure of an unstayed mast, this would be the proper time to do it. The second system involves reefing both sails in the standard jiffy reefing fashion, and this has the advantage of spreading the load onto two masts and bringing the load well down, but the disadvantage lies in the fact that the sail will have to be pulled down the mast — it won't slide down with as much ease as slides — and of course there is no boom for the sail to settle onto and be tied to and the whole thing tends to hang there looking like "a pair of socks that have slipped down rather skinny legs." Some people do a quick lacing between the two arms of the wishbone to create a temporary net for the sail to rest in, while others use standard reef points to

bundle the whole thing neatly together. The latter seems to be the most sanitary, if the most time-consuming approach.

In close quarter maneuvering the boat is a gem, for you can sail up to a dock or buoy with the wind behind you and if you want to stop you just let go ten miles of sheet and let the sails go all the way forward and spill the air.

I was told of a miraculous ability of this rig and I suppose it is conceivable, it goes like this: If you run aground beating or reaching you can usually centre the sail and pivot so you will face dead into the wind. Then you can set your sails wing and wing by running a line from the end of each wishbone forward so that the boat will actually sail straight backwards and off the reef or bar. Now some will say, "Why not just tighten the sheets and heel the boat and sail off?" But that is not always as easy as it sounds, for most keels get deeper as they go aft, so the more you proceed for-

ward the more draft you will need. As well, you will usually be going into shallower and shallower water. To illustrate. Candace and I were beating through a narrow turbulent pass under sail in good winds going with the current, trusting the bloody chart. Candace was at the helm and yelled out, "Maté, I can see bottom." Now for Caribbean sailors that's no big thing because they can see bottom at fifty feet, but for us Northwesterners when the bottom shows it's definitely Hail Mary time. I felt the first soft bump, but I don't panic easy (most slow witted people don't), so I said coolly, "Just sheet in and keep sailing." So we sheeted in and we kept heeling and we kept sailing, and the old bottom was getting so clear you could see the barnacles picking their teeth, but old *Warm Rain* with her five foot draft just put her rail down and kept on sailing, and we never actually touched bottom

again until we came to a sudden stop in three feet of water.

"That was a very good idea, Maté," Candace said quietly, "You should put that in your next book." So perhaps heeling and sailing off is not always the best of solutions.

Back to Whistler. If you are still not convinced about the rig, she is available as a sloop.

The lines show a hull with a fine entry and powerful aft sections so she will be able to cut through head seas and carry her canvas well. With the centreboard up she draws 3 feet 7 inches and that is almost thirty per cent less than most boats of her size, so she is ideal for East Coast and Bahama Islands sailing and would sure open up cruising potential for us Westerners in secluded little bays and river deltas, not to mention shallow South Pacific lagoons. The operation of the board

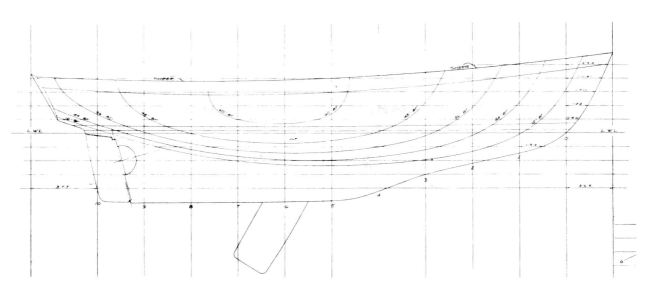

Whistler's lines show how well Chuck Paine balances his hulls. The entry is moderate and the quarter sections show good power.

is extremely simple, using a recessed socket fitting in the cockpit and the boat's standard winch handle, and as the builder Crow Fox showed me, they have done some improvements that make the whole thing as foolproof as possible, involving only two blocks and a wire drum.

The deck layout is straightforward with good side-decks and a good foredeck, the only problem being with the latter, that one will encounter much difficulty installing a windlass. This should be no major problem because all things being equal — and by that I mean your back being exactly as strong as you think it is — you really shouldn't need a windlass for a boat of this displacement. If you intend to use all chain, you can probably make do with a chain pawl into which the links of a chain can be hooked while the old back is taking a rest. There is of course no anchor-well because the forward mast lives in the space where the anchor-well and chain locker usually are. There is sufficient room around the mast — which is stepped down below — for ropes, but one would be ill advised to stow chain here unless a fine sheet of copper were used to wrap around the fibreglass mast to protect it from chafing. But this is really too far forward to stow chain anyway.

The cockpit is a typical Chuck Paine design, with deep seats and high backrests, all of which make for comfortable seating but also a cockpit that holds a lot of water. The seats are long enough for sleeping and the wheel is designed so that it is comfortable to stand behind or get around, and un-

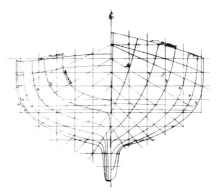

fortunately the wheel is mandatory because the rudder post is so far forward that a tiller would take up the whole cockpit. The lazarette is large and the sail locker to starboard enormous, with a removable panel to give you ample access to the engine — but not before you empty the locker.

Whistler is an ideal single-hander, with everything led back to the cockpit including outhauls, so the only thing that will make you go forward will be the need to douse the sails.

Visually the exterior is elegant, with a broad sheer stripe to accentuate the length and a sensible amount of exterior teak in the form of hatch trims, grabrails, caprails and Dorade boxes.

Down Below

The Whistler is built by Crow Fox and his handful of cronies (sorry, I couldn't resist) in a fine big boatshed behind his house that is just up the road from Tom Morris' yard and just across the

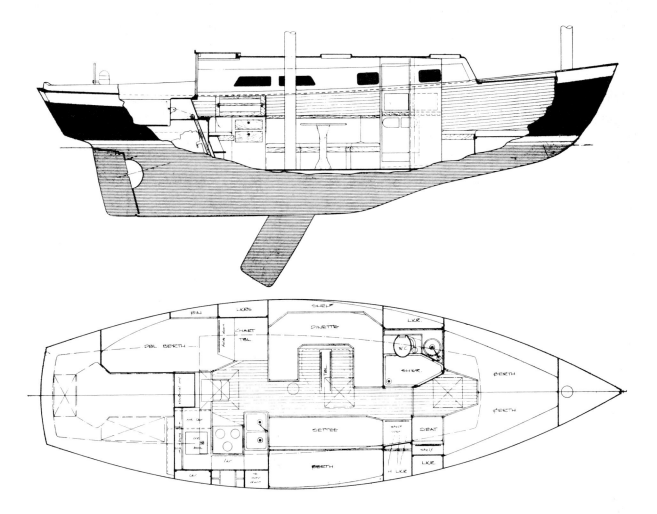

The layout of Chuck Paine's *Whistler* shows a friendly dinette which converts to an airy double and a very large forward cabin with a seat and a locker made possible by pushing the starboard forward bulkhead about 18 inches aft.

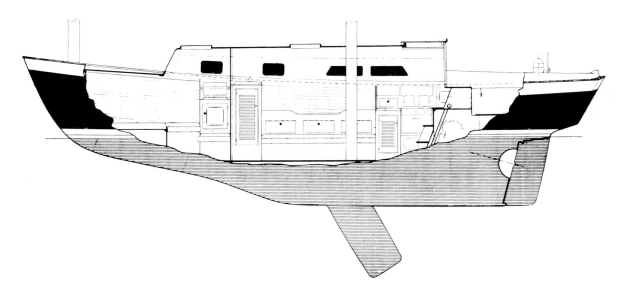

Whistler's centreboard stows fully under the cabin sole thereby not interfering with the accommodation plans, unlike many centreboarders whose salon is dominated by a large centreboard box.

harbour from Hinckley, and that's some mighty strong influence, and indeed pressure, to create very fine yachts or be laughed out of town, and since Southwest Harbour is home to but a few hundred souls it wouldn't take long for the word to reach every ear. But whatever the reason, Crow Fox's boats are as beautifully built as any in the harbour. Much of the interior is painted white and with the two Bomar hatches in the salon and forepeak and with the Lexan mainhatch, the feeling below is that of airiness and light. But the Whistler is by no means stark or cold, for her cabin sole is made of wide teak planks, which need but scrubbing to be beautiful nonskid surfaces, and all her cabinsides and ceilings and doors and drawers and table and ample trim are all hewn from, and meticulously finished in, the finest North Carolina cherry. The lighter colour effect is truly beautiful and I must say has a more interesting feel about it than teak.

The detailing in the boat is first class, down to the cherry wood toothbrush and cup holder, and the teak grate in the sole which sits above a small removable fibreglass pan into which all dirt can be swept and lifted out — obviating the need of a dustpan that is always lost or always in the way, and saving on dampened paper towels which I, alas, have used all these years to dab up the dust.

To continue with the sightseeing, stick your head into the hanging locker and find it lined with aromatic cedar, and take a glance into the head and see the cherry trim rings around the holes in cabinets and bulkheads where hoses penetrate. It's enough to make you turn emerald with envy.

For those considering building anything of cherry, a warning from Crow. Cherry is an extremely hard wood and it will literally burn as it's being cut with a saw, leaving black scorch marks. These can be scraped off with a piece of glass so that no trace will show, and this is faster and easier to do than using sandpaper.

Now for the complete guided tour from stern to stem. The quarterberth is ample and spacious and although Chuck Paine calls it a double, I promise you the only way two people will ever sleep in that berth is in shifts. For God's sake, Charles, even a phone booth is wider than that. Anyway, there is a nice stand-up chart table of modest size, but its aft end does have a flip-up extension which

makes it a fine size indeed. The problem is that someone unwisely decided to put a searail between the two pieces, which is precisely ¼ inch high, just the right height to bugger up any plotting over it. While I am complaining I might as well mention that the searails in the boat were generally too low — the proper height being over 1½ inches, anything lower will serve only to help cans and glasses tip over the edge instead of sliding straight off and what consolation one can get out of that I really don't know.

The galley has been made workable by again shifting the companionway slightly off centre and having the ladder start from the counter down, giving you very fine counter space. Unfortunately, Chuck Paine makes his cockpits so comfy by lowering the seats and thus having high backs, that the space below the bridgedeck, although well utilized as part of the galley, is just a bit too low to allow the hinged icebox lid to open, which means you have to lift the lid off and set it somewhere, and that is a pain in the wrong place.

Some very useful changes have been made in the galley area since Chuck first drew the plans. The skinny wet locker has been left out beside the icebox, so that the icebox was increased in size by about fifty per cent, and the wet locker has been moved to just forward of the stove where it has become much more voluminous and useful, and has also created a very fine flat surface above it, giving additional counter space to the galley. True enough, this does eliminate one berth, but my God man, how many do you want on a 32 foot boat anyway?

The U-shaped dinette works out well on Whistler and Crow now uses a telescoping aluminum leg so that the table can slide down to turn the whole thing into a true double with lots of air above for frolication. The pilot berth is not too narrow nor too wide, in other words typical Chuck Paine sensible. To increase the feeling of space in the boat the main bulkhead is cut away at the forward end of the starboard settee. Forward of the bulkhead is a large hanging locker and I can't recall exactly where, but the hieroglyphs in my notebook tell me that hidden somewhere here is a liquor cabinet with a — you guessed it — cherry wood bottle rack. The head is generous for a 32 foot boat, with a shower pan that is actually wide

The yachtsman-like interior of the Chuck Paine-designed, Crow Fox-built Whistler. The wood used to finish the interior is North Carolina cherry which has a lovely yellowish glow and beautiful grain, and is harder than hell to cut.

enough to be usable.

The forward cabin is truly that, a cabin, and if you look closely at the accommodation plan you will see why. The forward bulkhead on the starboard side has been pushed aft, and if I could find my scale under all these heaps of rubble in this godforsaken room, then I could happily measure it off and tell you just exactly how much it was pushed, but if we wait until then I'll be too old to write and you'll be too old to read, so let's just take a plunge and call it a foot and a half. Into this newly conquered territory Chuck drew in a comfy little seat which is wonderful for private reading or sock removing, or just hiding from your guests who have overstayed their welcome. The floor space in here is very good, and even if a filler was put into place to make the berth a huge double, you would still be able to open the door or put on your pants standing up, instead of lying on your back and wriggling on your belly like a snake.

Stowage is good behind the settees and across from the head. Galley stowage is ample with a pretty cherry wood dish rack, and a couple of nice deep and long drawers below the chart table. A 40 gallon water tank is under the settee because the centreboard and internal ballast fill up all the space in the bilge, leaving only bits of room for hoses and their valves and connections.

Construction

Whistler is built to the same high specs as all of Chuck Paine's boats. She has a double layer of 1½ ounce mat against the gelcoat which will make for a very fine gel finish and even a dark hull should not have the roving pattern showing through. Next to these are three units of alternated 24 ounce roving and 1½ ounce mat, then starting 4 inches above the waterline an extra unit is added, then four more units are added through the centre and the keel area.

The deck has a ½ inch plywood coring, sandwiched between two units of mat and roving, with extra reenforcement added in the area of the foredeck where the mast goes through. Again I remind you that Crow Fox's yard is a custom boatyard, so if you request heavier lamination, which would be warranted if you were planning to use the boat as an icebreaker or a bulldozer, then Crow will be only too happy to put it in for you.

The hull flange is made up of all the laminates turned over, plus a 12 inch wide strip, and the deck is bedded and bolted to it with ¼ inch stainless steel screws on 12 inch centres, which should be reduced to 6 inch centres.

The floors have twelve mahogany timbers 1½ inches by 3 inches and are doubled up at bulkheads. A ½ inch plywood sole is laid and bonded around the edges of the hull, over which in turn the ⅜ inch teak is laid.

The engine is set on heavily laid up fibreglass bases and I'm sorry but I don't recall if there is an engine pan or not, and if there isn't tell Crow you want one. The shaft is nice and short so vibration should be minimal, the fuel tankage should get you about 250 miles, and as a very fine precaution all bronze through-hulls are bonded together with copper strapping to stave off electrolysis.

The hollow mast is a combination of carbon fibre and fibreglass. For those who don't know but want to, carbon fibre is very long fine threads, which when stiffened with resin has a tensile strength that staggers the imagination — more than six times that of stainless steel. Weight for weight carbon fibre is sixteen times as strong as aluminum. Of course, this refers to tensile strength and since the masts aren't stayed, it is that strength that you need, for compression loading on a free standing mast is negligible. With the masts of Freedom yachts, which are essentially the same, you get a lifetime guarantee, and that sure shows a lot of confidence and puts aluminum mast builders to shame. The main mast is 8 inches in diameter at the base and its wall is 1 inch thick — more than a third carbon fibre and the rest fibreglass.

The boat I crawled through was hull #2 and the mechanics were done in a hurry so some of the wiring was haphazard with connections exposed to stray water below, but I am sure with Crow's eye for detail and insistence on quality these will be corrected on future boats.

Designer Chuck Paine with a half model of Whistler's hull.

11

Baby Face
Westsail 32

It is very hard to part with a first love. It is fun to be lured and excited by the new, and be seduced by the mystery of the unknown, but the memories of things shared just won't give way that easily.

So it is with *Warm Rain*. We built her from a hull and deck, Candace and I, and she has carried us thousands of miles to a hundred ports, and she comforted us when we were tired and sad, and she relied on our help in many gales, and she shared with us the joys of victory and the glooms of defeat; and those things you can't just brush off and forget, or if you can, then there is something lacking somewhere.

She has her faults or at least her weaknesses, but my God if we can abandon her for that, then she could have rightly cast us overboard years ago for ours.

So she is still our sailboat after much ogling at longer, sleeker boats, and she still fills us with joy every time we look at her.

She is a heavy boat indeed, a descendant of the old Colin Archer breed, drawn by Bill Atkin in the '30's, into a boat he called *Eric*, and rejuvenated by Bill Crealock in the early '70's into a Westsail 32. Her lines are chunky but to us beautiful, with a sweeping sheer, spoon bow and finely drawn low house, and the view of her stern sitting low and beamy in the water just makes you shake your head and mumble, "Okay ocean, let's see what you've got." (Just joking of course, Mama Ocean, just wrote that because it looked good on paper.)

She is a beamy 11 feet and a heavy 19,500 pounds, and full-keeled with not the finest of entries above the waterline, but she is without doubt one of the most seakindly boats around. Her motion is gentle, making her an excellent long distance boat that will not fatigue her crew with that nervous, twitchy motion that many a lighter boat will have, a twitching that will cause you to feel always just off balance, requiring in turn twitchy muscle ajustments. With a proper drifter she will ghost along even on a day when the water is flat, and in heavy seas she will feel like she is part of the ocean. I haven't sailed on a great number of boats, but I have sailed on more than a few, and not very often did I welcome the motion of an angry sea, but I do with *Warm Rain*. I have been aboard her beating into gales with a staysail and double reefed main, and eased slightly off the wind she did fine, and I ran for two days and two nights

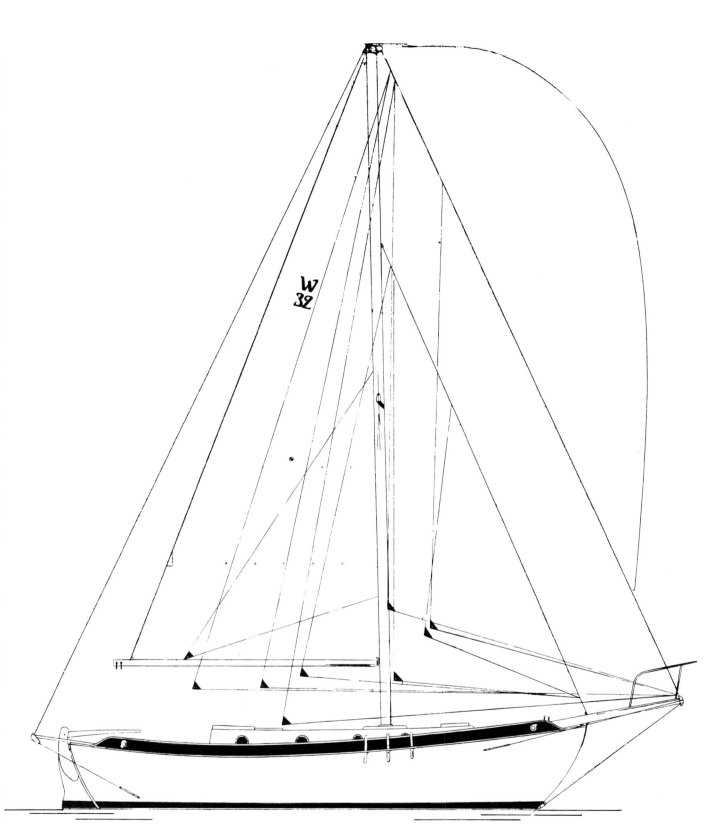

Westsail 32 — W. I. B. Crealock
LOA—32'0"   LWL—27'6"   Beam—11'0"   Draft—5'0"   Displ.—19,500 lbs.   Ballast—7,000 lbs.   Sail Area—663 sq. ft.

from an autumn storm that twenty-five miles from our position blew the instruments off the weather ship at 90 knots, and in the same storm we saw a half loaded freighter about 500 feet in length and of massive beam, roll from gunwale to gunwale in the berserk seas, and on we sailed with storm jib only, happy at 7 knots, surfing night and day, taking water in the cockpit only once, in a squall. The other times her pointed stern gently split the seas without a hint of her wanting to broach, and she required a very firm hand on the tiller only when surfing hard. In another storm off the Oregon coast in a sister ship I was sick with stomach cramps and fever of flu, yet the motion, although excessive, was so flowing, that not once did I get seasick, weak as I was.

In less violent places she has carried us at a steady 7 knots for a day on a reach, while sister ships have done the same for days on end. One sister ship did the 2,250 mile Newport to Hawaii run in fifteen days, ten hours; an average of 6 knots.

Of course, she has had her bad times. Off Point Conception with 35 knots of wind on the nose and a vicious steep chop pounding away at her, and with yours truly stupidly dislocating his shoulder during a sail change, she did slow down to a depressing 2 to 3 knots at which point we ran for cover of the cove until the pandemonium died down, and at three in the morning, after a fine dinner of crab and wine, off we went in a breeze under starry skies. All's well that ends well.

It is beyond doubt that a boat with a finer entry, fin keel and an inboard rig, will sail windward at a better clip and point higher than *Warm Rain*, although in a good blow and normal waves she has no trouble staying at 6 knots with a small genoa, staysail, and reefed main, but her fate will be greatly influenced by the amount of weight in the bow and the amount of sail the crew is willing to carry. With that genny and staysail and reefed main she will keep on slogging away after many a boat is bobbing under power with bare poles, and she will defy all the silliness one hears, like that she won't come about and won't go to windward. Most comments of this kind come from people who have either never sailed her or have sailed her badly.

As for her light air sailing, I am not sure what to say because it all sounds idiotic, but here it is.

Her wetted surface is great with that long keel, although it is somewhat reduced by her slack bilges, yet in light ghosting airs she is a joy. We broke her in on Newport Bay, which is about three miles long and but a few hundred feet wide, and we used to tack up there like madmen, Candace and I, coming about so close to docks that you would look over the side to make sure there was still gelcoat on the hull, and she handled just fine and on many occasions embarrassed the hell out of lighter and sleeker boats of her size by sliding right by them. How she does it or why, I don't pretend to know, and as Bruce Bingham said about his Flicka, "It's beyond reason." She has done the same thing in her home waters, leaving the crews of lighter craft scrambling and guessing in their cockpit. One logical explanation may be her weight, that because she is so heavy she does take a bit to start from a standstill, but boy, once she moves, it takes a lot of dead air to slow her down. Since much light air tends to be fluky, maybe she manages to drift through the dead or slow spots with her great momentum, while lighter boats come to a standstill from which it takes a lot longer to accelerate. Now that I think of it, this is not such a stupid notion, for it is this exact principle of penetration that racing sailplanes use. In competition soaring we fill up the wings of Candace's fibreglass sailplane with about forty gallons of water (250 pounds) which increases the sailplane's weight by fifty per cent and enables her to penetrate much better and fly faster and glide farther. This is not a quirk, every soaring pilot does it and they fly at close to 120 miles an hour, and without the built-in buoyancy like sailboats have — they stay up only because of the lift in their wings — and if they can gain by increasing their weight why shouldn't a boat? A valid comparison would be the difference of distance travelled by a ping-pong ball that you throw with all your might and a rock of the same size thrown with equal force. Perhaps you can't compare sailboats with ping-pong balls but then perhaps you can.

Warm Rain's draft is moderate at 5 feet giving pretty good access to most areas, and indeed a friend sailed his 32 in the Bahamas for some years with only a few groundings, which is pretty good considering this is the domain of centreboarders. The rudder has been changed from the original *Eric* and even from the original Westsail, which

I can't believe it. After 6 years of sailing we had to arrange a photo session to get a picture in time for this book — and of course we got light airs.

had a scimitar-shaped rudder with not much meat at the bottom where it counts most.

The bottom of the keel is wide enough so you can set the boat on it for bottom cleaning in far-away ports by tying alongside pilings. The rudder is mounted a couple of inches higher than the heel of the keel so no harm should come to it when grounding, intentionally or otherwise. Candace and I have encountered a couple of groundings of the "otherwise" variety, both times through over-estimating the accuracy of charts, but neither time did the rudder suffer a scratch.

The deck layout is of the simplest kind, with but a foot-well for a cockpit, which is wonderful for holding very little water in case of being pooped, but because it lacks any kind of back support or coaming, it is without doubt the most uncomfort-able cockpit ever devised by man, unless of course you have very broad, very flat cheeks and a self-righting torso. I don't, so I squirm and I twist and I lean against the lifelines — which is about as com-fortable as being hit in the back with a broom hand-le — but somehow I have survived all these years even though I am an obsessive helmsman, to whom an eight hour turn at the tiller is just fine. However, construction of a simple coaming about 10 inches high at the forward end, made up of say three layers of ⅜ inch teak would be simple enough to fabricate, reaching nearly straight aft from the corner of the house and ending up a foot or so from the bulwarks. This would make for a good back rest and keep the seats of the cockpit occupants dry as well, although if you are taking water on deck you will probably have your foul weather gear on anyway, so it makes precious little difference whether you are sitting in a puddle or not.

The visibility forward is very good (and it should be since you are sitting on the damned deck) but there is no way on earth you can seat more than four in the cockpit, and even then one person will have to do Chinese fire drills with the helmsman when tacking in a blow. The side-decks are quite comfortable, being narrow only at the aft corners of the house, and they are only a problem if you are as dim as I am and leave your extra-long bronze portlight casings sticking an inch out of the house. This witless procedure has three distinct disadvantages: a) the portlights will hold twice their usual amount of water, b) the genoa sheet will

get caught on the two forward ones on almost every tack, and c) every time you walk down the side-deck, the protruding casing will hit your ankle bone so hard that your entire lower leg will go numb for an hour. So cut the things flush with the outside ring — it might not look as "classic" but it will add ten years to your life.

The house is all Bill Crealock's design and his lines are certainly a witness to his fine eye. The bulwarks are very high, averaging about 8 inches, which makes for an extremely secure feeling in all deck areas; and they also provide a most secure mounting place for the stanchions whose upper and lower base bolts are 4 inches apart.

The high bulwarks and the sweeping sheer do make for a dry boat windward, although the high bow carries a lot of windage which is an in-calculable disadvantage under sail and a definite hair raiser at anchor in a blow if you are not using all chain anchor rode. For local cruising we keep only 50 feet of chain in the bow (to keep her light) and have spent many a windy night tacking back and forth in a harbour like a banshee. She can become quite uncomfortable in the process since she will tend to end up beam to the wind near the end of her tacks, and if there is a sea running she will tend to roll; this is hardly a joy when we are adrift in a double berth in the forepeak. So if a gale is forecast we haul out the chain from below the showerpan amidships and set it and the 35 pound CQR and sleep like babes.

The foredeck is spacious when the dinghy isn't there, and we have thrown away the knee-killing staysail boom, making it safer still. The bowsprit has a very good platform on either side with double rollers for two anchors, although storing anchors here during a crossing would be foolish because the extra weight will induce hobbyhorsing when beating into a seaway, thereby greatly slowing progress. The pulpit is sturdy and safe as are the gallows aft which are a godsent thing to cling to on a stormy night and a blessing during reefing, when the boom can be set firmly in them instead of flail-ing madly about.

The companionway opening is small, which is good if disaster strikes and the sea wants to come below, but the sides of the opening are so sloped that you have to lift the boards but very little to get them out, and if a big sea comes aboard, the boards

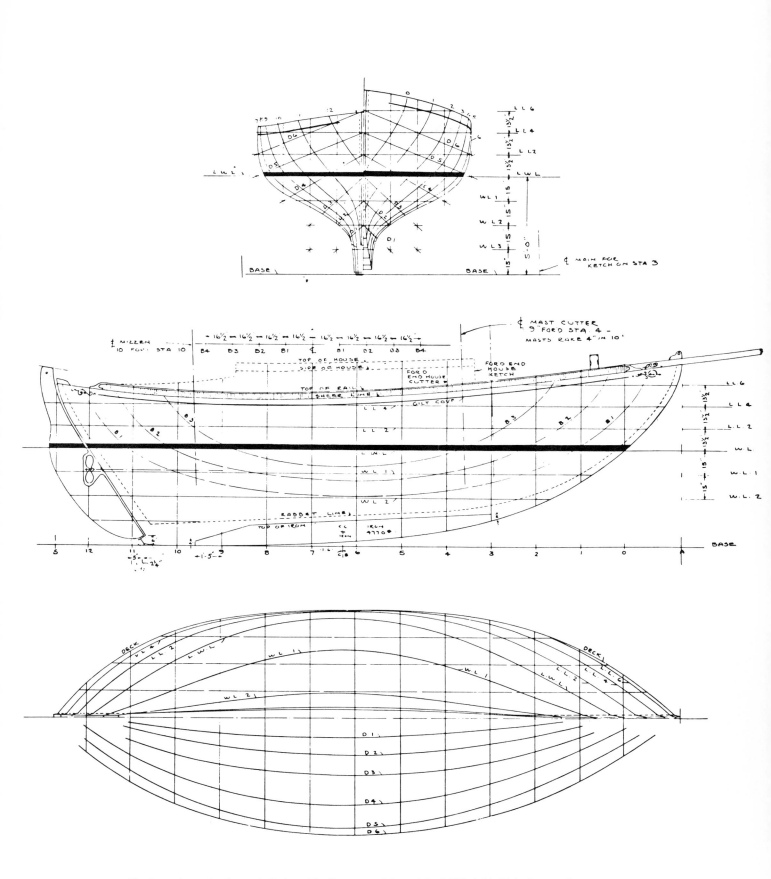

My favourite pudgy boat of all time. The lines are of the original Bill Atkin Eric drawn almost 60 years ago. The hull is perfectly balanced, but the entry could be finer for better windward performance. The original Eric sheer is more pleasant with less freeboard forward, and lower, more elegant bulwarks.

can lift out and float away unless the hatch is completely shut and locked. Since keeping the hatch locked is a great inconvenience and more likely to be forgotten than not, I like the idea of mounting a couple of barrel bolts on the inside of the top board and sliding them in place about the time your knees start to shake.

The cutter rig is a handy thing indeed when it comes to reducing sail in a blow, but the forestay (the staysail stay) is a downright nuisance when tacking in light airs. Although we managed not badly in our Newport Harbour days, I will, any day now, have a simple modification done to the forestay turnbuckle, enabling it to release quickly and enabling us to store the stay back by the shroud somewhere, out of the way. Until then we will just go on tacking and wait patiently for the genoa to feed through. Tacking is, of course, much easier if you keep the staysail up and tight, so the wind *has to* blow the genny through the slot between the stays, otherwise the sail just straddles the forestay and flogs itself to death. Another modification I am threatening has to do with the backstay arrangement. A boomkin is used for the backstay base for two reasons, a) to get around the tiller box at the rudder head, and b) to enable adding more meat to the leech of the main.

Now we know that the former can be circumvented by splitting the backstay or using a well reenforced stern pulpit, and we also know that high aspect ratio mains (tall and narrow) are better wings, for Mr. Baader in his book *The Sailing Yacht* tells us that tests have proven that a five to one ratio makes for the most efficient wing. So the question arises, why is the boomkin there at all? Boomkins look great, but with all the fittings on the wood they can rot undetected, and the boomkin stays necessitate four unnecessary swedges along with two extra turnbuckles which are not only costly but are also points of potential failure. To make things worse still, one of the whisker stays is located directly above the exhaust through-hull so all the yummy corrosive fumes ensconce themselves around the swedging, and God only knows what kind of rude things they do there. I did hear from the crew of one ship — not a Westsail but a boomkinded double-ender — that they were dismasted in the China Sea because a swedge parted on the boomkin stay just above the exhaust. This of course should not cause a world-wide panic,

for it is only one instance, but a boomkin should be eliminated if at all possible, at least as a base for the backstay. It makes for a fine mounting platform for the Aries Windvane though, and it can be left for such a purpose, but as a base for the backstay it should definitely go. I will get on the phone to Bill Crealock tonight to see what he thinks of all this and let you know the outcome in the morning.

Well, it's morning. I talked to him and I had hardly gotten the phrase, "Get rid of the boomkin" out of my mouth when he said with much exuberance, "Great."

Other than that *Warm Rain's* is a dandy single spreader rig with a heavy walled mast, $\frac{9}{32}$ inch standing rigging, and running backstays which you only need use if you are going hard to weather for prolonged periods. The one problem we found with *Warm Rain's* running rigging was fair-leading the genoa or more specifically, locating the genoa track. The original deck layout calls for this track on the deck close to the house, where it has to be for the jib and yankee jib because they get sheeted inside the shrouds, but for the genoa itself whose sheets lead outside, we were loath to bring the sheets back inboard, then out to the caprail where the winches were, for it would have meant more lines to trip over in an already narrow part of the deck. So we experimented with tracks on the caprails and tracks next to the bulwark until the whole boat looked like a model railroad set, but the lead from the high caprail would foul in the winches and the lead from beside the bulwark would chafe the caprail, so after six years we are still out there switching and shunting in an everlasting self-propagating confusion of alternatives.

Down Below

Belowdecks *Warm Rain* is a perfectly cozy and spacious galleon, and a termite's dream. There is, you see, an entire wooden boat inside the fibreglass boat and I don't mean plywood, I mean wood wood. We used over 500 square feet of $\frac{3}{8}$ inch tongue and groove teak on the overhead, cabin sides, bulkheads, ceilings, and settee faces, until the whole boat looked like the inside of a Taiwanese barrel. You may sigh and say, "My oh my, but what a piece of beauty that must be," and she really is a dream, especially if you happen to be a mole and love eternal twilight, for that is what all

Warm Rain's *all wood interior — a carpenter ant's dream come true. The area across from the head has been changed into a large writing-desk with seat and stowage. The main bulkhead to starboard has been cut away because I never fancied writing in a closet.*

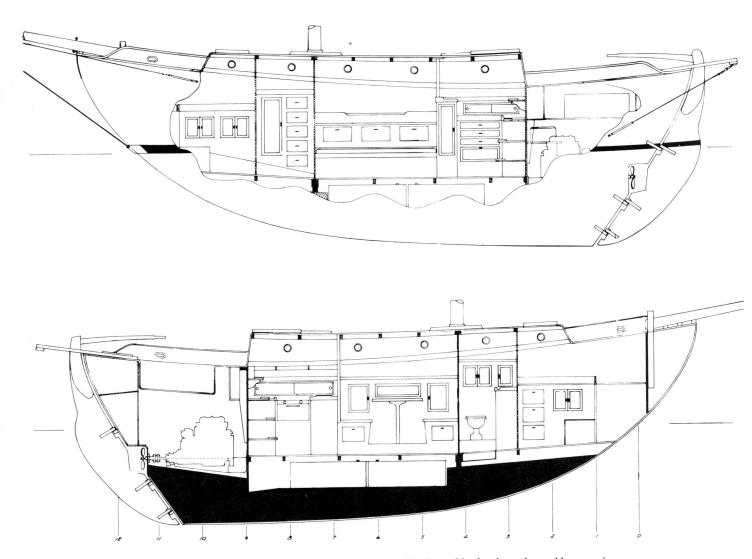

The Westsail 32 with what one can safely call a "full keel." The rudder has been changed by squaring off the bottom which makes her less pretty for the fish to look at but helps to steer her better.

the dark wood created. We alleviated the gravity of the problem by cutting a skylight over the salon table, lining the cabin sole and countertops with light and varnished ash, and painting the galley, chart table area and the head white, but on rainy days — of which we get a good number here — all you want to do belowdecks is light the fire in the Chummy stove, crawl into your bunk and catch forty winks until the sun comes out. There is, of course, basically nothing wrong with that, but were I to do it over again, and one of these days I will, I think I would do a traditional yacht interior, which had acres of lovingly painted white surfaces with varnished teak used as trim only. Good white paint, if well done, will last virtually forever, is

very easy to keep clean, and creates a feeling of fresh airiness belowdecks, but it is a true pedigreed son-of-a-bitch to apply. It involves taping and sanding, and painting and sanding, and sanding and sanding, over and over again until you begin to feel as if you have done nothing but that all your life. But it sure can't take as long as lining a boat with narrow strips of teak. It took Candace and I exactly one month of full time work to do just that, and that, if you want to know, is four hundred man hours of labour, and that, if you want to know, is stupid — *and* expensive, which makes it more stupid still. So get out a can of paint and a sleeve of sandpaper and go to it. If you don't mind a paint job that is not quite Chinese lacquer, you will be

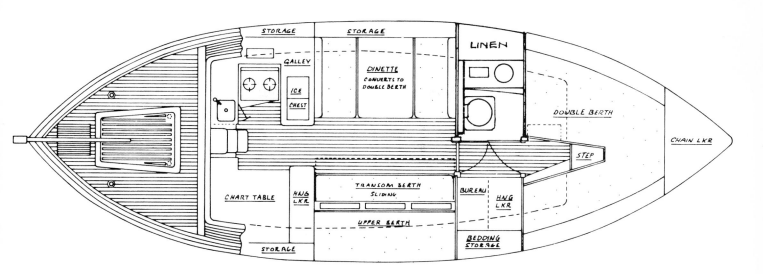

The original Westsail layout prettily drawn has a fine galley and chart table, a good pilot berth and a totally useless dinette, which is too cramped at anchor and a dead loss at sea. A settee berth with a double leafed centre table is infinitely better. In the forepeak the berth is too high; it should be dropped 4 to 6 inches. The water tanks are in the bilge so the stowage elsewhere is enormous, especially if the bloody dinette is yanked out.

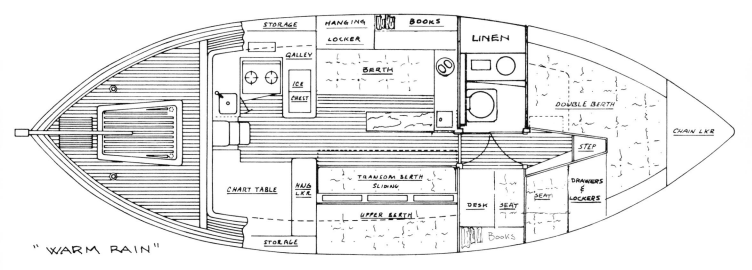

finished in a few days.

Back to the job at hand. The advantage of a beamy boat with the beam carried well forward and well aft is the amount of volume belowdecks. For a 32 foot boat *Warm Rain's* volume is great indeed. The chart table to starboard of the companionway can be made good and large, which we did. This is a stand-up chart table with three wide drawers below that hold double folded charts. The surface itself is so large that you can fully open a chart up for circumspection and even plotting, and only the very edges will be a little curled. This we achieved by having the chart table top project aft over the engine bulkhead into the engine room about 12 inches. Besides creating a larger surface this also helped us gain some accessible storage through a long lid in the aft end of the chart table, to a deep and long locker which is now our rope locker. We have done the same thing behind the galley counter, and not only has this created more open counter space in the galley, but it has given us a locker to hold small pots and lids and sieves and the like. The galley is U-shaped and has good counter space with plenty of stowage even for Candace, who has more oils and spices, vinegars and mustards than all the Burgundy region and Northern Italy combined. This plentiful stowage is achieved by stowing all dishes, mugs, and tableware in a dish rack above the icebox (see *The Finely Fitted Yacht,* Volume I). The icebox we found too large, so we divided it into two sections, separated by a wall of plexiglass-covered foam, which lets us make maximum use of our ice supply. With the poured foam icebox having 3 inch walls and a 3 inch bottom and a 3 inch thick lid, we have had six blocks of ice last as long as two weeks, with a little shuffling, at the end of which time almost two blocks were left.

The wetlocker forward of the chart table is good and high but only 12 inches wide, which is just about enough for three sets of gear and no more, but it is deep so that the three sets hang free with boots, etc., under them or behind them and out of the way. The salon is very ordinary with a godsend of a pilot berth, where the off watch crew can sleep in peace out of traffic and commotion. I prefer pilot berths to quarterberths for although they are usually about 12 to 16 inches higher than a quarterberth, making them a little less comfortable when you are flying downwind and rolling about like a pig in a puddle, they do allow the off watch crew to be out of the way of everyone else, especially the navigator, who with a quarterberth situation (where the chart table is usually located at the head of the berth) would have little choice but to deposit his behind on the sleeping crew, greatly inhibiting the sleeper's breathing. For a pilot berth *ultima* see the Spencer 1330.

The starboard settee looks narrow, but it is comfortable for sitting and does pull out for better access to the drop leaf centre table. The port berth has a foot-hole which is excellent for stowing bedding. The "Chummy" wood stove sits on the shelf over the foot hole. Ideally, a heating stove should sit right at cabin sole level, but this would have involved running miles of pipe from just beside the mast, which was the only other available spot, especially as we wanted the chimney well outboard so that it would not soot the boom and mast or set the mainsail on fire.

So the stove went up and outboard and the space by the mast became a woodbin. The hanging locker is aft of the bookshelves and finessed in so that the clothes hang down behind the settee back.

Forward of the settee is a head of usable size,

with a shower pan (which we have never used, taking our teakettle baths in the cockpit) inboard of it. Across from the head is something I wanted for my own - a built-in writing desk with storage under the lid and seat and on shelves outboard of it. We have cut away part of the starboard bulkhead between the desk and the salon and this made a visually spacious area even more so.

In the forepeak is a seat with a long comfortable back that is fitted to the hull, a 44 inch wide double berth and a set of drawers to starboard. The anchor chain is fed aft through a system of pipes to an area below the berth, so only rope and light stuff is kept in the peak locker.

Storage is plentiful (we have five sails in two lockers under the berth) and there are great volumes of stowage in the salon below the settees, the pilot berth, and behind the port settee. Small lockers are everywhere in every accessible space.

The engine room is a tinkerer's dream. The cockpit sole lifts up creating air and light below, and there is good room all around the engine for any kind of work. Interior access is gained through dropboards from the galley. 75 gallons of fuel are located on shelves in the engine room, but the tanks are rather high up and well aft, so next time I think I would eliminate the port tank and stick the other farther forward, like underneath the chart table, to counter the weight of the galley stove and icebox. Two water tanks of 40 gallons each are below the cabin sole in the salon.

In all it is a very functional and comfortable layout, excellent for long cruises for two or three, long crossings for four, and local family cruising for five.

Construction

The 32 has come home. It started life in the early '70's in a dusty lot just up the hill from the glistening yachts of Newport Bay, when Lynne and Snyder Vick bought the mould for the hull at a sheriff's auction for a grand total of $1,200.00 and named their new baby a Westsail. There was no deck mould then and the first decks were built flush like Atkin's original *Erics* with barn-sized accommodations below and very good deck space above, although the overall look was a little graceless to say the least, unless you had an insatiable lust for hippos. Anyway, a deck was

designed by Bill Crealock and things really started popping in the little dirt yard with a trailer for an office and a porta-potty out back. The Westsail name spread like wildfire, partly through Lynne Vick's advertising genius, but also because the boat was thoughtfully built and strong, well finished and strong and simple and strong, all at a time when most other builders were turning out day sailers of up to 50 feet with chopper guns and pop rivets. Within a year Westsail moved to larger premises next door and at the end of two years had already built a hundred boats. They expanded then and began a 42 foot boat and *Time* magazine did a centrefold on Westsail and enquiries poured in from Ceylon and Brazil and Cape Town and Zanzibar and people stood in line at the factory literally waving their money, but it was no use, if you wanted a Westsail you just had to wait, at one point up to fourteen months. And Westsail moved again. They took over the bankrupt Columbia facility which was the size of the Houston Astrodome, complete with miniature railways and

miniature cranes and teak panelled executive offices, and the crew grew from the modest 8 two years before, to 250 out back and almost 40 up front among the teak panels, and they opened a factory on the East Coast, and the sun shone and out came the boats and out came hull number 800, and then somehow the bloom started coming off the rose.

It was hard to say why, but things kept going wrong; boats were late, competition was growing and all of a sudden everyone was building a "high quality heavy cruiser," from Florida to Taiwan, all of them telling potential clients just how much better their boats were than a Westsail. Meanwhile Westsails were being built at inflated costs but sold at prices guaranteed a year before, and everything moved so fast no one knew how much things *really* cost, and people were coming and going in the front office until few knew exactly who was doing what, and then somehow things slowly but surely came apart. Dealers left and workers left and creditors closed the doors, and with the creditors came rumours that would plague the company through its death throes into oblivion. New owners were found and new money was found, but the name was cursed and everything finally wound down and the moulds were auctioned off and the pigeons moved into the empty bowels of the Astrodome of Costa Mesa.

The great American dream was dead.

And then along came Ed. He came full of earnest integrity and goodwill and a profile lower than a feather lying down, and he rented the little dusty lot on the hill that overlooks the sparkling yachts of Newport Bay, and he bought the moulds of the Westsail 32 and brought her back home to the sunny little field where she was born ten years before. Here Eddy and his friend Mendosa build the 32 slowly, one boat at a time, and they have working with them a few people with many years' experience, plugging away in the sun contentedly, without dreams of grandeur or glittering production lines or long miniature railways; they just build good boats, simply and heavily, that can humbly withstand the winds and the seas and that's all.

The hull is laid up in one piece and laminated of four units of mat and cloth and mat and roving, and below the waterline another unit of mat and roving is added. All these laminates overlap about 6 inches each side of the centerline, resulting in a full 1 inch thickness at the keel. The hull flange is made by turning the last laminates over, and is reenforced with a 12 inch wide run of mat and roving.

The deck is set on the flange in a layer of polysulphide, that dries so tough and rubbery you have to cut it with a chisel, and that's no lie. I once tried to remove a set of spun brass hawse pipes from *Warm Rain*, that had been set in polysulphide five years before, and after the screws were out it took me thirty minutes to chisel, pry and claw hammer the little bugger out of there and I wasn't being Gerry Gentle either, because the hawse pipes ended up looking like they had been dynamited out. Now there's a thought. Anyway polysulphide works. The hull is attached to the deck with ¼ inch stainless steel bolts on 4 to 6 inch centres, and then of course when the caprail is screwed down another two million number ten stainless steel screws go into place so it may just hold.

Ed and Mendosa use ⅝ inch balsa to reenforce horizontal surfaces in the deck, and to reiterate, this has, as everything in boatbuilding, its plusses and minuses, the plusses being lightness of weight, good insulation, and no delamination because the resin does saturate the end grain balsa well; and the minuses being higher cost and a need to reenforce the stress areas of cleats and winches with large backup plates. All in all the balsa is the better solution.

The ballast can be either all lead or 2,000 pounds of lead and 5,000 pounds of steel punchings, and I would certainly vote for the all lead because it lowers the centre of gravity slightly, creates more space under the mast for long term chain stowage and eliminates any potential rust problems, although with well resined steel punchings poured in shallow layers and topped off each time by resin, then bonded over, the likelihood of problems is extremely minimal.

Bulkheads are ¾ inch and I can't remember whether Ed likes using foam between the bulkheads or not, but tell him that if he doesn't you will break his glasses.

As for liners, there was a full liner with the 32 before Ed bought the moulds, but liners create all sorts of misery and they do little to reenforce and strengthen a hull, so Ed has wisely forsaken it for a simple cabin sole and a moulded engine pan which may or may not suit your desires. If you are at all unsure, don't get the cabin sole mould. All rigging and hardware is to the old Westsail specs and that's good but for God's sake get rid of that boomkin.

Except for one more thing, the 32 is a custom boat from here on in and Southwest Marine, who share the premises with Ed, do very fine woodworking and they can do whatever more you desire, including a completely and very finely finished boat, so it would be futile to discuss any more construction details here. Except that whatever you have done make sure each piece of plywood that makes up your bulkheads, cabinets, shelves, knees — in other words everything that touches the hull — is double bonded, i.e., bonded both sides and bonded well.

The one more thing that should be hashed over is the stepping of the mast. Many of Bill Crealock's boats have deck-stepped masts and this is of no

detriment *if* the compression load, which is the primary force to be encountered, is carried down all the way to the keel. On the Westsail this is done by use of a reenforced plywood coring in the deck, measuring 12 inches by 20 inches by 2½ inches in thickness to spread the load. Next, a wood post of whatever size you please (we used a 3½ inch by 6 inch teak post) is attached to the main bulkhead directly below the mast and this post will have to be shimmed up below the cabin sole, tight to the keel. This shimming should have a wide surface and it should be of treated wood to prevent rot; and

it must be *tight*. Even so it should be checked every year for rot and potential looseness through shrinkage. And of course if your mast is deck-stepped it can be hinged and lowered for canal travel or repairs.

So that's our boat. Perhaps I'm still infatuated but I cannot close without saying that *Warm Rain* is as sweet-looking and as seakindly and as honest a cruising boat as you will find anywhere; she may not be a demon on the race course but she has been the most forgiving and the kindest friend we could ask for.

12

La Famiglia Cherubini
Raider 33

Once upon a time life must have been simple — when families worked the fields together, or raised cows, or built furniture, when there were lots of hands to frame a house or loft a boat or dig a pond, when pain wasn't so bad because the whole family shared it, and laughter was louder because the whole family laughed, and there was always someone else to blame when you left the coop door open and every last damned chicken ran off over the hill forever.

Life must have flown in a reasonable order, helped along by the wisdom of a houseful of generations, when home was a place to rest the body and the soul, not some rowhouse hastily raised and as hastily abandoned for another and another as if four new walls would somehow fill up the emptiness of the old ones.

But those days seem to have gone, and maybe they never were, except in wishful tales, but they say if you believe hard enough, tales can come true, and for a family named Cherubini it seems to have worked. It all started back in Italy with Leon Cherubini, who came to America and raised a family that stuck together even while it worked for others, and when they got tired of that they

started their own boatyard, and why not — there were enough of them.

Leon Cherubini started building wood boats in his backyard to make ends meet, rowboats and custom boats, and 17 foot sailboats, and after the war they really went at it and built wood power boats and class sailboats like Dusters and Comets, and a little 26 foot sailboat designed by John. When this little boatyard slipped away the family drifted apart and back together a number of times, at one point most of them ended up working for Essex Sailboats while others like son John, who started drawing boats at the age of seven and whose love and dreams were always sailboat design, went to work at Boeing Aircraft where he spent most of his time in the wind tunnels, and brother, you just know he wasn't testing only wings.

Near the age of sixty Leon Cherubini retired from boat building and took to teaching classical guitar, while son Frit and his son Lee opened the Cherubini Boatworks and proceeded to build one of the rare works of art on the continent, the Cherubini 44, designed by brother John. John kept on designing boats; among his best known projects

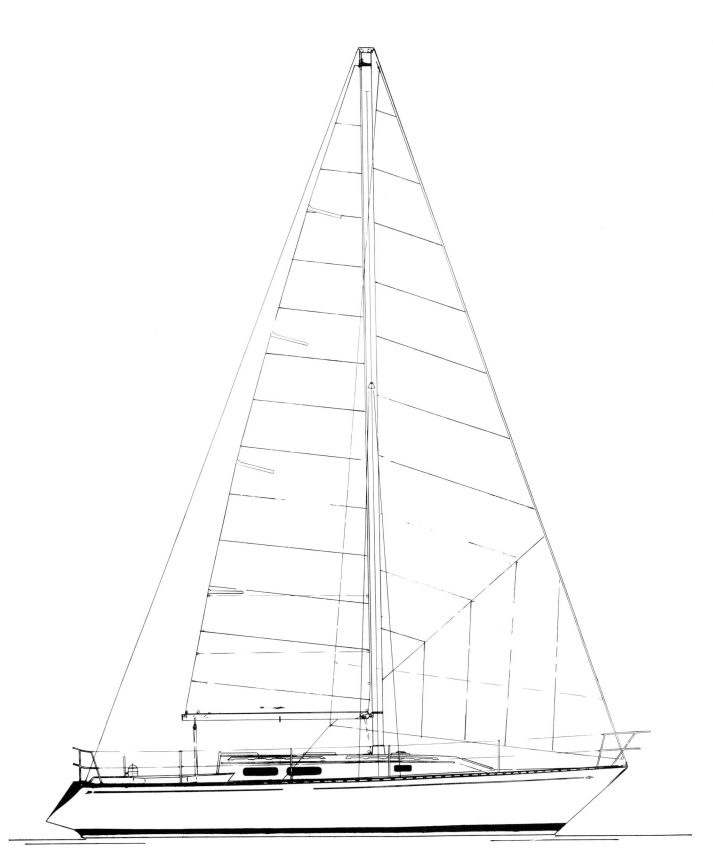

Raider 33 — John E. Cherubini
LOA—33'4" LWL—27'0" Beam—10'7" Draft—4'0"/5'8" Displ.—9,300 lbs. Ballast—4,100 lbs. Sail Area—498 sq. ft.

The Raider under spinnaker is kind enough to put her rail down so we can have a good look at her decks.

were the whole line of Hunter boats, including the now famous 54 which he co-designed. He also designed a very fine ¾ tonner for his brother Joe Cherubini who, with his whole family, started Raider Yachts and builds the little 33 footer among the rolling green hills in New Jersey, near the Delaware River. Raider Yachts is a one-building operation that is owned, run, and swept by the family, and only the family. You have no doubt of this as soon as you walk in because the place is so tidy and clean you could eat off the floors. "It's those boys," Joe says, "they can't stand dirt or mess."

So son Peter sweeps and does the fibreglass

lay-up and it is done to such perfection that I just kept walking around shaking my head. His sister Phyllis, who takes photographs for the brochures, is the newest of the crew, and she works with Peter laying up the boats. "At first she didn't understand why it had to be so perfect, but now I've got her believing."

Papa Joe and son Brian share in the rest of the building of the boat, which is done as thoughtfully and perfectly as the lay-ups.

You may look at the exterior photos and glance at the lines and say, "What an ordinary looking boat, why bother with it in this book?" But what you don't see is the high quality of workmanship and the pride of the family that is designed and built into each one.

I guess the best place to start is in the beginning, or more precisely the bow. Now you always hear designers and builders talking proudly about how fine the entry of their boat is, and in most cases this is true enough as far as the sections of the underbody are concerned, but very very few have anywhere as sharp a stem as the Raider's, which is like a razorblade. This is no great benefit in calm waters, but once head seas build and the bow begins to go under, all things change, and while many a boat will butt its way through the seas, the Raider just slices through, so the water hardly even knows it's been there. I will grant you that laying up this fine a stem is no easy chore, but as long as the lay-up man's and woman's hearts are in it , as Peter's and Phyllis' are, the result will be nothing but perfection. As for the rest of the hull, it has nice overhangs for a cruiser-racer, though some may think a bit too much, putting extra weight at the ends where it does no good, in sharp contrast to the more plumb stems or even chopped

noses like the America's Cup 12 Meters. Her stern is fined down as well, unlike the obese chain sawed sterns of new IOR boats, but what minimal amount the Raider gives up in IOR rating she makes up for in beauty. Adding to her grace is a good amount of tumblehome, the nicely curved stern, and the well proportioned deckhouse. Its portlights should be chosen with care though, for any that are higher than the ones in the drawings will add an unpleasant visual bulk to the house. The 33 I was aboard in West Bay, Connecticut, had large opening ports with black anodized trim rings, and it certainly took away from the good looks of the yacht.

You can see in the profile drawings and the lines, a fine keel, very tall and very slim skeg, and a bottom rather more "V"d and less flat than more current racers. A "V"d bottom gives you a bit more bilge space, and more importantly, a much stronger bottom than a totally flat one which will require more reenforcing. On the negative side, this "V"dness probably dampens the boat's planing potential, but then don't forget she is not designed as an ultra-light downwind flyer, and if that's what you want you should flip the pages and see Bill Lee's Santa Cruz boats.

Yet Raider is no heavy boat, having a waterline to displacement ratio of 203, which means she will be easily propelled and yet have fairly nice motion. The deep draft version draws 5 feet 8 inches, rather limiting for a cruiser, especially for the eastern coast, but a shallow draft version drawing 4 feet is available.

While on the hull, I must warn those who look for the full and powerful and unpleasant looking aft sections, that the Raider has none, but then neither does Doug Peterson's Ganbare type and it does extremely well on the race course even today,

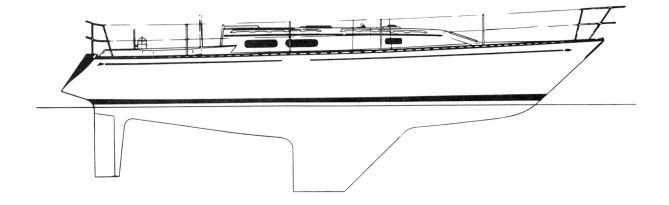

although it's almost ten years old.

On deck the Raider is a sailor's ideal, with a well shaped cockpit with excellent room behind the wheel to spread one's legs and bend one's knees to absorb the kick of the seas. Unfortunately too few boats have such good space, having shaved it so narrow that the helmsman would have to be made of pasteboard to fit in. The seats are comfortable for a crew of four, and although the edges of the cockpit moulding aren't as good to lean against as some of the over-radiussed ones in vogue with some designers, I say better a million sharp beautiful edges than one great round roly-poly one that is reminiscent of inflatable furniture. Now I know you will think me out of my mind, but I promise I actually feel sea-queasy just looking at these rotund bulbous growths.

Other fine touches in the cockpit include seats that are long enough and wide enough to sleep on; a split backstay which gives the helmsman more headroom and also provides access to the boarding ladder aft, built into the stern pulpit. There is a recessed mainsheet traveller trough on a 12 inch wide bridgedeck; this is a practical width, for anything much narrower than that will result in a lot of slipping and tripping. This is only true of boats over 25 feet, where you become used to a certain feeling of security of movement allowed by the larger surfaces, but in a smaller boat, where you are forced to adapt to smaller more calculated steps, narrower bridgedecks are quite acceptable. The 24 inch wheel felt a little small, but perhaps because of the good balance of the boat, that is all you need. I do have a quibble about the main hatch. It has no cover built over it, a cover which would make the hatch more watertight and create more firm standing space on the house for reefing and sail handling. The main hatch is made of solid fibreglass, blocking a lot of valuable light to belowdecks. This is very noticeable in the Raider whose interior is all teak, making it rather a lot darker than boats with white interiors. The hatch as well as the drawboards should be Lexan.

Aside from the big lazarette, there are two lockers in the cockpit, one of them a deep one for fenders, sails, etc. This locker also houses the batteries. This is both good and bad, because here they are quite exposed to weather, as well as to punishment and burial by whatever spares and junk get heaved in here, making servicing very difficult.

But once the junk is removed, checking of water levels and cleaning of terminals, as well as removal of batteries, will be very easy, and if you don't think these are important points then you obviously haven't had to refill your batteries out of a baby bottle for lack of space above them. I have. The other cockpit locker is a shallow 7 inch deep one over the quarterberth. This is an excellent depth for bits of gear, flashlights, binoculars, suntan lotion, and rosaries for when the going gets tough. Since this space is almost 2 feet in length and 16 inches in width, it could quite feasibly be divided up into a number of 4 inch or 6 inch wide compartments by the use of baffles (of plexiglass because these places can get water in them) to make the spaces more functional by limiting the size of potential messes.

The side-decks are good and wide, 16 inches at the narrowest and 30 inches at the widest, leaving lots of room to get by the inboard shrouds. But the foredeck is narrow, limited by the fine sections of the entry. There is a foredeck-well with direct access to the rope locker, which could be well used especially if a place is built to stow a Danforth anchor out of the way against one of the sides.

While on the foredeck, an interesting point of design should be touched on. The Raider's deck mould does not go all the way to the tip of the bow as it does on almost all other boats, but instead, the first 8 inches of the foredeck are laid up in one piece with the hull laminates. This results not only in an extremely beautifully finished bow, but also in a stronger, more unified piece, not dependant for its integrity on fasteners and bedding compounds.

The rig is kept simple, with a single spreader and a very high aspect ratio main, close to 3½ to 1. John Cherubini has drawn two rigs for the boat; a masthead and a fractional one, and you can choose depending on your tastes. It would take forever to discuss the pros and cons of each rig, so I will just mention the obvious, like that the fractional rig will allow you more mast bend, thus a better mainsail shape, as well as make for smaller headsails, which are easier to handle and cheaper to buy, and this is no small consideration for racing, when you are looking at six to ten headsails as opposed to a couple of mains.

The boat is well rigged for its displacement, with the cruising masthead rig having a total

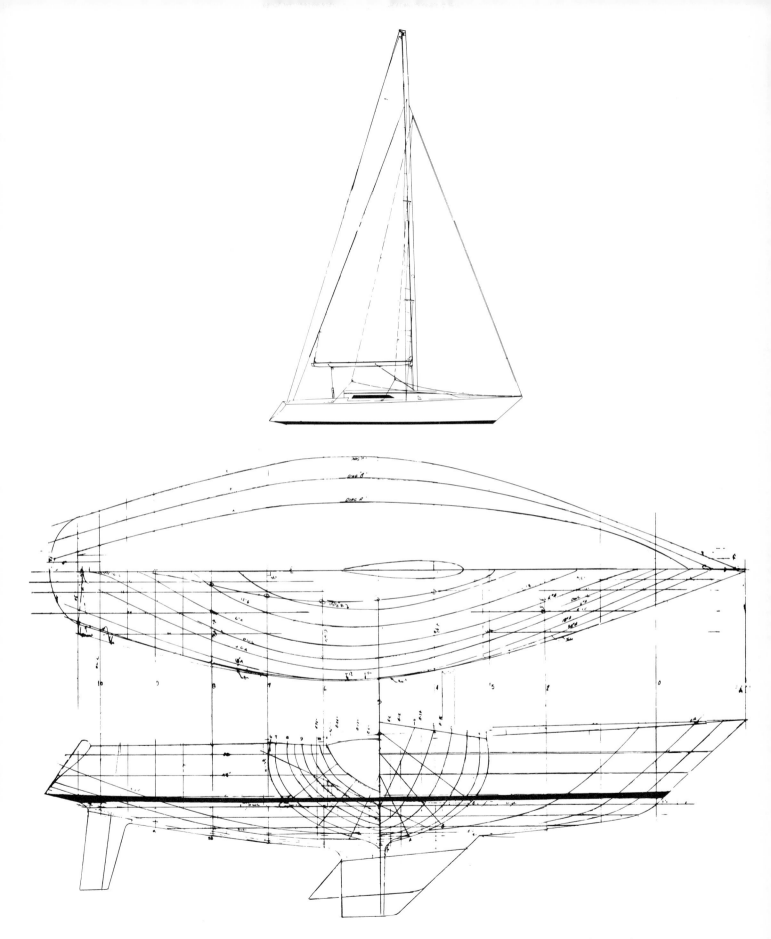

The Raider designed by John Cherubini, shows a hull form not dissimilar to Doug Peterson's Ganbare, although her small skeg gives her more directional stability and her optional shoal keel better access to shallow cruising grounds.

square footage of 497, for a sail-area-to-displacement ratio of 16.7. This means she should do fine in light airs yet not be easily overwhelmed when the wind comes up. A 33 has done well in P.H.R.F. racing with seven of eleven class victories at the Rariton, New Jersey, Yacht Club. The ⅞ rig has a mast that is 7 feet taller with double spreaders swept back so the stays come to a single chainplate. The total sail area is increased from 497 to 554, increasing the sail-area-to-displacement ratio to a whopping 19.7, and that in light airs will make her move, but once she starts to blow you had better get your reefers ready.

While we are talking about a racing version we may as well discuss potential changes in the deck. If you insist, you can have the deck and house reworked to a racing cockpit to accommodate more crew easily and get the weight closer to amidships. As you can see by comparing the drawings, the house is cut short, the helmsman pushed forward, and the cockpit broken up into two halves with the mainsheet traveller between. The interiors are vastly different for the two boats as you will see.

Down Below

Once you go below, the lean and hungry aspects of the boat are forgotten as soon as you see the acres of teak. There are no liners in the boat, all cabinetry is teak ply that is very well fitted and trimmed. All ceilings are covered with strips of teak and the underdecks are lined with a tastefully textured and coloured foam-backed fabric. The house sides are lined with teak and the sole is teak and holly, and even the genoa tracks are backed below with a teak strip to add a nice detail under the nuts and washers. The quarterberth is good and airy, with a hinged, fold-down chart table over it, not the strongest or the best of solutions, but better than nothing at all. There is lots of height above the quarterberth for a chart rack to be installed, and lo and behold there is even a real wet locker.

The galley is compact, but helped by the fact that the companionway ladder starts only from the countertop down, so that the counter above it becomes a functional part of the galley. The fold-down chart table can also be used if a feast for kings and queens is being prepared. There are plenty of elegant, well-proportioned and well-positioned teak cupboards above the counters, the stove is small but gimballed, and the icebox is only a couple of cubic feet — ideal for short holidays, but it will need to be supplemented for long ones.

The salon layout is a perfect mirror, with very comfortable settee berths and some very useful small cabinetry above them. There is an opening hatch above the centre table, the table being a folding type and nicely built, although I prefer permanent sturdy ones for supporting abject bodies. Everywhere I looked I was impressed by the good taste of the Cherubinis, even down to the extra thick velvet covered cushions. The head is very generous with a usable shower pan and there is good storage across from it.

The forepeak can be closed off by a sliding door for privacy, and the forepeak is good and airy, but with such a fine entry the berth is a little narrow at the foot, so unless you are good at toe braiding, look out. Raising the berth top a few inches would help a lot, for every inch you raise the top you gain almost an inch and a half in width. Sure the hull's slope is steeper than 45 degrees, but then there are two halves remember, Noodlebrain. The holding tank is below the berth, taking up most of the space there, but the berth is so far forward and the bow so fine that you wouldn't gain much stowage by putting it elsewhere anyway. Two narrow *necessaire* shelves running along the hull above each bunk, are well bonded for extra hull stiffeners.

Tankage is 30 gallons of water and 12 gallons of fuel, which should be good for about 200 miles with the 2 cylinder diesel. The fuel tank is aft of the engine, the water tank below the starboard settee.

The only real complaint I have with the boat is one that is unfortunately common with too many, and that is the engine room. I know it's very hard for builders and designers, the best of whom are genuine artists, to get worked up over battery cables and fuel lines, but engines appear to be here to stay, at least for a while, so their installation and serviceability should be of serious concern, to save the poor owner the agony and frustration caused by things that are at best inaccessible and at worst totally forgotten.

First, the Raider has no engine pan, so all of the drippings proceed to the bilge. Now a bilge is a detestable enough place as it is, without mucking it up with more goo. There is good access to the engine water-intake seacock and the galley drain

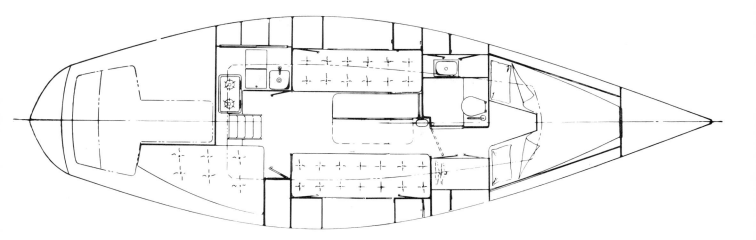

The standard cruiser-racer version of the Raider 33 has kept the number of berths down in the salon to two, allowing for good stowage above them, and this is certainly necessary on a boat with shallow bilges for there is no room for water tanks here, forcing them into the salon under the berths. For a boat with such a fine entry the accommodations and stowage have been made adequate indeed.

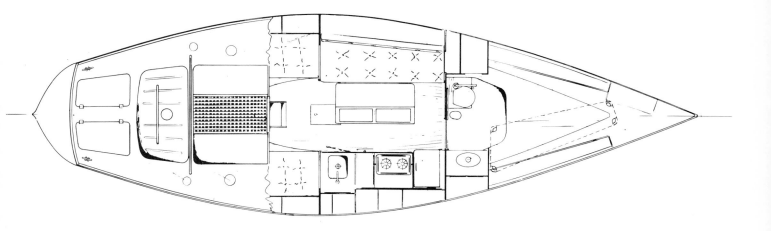

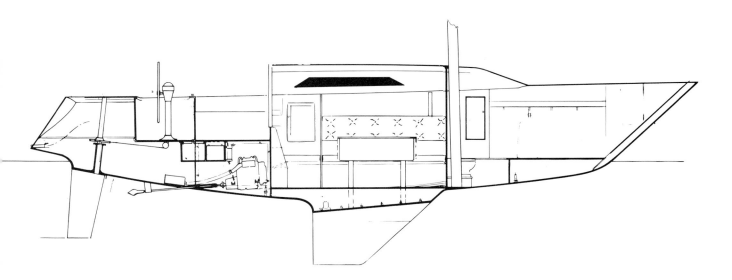

Another classic Maté photo—this time victimizing the well finished interior of the Raider 33.

seacock from the front, and decent access to linkage (gear and throttle) from the quarterberth, but unfortunately the injectors are located on the other side and are inaccessible; and this could cause you to tear great handfuls of hair out if you ever get air in your injectors and have to bleed them, or worse yet, if you have to remove them for service. You can clamber in through the cockpit locker, or hang upside down if you are slothishly inclined, but much of this acrobacy could be preempted by having the top of the counter over the engine hinged or removable. By closing off the engine room the way it is, a major expedition will have to be mounted to find the back of the electrical panel, and most of this will have to be done in an undignified position. How well the wiring and plumbing were done in the boat I could not tell since my neck is only of normal length and my eyes are permanently entrenched in their sockets.

Again I emphasize that all the above things are common failings, even on some other excellent boats, but that certainly is no excuse.

The above points notwithstanding, the Raider is a fine yacht, and remember that the Cherubinis are custom boat builders and will happily make modifications and improvements for you, to eradicate the above annoyances. Either that, or they will come and break both my legs and cast me as a bridge footing in the Delaware River.

Construction

As I mentioned before, the Cherubinis are boat builders of the best intent and the construction of their boats reflect that. In general, the glasswork is superlative and the finishing excellent. In particular, the hull is light but very sturdy using 24 ounce Fabmat, which is a layer of woven roving and a layer of chopped mat in one sheet. Along with a couple of extra runs of mat next to the gelcoat, the boat has two layers of Fabmat through the sheer with an extra 8 inch wide strip added along the hull flange. There are four layers of Fabmat through the waterline, six layers below that and through the stem as well, ending up with eight layers in the sump and sixteen layers in the keel area, and what's most important, it is all perfectly squeegeed to get maximum glass fibre to resin ratio, and that of course is what gives all the strength.

The skeg is moulded separately and bonded

and bolted on with a ¼ inch thick reenforcing stainless steel plate in the skeg, but this is really only a backup plate for the bolts that bolt the skeg to the hull, when the best practice is to have a vertical plate in here as well, running down the centre of the skeg to stiffen it. If your skeg is stiff, it can take a lot of strain off the rudder post. The 4,100 pounds of cast lead ballast is external, and is bolted in place with nine ¾ inch stainless steel keel bolts. The area of the hull where the keel bolts penetrate is 1¼ inches thick.

The hull has a customary flange, 4 inches wide, and the deck is bedded and bolted to this with the aluminum toerails as backup. The bolts are ¼ inch stainless steel on 6 inch centres and they should be no farther apart than that. 4 inches would be better.

The sole is reenforced with two vertical floor members bonded over with two layers of Fabmat, then the sole-base is laid of ¾ inch ply and the whole thing is bonded over with two layers of Fabmat. Then comes the teak and holly over this.

The bulkheads are all half inch, as is the cabinetry, and every little knee and piece is thoroughly bonded and that is what will give the boat long life.

The chainplates are ¼ by 1½ inch stainless and they are footed as follows: The uppers foot on the main bulkhead, which gets an additional layer of ½ inch plywood reenforcement, bringing it to a total of 1 inch. All this is covered over with three layers of Fabmat each side. The lowers foot on knees that are made of ¾ inch ply, 12 inches deep and 3 feet high, again with three layers of Fabmat on both sides bonding the knees to the hull. This is about as good as you can get.

The deck is stiffened with ⅜ ply and reenforced with ¾ inch ply where winches etc. are placed, which is all very good, but the foredeck is a little springy and it should probably be reenforced with ¾ inch balsa instead, for added stiffness. This would be lighter than the plywood, and take a little weight out of the bow. The deck has no nonskid pattern moulded in, which is just as well for the

The Cherubini family's small boatyard in New Jersey is so tidy and clean you can eat off the floors. The boat they build shows family pride. She's a very pretty 33 foot racer-cruiser with much tumblehome and graceful ends.

Woolsey deck paint they do use along with the Woolsey nonskid silicone or ground walnut shells or whatever it is, make a much higher-traction surface, which is of course easily repairable.

For the owner-builder the stanchion and hardware locations are all in the mould and all deck and housetop areas to be nonskidded are raised, so that taping off in the right spot will be child's play.

The mast is anodized and stepped on the keel and grounded to it. It has ¼ inch stainless steel standing rigging, which is spiffy indeed, and the halyards are internal. The through-hulls below the water are all bronze, as of course are the seacocks.

There is one note about internal halyards worth mentioning here. Whatever boat you get, be sure your mast is soundproofed for internal halyards, and make sure that the wire harness in it has been well attached and padded. I have spent many a sleepless night on boats that had no such precautions taken, and with a gentle groundswell running, there was a sombre little bell going ding-dong, ding-dong, unstoppably a couple of inches behind my eyes. I'd rather be basted with honey and strapped to an anthill than go through that again. Oh yes, the grabrails are too light.

In closing, I remember something Peter Cherubini said as I was leaving, and perhaps it gives a clue as to why there are such fine boats still on this continent, and perhaps it tells us for what rewards the builders continue to build. He stopped at the door and looked back at a boat sitting there and said, "You know, it's so much hard work and sometimes you get so discouraged you're ready to quit, but then people come and look at the boats and they really appreciate them and that makes everything alright."

With the main reefed and genny flat, the Raider 33 claws windward.

13

One for the Heart
Luders 34

It is hard, if not impossible, to get sailors to agree on many things, or for that matter really anything, especially when it comes to the subject of *the* beautiful boat, yet nearly all who have at one time or another set a sail, will stop in their tracks, get a glimmer in their eyes and feel a quiver in their hearts at the sight of a sleek, elegant metre boat. Now, it is true that square riggers look full of adventure, and schooners speak of romance, and new racers of bare breasted ladies and warm Antiguan nights, but nothing looks quite as much a part of the water as a long narrow metre boat. With its graceful fine ends and freeboard very low it looks as if it will barely disturb the sea, slicing its way with precision and care, leaving nothing behind it but the whisper of its sails. Bill Luders has designed as many beautiful metre boats as anyone. He drew over fifty 6 and 5½ metres and, of course, the beautiful 12 metre *American Eagle*, and the beauty and grace he drew into those seemed to have seeped into his veins, for those characteristics appear in almost everything he does.

His famous 44 foot Naval Academy yawls, which he designed and some of which he built at his own yard, were without doubt some of the most beautiful all-round yachts ever launched, and as for their longevity, well, the Navy kept them for their midshipmen for over twenty-five years and as Roger Taylor in his *More Good Boats* says, "They were sailed every day from April 1 through November 1 and by the nature of their purpose, they had been sailed and maintained by people less experienced around small boats than the average private owner. That they have survived so long and so well is a tribute to their design and construction by Luders."

That Bill Luders designed and built easy to manage, well balanced and finely crafted yachts should be enough for one man for a lifetime, but his yachts were often menacingly fast as well, and none more so than *Storm*, the beautiful L-27 he designed in 1955 of which "Judd" Henderson in his *Choice Yacht Designs* said, "For over a decade she all but dominated the racing scene in the vicinity of Long Island Sound, and repeatedly won or did exceedingly well in such events as the Vineyard Race, New York Yacht Club cruise, Block Island Week and the Whitmore Trophy series. The latter, a hotly contested series spread throughout the summer, was won seven times in a row by *Storm*." Oh yes, I almost forgot to tell you who the skipper

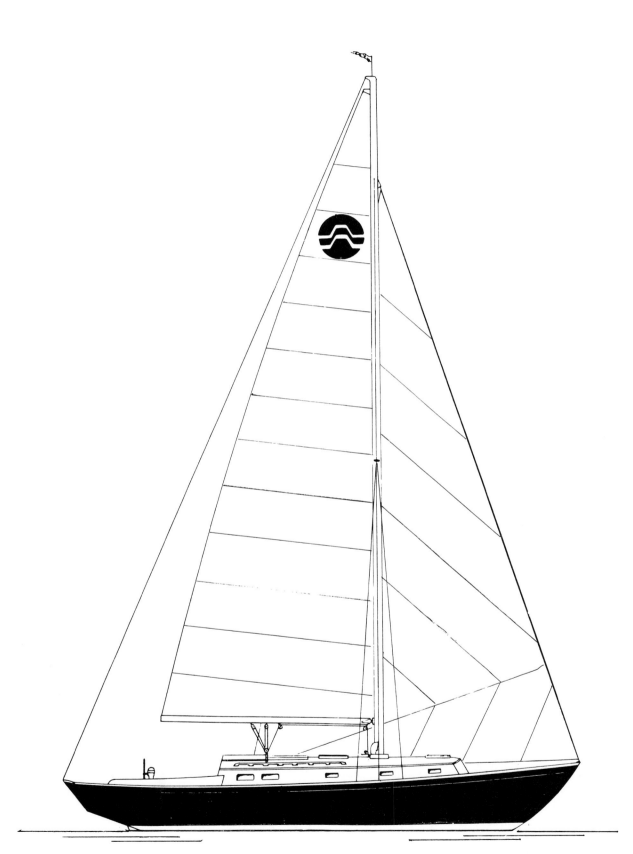

Luders 34 — Bill Luders
LOA—33'10½" LWL—24'0" Beam—10'3" Draft—5'0" Displ.—12,800 lbs. Ballast—5,000 lbs. Sail Area—532 sq. ft.

was aboard *Storm* for those years — a man called Bill Luders.

One's first impression upon hearing all this achievement is quite normally to admire the man but then dismiss him as a probable egotist, yet I was assured of exactly the contrary by Ted Brewer, one of our finest designers, that Bill Luders is one of the kindest, most benevolent men around, gentle and soft spoken. And Ted ought to know — he worked with Luders for many years as second in command, doing among other things all the drawings that *American Eagle* was built from, and supervising her during construction. He also sailed with Bill Luders for seven years aboard *Storm* when together they terrorized Long Island Sound, and even in the most heated moments gentle Bill kept his composure up and his voice down, and only when things went really badly did he say very softly, "Now boys, you have got to do better than that." No wonder the crew performed so well; anyone who is that composed has to be latently dangerous.

That is not to say Bill Luders is not outwardly competitive. You don't win that many races with just smiles, and there is one story told that Bill Luders had an operation at Thanksgiving, major enough to keep an ox in bed for months, but Bill got bored so he went skiing that Christmas. I told you the man was dangerous.

Over the years his name also became associated with sensible, well mannered, seakindly and very balanced cruising boats, and I am very glad that he designed a 34 footer last year, and that it is available as a semi-custom boat from Ryder Custom Yachts of Rhode Island.

In a book like this it is hard to pick favourites, and since the variety is so great it is easy and perhaps permissible to like them all at once, but for all-round grace and modest good looks, I would have to pick the Luders 34 as one very dear to my heart.

She is very sweet of sheer, and has those perfectly balanced graceful overhangs that one feared had died away years ago, with the arrival of the mania for ten room split-levels in a 30 foot hull. The house of the 34 is simply and cleanly drawn with no steps, no humps, just general excellent proportions in height and length. Her beam of 10 foot 3 inches is moderate indeed for a 34 footer, which means that she won't be as voluminous

below as she could be, but neither will she need to push a lot of ocean out of her way to get by. Her stern is fine and not bulbous or saggy, which means that she won't be quite as powerful as she could be, but who gives a damn about power when she is as pretty as she is, and that is what really matters on a sailboat anyway, for a sailboat should be chosen like the women of our lives, with our eyes and with our hearts and not with a measuring tape and a pocket calculator.

Generally

For her length of 34 her waterline of 24 is by modern standards short, but her easy bilges mean she will pick up waterline length as soon as she heels, and her easy bilges also mean less wetted surface, thus more speed. Her draft is 5 feet exactly and with her 5,000 pounds of ballast, which gives her a ballast-displacement ratio of 40 per cent, she should be stiff enough to stand up to her sails. For those who prefer stiffer bilges for more initial stiffness, please remember that the harder the bilge the harder the "snap" when the boat rolls, and the harder the snap the quicker the breakfast starts on its return trip. Where the fine line should be drawn regarding this matter is rather hard to say, but generally a hull of moderate form will have the most seakindly characteristics. Her forefoot has been smoothly cut away and the leading edge of the keel has been well faired, although the keel itself has been left fairly thick to enable proper positioning of the ballast. For added stability the very good sized 70 gallon water tank was nicely fitted over the ballast. The show of a sure hand continues with even relatively minor details, such as the beautifully shaped propeller aperture. In general, all her lines and curves are easy and smooth. She has plenty of rudder surface deep down which means good control on any heel.

Her overall displacement of 12,000 pounds on her 24 foot waterline gives her a displacement-to-waterline-length ratio of 408 which is hefty indeed but then she will give you the most comfortable motion this side of your cradle, and remember very few family members have ever disliked sailing because the boat's speed was 2 per cent less than it could have been, but thousands have hated it because of the boat's motion — and who could blame them, for what fun is it hanging doubled

over the lifelines heaving worse than the ocean below, reprimanding God for not breaking both your legs the moment they carried you aboard. That is why many families don't sail together, and that is why a friend who spent all her time begging Death to hustle it up whenever she was aboard their light displacement boat, stepped aboard *Warm Rain* and fell in love with sailing again, for *Warm Rain* felt as stable and gentle as the old boats she had sailed years before as a child.

And don't think for a minute that the Luders 34 is slow. Remember she is designed by a man who knew all about fast hulls and fast boats, and that has been proven out by Gary Lanagan who has been sailing his 34 out of Newport for a year and has done extremely well in all the local races.

The fractional sail plan looks totally modern on the Luders 34, with a high aspect ratio main, inboard shrouds and an adjustable backstay, and none of this should surprise you for Bill Luders has always been in the forefront of creative rigs. It was he who one season campaigned *Storm* with a 95 square foot mainsail, just to point out to the Cruising Club of America a major loophole in their rating rules. And lest you think him a brute for that, he very nicely wrote them a letter first, pointing out the obvious *faux pas*, to which the C.C.A. kindly replied something to the effect of "drop

The grace and simplicity of the Luders 34 is evident on Emily. *Amazing how a few touches like teak toerails, eyebrow and bits of trim can make a handsome yacht even more so.*

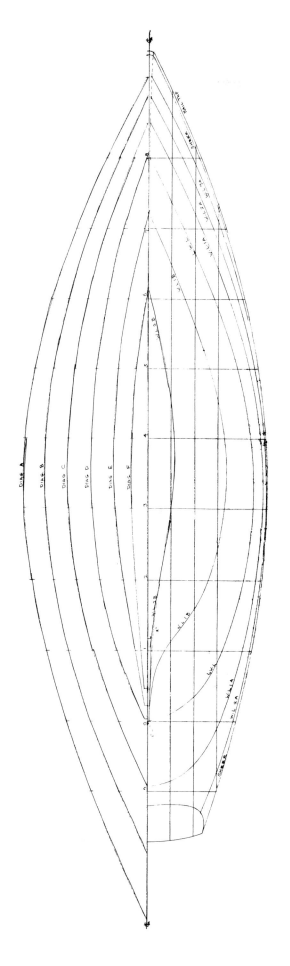

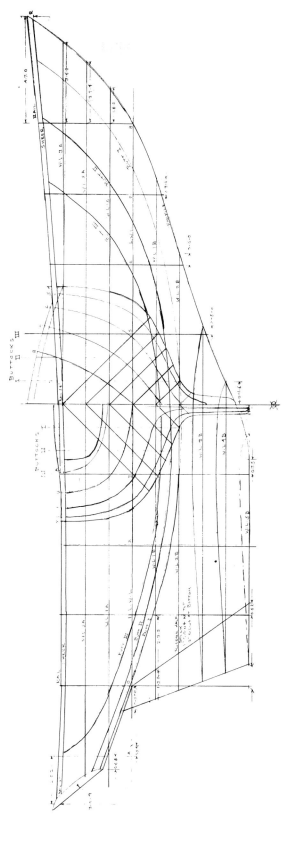

Moderation in every way is the main feature of all Bill Luders' lines in his 34. She is a very fast, as well as a most seakindly, vessel.

dead.'' So up went the 95 square foot main, and out went *Storm* and beat the pants off the fleet; and the crow population around the C.C.A. offices still hasn't recovered from the decimation it suffered that year.

At any rate the fractional rig gives you more mainsail shape control through mast bending, which is accomplished by adjusting the backstay, which in turn is accomplished with the simple mechanical device that you see in the photo. It is made up of a block system much like any mainsail sheeting, with a cam-cleat on the lower block. The tightening adjustment is made by simply pulling together the two halves of the backstay that had been split just a few feet above the edge of the picture. The system is much less expensive than a hydraulic one and infinitely easier to service and repair, although admittedly you cannot get as much torque out of it.

The rated sail area is 532 square feet, split into a manageable 282 square foot mainsail and a 230 square foot jib. With the small foretriangle, even a Number One genoa is kept down to 363 square feet, meaning quite easy handling even if left on a little past shortening down time. The Luders 34 has a nice little cruising spinnaker of 735 square feet (the regular spinnaker is 865 square feet) and if you haven't sailed with one of those you haven't lived. Sadly enough I have had the pleasure but a few times, and keep threatening to get one for *Warm Rain* as soon as I win some lottery or other, but that won't be for a while because I haven't started buying tickets yet.

On deck, as you can see in the photo, the Luders 34 carries on in her genteel ways. The lazarette is very large and for a nice change it has a large enough hatch to give you good access to its outboard extremities. The helmsman's seat is broad, although the wheel is a little tight to it. The cockpit is comfortable for five adults and good access to the area below the seats is gained through two additional hatches, one leading to a shallow compartment for small gear, the other to a huge one for sails. The winches are mounted on moulded-in pads, with the mounting bolts accessible from below for tightening or removal, but the cockpit coaming is not moulded in and this gives the boat an elegant touch with a coaming of solid teak. As the photo shows, this is a very simple affair with the gentlest of curves (home builders

should have no problem with it at all) and good support at the forward end where it fits into the house moulding, and in the middle where the winch base lends a hand. Since the seats are a few inches below the deck level, the teak coaming has good basic support all the way along; and of course even the slowest witted builder would have no trouble figuring out where it goes with the fibreglass lip where it is.

I am a bit apprehensive about the narrowness of the bridgedeck, which (at least on the boat in the photo, but not on the drawings) shows the mainsail track on it as well, so that very little "sure" footing is offered. Perhaps in this case the narrowness of the bridgedeck should be enough to prompt relocating the track to the the house top. For arguments pro and con about this, see the chapter on Tom Gillmer.

If you look closely at the photo, you will see evidence of an age-old problem, which is — how to have a lower lifeline aft without having it interfere with the winches? In many boats, *Warm Rain* included, you cannot make a full turn of the winch handle if that lower lifeline is in place, and not only does this mean that you can only get a half turn at a time — which is really no big deal because it's easier to pull than to push a handle anyway — but what *is* bad is that you cannot use the higher gear of the two-speed winch, for you will have to be in low every time you crank the handle "back." What the solutions is I don't know, although the problem is not as serious on the Luders with its good cockpit coaming as it is on some with no cockpit coaming, for if you remove the lower lifeline, then begin to daydream and lean back, the next thing you'll know you'll be hanging over the side like Raggedy Andy. If you have any good suggestions, send them to a good sailing magazine and tell them to stop the presses, you're saving the world.

The side-decks are wider than they look, being a good 16 inches at their narrowest, and the foredeck is clean and uncluttered with a cleverly placed cowl vent that will ensure ventilation throughout the length of the boat. The anchor roller is made of a simple piece of stainless steel channel. The entire deck is made safe with a 2½ inch high toerail that is nicely capped off with a piece of teak, and this is probably as good a time as any to discuss the elegant touches on Bill Luders' little yacht. It is absolutely astonishing to me, how

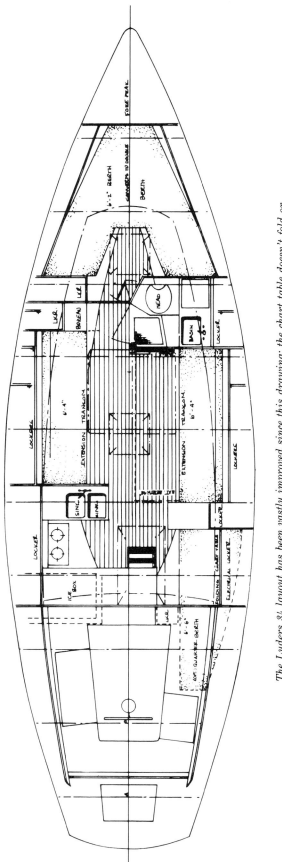

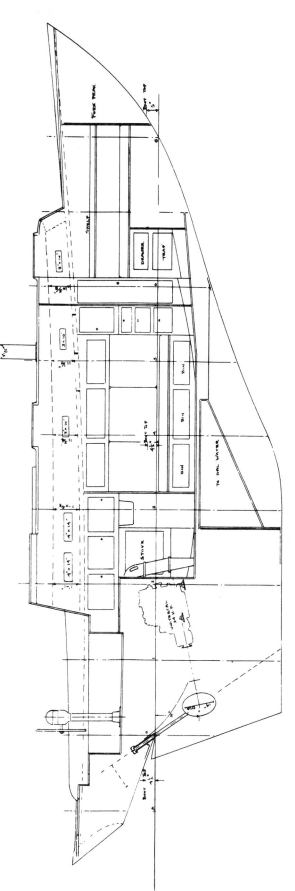

The Luders 34 layout has been vastly improved since this drawing; the chart table doesn't fold or mutilate anymore; it is permanently fitted athwartships at the head of the quarterberth. Everything else is plain and sensible with abundant stowage in a good variety of lockers.

The classic underbody of the Luders 34 with efficient high rudder, well-faired in aperture, and the most perfectly fitted water tank you have ever seen.

Although the Luders uses a liner, there is still much wood cabinetry everywhere. A nice touch is the broadly radiussed teak cornerpost in the galley corner. Clark Ryder's boatyard does some of the best glasswork on the east coast.

much warmth and good feeling can be added to a nicely drawn yacht by a few pieces of varnished teak, which all but the most severely disoriented should be able to maintain with a few half days of work a year. Apart from the mentioned toerail and cockpit coaming there is teak trim on the main hatch, a teak eyebrow on the house, teak grabrails and two teak Dorade boxes, yet the vast difference between a Luders 34 and the average 34 foot bleach bottle — whose designers, owners and builders must have at one time decided that teak is too unmacho for them — should be obvious to all but those with hearts of stone.

The main hatch has a moulded cover that has been kept mercifully low, as have the bases for the two transparent hatches, one in the salon and the other up forward.

One small digression before we continue. Elegant details, like a teak cockpit coaming and the Dorade boxes, not only add to a boat because they are there, but they also displace moulded fibreglass blobs which *would be* there were the teak removed. Plain slabs of fibreglass are unfriendly enough, but when topped off with a protrusion here and a herniation there, the whole house takes on a frighteningly octopusish effect, reminiscent of the painting of the warted, welted man you used to see in front of the tent of the carnival freaks.

But I do have one complaint, or rather perhaps a puzzlement about the Luders, regarding the two aft portlights which have been pulled tightly together instead of being spaced evenly with the other portlights. Now I know that they are where they are to provide the needed light for the chart table and galley, but then a little blindness is a small price to pay for beauty, especially when the amount of light that the clustering provides could be increased tenfold by making the main hatch of transparent Lexan.

Down Below

As the thorough interior photos (not mine, needless to say) show, the layout is simple and straightforward, with a trim U-shaped galley that has access to every nook and cranny, and good counter space, helped out by the space behind the ladder just under the bridgedeck.

One should take a good look at the photos, for many improvements have been made or added that don't appear on the layout drawings, the most major one being the chart table. The drawings hint at a collapsible affair of which one should always be suspect, but in reality there is a very spacious and

The new interior of the Luders with a fine fixed chart table, and an innovative companionway ladder. Notice handholds everywhere, and how the galley counter space is enhanced by encroaching into the engine room area. Oh yes, the breaker panel is hinged to give you quick access to its back for quick repairs.

workable fixed chart table with good storage in it, and a couple of very useful drawers below it. The forward end of a broad quarterberth is used as a seat for the chart table, and the ceiling outboard of it is lined with pine or fir — I forget which, but some relatively inexpensive light soft wood which looked just fine. The breakers are well incorporated into a hinge-down teak panel behind the chart table, and the imaginative companionway ladder frees up the counter space behind it. Note the handholds in and above the ladder.

Other nice touches are the grate at the foot of the ladder where all drippings from wet gear can pass, and the removable fibreglass dustpan recessed in the cabin sole just forward of it.

The rest of the cabin plan has been kept pretty much as in the drawings, with the settees left slightly asymmetrical. To support the mast, the starboard main bulkhead should stay where it is, which means you can't really make any major changes unless you are willing to chop the galley, which would hardly be worthwhile just to align the settees. Although the drawings don't show it, the starboard settee pulls out into a double that I guess you use when you want to turn your boat into a hotel. To accommodate this pulling out, the table is a foldaway kind, which is a plus if you are incorrigibly obsessed with square dancing. If neither of the above is a major component of your normal existence, I would nail the berth shut as a single, and make the table into a permanent drop leaf centre table, to make life much more simple and provide something solid to lean onto when you are staggering around below in a blow. The bureau full of drawers and the little locker above it add nicely to the feeling of spaciousness in the main salon, as well as provide plentiful storage spaces.

My notes say that the head is very fine, but that is *all* they say, so if you want to find out why it is fine you will have to go and see. I suspect there is probably some pretty fancy tooling in the fibreglass liner if I know Ryder Yachts.

The forepeak has good space with a locker to port, and decent clearance above and decent clearance at the feet, and that is important unless you are a retired ballerina and sleep with a permanent double *pointe*. The little *necessaire* shelves you see running along either side of the berth in the drawing are there in real life, and they are a true gift.

Access to the engine is very good through a large 2 foot by 2 foot opening behind the companionway ladder, letting you reach injectors, filters, linkage, etc. You would have to go in through the cockpit locker to get at the stuffing box, but if it is checked periodically you should encounter no great difficulties. Still, it might be a good idea to keep that locker well organized and to have a couple of good sized pipe wrenches ready just in case.

As you may have noticed, there is no mention of a wet locker so far, and I have left it for last, hoping my brain would come up with a good solution, but it didn't, so here is what there is, and it's not very good, so try to figure out an alternative. If you look hard at the photo with the companionway ladder in it, you will see a section of louvers between the ladder and the quarterberth. No, Elmer, that is not the whole thing but this once you are close. The louvers are the top part of a door to the wet locker, which is a decent height going from sole to bridgedeck, but what isn't decent is its depth which is but 12 inches, meaning no coat hangers (plastic of course) will fit in to allow you to take out one gear at a time. Instead, you will have to line the walls with wood pegs and suspend your suspendibles there. Other than that, the boat is plain, simple, elegant and completely good for the eyes and the heart.

One last note before we go on to construction. I have been intrigued for some time with the drawing I saw of a new interior Tom Gillmer drew for his 37 year old design of *Calypso* (see drawing). This has stuck in my mind ever since, and although I am not absolutely certain it would work on the Luders 34, I think it might be close enough for someone to spend a few days to see if it could be made to fit. The quarterberth chart table that is now in the Luders should be left, the rest should be tried *à la* Tom Gillmer. The mast would, of course, have to be stepped on the keel for it would be coming somewhere through the centre of the table. Do check with Bill Luders regarding the bulkheads. before you start.

Construction

The Luders 34 is built by Clark Ryder in Bristol, Rhode Island. He has many years' experience with both custom and semi-custom boats, and he is renowned for high quality glass work and

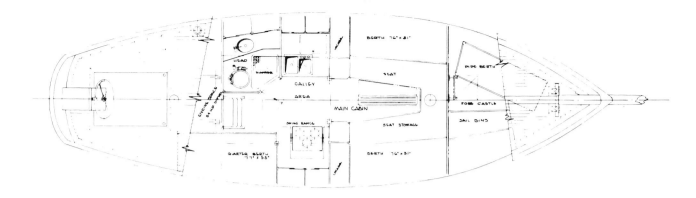

he is getting very good at finishing detail as well.

Unfortunately, but understandably, Clark Ryder is reticent to release his lamination schedule, for he has worked hard and has run many tests to perfect it, so he asked me not to publish it, and that's a bit of a pity, for his boats are built very well. I will try to tell you as much as I can without giving away the secrets. The hulls are laid-up as a single piece with Airex coring (you can get single skin if you want), and the outside laminates have enough layers of roving for a strong 25 foot boat, so the construction so far is nothing to write home about, but what is worth writing about is the fact that the inside laminates (inside the Airex) have enough layers of roving for *another* 25 foot boat. Now, as you know, the important point is not just how many layers are in there but how well they are put in and here again Clark Ryder excels. First, he excels because his is a relatively small yard (although by far the largest in this book) which works on customer orders only, which means the hulls don't have to be rushed out of their moulds. Each set of laminates is therefore given a chance to go off slowly and set up well before the next one is applied. Thus, the resin will cure under ideal circumstances, whereas if the laminates are heaped on one another like they are on some production lines, much heat will be given off during setting, the extreme result of which can be hull distortion or very brittle resin that "cured" too quickly.

Second, the ½ inch Airex is of the scored variety which conforms to the hull curves better than the unscored one, and it is set in wet mat and pressed into place, then allowed to sit while the resin goes off. Once it has cured, someone comes around and taps each square with a mallet to make sure all pieces have adhered perfectly, and if there is a hollow sound indicating that they haven't, the Airex is cut out with a knife and rebedded in resin.

Apart from the normal laminates, an addi-tional 18 inch strip of mat and roving runs around the sheer to strengthen the flange, and a full width pass of mat and double 18 ounce roving runs athwartships in the chainplate area from sheer to sheer. The hull and deck are bolted together with ¼ inch stainless steel bolts on 6 inch and 4 inch centres and that is good.

I am not sure how to react to the fact that the Luders 34 comes with a liner. This is not the ideal solution for longevity since a liner cannot ever be bonded as well as individual bits of cabinetry (see *The Little Yachts of Tom Morris*), although I must say that the liner of the Luders is built as stiff as any liner I have seen and everything is bonded as best it can be, *plus* many knees and dividers of plywood have been installed into large areas like behind and below the bunks, and all of these are well bonded, so perhaps a Luders liner is a rare exception. If you are building your own boat, however, I would forget the liner altogether (except for the head and the engine pan) because a layout as simple as this one (still requiring a good bit of cabinetry work after the liner is put in) can be roughed in by any shipwright worth his salt in about three weeks' time. The factory wants $2,800.00 for their liner so if you pay your man $1,500.00 and spend $1,000.00 on material you will still be way ahead and have an optimally strong boat if you bond every piece to the hull both sides, and you can make whatever changes you like to the layout. What you should get *en masse* from Ryder though are the beautifully rounded teak corner-posts. You will find them in the photos of the galley if you look hard.

In all, the Luders 34 is a solid elegant yacht worthy of a true master of yacht design. Bill Luders has been designing yachts for well nigh fifty years and the sailors of the world are much better off for it. One can only hope that he will go on enriching our harbours for many years to come.

14

Go Find the Golden Fleece

Jason

It is funny how some associations leave such a strong imprint, but they sure seem to. In the case of Ted Brewer, his years of working with Bill Luders left their mark and all for the better, because through all of Ted's designs flow the graceful lines, moderate proportions and elegant overhangs that Luders was so well known for. I am not speaking of the overhangs like the 44 foot yawls Luders designed and built for the navy in the thirties, for they had a total of 14 feet in overhangs with a beautiful long counter, but I refer more to his recent designs where the beauty of the overhangs has not been dampened by the reduction in their length.

I have always liked Ted Brewer's designs and was very glad when I had an opportunity to sail one of his boats, a sleek fin-keeled cruiser-racer, the Morgan 38. That all came about when I was doing research for a book in the Caribbean and the very generous people at Nautilus Yacht Charters of St. Thomas in the Virgin Islands, put at Candace's and my disposal for a couple of weeks, the pride of their fleet, a perfectly kept 38. It was one of the simplest and cleanest designs around then, without any pretentions or razzmatazz, for

everything had been "designed away" so all that was left was a plain trunk cabin, a large simple cockpit, and a pretty, and bloody fast, hull. There was nothing mechanized on deck, no furling jib or self-tailing winches, yet featherweight Candace and I proceeded to terrorize the charter fleets from Charlotte Amalie to Virgin Gorda, and certainly not because of our modest sailing abilities, but because of the excellent performance of the boat.

The Trades got angry a few times during the cruise, but with a genny and reefed main the boat stood up well and kept moving like a freight train. The rig balanced perfectly, the hull moved effortlessly, and handling was so excellent and positive that it reminded me of an old Porsche I used to have. By that I mean the boat responded to every shift of the wheel, and it responded immediately, not twenty minutes later, and it stopped responding right when you stopped moving the wheel, without wandering off another few degrees like boats with poorly balanced underbodies and rudders are wont to do — as a nasty little 35 footer we sailed for ten days previously, most assuredly did. That was a heinous little beast of a boat, whose wheel you could turn hard over and absolutely

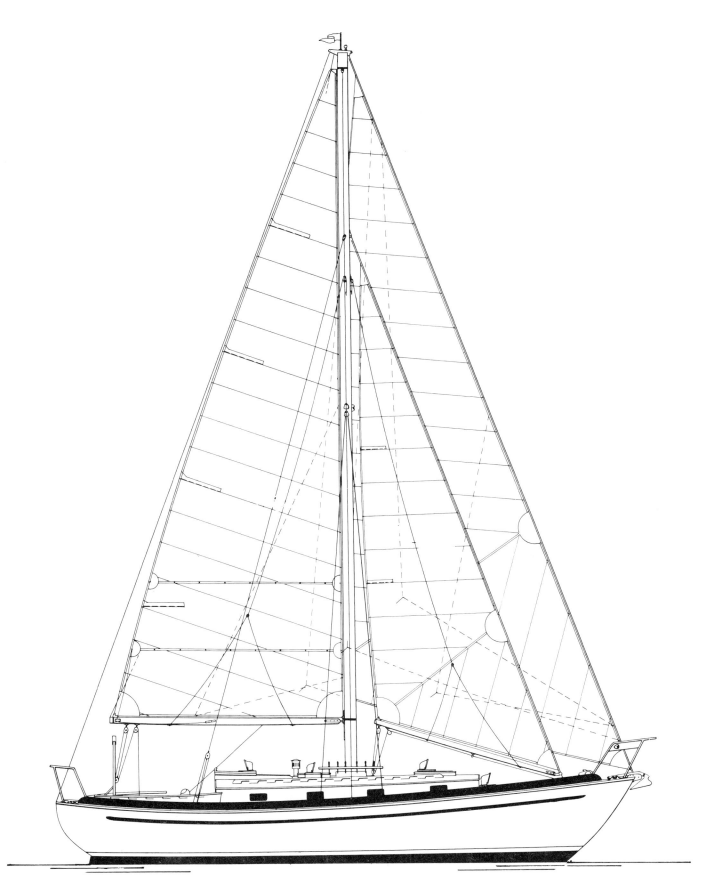

Jason 35 — Ted Brewer

LOA—34'6'' LWL—27'4'' Beam—11'2'' Draft—5'0'' Displ.—16,800 lbs. Ballast—6,200 lbs. Sail Area—634 sq. ft.

nothing would happen, then as you looked over the stern to see if the rudder had fallen off, the cheeky little bastard would spin as if the bow had been kicked by an elephant, and God have mercy on your soul on a hard run in a blow, for she would be all over the ocean looking for a place to roll over.

What does this all have to do with the Jason 35 you may rightly ask, and the answer is everything, for unless a designer goes senile unbeknownst to all, his understanding of performance, handling, and general hull behaviour will neither crumble nor vanish, but will carry over and in most instances improve from one design to the next.

The Jason falls somewhere in the middle of Ted Brewer's career, being design #83 (he is now past 160) and she seems in all aspects to be a sensible cruising yacht.

Her sheer is lively with her bow low enough to look good but high enough — especially when combined with the bulwarks — to keep the boat dry in rough beating. Her entry should not be compared to that of traditional double-enders, as it is fine indeed, which means she will cut through the waves instead of beating them to death. Ted has balanced the hull by fining down the aft sections as well, which should give her an easy even motion. The tumblehome makes for very pretty sections and rounds off — excuse the pun — a very finely realized hull. The bilges are on the stiff side, giving her more stability than her 36 per cent ballast-to-displacement ratio would suggest. Just for fun I ran through a pile of designs Ted sent me and through all of them the ballast-to-displacement ratio hovers between 36 and 38 per cent. Well, I guess if something works well for you, you had better leave it well enough alone.

The keel configuration is possibly the most interesting aspect of the Jason, for although at first glance one would tend to say, "Oh, yes, another one of those full-keeled boats," one had better open one's eyes, because this is a Ted Brewer version of a full keel, in other words it is no full keel at all. The forefoot has been so drastically and so sharply cut away that if you cover up the aft portion of the profile plan with your hand, you would think you are looking at the underbody of a fin-keeler with a bizarrely swept leading edge. Now take away your little hand and you will see that Ted has taken a "bite" out of the after portion of the keel as well. When I asked him why on earth he didn't just take

another small bite to give it a simple fin-keel-skeg rudder, Ted snickered and said, "You shouldn't put this in print but, a client insisted on a full-keeled boat, so I pared away everything but the illusion." Then he laughed out loud and said, "What the hell, print it."

The client was happy and so he should be; he got the best performing full-keeler around. Not only has the wetted surface been greatly reduced, but with the forefoot gone and the bite gone, the boat will respond much more quickly to the helm, a true blessing when tacking or maneuvering in light quarters, and she will still track like a choo-choo and sit easily on her keel in old-fashioned marine ways, or sit in the sand tied to pilings in far away Chinny-Chinny land.

The rudder is large with all the meat down low out of turbulence. Ted Brewer has vast design experience, having been for many years Bill Luder's right hand man, working on designs that ranged from the most conservative of cruising boats to the America's Cup 12 Metre *American Eagle*, so when he comments on one of his own designs he is well worth listening to:

"This was a custom boat for a West Coast owner who wanted a seaworthy long distance cruiser. He knew, from experience, exactly what he needed in such a vessel. As a result she has features in her design that make her safe, easy to handle and comfortable, i.e., a small cockpit-well, permanent boom gallows, running backstays, double head rig, exceptionally large salon and ample stowage space throughout. Auxiliary power is an economical 10 horsepower diesel with a 27 gallon fuel capacity, although a larger engine can be fitted. Water tankage is 95 gallons in three tanks."

Jason's displacement is heavy for her waterline length; the ratio is 375, which means she will have such a lovely motion that you will think you are aboard some beautiful old cruiser, and if you are going to do serious long distance cruising, all the goods she is able to carry will certainly be needed, and remember this boat was designed for a man who wanted a long distance cruiser.

Her sail-area-to-displacement ratio of 15.6 is about what a serious cruiser's should be, one that doesn't have to reef in 12 knots of wind, and to bear me out Ron Holland's Swan 375, which is not intended for slouching about, has an almost iden-

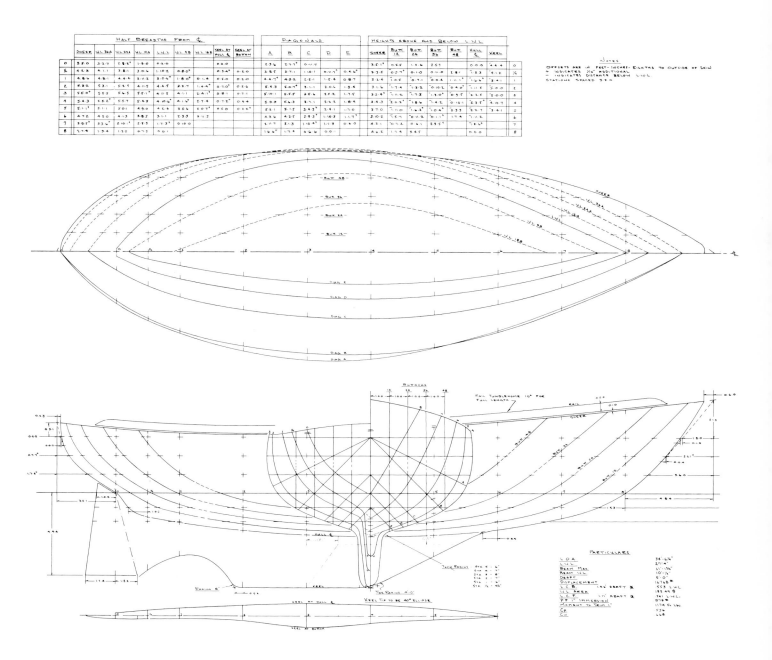

Ted Brewer's 35 foot Jason showing off her pretty tumblehome, moderate bilges, fine entry, and reserve buoyancy aft.

tical sail-area-to-displacement ratio at 15.4. And do keep in mind that this ratio is an indicator of light air performance basically, for once she starts to blow it just means that the higher the ratio the quicker you reef. For long distance work it makes more sense to be able to carry sail longer, for who on earth wants to go through the trades with a reef tied permanently in his main. With a short crew I would rather mess about with big light air sails when things are calm and friendly, than have to put in and shake out reefs just because the wind happens to want to have a little fun.

Ted Brewer has very wisely kept the whole rig inboard with no bowsprit or boomkin to maintain or replace when rot strikes. Bowsprits and boomkins also have extra stays — two whiskers each, as well as a bobstay for the bowsprit, and the more fittings you have the more things there are to fail, and the more fittings you have the more holes in the hull, and who needs that.

The rig is modern with a tall, skinny main having an almost 3 to 1 luff-to-foot ratio. The cutter rig is handy for reducing sail, but the slot between the headstay and the forestay is not much over 4 feet, which means you will have a pretty tough time tacking with a genny. For coastal cruising I think a quick-release to the forestay would be in order to foot the critter off by the shroud somewhere, so the genny can go back and forth quicker than a belly dancer's belly button.

Now I realize that a regular quick-release mechanism is an expensive little bit, costing around two or three hundred dollars, which is enough to make you want to leave the staysail stay in place until the hull rots from underneath, but a simple inexpensive device can be made up to do the job. All you need is a small handle attached to the turnbuckle of your stay, by means of a pin through the centre of the turnbuckle. This handle, which is made of channel stainless steel, can be flipped up and stored against the turnbuckle out of the way and when needed just flipped down and turned, loosening the turnbuckle and allowing you to release the $20.00 quick-release pin that you have installed instead of a clevis pin in the bottom of the turnbuckle. Our local mast shop does this modification for about $30.00, so for a grand total of fifty bucks you have yourself a simple and very operative means of disposing of a stay which, especially for coastal cruising, is used but half the

time.

The deck layout certainly reflects Ted Brewer's concern regarding offshore safety. The cockpit will hold about a cup of water, for as you can see in the drawing it's a miniscule foot well that seats four cosily, with comfortable wood coamings added on for backrests. The deck house profile is a very low 12 inches all along, offering very little resistance to unmannerly waves that choose to come aboard, and if you don't think that this is an important point, ask the owner of the Westsail 42 which had a 2 foot high house before the remnants of Hurricane Annie hit her, but had become a big open day sailer by the time she left. Somewhere along the way someone seemed to have misplaced the house.

The companionway opening is only 12 inches high, and I hate to bring this up again, but a large opening that can lose its dropboards is by far the single most vulnerable point on a well built vessel. In case of a knockdown, tremendous quantities of water can enter a boat in the minute or more she may take to right herself, so much water that the boat will not be able to rise to the waves that follow but will be continuously overwhelmed by them.

The side-decks are broad and made extremely safe by the 6 inch high bulwarks that border them. A freestanding bulwark arrangement that you saw on the Bristol Channel Cutter is used here, with very fine bronze castings finishing off the ends, and bronze base castings, that also foot the stanchions, spaced in between. The actual bulwark itself is ¾ inch teak bolted to these castings, and not only does this make for a very attractive detail, but it allows unlimited deck drainage, for the teak boards are raised slightly from the deck, making the whole thing one long scupper. Ted has ended his house well back of the bow and not only has this created a spacious and clean foredeck, but it has also helped the looks of the boat. Some designs in their quest for more accommodations below, carry their house too far forward, and as in the case of a very popular cruising boat whose name I won't mention, the house ends up awkward and ungainly looking, like the deck of a freighter whose containers have not yet been unloaded.

The side-decks are very wisely kept parallel, so laying of teak decks is simple with a most attractive result.

The stowage topsides is good, the lazarette is

The fine stern and even finer rudder of the Jason 35. The backstay is split and footed on the double chainplates on the hull.

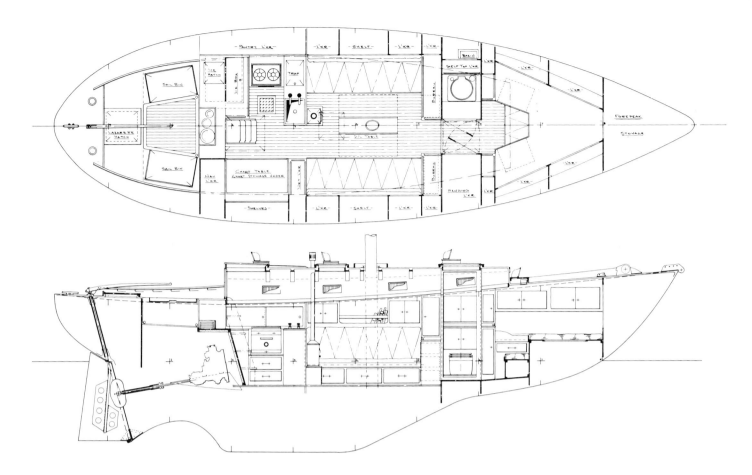

The profile of the Jason 35 shows Ted Brewer's interpretation of a "full keel" with a greatly cut back forefoot and a "bite" taken out of the aft portion of the keel. The rudder post is angled to keep the tiller well back in the cockpit and below there are enough locker bins and shelves to satisfy even the most retentive among us. To give good space in the galley and provide a chart table almost big enough to sleep on, Ted has made the head narrow by using a slide-out or flip-down (your choice) sink. Note lids in cockpit-seats to cavernous sail bins. Note how far aft the mast is located, allowing for a generous fore-triangle without the use of a bowsprit. Ted Brewer is one smart man.

very large, and there is a sail bin of a very generous size to port.

Down Below

The original boat drawn for Mr. Pertner shows a most sensible interior, and Mr. Pertner certainly seemed to know what he wanted. He had a giant stand-up chart table built starboard, and only single settee berths either side of the salon with storage above. The only other berths were the two in the forepeak. This makes for ideal accommodations for a couple going long distance cruising, but you would have a problem if an additional crew was taken aboard, since the forepeak is most uncomfortable when going to weather. I think I would prefer the new interior that Earl Miller, who now builds the boats using fibreglass hull and deck

moulds and customizes the interior to your taste, is putting into the Jason 35. He turned the chart table athwartships, and put a quarterberth aft of it. According to some rough measurements I took off the lines, it should be possible to slide a quarterberth another 16 inches aft to give the chart table its own seat even when the berth is occupied. As it is, the quarterberth is 36 inches at the shoulders, with a 32 inch clearance above. The chart table can be 27 by 44 inches and that is very good indeed.

The engine is hemmed in by bulkheads on the sides, but access could be cut from the quarterberth. The galley is well laid out and because the companionway is slightly off centre it has enough room so that the cookie can work out of the traffic undisturbed and safely strapped in place. The icebox is 22 inches wide and 28 inches long and a foot and a half deep, an average which gives you over 6 cubic feet, which is a lot, but Earl Miller, the builder, pours 4 inches of foam around it all, so ice should last a long time, especially if the lid is insulated as well. We have used a similar system of insulation on *Warm Rain* which has a comparably sized icebox, and six blocks of ice will provide perfect cooling for up to two weeks, at the end of which we usually have a block and a half or two blocks worth left. *Warm Rain's* icebox is in truth divided in two halves which means once your ice starts to go you can concentrate all of what is left in one compartment, thereby extending its life considerably.

Ted Brewer pushed the upper part of the galley aft over the engine room bulkhead so there is plenty of counter space and good storage for dishes behind the ladder.

The salon is laid out in the original Jason with two settee berths, but Earl has made some liners with 22 inch pilot berths each side as well, and that still left 20 inch settees. What you choose here is up to you. Remember, Earl Miller is a custom boat builder so he can readily change the accommodation. The head is kept small but functional, although it is even smaller in the original plan. I saw the original version put to use in a beautiful fully finished boat that Gary Peerless and his partner Ann built from a hull and deck (including their own ballast, but more of that later) and they used a slide-out sink with flexible hoses, and thereby managed to squeeze the head into a space measuring 27 inches between bulkheads. With such tight quarters as that, the throne might be the snuggest, safest seat aboard in a blow.

Across from the head is a voluminous area, excellent for a giant hanging locker or other stowage, or even a "Maté"-desk if you plan to do a lot of writing or prefer your daydreaming with a blank piece of paper and pen in front of you.

The forepeak makes into a great double and has 34 inches of clearance over it so that the lockers Ted drew above the outboard edges should hold significant quantities of small goods. As you can see from the drawings, the rope locker is large indeed, and could easily be used to stow a drifter as well. The chain should be led aft to stow below the berths, and if you install your windlass where the drawings show, it should be easy to lead a pipe

through the bulkhead just below, or right at, the bunk's top.

Construction

As I said, Earl Miller of Miller Marine builds the Jason and has now built forty-one in all. Earl is known throughout the Northwest as a builder of excellent quality (and by no means inexpensive) custom boats, mostly in the large category. When I was at the yard they were lofting the lines of a 65 foot Robert Perry designed ultra-light. They are out in the woods of Bainbridge Island, which is a twenty minute ferry ride from Seattle, and what a pretty setting it is.

The glasswork coming from Miller is truly first class—I can honestly say I have seen no better anywhere. The hull is laminated mostly with athwartship runs of glass, which seems to be a Northwest way, and for results of what this does please see the Cape George boats.

The hull laminates graduate from six layers of 24 ounce roving (mat is used only against the gelcoat) at the sheer to more than double that in the keel with the overlapping ends. If properly squeegeed, an all-roving hull will give you a much higher fibre-to-resin ratio — hence more strength — than a hull using alternate layers of mat and roving. (See Ingrid, Blue Water Boats for more.) As is, the Jason has one of the best built hulls in this book of boats.

All laminates are turned over for a 4 inch flange upon which the deck sits. The deck is totally flush along the sheer, so there is no trick to bonding the two together from below with double runs of mat and roving, which is what Miller does. With the kind of glasswork he does you should get a perfectly leakproof joint, as good as any in the industry.

The deck is also hand-laid-up with a ¾ inch core of balsa. If you wish, for an extra $2,000.00, the hull can have balsa or Airex core *added* as well for insulation, for the hull certainly doesn't need more stiffness.

As if the hull was not built heavily enough, Ted Brewer designed eight fibreglass beams hung athwartships below the cabin sole. Three are 2 inches by 5 inches, and the other five beams (the ones under the mast step and adjoining bulkheads) are 4 inches by 5 inches. Miller makes the beams hollow — as if a boat of this displacement would

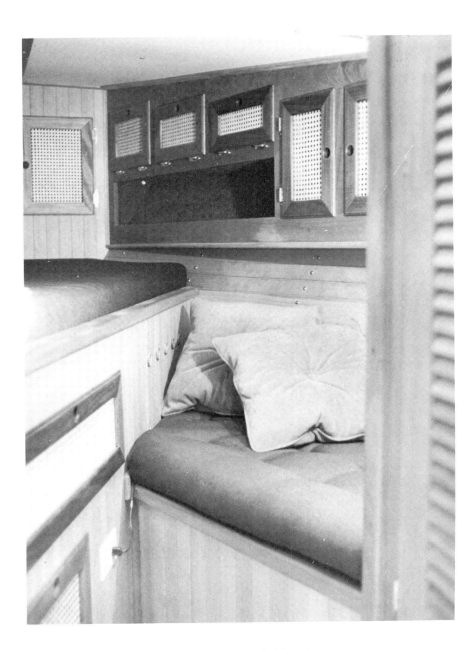

Freja's *lovingly finished interior.*

sneeze at solid beams — by using two wedge-shaped pieces of wood to lay the glass around. These are heavily waxed and slipped out once the resin has set. The beam walls are made up of two layers of mat and four layers of roving, and are of course bonded to the hull.

The ballast is all lead, and when I was told of how it was installed I almost had a coronary right there and then, so before you start reading the next bit you should sit down and breathe slowly.

First they get a little heap of lead pigs — brick sized, instead of the normal large castings — and they put these little pigs into the hull one layer at a time. Then — take a deep breath — while the hull is cooled from the outside with fans and hoses, they actually pour in molten lead to unite the pigs together. Now you have got to admit that that takes a lot of *cojones*. But while you are still laughing, remember they have done this for many years and it does work, as long as enough cold water is circulated onto the hull. (See Cherubini 44 for more on this.) Gary and Ann did their ballast themselves using this method, and they had no problems and the task was not terribly demanding, unless you consider demanding, the lugging of 6,300 pounds of lead up a ladder and down a ladder, piggy by piggy.

Once all the ballast is in, it is all bonded over to seal it off. But keep in mind that lead shrinks as it cools, so it should be given time to settle, and the space between the hull and the ballast resulting from the shrinkage, should be carefully filled with resin mixed with a bit of microballoons or some other such thickening agent. When the space is all filled solid *then* the bonding can be put over top.

I just found in my notebook a couple of lines about the rudder, they read: excellent tooling, fine trailing edge, nicely faired for wash. That last part refers to the aperture where the propeller lives, which is nicely faired both in the hull and the rudder, which in turn means that the water will flow around this area smoothly and give the prop a good solid water to bite, and once bitten, it can flow out past the rudder without meeting unnecessary resistance. This is a constant problem with boats whose propeller is located in an aperture, and even a greater problem with boats with substantial deadwood. This deadwood must be faired down otherwise there will be much turbulent water and the prop will then cavitate and vibrate and lose

much potential power *and* wear out the cutlass bearing. Similarly if the rudder right behind the propeller has too much meat to it, the water the propeller is trying to push off will meet with unnecessary resistance which will result in a power loss. These points are even more important for those who seldom use their engines, for the turbulence that badly done fairing causes will add much drag and slow a boat's speed substantially.

The bulkheads are ½ inch plywood, generously bonded in, but no foam "shock absorber" is used between the bulkheads and the hull. Again at the risk of being redundant, almost all of the builders who have been around for a long time and have seen what a hard bulkhead can do to a pretty hull, all use foam, so twist Earl's arm a bit and I am sure he will go along with you. The coring in the decks is ¾ inch balsa with plywood reenforcement where needed for through-bolting.

On the last three boats, a four-piece interior liner was used, and I keep saying that liners are a weak point because you can't properly bond everything to the hull for added stiffness, but Miller's liners are so heavily built and so well bonded on both sides, inside and outside of the cabinetry, that in this case the good things about the liner (low maintenance, and simple completion) may just balance the disadvantages of extra cost and lack of flexibility in altering the layout. The latter is of course somewhat flexible in this case, even if the liner is used, since the thing is in four pieces, hence you can have the parts you like and leave out the ones you don't. All, truly all, horizontal surfaces in the liner are reenforced for stiffness with ⅜ inch balsa coring, and the parts that are not are an incredible ¼ inch thick in most places, and with that much glass, how the boat doesn't sink below her designed waterlines I will never know, but of course having balsa in the tops helps. As I said, the liner is bonded on both sides everywhere it touches the hull and reenforcing plywood knees are installed (and honestly bonded) in all long spaces, like below and behind the berths.

The tanks I thought were a little lazily located. The water tanks are below the berths in the salon, where they are higher than they should be, and take up much valuable storage space, while the fuel tank is above and aft of the engine, where again its height reduces the boat's stability, and its weight aft adds to hobbyhorsing potential which will slow the boat. Mark Julian (who looks after the shop in Earl's absence) and I measured out the unused volume below the floor beams and found above the lead ballast a space averaging 14 inches in height, 16 inches in width and 7½ feet in length, which could house 11½ cubic feet of tanks or about 86 gallons (7.5 gallons per cubic foot). Now 86 gallons of water is a goodly amount in a small cruiser. Another space aft of the ballast could hold a 27 gallon fuel tank, which, with a small engine and some dedicated sailing, could last a long time, close to 54 hours with most 2 cylinder diesels running at around 1,800 R.P.M. Now 54 hours of rattling, banging noise should be rationed by even the most dedicated masochist, so the fuel will last a good long while.

In all, the Jason is a thoroughly fine yacht, and my one large regret is that there aren't more beautiful Ted Brewer boats built on a semi-custom basis. The plant building his lovely 39 foot cruiser-racer — which was perhaps one of the few "perfect" cruising boats — was closed down by fire. Jason is carefully thought out and very well built by Earl Miller, who will build her for you any way you like, and to whatever degree of completion you like, and the ferry ride to and from Bainbridge Island is such a joy that you might as well go and see his place just for a good outing if nothing else.

The Jason has no bulwarks laminated into the hull; instead it has cast-bronze stanchion bases and cast-bronze ends supporting teak or mahogany 'wale boards. This looks very fine and also lets the deck drain quickly.

15

Windward
Peterson 35

Doug Peterson didn't exactly stumble into yacht design, he clawed and pushed his way in. He started sailing on his father's 100 foot four masted schooner at the age of twelve, raced dinghies in the San Diego Yacht Club until he was fifteen, then raced offshore as crew after that, helped out designer Skip Calkins after high school, and was in his first long distance race when he was twenty, sailing in events like the Acapulco race, Transpac and the Tahiti race. Then he read everything there was about designing boats and at the ripe age of twenty-nine, drew the lines of his own first boat on the living room table, had it built in five weeks, dropped her in the water and promptly won the North American One-Ton Championships, with himself as skipper and designers Ron Holland and Bill Green among the crew. They came in second in the World One-Ton that same year in Sardinia.

That was all done in 1973 in a boat he called *Ganbare*, whose basic ideas he had worked out during a Tahiti race. "It was a pretty rough race and we pounded like hell. There had to be a solution, I thought, a way to make a light boat go to windward. That's when I started to evolve the U-bow. I knew the V-bow was slow because if the 'V' has a

20 degree angle, when the boat heels it becomes flat and the boat pounds." Well, *Ganbare* had a U-bow, that's for sure, and she made history "because of her bow and pintail stern shape she could point high and go through the chop. The theory was to have balanced ends so that the keel stayed in correct relationship to the rig as the boat heeled. With a wide stern the keel pops up and goes on a negative angle of attack . . . The boat gave me instant recognition."

He has since designed boats like *Acadia*, that won the SORC, *Williwaw*, which won the World Two-Ton Cup, while his *Solent Saracen* won the Three-Quarter-Ton Cup and *North Star* the Half-Ton. And they were all along the *Ganbare* line, with slight evolutions like an increasingly broader stern.

The Peterson 35 is a true *Ganbare*. The hull, having been designed almost ten years ago, has more overhang in the bow than newer boats and a moderate pintail stern, resulting in pretty profile lines and an elegant transom. The latter will of course make the 35 a little less powerful once heeled, (power meaning standing up and carrying more sail longer because of the buoyancy added by

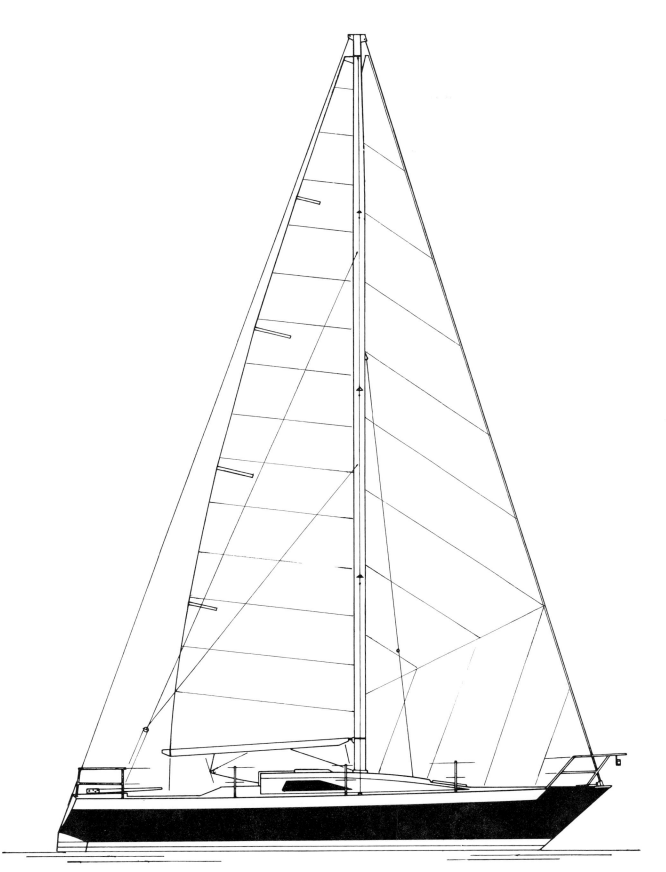

Peterson 35 — Doug Peterson
LOA—35'5" LWL—28'6" Beam—11'3" Draft—6'3" Displ.—13,200 lbs. Ballast—6,500 lbs.

a broad stern) and she will not pick up as much added waterline length as the newer butt-draggers, but then she doesn't look as distorted either. The entry seems to be a classic, and a little different from the many racers whose designers tend to cut away almost all of the forefoot to reduce wetted surface, drawing an almost straight line from just below the waterline back to the leading edge of the keel, much like a Hobie 33. I say that the entry is a classic because designers seem to be coming back to this deeper forefoot now, among them Britton Chance Jr., who wrote about his latest thinking about IOR/club racers in reference to his 34 foot *Alethea*:

"I was after a boat that would not only be fast, but would also be easy to put and keep in the groove. The hull shape is therefore designed to be insensitive to angle of heel; she has a deep, very fine forefoot and a deeper bustle aft than my earlier designs."

Perhaps it is this deeper forefoot (combined with a very fine entry and a slight U-shaped forward section) that make the 35 a more pleasant racer to sail. Its bottom becomes very flat and broad starting from the forward edge of the keel, so much so that the cabin sole between the port and starboard settees is over 4 feet in width and the bilge space below it so shallow that if you spill your Scotch you will have flooded the cabin. The keel has a very high aspect ratio and has been thinned down and made even a little deeper by builder Don Martin in the newer model, although the hull went unchanged in order to be able to use the age allowance in her rating. The rudder was also thinned and deepened, probably resulting in slightly better lift. The cockpit has been changed drastically. Nearly 2 feet was chopped off the aft end of the house, replaced by a humped bridgedeck under which the athwartships part of the U-shaped settee is located. There is now much more cockpit space for a rapidly moving racing crew and a more innovative layout belowdecks.

One of the best evaluations you can get about a boat is to talk to a knowledgeable owner who has sailed and campaigned her for some time. Vic Bishop, who owns Pride Sails Northwest, bought his Peterson 35 *Brigadoon* just over two years ago and his has been the winningest one-ton boat in the Vancouver area since. He has won the gruelling 135 mile Southern Straits overall, in a year when

masts broke like reeds, and he has won the division title in a year when it blew from zero to 30 knots and everything in between. He took the division title in the Swiftsure race, and has won a lapful of races in the Winter Series.

To do all this he has been less than gentle with his boat, cranking the stays and hydraulics to their limit "until the rug was coming through the deck," and he has been in too many knockdowns to count and he has even been attacked and rammed on two separate occasions, yet *Brigadoon* always finished the race, which says a lot for Doug Peterson's design and Don Martin's construction. He has had no structural problems or failures and no leaks, save for seacocks which were unfortunately orlon or nylon or some such thing, and he has changed O-rings and levers and he has tightened them and loosened them until he has used up every blasphemy in the English language and still they leaked. So out they went and in went real bronze seacocks, the kind that should have been there in the first place. This is no place to save weight, even on a racing boat, and if you are that desperate for lightness, take the grommets out of your deck shoes or leave your dentures at home, but for God's sake don't chintz on your seacocks.

Back to *Brigadoon's* adventures. One time, Vic was crossing tacks with a C & C 39 and Vic had the right of way so he kept on, and the C & C thought he had him beaten, so *he* kept on; then at the last minute the C & C decided he had better fall off, but by then it was too late to fall off because his bow had climbed over Vic's lee rail and come down crash smash boom, on the house, and to add insult to injury, the pulpit went clear through the mainsail. Well, Vic was so upset and distraught that he finished only third in that race.

Another time he carried the chute too long and got knocked down on his *dakine* so hard and so flat that he was down three or four minutes before they cut loose the sails and she righted herself, but still nothing broke, and another time a boat was going to cut across his bow but changed its mind and slipped off a wave and rammed him instead. There was no holing but there was a goodly crack indicating delamination, and here perhaps I might digress and tell you how repairs can be done on a cored-hull where no major holing or destruction of the outer skin has taken place.

To approach the repair with any thought of go-

The Peterson 35 Mk II with a deeper, finer keel and rudder and updated short house with broad crowned bridgedeck making for a more functional cockpit, and bringing crew weight closer to midships.

ing in from the outside is just plain folly, for you will have then destroyed the original shape of the hull and only some very miraculous and time-devouring effort will make it look like new again. Repairs should begin from the inside by cutting away, with a small mineral blade, (attached to a drill motor or side grinder) the inside laminates, being careful not to penetrate past the coring in the hull. Don't be too conservative with how much width you cut out, because this inside skin hole has to be considerably bigger than the outside skin damage so that the outside damage can be removed and the new laminates put in its place, reaching a good 18 inches all around the undamaged areas.

Once you have cut the inside hole, remove the foam carefully over the area and begin, with the mineral blade, to cut away all the delaminated outer parts, *but do not go through the outermost layer.* You must remove all the delaminated material, and fair back with a grinder all edges, but you *must* leave this outermost layer intact, for that

is all that is retaining the original shape of the hull. Once all the delaminated laminates are off, and the edges are faired in and an 18 inch wide path cleared off all around the damaged outer layer, you can begin repair by filling in with however many laminates you need to replace, one layer at a time. Make each consecutive pass 4 inches to 6 inches larger than the last one all the way around until all the faired area plus the 18 inch cleared area around it is rebuilt. Do not mix your resin too hot (too much catalyst) and *do* wait until one layer has set completely with no more heat being given off, because if you get the hull too hot you may distort the remaining thin outer layer. Next, fill in with foam or balsa coring, whichever you had to start with, and rebuild the inner layer in a similar fashion. Now you can go outside and do whatever minimal cosmetic repair the hull will require, usually just a bit of sanding, filling and sanding along the crack. Paint it — leave the job to someone who has had experience with air guns — and you will be as good as new.

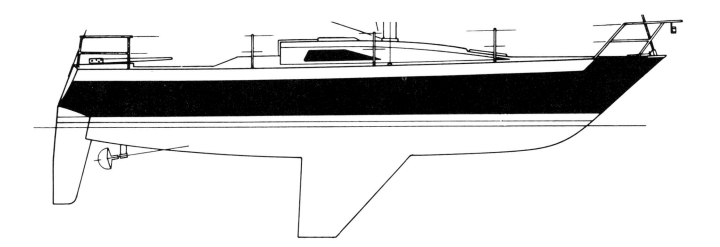

I knew I'd backtrack my way to *Brigadoon* somehow and I did, for while we are talking about filling and sanding, it's worth while to mention one of Vic Bishop's most highly stressed points, which is that if a boat hopes to gain that extra $\frac{1}{10}$th or $\frac{1}{8}$th of a knot that most often separates the winner from the non-winner, then the whole keel, rudder, and bottom must be as smooth as a baby's. Very few sailboat manufacturers can, or even try, to achieve a perfect bottom, so this totally unrewarding task is left to the ardent skipper and whoever else he can con into doing it. This is really no different from skiers filling and refinishing or waxing their skis, or the devoted competition soaring pilot sanding and filling his visually perfect sailplane wings. It's all part of the game to those who care a lot about winning.

So anyway the Peterson 35 is tough and she is also fast. Boat for boat she will normally beat older C & C 39's and the newer 38's and as often as not the C & C 40's. She does have a very tall rig, almost as tall as the C & C 39's, but with this much sail and the flat bottom and not even a hint of a skeg, the boat does become "squirrelly" downwind in a blow, and after 20 knots or so she gets so spinny that you have to carry a blooper. Vic has had the chute stuck on a jammed halyard at close to 40 knots and nothing much happened except that a lot of his hair went grey and some of it even jumped overboard in fright.

The skittishness of the 35 is not a unique phenomenon in racing boats; if you flatten the bottom and reduce wetted surface by removing skegs and bridging between keel and rudder and shave the forefoot away, then indeed any boat will "slide around" at high speeds, but nevertheless that does not alleviate the problem at hand, which is that, running hard with a lot of sail the Peterson 35 is not a boat for the novice or sightseer.

To exercise as much control as possible, the use of a tiller is mandatory. Vic has spent more than a few races running with another 35 whose helmsman was at least as experienced and able as himself, but whose helmsman was also cursed with a wheel, and on many an occasion ended up skedaddling all over the ocean instead of steering a fairly steady course which Vic more or less managed. His only explanation for this (for they usually carried similar sails) was the presence of the wheel, for no matter how well adjusted a wheel's steering is, it simply cannot have the feel and sensitivity or even the accuracy of response that a tiller has. With a tiller you can feel *exactly* how much push the following seas are giving the hull and you can respond accordingly, and it can respond quickly. To say that this is a lot of boat to handle with a tiller is less than accurate for there are much larger ocean racers around today, some over 40 feet, and they manage well with a tiller; a long tiller, mind you, but a tiller nonetheless.

So much for downwind misbehaving, for whatever creases the 35 will furrow on your face on the run, she will iron them all into smiles on the wind for that is what she excels at as all good racers should, for according to Baader in *The Sailing Yacht*: "The overwhelming importance of windward performance is evident from the fact that of the total time spent on all points of sailing, about fifty-five per cent is to windward, twenty per cent reaching and only twenty-five per cent

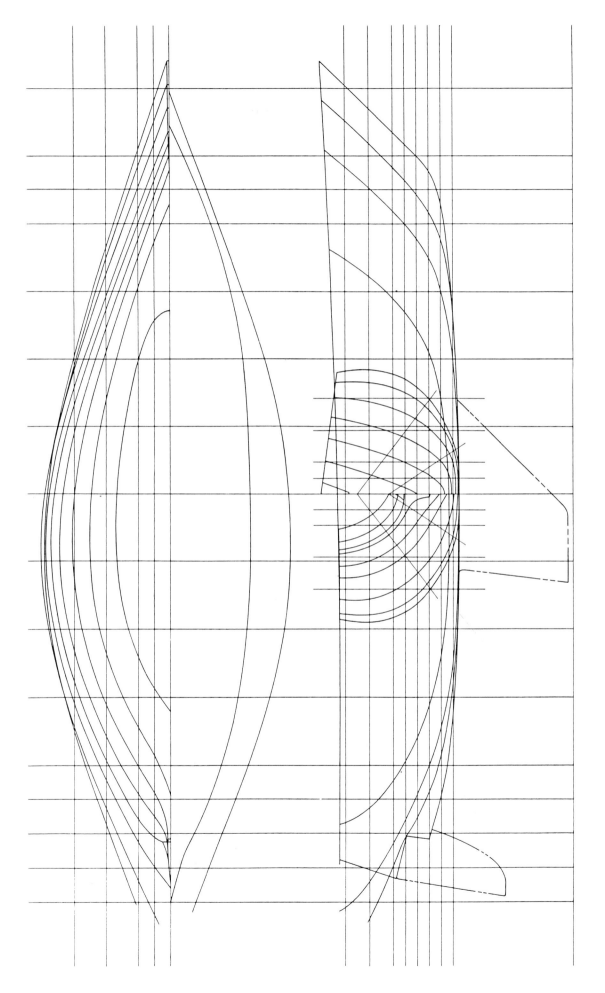

Doug Peterson's Ganbare, which he launched, reciprocated by launching his career almost ten years ago. According to Peterson, the U-shaped forward sections kept her from pounding to weather, while the balanced lines aft gave her better keel lift, by maintaining the proper angle of attack even when heeled. Her bottom amidships is as flat as a pancake, although not quite as flat as the much never Frers 40.

running.''

That fifty-five per cent of the time the Peterson 35 is a demon. She does very well in light airs, hits hull speed in 8 knots of wind, and in 10 knots you can balance the sails and the boat will steer herself. Vic has done this in fairly smooth waters, then left the tiller for thirty minutes just to prove a point and the boat wandered but 5 degrees each side of her course line. Of course you will say that any owner will rave about his boat, but Vic has a pile of trophies to back up his claims. And if you think that this is a single regional aberration, then think again — I just read that an old Peterson 35 placed seventh in class in this year's SORC ahead of a couple of new New York 36's, C & C 39's and a Soverell 36. Not bad for a ten year old design. One last note before we leave *Brigadoon*, for those who think races are won mostly by equipment. *Brigadoon* has achieved her feats with one set of primary winches, using stops for the sheet, not being cranked. This might result in a lost second here or there but can be made up by an attentive crew, and a pair of stops are a hell of a lot cheaper than a pair of Barient 32's.

The rig has also been changed on the 35 this year. Martin reduced the mast section slightly and went to triple spreaders and split running backstays, and this, combined with a hydraulic back and babystay, ought to give very fine mast bend control. The mast is from Sparcraft in Costa Mesa and they certainly do some of the finest welding and the most thorough and cautious assembly on the continent. The rod rigging and hydraulics are all Navtec.

Down Below

The new interior concentrates on locating all major weights: galley stove, icebox, etc. amidships to keep the ends as light as possible. The engine is aft of the athwartship settee along with its small fuel tank, which puts it far enough forward to allow for a straight drive, eliminating the potential problems one can encounter with a V-drive. The engine is boxed in and insulated with sheet lead and foam, admittedly bad as extra weight but it sure is good for the soul. Access to the engine is excellent from both sides. A pair of quarterberths can be installed either side of the engine box and if you wonder how you get into these, then I will tell you.

The aft backrests of the corner pieces of the settee slide out like drawboards. The settee layout — a watered down version of the New York 36 where the whole thing is slid back under the aft deck — seems like a good idea, in that it will snugly seat six people around the table (keeping the crew's weight below roughly where it was above) and the seats are wide enough and comfortable, but the only problem is that, as someone comes down the open companionway ladder, all the grit comes trickling down into your soup bowl below. This problem can be corrected by building a closed off ladder, one that has a solid back, but then the settee area would feel rather closed off and darkish. To prevent this the backpiece could be made out of a piece of plexiglass, opaqued on the side facing the steps so that scratches and scuffs won't show.

The other problem is with regards to navigation, (for it is this same table that is to be used for chart work) for rain and spray coming down the hatch can raise havoc. I suppose if you want you could work your charts on the icebox lid where you are out of the weather and in a place where navigation gear can be easily mounted, but then you will be a very long way from the cockpit.

As I said, the settees are fine and their backs are hinged and can lift up to form pilot berths either side, but this is accomplished with a block and tackle gear like Roman blinds, and I wouldn't trust that unless I was terribly well sauced, in which case I could probably levitate without the damned pulleys anyway. The second poor aspect of this arrangement is that in order to get into the lockers behind the settee, you have to hold this hinged guillotine-of-a-back over your head. Since the thing weighs about fifteen pounds, it can gather pretty good momentum in a good seaway and give your noggin such a whack that you won't know whether to weep or go blind. I think I would put in the quarterberths and forget about the pilots, but then to each his own. As I mentioned before, the sole space is enormous, with lift-up access to most of the keel bolts.

The galley is minimal but with the icebox lid serving as counter space, two people can work in it which is a great advantage when feeding a large crew. The head is small but serviceable with a large sliding door between it and the main salon. This can be easily lifted out of place for racing to save weight, or an even better solution would be to use

The Peterson 35 is built along the lines of Ganbare, *which Doug Peterson designed on his living room table and launched in 1973, just in time for the North American One Ton Championship held in San Diego.* Ganbare *won the event, and came in second in the One Ton Cup in Sardinia, but won the event in both '74 and '75.*

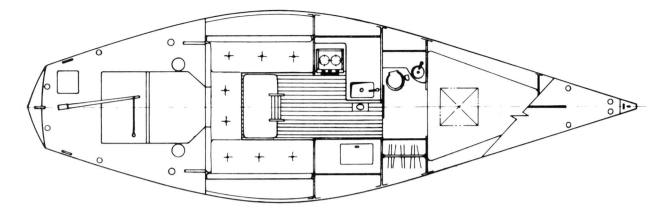

The interior of the Peterson 35 has the dinette area aft with the athwartship seat located under the bridgedeck, a sort of moderate version of the new New York 36. Not shown in the drawing are the two good quarterberths. There is a lack of a decent navigation area.

foam-cored plywood which weighs next to nothing and can be left in permanently. There is a good sized V-berth forward, consisting of two pieces of ⅜ inch plywood slipped into place, and again this can be lifted out and left ashore for racing, saving a few pounds.

As you can tell from the description, this is a minimal interior and for a racer it has to be, but it is by no means visually stark since no liners are used and the furniture and even the sole is made of plywood, the latter having a thin veneer of teak and holly. This is now the trend to save weight and cost in most boats from the elegant Swans to the lowliest bounce-abouts.

The overhead does, however, have a nicely tooled and slightly textured fibreglass liner and I must say this looks much better than the soft naugahyde that many builders use, which hangs and droops and glitters like Tijuana seat covers. This liner looks solid and structural and can be nicely finished off at the portlights etc., by simple filling and sanding instead of having bits of trim everywhere. Very good access has been left all around to the bolts of stanchions, winch bottoms, and deck hardware, and all this is vital especially on a racing boat, for with the loading this hardware undergoes, slight working and leaks are not only likely but guaranteed. So you have to be able to get at everything to tighten and re-bed if necessary.

The stowage for personal gear is, as on most racers, scant to nil, consisting of an open hanging locker across from the head and whatever space there is behind the settee backs. The space below the settees themselves is minimal because they are so far outboard that the turns of the bilge begin here, and anyway a bladder type water tank lives in each of these spaces. But then this is where the beauty of finishing your own boat comes in — you can do with the interior whatever you please.

Construction

The basic thought behind racing boat construction is to achieve as stiff but as light a hull as possible. There seem to be four common factors that the builder and designer can manipulate in various degrees according to their beliefs, their daring and their budget. How far you can push each and in what proportion to the others is beyond me, and the more designers you talk to and the more builders you ask the less clear everything becomes, for the opinions of one seem totally contrary to those of another, to the point where you begin to think that they are all crazy and all of their ships will come apart and sink at exactly the same moment, but all will do so for totally contradictory reasons. So maybe all you can really say with any sense of accuracy is to read the magazines and see who wins the races, then pick a colour you like and buy one and rely on the fact that most of them stay together most of the time, in spite of best efforts of the crew to pull, torque and tear them to pieces.

Anyway, the four basic ways of giving strength to light hulls are:
1) Coring — using a light core of various forms like Airex or balsa which will give rigidity

Metalmast Marine of Connecticut makes a boat virtually identical to the Peterson 35. The hull is kept light and a nicely engineered athwartship beam of aluminum is made up to act as mast-step. The chainplates tie in to the turned-up ends of the beam, so in essence the mast is holding itself up.

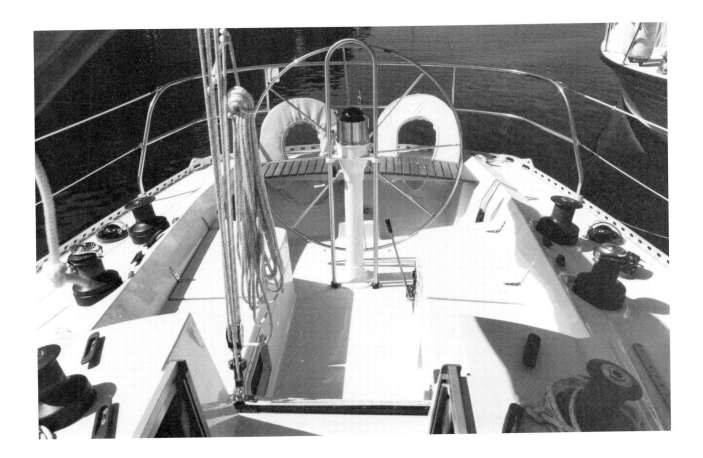

without the weight of heavy fibreglass.

2) Adding stiffening members — either basic longitudinals through the bilges, complex transverse ones or grid-like floors or all of them.

3) The use of high strength unidirectional fibres.

4) The use of ultra materials such as Kevlar and carbon fibre, which are very light and extremely strong and devilishly expensive, in areas that would otherwise require heavy reenforcement.

Kevlar and carbon fibre are used almost exclusively on one-off or extremely limited production yachts and have led to some unique breakthroughs in lightweight masts and booms. Unfortunately their use has also led to some disasters, such as in the 1979 Fastnet race, where their applications were in the wrong areas and many rudder stocks snapped in the storm, leaving the boats helpless in the seas.

The other three strength producing methods, however, are commonly used on many racing and cruising boats and they are all used on the Peterson 35.

The hull is laid up with opposite diagonal layers of unidirectional roving, then reenforced with ¾ inch Klegecell foam, then stiffened with longitudinals along the bilge, that go right into the stem. It is then reenforced with unidirectional roving layers over the floor beams. The actual hull lay-up goes something like this: Gelcoat, 1 ounce mat, unidirectional diagonal roving, opposite diagonal roving, 1½ ounce mat, ¾ inch Klegecell, 1 ounce mat, 18 ounce roving.

The transom has no Klegecell in it but it does have four additional units of 1 ounce mat and 18 ounce roving. The keel area also has no coring, instead it is built up to a thickness of 1 inch with layers of 1½ ounce mat and 24 ounce roving. The coring stops about 4 inches below the sheer and the laminates are turned over to form a 2½ inch flange to which the deck is attached. Klegecell foam is said to add more stiffness than Airex, but it is not as resilient. It has the advantage of being dark, so that air bubbles can be detected more readily during lamination, but its competitors claim it to be less stable — that is it may *work* in very hot climates, especially if encased in a black hull. This latter point I think needs more investigation before a final decision is made.

The first Peterson 35 was built without a reenforcing floor grid, and although it suffered no ill effects during racing, the hull visibly sagged from the pull of the keel during haul out, so the reenforcing grid was put in. This is all the more important on a boat with hydraulics where enormous forces up to five or six thousand pounds are in play trying their utmost with backstay, vang and babystay to bend the hull into a pretzel. As a test that all this stiffening and strengthening works, Vic Bishop casually sailed *Brigadoon* in 25 knot winds through a broken log boom (in the dark of night) and he bounced and rammed merrily along for some time and suffered no damage.

The longitudinal beams are made up of 2 inch by 4 inch foam placed on edge to give the shape, and are then bonded over with six layers of unidirectional roving. The backstay is footed on the longitudinal beam. The lateral grid is built over 2 inch by 3 inch foam, laid onto the hull laminates and again covered over with six layers of unidirectional roving. The twelve keel bolts, ¾ inch in diameter, are scattered among the beams.

The rudder has a 4 inch diameter aluminum stock, with a 2 square foot reenforcing plate of ³⁄₁₆ inch thickness in it. The bulkheads are ½ inch thick and are bonded to the hull without the use of foam, which in this case is acceptable since the hull is cored with foam anyway. The deck is bonded and bolted (¼ inch stainless steel bolts on 4 inch centres) to the hull, and this operation is best left to the builder since the beam measurement is critical for the IOR rating.

The design and installation of the chainplates is noteworthy. The plates are based and bolted to the longitudinal bulkheads running outboard of the galley to port, and outboard of the icebox to starboard. These half bulkheads are bonded not only along the edges as most bulkheads are, but are covered with six layers of unidirectional roving that come down the hull, go up, over and down the bulkheads, and lap another 12 to 18 inches down the hull. This results in *beam* that is well over 1 inch thick.

The chainplate itself is ¼ inch stainless steel, 4 inches wide, and it is bolted with eight ⅜ inch stainless steel bolts to a long aluminum plate (½ inch by 3 inches) that is in turn bolted to the mega-reenforced bulkhead with twelve ⁵⁄₁₆ inch stainless steel bolts. Now *that* you can torque to your heart's content.

An interesting idea is used for the interior backup plates for the sail tracks. Instead of using one washer per bolt, Don Martin uses an upside down ¾ inch aluminum channel. This distributes the load better and houses all the bolt ends which might otherwise protrude and gash skulls. He rounds the ends of the channel well, to render the corners harmless.

Topsides there are a couple of minor shortcomings. There is no collar around the mast to which blocks can be snapped; instead each block is fastened individually through the deck. This can cause many leak problems and if a block fails during a race its replacement will be a major undertaking, whereas with a collar, a new block could instantly be snapped into place.

The other thing I question is the T-bridge that holds the mainsail track. This is built of 1 inch teak 4 inches wide and screwed to blocks on the cockpit sides which in turn are screwed through the cockpit. This is just too much screwing for my taste. You can replace all these pieces with a single aluminum I-beam with a plate welded to each end. The plate can be through-bolted to the cockpit side with a large single backup plate behind; a much simpler and stronger arrangement. Apart from those points the boats are very fine and the help you get from Don Martin's shop is good indeed, judging by accounts of owners who have worked with him. His help is based on experience, having built the 35, as well as two boats of his own design, for six years. The shop is small and usually open to customers who have problems or need anything, whether it be plywood parts, paper templates, or just a pat on the shoulder. Happy racing.

16

Deceptre
Sceptre 36

I have had my eye on this critter for over a year now, often slowing and sometimes stopping as I row by on my constitutional through our cove, and every time I do I wonder in puzzlement why I find this boat so attractive. I have watched through the telescope from the house as, on blustery cold winter Sunday mornings with snow drifting down, thirty or forty hearty skippers from the yacht club edge out of the channel into Georgia Strait for the race, and I usually shake my head and say to Candace, "Now those are real sailors." And out of a deep feeling of empathy I pull my bathrobe tighter, put a log on the fire and stuff another croissant in my face. To each his own.

I kept watching the progress of the Sceptre in the races, and this is not hard because going windward up the Sound they often come so close to Parry Rock, in front of the house, that a great flock of gulls and grebes and cormorants living there, take to the air shaken from their slumber; and then of course there is the stern. The chopped stern is not an easy thing to miss. When I asked Hein Driehuyzen, the designer, about its *raison d'être*, he went into a dissertation about a better angle for the boarding ladder and less chance of damage to the stern, then he stopped and his eyes shone mischievously and he said, "And I thought it might make a good trademark." So anyway, I kept my eye on the Sceptre and noticed how, on one Sunday, it would do well against the C & C's and a Yamaha and other boats I could hardly make out through the mist and snow, and the next Sunday would come limping home just before dark. And so it went through the winter, until one Sunday I ran into a man on the beach who was watching the race, and in the progress of our conversation he informed me that his wife was the skipper on the Sceptre today, while on other Sundays each of the crew takes a turn skippering.

And that is the kind of boat the Sceptre is. She has all the potential of a good club racer, yet she is forgiving and well mannered enough that when a green skipper takes the helm in a race, she won't immediately roll over on her side and kick her feet in the air. Most of this is attributable to a well balanced hull and a deep though narrow skeg preceding the rudder. With that skeg the Sceptre probably gains enough wetted surface to handicap herself against skegless boats, but boy, it sure makes her a lot more manageable in a blow down-

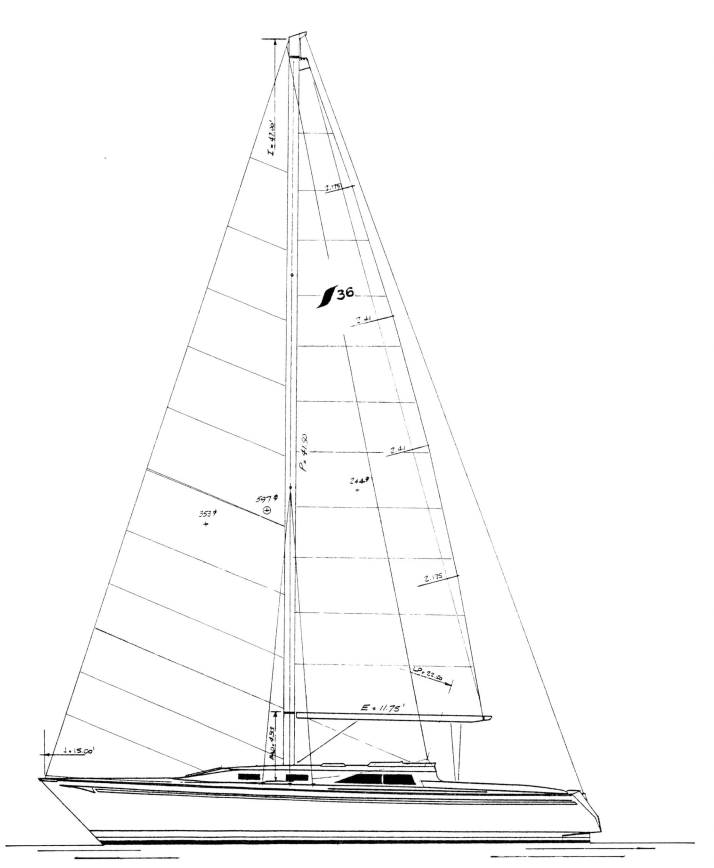

Sceptre 36 — Hein W. Drienhuyzen

LOA—35'6'' LWL—29'1'' Beam—11'5'' Draft—4'11''/6'0'' Displ.—12,000 lbs. Ballast—5,500 lbs. Sail Area—597 sq. ft.

wind. In short, she is a good club racer and one fast cruising boat.

Her displacement of 12,000 pounds is low compared to a Crealock 37 or Bob Perry's Reliance 37 or Ted Brewer's Morgan 38, all good cruisers with skegs and all displacing over 16,000 pounds. The Sceptre's displacement would put her closer to the C & C 36 and the Swan 371, both categorized as cruiser-racers. The displacement-to-waterline ratio is 220 which is getting pretty low for an open sea cruiser, but it will make a great boat for coast hopping. When I say low for an open sea cruiser I don't mean for a minute that she will be physically incapable of making the journey. I mean simply that her motion will be less comfortable than a boat with a ratio of over 300; also, she will have more difficulty in carrying the ton of stowed goods that seems to find its way aboard a long distance cruiser.

The rig is a modern masthead, with a tall skinny main, and rod rigging footed well inboard, enabling the Sceptre to point well into the wind, and also allowing for good wide decks outboard of the chainplates.

I sailed the boat only once, and that was in light airs with a 150 genoa, and in those airs her 18.2 sail-area-to-displacement ratio proved noticeable for she was quick to accelerate and had a good turn of speed in winds that never topped 10 knots. The rig balanced easily and with her ample ballast (46% of total displacement) she sailed almost upright, with the inclinator only seldom hitting 10 degrees. She was very responsive to the helm, too much so in fact for yours truly, who managed on his first touch to oversteer by 20 degrees. It was unfortunate that we had no opportunity to sail her off the wind in a decent blow to see just how much stability the narrow skeg adds, but I was assured by the owner that the boat handles well indeed, and he has sailed her through a couple of gales in his over 2,000 logged miles.

The one thing I did miss — and here I have to consider that the winds were light — was a feel to the helm. The boat I was on had a 36 inch wheel, while some Sceptres have 32 inch ones. I think for average coastal cruising I would choose a 32 since it gives a little better "contact" with the pressures on the rudder, but then this is really a matter of personal preference; it you like power steering, get the bigger wheel; if you want biceps, get the small

one.

We did, on our leaving the breakwater, encounter some steep 2 to 3 foot slop left over from the front that had passed (helped out by a goodly counter tides) and we pushed the boat into it to see just how she would rise and she moved well, taking only spray over the bow. Another owner told me he had beaten twenty miles one day into a small gale with reefed main and a big jib and the boat moved very well, and with her very fine entry and plenty of sail she should. When on a beam reach in the slop one could notice a few "corky" movements, attesting to the fact that the boat is leaning toward moderate displacement.

As I mentioned in the beginning, the Sceptre is certainly an eye-catcher and not just because of her chopped stern either. Her moderate freeboard gives her a very graceful look in real life, that is not evident in the drawings, ironically enough for the very reason that they are moderate, which in turn creates the need for a heavily crowned deck. This crown creates a line (just above the sheer line) on the profile drawings, not at all doing justice to the sheer, which actually has a very pleasant though modest spring. Look at the photos and you will see. The forward section of this sheer is drawn perfectly straight, but then this goes very well with the crisp lean look of the rest of the boat. I particularly like how nicely the house is worked into the foredeck, a welcome change from the hogged or Mongoloid brow look that too many modern designers seem to find irresistible. The fineness of the house leaves ample side-deck and foredeck space. A good sized anchor-well is on the foredeck along with a roller on the bow fitting for an anchor.

The cockpit is well set up, cross-shaped, with excellent forward visibility not only from the curved helmsman's seat but from the other seats as well, and this is important indeed. I find that I quickly begin to feel helpless and apathetic being aboard a boat in which I am unable to see anything up ahead. If you want your crew to be interested and involved, the first step is to make sure they can see where they are going.

There are many excellent "small" things designed into the deck by Mr. Driehuyzen which make the boat a joy to sail. The mainsheet traveller is recessed into the bridgedeck so you won't have to do the standard jackknife down the companionway. The genoa tracks are also recessed on their

The Sceptre's low freeboard makes her look long and sleek. She's a comfortable family cruiser and a very able club racer.

outboard side (they are almost against the house and cockpit coamings on the inside) so their toe stubbing days are over. The deck is laid out (and reenforced) for all hardware, turning blocks, stops, winches and cleats so that halyards and reef lines can be led aft to the cockpit if so desired, or handled from the base of the mast. Even this second method has been given some thought by Mr. Driehuyzen, in that the halyard winches are located in the cabin top and not on the mast. This system is worthy of consideration for three important reasons. First, you can work the halyards from the wide decks, for bracing is easier and you are enclosed by lifelines and shrouds. Second, your centre of gravity is lower so balance will be better kept in rough seas, and you can even get on one knee if you like and still work the winch handily. Third, with the cleat for the winches aft (about where the three turning blocks are shown for the

cockpit-led halyards) you will not have to lean *over* the winch handle when you are cleating the halyard, like you do if the halyard winches are set in the mast. It is the leaning over the handle that causes broken noses and chipped teeth, for once in a while the line will slip and the handle spin and bang — it's lights out.

Back to the companionway. The single Lexan hatchboard fits nicely over the hatch which can still slide away under the hatch cover. So much for the problem of where to stow hatchboards. While you are looking at the deck layout drawing also note the two small deadlights, port and starboard on the cabin top just forward of the mast. These bring added light into the head and forepeak. Note also the two small deck drains near the aft ends of the genoa track. Many designers and builders don't bother with these on boats without bulwarks; this often results in little pools of water that are very slippery and leave great dirt stains where they sit and dry instead of draining off.

A very nice touch that is more evident when looked at in combination with the profile drawing, is that the forehatch (which is an ample size for the passage of sails) is on the sloping, forward part of the deckhouse. This makes it easy to keep an eye on what is up ahead when you have to go below.

There are a few minor things that seem to me objectionable and worth correcting. First, the red and green nav-lights are set into the hull a few feet aft of the bow, where they are vulnerable to salt corrosion, and one owner I talked to has had problems. Also, as they are this low down, the lights are very difficult to see in the seaway. The often-used location high on the bow pulpit seems infinitely preferable.

Second, the wheel is located too close to the two raised seats/lockers in the aft end of the cockpit, so when standing at the wheel in a seaway it is most difficult to brace yourself against the pitching motion of the boat. Hanging onto the wheel for balance is less than ideal for keeping the boat on course or for keeping your balance. Anyone over six feet will have a bit of trouble standing at the helm for the backstay would forever be parting his hair. This could be solved by splitting the backstay, but then installing hydraulics for the racing skipper would pose a problem, although it would certainly allow you to install a much less expensive mechanical backstay tensioner.

Third, the fuel tank fills are in the cockpit sole and this makes the possibility of water getting into the fuel tank just a little greater, since the cockpit will hold water for however short a time, and if your deckfill is not torqued down by an elephant, water may get into your tanks. This location does put the fill directly over the fuel tank, which makes stick measurements of fuel supply easy, but then a good skipper doesn't rely on this anyway, since he keeps an accurate track of consumption through the hours on his engine. Right? . . . Sure.

Oh yes, the Sceptre uses rod rigging, a tapered mast, internal halyards, with a long aft turnbuckle to accommodate a hydraulic cylinder for the backstay.

Down Below

As can be seen from the accommodation drawing and the photo, the layout is very traditional, but again Mr. Driehuyzen (the Dutch always seem to be able to use every square inch of space to advantage) has paid great attention to the details which make living and cruising aboard a pleasure.

In the galley the icebox is large and reaches out into the area below the cockpit where access to a second lid can be gained by lifting up the cockpit seat lid. This saves trips below for food and drink and saves dragging blocks of ice through the galley.

Right beside the second icebox lid is another fine idea. A regular size rubber garbage pail, that takes the handy little white garbage bags, is located *in* the engine room in a snug space where it cannot spill and is out of the way. Garbage can be dropped into it through a hinged flap door set in the bulkhead just above the counter. Now that is good thinking.

The galley stove is fitted with a simple, sliding, formica cupboard top, that can be used to increase counter space, or slid out of the way in its little sloping tracks and stowed behind the stove. Small, useful upper cabin space is everywhere. The chart table is a good size with chart stowage in it, and access to it, as well as to the side of the engine, is made easier by notching a corner out of the quarterberth. The quarterberth can be enlarged with a filler. What is even more impressive is that finally someone has actually installed an opening portlight at the aft end of the quarterberth, opening into the cockpit and bringing in light and good ventilation. The skipper of the boat I sailed told me that he often sleeps underway with his head at the aft end of the berth near this open portlight, for he gains much privacy and will not be awakened every time someone rattles down a companionway or rummages around in the galley.

Access to the engine is good; the whole companionway box comes away in one single piece, and there is a door opening into the quarterberth as well. The salon settees are comfortable and deep (about 20 inches). The centre table dropleaf is wide enough to be used comfortably from the port set-

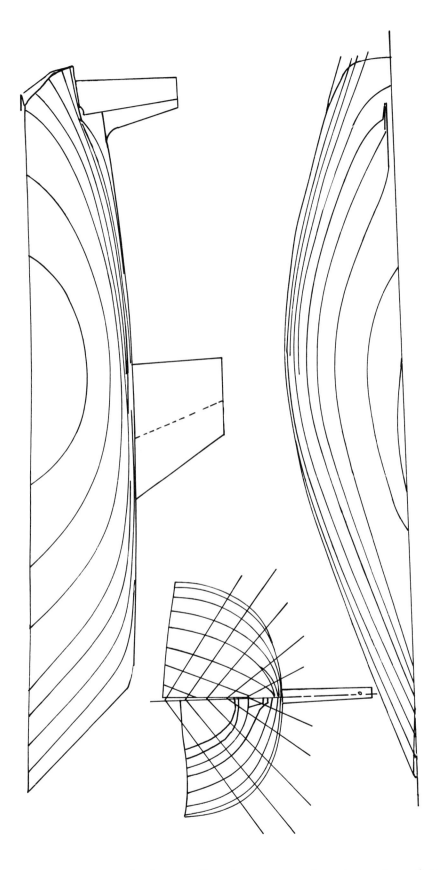

The lines of the Sceptre 36 reveal a close resemblance to many racers of recent years. A very fast family cruiser indeed.

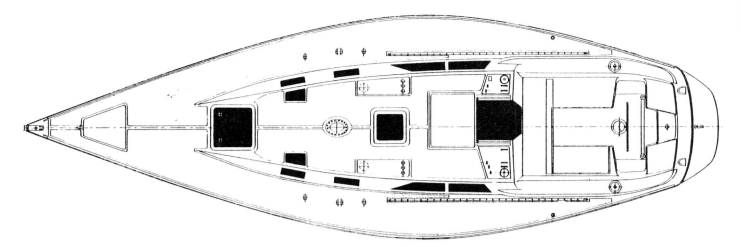

The Sceptre 36 deck-plan shows how well inboard the shrouds are footed, leaving good deck space outboard and putting the genoa tracks against the house, well out of the way. Provisions have been made to lead all lines aft to the cockpit, and you'd have to look far and wide to find as much good light as provided here for belowdecks.

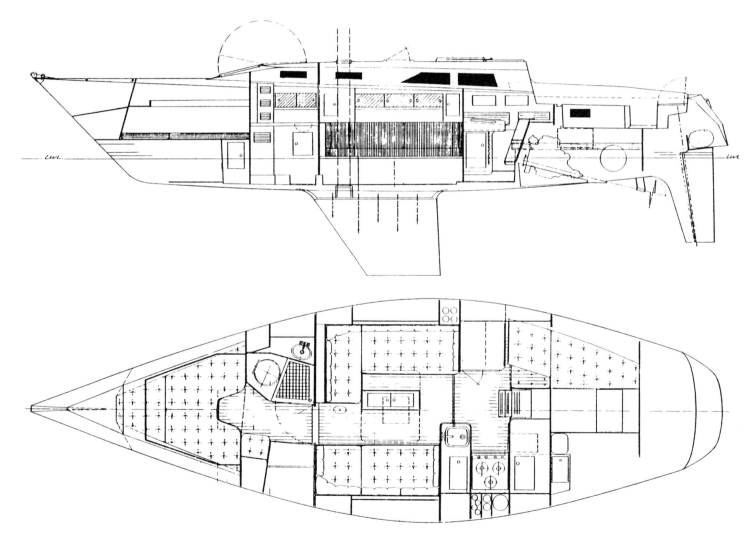

The profile of the Sceptre 36 shows a narrow skeg and fin keel, and that easily recognizable chopped transom. The interior plan has luxuriously deep settees, a good chart table and fine galley whose usable space is extended aft below the cockpit for extra stowage of rubbish and ice. The forepeak is made good and useful with a seat and ample floor space.

tee, and if you don't think this is important you obviously have never had to eat sitting on a berth edge leaning forward over an abyss and dropping every second spoonful of goop into your lap. Speaking of tables, I almost forgot — the cockpit has a simple, narrow one that hinges down from the pipe protecting the binnacle compass. It is held by an arm in the up position or it snaps flat against the pipe completely out of the way in the down position.

Now where was I? Oh yes. The salon table has a single 3 inch aluminum leg, you know the type, and with a half twist of two levers, off comes the table and then the leg and the whole thing stows neatly in a space built for it behind the short leg of the L-shaped settee. The long leg of the settee pulls out into a double that measures a comfortable 6 foot 10 inches by 46 inches.

To give privacy to two couples aboard, the head door closes off the salon from the forepeak. A nice addition would be the installation of a ship's curtain athwartships from the forward end of the hanging locker to the knuckle in the fore and aft wall of the head, to close it off from the forepeak.

Speaking of hanging lockers, the boat has a very modest one for foul weather gear, if you accept Mr. Driehuyzen's nominal enclosure under the chart table. If you don't, then you can sit and stare at the plan until your eyes bug out, for you won't find space for one. I sure didn't.

The forepeak double berth is good and wide aft, but because of the fine entry you had better agree in advance about whose toes go where.

Construction

Mr. Driehuyzen owns Sceptre Yachts and he often tools and sometimes builds them with his half dozen crew in an old hangar at Vancouver's old airport. The craftsmen he has managed to corral are very good indeed, one of them having been head of the finest woodcrafting shop in town for many years. He and I go back millennia to old houseboat days in the floating catacombs of Vancouver, and he was a fine craftsman then and he seems not to have gone to seed in the least. And boy, does he have a beautiful daughter. Cover your face Mariel Hemingway.

But back to work. Mr. Driehuyzen, who has run a number of boatyards in town and has picked up much experience and a headful of grey hair, insists that the boat is designed primarily for weekend or holiday cruising, yet her construction falls very much above that of the "pop-out weekender," and a good thing too, otherwise it wouldn't be in this book.

The hull lay-up is as follows: 2 layers of 1 ounce mat as skin, three units of 1½ ounce mat and 24 ounce roving, a fourth unit starts 6 inches above the waterline, units five, six and seven start about 18 inches further down, then in the keel area the seven units are doubled up to give you a thickness of over 1 inch throughout the keel stub.

The keel area is reenforced by three transverse beams about 6 inches wide each, built up of foam and covered over with about 1 inch of fibreglass. There are seven 1 inch keel bolts paired and staggered, with 2 inch square backup plates, although the skipper of *Chentelle* found some well laid up ½ inch thick fibreglass pads, cut them to about 3 inch by 4 inch slabs, and used these as well as the plates. And why not?

The hull-to-deck attachment is equally strong. Mr. Driehuyzen is quite proud of this system. This involves trimming the hull flange with the aid of a guide to exactly 3 inches, then covering it with a butyl rubber caulking, then laying over this a vinyl rubber gasket, the inboard lip of which snaps over the hull flange. Then more butyl is added, then the deck is laid on, then the aluminum toerail is laid on, and then the whole thing is through-bolted with ¼ inch stainless steel bolts on 4 inch centres. Sounds very good to me. This is a system that C & C Yachts use, and it has worked well for them for many years.

The boat comes with a three piece fibreglass liner: forepeak, salon-and-galley, and engine room, but the main bulkheads *are* glassed directly to the hull and the deck. Also, the liner is quite shallow, coming at its highest point just above the waterline (height of the seats in the salon). As you know, I strongly disagree with full liners, which although bonded to the hull at the upper edges, are pretty much adrift within the boat. Virtually all of the boats in this book use no liners at all; instead they are already strong hulls built into a completely reenforced, honeycomb-like structure, by bonding every bulkhead, every berth top, every partition, and every shelf directly to the hull. It doesn't take much imagination to see how much less support a hull would have if it were left to fend on its own. In

A just completed Sceptre 36 showing her not unusual interior, but what is there is well done.

the case of the Sceptre the liner is comparatively modest in size, and all the accessible knees and partitions within it are bonded directly to the hull.

The mast is keel-stepped, footing on one of the reenforced beams mentioned in the first part of this section. The skeg is moulded separately from the hull and is fastened to it later with two ½ inch stainless steel internal rods, and exterior laminates. The rudder stock is 2¹¹⁄₃₂ inch diameter stainless steel.

The deck lay-up and its engineering I found very impressive. The deck is balsa-cored *everywhere*, including the cabinsides and cockpit bottoms and sides, for stiffness and lightness and to prevent condensation. Many manufacturers don't bother with this and consequently not only does it almost rain inside their boats from condensation, but decks and cockpit soles creak and crackle viciously. Plywood coring ½ inch thick, replaces the balsa in stress areas — winch islands, tracks,

hatch coamings.

The engineering of the deck is a home builder's dream. All hardware locations are marked in the mould-tracks, winches, cleats, stanchion bases and chainplates-eliminating almost all measuring and certainly all guessing, letting you go at it with drill and caulking gun. This can save you literally days of preparation and nights of sleeplessness.

The design of chainplate reenforcement has some good original notions, using a number of straps, plates and knees. I am going to try to describe it to you, but you have got to be patient. Remember, English is my second tongue. First, the chainplates aren't really chainplates (remember I warned you), they are actually ½ inch caliper Navtec U-bolts installed upside down in the deck. The clevis pins (the little rod-type things that hold the turnbuckles in place) slip through these. Now belowdeck the U-bolts are not backed up by washers or small back-up plates, whose stress would be distributed over a small surface only, but by a ½ inch thick aluminum plate that is 6 inches wide and 2 *feet* long. Don't congratulate yourself yet, Elmer, I'm just getting warmed up. Now, the plate isn't really a plate but an I-beam sawn in half (so now it is actually a 'T'), then laid against the underdeck so that an integral vertical flange protrudes down into the cabin. Now, in turn, this reenforcing plate is anchored firstly to the main bulkhead with a chainplate, and with the help of another, wider, triangular piece of stainless, to a knee that is bonded into the bulkhead. There are a few details that I have left out, but I figure you have had enough. If there is anything in the above that you don't understand, have a good stiff Scotch, as I did, and the whole thing will become as plain as the nose on your face.

Before the Scotch wears off, let's get something else straight. I don't like soft plastic overheads, and I don't care whether they sparkle or swirl or look like ancient marble or new leopard skin; the proper material to use is a fine wood liner which can be bonded to add strength (see Santa Cruz 50) and which can be painted white for light reflection. Hinckley does something even nicer, and it could be done here as well. They leave the deck in the mould and fill the whole overhead with a light pasty mixture of microballoons and resin, in other words, putty. This of course is done with a very broad putty knife — the kind that plasterers use — or a squeegee, so a moderately quick and easy job can be made of it. Whatever irregularities remain are sanded off, then the thing is painted or left flat white. The finished feeling is that of a solid, integral structure, with nothing hanging or wrinkling, or sagging in the heat like an old udder. And it looks beautiful. You will of course have to use cap nuts on your deck hardware bolts, but so what, the thing is a boat, why not show how it is put together?

There is a hitch, of course. To try to do this once the deck is right side up would be pure madness, because you would end up with either stalactites dangling down, or a lungful of irremovable dust from grinding. So the thing to do is to convice your boatyard owner to do it himself in the mould. Most of the yards in this book are very small so probably very few of them have to worry about idle mould time, and most of them are flexible enough so that a little convincing might work. Give it a try, who knows, their boats might end up looking like Hinckleys, instead of Aunt Gertie's rolled-and-pleated laundry basket.

When I was writing this, there was much of this stuff in the Sceptres, but maybe since then Hein Driehuyzen has seen the light; he certainly shows good taste in the rest of his boat.

The quality of materials in the Sceptre is first class, including the mahogany plywood (with bullnosed edges) used for bunktops and undercushion dropboards. The beautiful cornerposts are solid teak and rounded to almost a 3 inch radius, which all has to be done by hand grinding. The good news is that all these parts are available precut and ready to fit, but the other news is that Mr. Driehuyzen insists that whoever buys one of his boats must show ability to do a fine finishing job. In most cases this is no problem, for most of the time a privately finished boat is superior to its yard-produced sisters, but at least you stand warned.

Well, that about covers it, except that the engine is a Yanmar with an 18 gallon tank, and if that small a tank doesn't show confidence in the boat's light air performance, then I don't know what does. The water tanks are a sensible 74 gallons.

One last note. If you peek at the lines you will see a sharp tuck or pinch in the hull just at the skeg, meaning once the boat begins to move through the water her waterline length will increase almost 3 feet over its measured and rated waterline . . . Just an old family cruising boat, huh?

17

The Master Builders
The Cape George Yachts

The springtime is the best time to go to Port Townsend, when the air is fresh and the sky is clear and the wind is chasing fat clouds over the sea, and the apple blossoms are out and the cherry blossoms are out, and the green leaves are so new and bright that, with the sun coming through them, you have to squint. That is the time to go to Port Townsend, to drive past glistening marshes and meadows of mustard flowers and hills laden with grapevines, down to the point where the old lighthouse and gnarled trees face the screaming winds of the Strait, winds that blow so hard that you have to hide behind deserted battlements to eat your Easter-turkey sandwich while you wait for the ferry that may never come because the waves around the point are now six feet high.

But the ferry's skipper has more guts than a canal horse, and he brings the old dear rolling and surfing through the foam, and you drive on and you wonder why the decks are wet on such a sunny day, but then the ferry pulls out and you know why, because as soon as it pulls out, the first big roller rolls aboard and four inches of water slide around the deck, back and forth, back and forth, until the ferry heels far enough for it to run off and

the next batch to roll on. So on you go swaying, as the skipper heads her south for a while to run away from the breakers, and you roll across the heaving sea with everyone on deck swaying and laughing and chattering feverishly to hide the fear, the fear that when the next big one hits, the tired old metal might not stop shuddering and the old plates won't stop creaking, but instead they'll come apart like a rotten old onion, and then down we'll all go, jokes and chatter and laughter and all. But we don't. We land with the sun falling toward the snowcapped mountains and the old clapboard houses glitter in its light. And then you think, well this has been one great day, and little do you know, brother, that you ain't seen nothin' yet.

Cecil M. Lange, Boatbuilder, is not a young man anymore, his work-hardened hands show the years, and so does his grey hair, but his eyes and his voice and his movements are quick, so quick I could hardly keep up with him down a long wharf. We walked past many old wooden boats, lovingly designed and beautifully kept, then we stopped beside a simple, rugged-looking cruising-boat, moderate and honest in every way, and Cecil M.'s eyes lit up and he said "That's her."

She was a true yacht, with high bulwarks and broad teak decks, a low elegant house, and a spacious safe cockpit, a gentle sheer and wineglass transom, and a massive aft hung rudder. She looked like she could not only take you anywhere in the world, but would also love going there with you.

There were touches of elegance everywhere — in the gently curved cockpit coaming and the beautifully made hatches, and even in the large skylight, solid and shaped like the old ones (but made in one piece and hinged like a hatch to keep it from leaking like the old ones) with bronze rods and acid-etched glass panels that show the vessel's name, and bespeak only one thing—that not only does Cecil M. Lange & Son build fine yachts, but they love building them.

The boat we were looking at was called The Cape George 36, but all three boats in the family, the 31 and the 40 being the other two, had the same ancestry inasmuch as they are all variations of the same timeless notions of William Atkin. The lines of all three are what Bill Atkin called "Atkinized," in that "all sections have a perfect continuity, a feature which produces an unusually well-balanced underwater and abovewater form. The hulls are designed to bring the athwartship sections in very exact continuity, and this feature undoubtedly accounts for the exceptional speed and ability of the Atkinized hulls; for, despite a very generous displacement of nearly 22,000 lbs., and a modest spread of sail of approximately 750 square feet, these are fast yachts."

Atkin received many letters from owners of boats of his design, some of them reprinted in his *Of Yachts and Men*. In one letter a Mr. Gamwell of Seattle, Washington, owner of *Venture*, wrote:

"As for speed she will outrun boats twice her length in light and medium airs. Reaching and beating she is also excellent. The remarkable thing about the boat is the fact that she will drift in extremely light going, and when a breeze freshens she continues to hold her own. *Venture* is consistently good in any kind of going. Most of the boats here that are very good in light weather, fall down in fresh breezes. These boats sail about even with us in real light going, but when it breezes up we walk away from them," prompting Atkin to say, "All of which goes to prove that a high coefficient of fatness does not necessarily mean a

The Cape George 36 with solid wood house and teak decks. Everything aboard is well thought out, simple and built with great care. Even the skylight has the name of the boat etched into the glass.

woefully slow moving yacht." And as one who owns a boat whose lines were drawn by Bill Atkin, I say, "hear, hear."

The Cape George yachts are what Atkin would call "a chunk of a boat." The 36 displaces 23,300 pounds and has 10,500 pounds of lead ballast in her. The draft is typically held down to only five feet, which will get into most cruising grounds. Her beam of 10.5 feet is modest by today's standards, which on average are a foot beamier, but her beam is carried well fore and aft so there is no loss of accommodation or power, since with the beam carried aft, she has full bottocks to help her carry more sail longer.

Her waterline length is long indeed at 31.5 feet which, in spite of her great displacement gives her a displacement-to-length ratio of 333 which shows that, although heavy, she is no ton of bricks. Her keel is full, as any blind man can see, and her rudder large and effectively deep. Her entry is on the moderate side and her bow flares substantially at the sheer which, along with her bulwarks make her a rather dry boat. All the Cape Georges have spoon bows and just enough tumblehome to give them an elegantly finished look, as opposed to hulls whose beams keep increasing and increasing right to the rails and hence look as if they are about to fall apart. This, of course, has very little to do with structural reality, but tumblehome is, at least to me, very pretty and it's a pity that so few modern designers besides Frers use it.

On deck, the 36 is a beauty. Her cockpit will sit eight for day sailing, and her coamings, which are twelve inches high and sloped, make the seats very comfortable; and what's most important, the seats are long enough to sleep on. I didn't measure them, but I lay down and it was long enough for me and I'm six feet plus a bit. There are two lockers in the cockpit, and a good broad, deck-height bridgedeck, which makes for a single dropboard companionway opening only 12 inches high. This is about as small an opening as you can get unless you buy a Swan, which is top opening. The visibility from the cockpit is very good. To make the deck safe, 5 inch high bulwarks rise above them, onto which the stanchions and chainplates are attached, but more about both of these later under *Construction*. The side-decks are 22 inches wide all along, and they are perfectly parallel, as they should be, for this makes the laying of teak decks much easier, allow-ing full-width pieces to be run without the necessity of painstaking nibbing (tapering the planks) to fit a narrowing deck. This is a very important point, for a single nib can take a good couple of hours to plane and fit, and if you have four nibs per side as we do on *Warm Rain*, then that's a couple of days of extra work, which could have been prevented if the designer had thought ahead.

The foredeck is small but clean, and it sports a monstrous samson post with a windlass forward of it mounted on a bowsprit. The house is kept to a low 14 inches with uncomplicated lines. This is probably due to the fact that it is built out of wood so it has to be simple, but whatever the reason, it *is* pretty.

The house has grabrails running its full length, and for nonskid the Langes used the best nonskid ever — finely ground walnut shells mixed into the paint. The main hatch did not have a cover on the boat I saw, but the hatch is of such a low profile, that one could be fabricated quite easily. The gallows have bronze end-fittings and are located well aft and out of the way. The main winches are mounted not on mediocre pads but on huge bases made of ½ inch stainless steel, which has been designed to base a cleat as well (see photo).

In general, standing or sitting at the tiller, you have the distinct feeling that you are aboard a well-built ship. This does not come from the fact that there is much wood around, for that can be found on many an oriental floating rec-room, but it's the simplicity and integrity of construction which create this feeling, and I'm afraid I am not an able enough writer to convey that. You will just have to go and see for yourself.

The Rig

The sail plans of all three boats show moderate aspect ratio mains and they are all cutters, meaning a very flexible rig that can be brought all inboard in heavy blows by lowering the jib. The 36 is available with a tall rig, about 2½ extra feet in the mast, which would help the boat, especially in light air, although its sail-area-to-displacement ratio is a healthy 16 which is within decimal points of very modern cruisers such as the Valiant 40, the Swan 371 and the Morgan 38. The rigging is all 5/16 inch stainless wire with Norseman fittings which are threaded on and not swedged. Many designers, if

Cape George 36 — Wm. Atkin/Ed Monk
LOA—36'0" LWL—31'5" Beam—10'5" Draft—5'0" Displ.—23,300 lbs. Ballast—10,500 lbs. Sail Area—781 sq. ft.

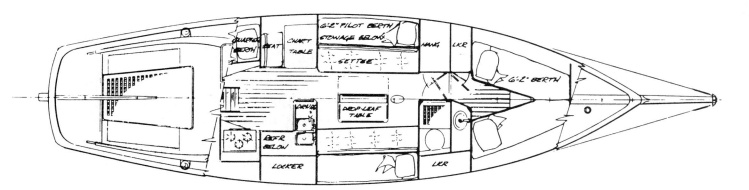

The Cape George 36 interior bespeaks a true offshore cruiser with a large workable galley, first class chart table and a quarterberth. The pilot berths are lovely to have, but they do displace shelf and bin space and make the settees a bit cramped. Maybe one should go or maybe both. The forepeak is large and airy and with a filler it becomes a vast double.

prodded enough, will tell you that this is the best for cruising boats, for a) repairs can be made easily anywhere, and b) there is no chance of failure with faulty swedging, a possibility which exists unless the swedging is done on a proper, very heavy machine.

As you can see from the renditions and photos, the boats have no chainplates showing, because Cecil M. decided to take a less conventional method which has worked well on the over sixty boats they have built. It goes like this. Since the inch and a half thick 6 inch high wood bulwarks are epoxied and bolted to the ½ inch thick hull, the boat at the bulwarks is 2 inches thick, solid stuff. With the hull reenforced and stiffened to the degree that it is throughout (see *Construction*), Cecil feels there is no need to take the load down lower on the hull with vertical plates. So he distributes the load longitudinally by bolting a 4 foot long by 4 inch wide by ½ inch thick stainless steel plate through the bulwarks. Short plates come up from this for the shrouds to hook to. This looks like a very fine idea, making rebedding and retightening of the plates child's play, and it is certainly more leakproof than through-deck chainplates. But remember this can only be done on an ultra-strong hull, with a very stiff deck and much reenforcing. Don't try it on your Marshmallow 24.

Belowdecks

Down below, the craftsmanship is not just evident, it is overwhelming, and the choice of materials used shows thoughtfulness and good taste. The overhead and bulwarks are plywood painted white, and with the skylight and all the portlights — eight of which open — the whole belowdecks was aglow, and I was there as the sun was setting. The beams (don't forget that this is a real wood house) are laminated out of Port Orford cedar and mahogany. The ceilings (the sides of the hull) are also Port Orford cedar, which is light in colour and in weight, much cheaper than teak, and something not as important but a nice touch, indigenous to the area where the boat is built. The cabin sole is teak and holly and the galley counters are maple.

The layout is very traditional but made first class through detailing and the shifting of inches. The galley is made uncommonly large by pushing the upper half of the engine room partition well aft so that the space under the bridgedeck becomes part of the galley, and half the ice-box (with its 4 inch thick walls) is effectively in the engine room. All this creates extra floor and counter space so that galley chores can be shared by two people at a time. The sinks are ample and deep and there is more stowage in this galley than in any boat I have

The Cape George boats are drawn after the lines of Bill Atkin, and they're all what Atkin would call "a chunk of a boat." Here the 36 is homeward bound in light airs.

seen under 40 feet. This is gained not through great amounts of volume but through the intelligent use of what volume there is, in other words, by subdividing large awkward spaces into small useful compartments, all of which in turn are subdivided by shelves and knees. It's no use having just great gobs of space, because although they will hold vast amounts of stuff, you will need a backhoe to unload them when you want to get something out of the bottom.

The chart table is a good size, with its own seat, so you won't have to disfigure or suffocate the off-watch crew in the quarterberth when you come below to do your navigation. The quarterberth is spacious and as an additional nice touch, the back of the engine controls are exposed into it, so maintenance and repairs can be quickly done — a most important point in emergencies such as linkage failure just as you roar up to your dock and search desperately for reverse that is nowhere to be found.

The access to the rest of the engine is equally good, and can be managed in differing degrees as need dictates. First, there is a quick-check lid, which allows you, just by lifting up a single small hinged lid, to have a look to see what mischief the noisy elves are up to, or you can lift out the companionway ladder and open two large doors and crawl right in and join them. There is good access to the Sabb diesel all around, and for the first time in many a year, I saw a mechanical bilge pump hooked directly to an engine pulley. Leaving this out of any offshore cruiser would be a great error. The pump is simple and cheap and nothing, but nothing, will pump in an emergency as reliably and as relentlessly as a diesel, which will run even if half submerged as long as the air intake caps point upward and not down. Cecil Lange even put in bits of storage for tools and spares in the engine room and hid the fuel tank low under the engine, but his greatest bit of creative engineering he saved for the electrical panel. Most boats I have seen, sadly enough ours included, have the electrical panels so mounted that the back faces some dark, narrow hole-of-a-locker or underdeck space, where repairs can be done only by an India-rubber man with radar-equipped eyeballs. Cecil M. put his electrical panel into a box of plywood that is 18 inches by 30 inches by 5 inches deep and lives underneath the bridge deck, well out of any weather and traffic.

But the nicest part of all is that the whole box hinges down, allowing you perfect access to the back of switches and breakers in the good light of the cabin, with lots of elbow room everywhere.

So far so good. The salon is straightforward as you can see from the drawings, but the salon dropleaf table isn't. It is made of solid ¾ inch teak, and its forward end is attached to the mast for good support, while the aft end has about 20 inches between it and the galley bulkhead; and here another piece of ingenuity is shown by Cecil and son Bob. A long narrow drawer fits under the fixed part of the table, and when I say long and narrow I mean long and narrow; it is 2 feet long and 4 inches wide and 4 inches deep and it slides lengthwise out, but it can't *fall* lengthwise out because it is about 4 inches longer than the space between the end of the table and the galley bulkhead, which of course means that you have to put the drawer in place before you install the table, but so what? This is, of course, the cutlery drawer, and being so it is divided into four proper sections with yellow cedar baffles that are so finely fitted and shaped, that I turned green with envy; and I bet that old geezer just slapped it all together half asleep, because every time I "oohed" and "aahed" about one piece of craftsmanship or another he'd just mumble and say with a little shrug, "Oh well, that's nothing, just a bit of something we threw together." Rub it in Cecil, rub it in.

The settees are comfortable with ample stowage below, where in his own boat, Cecil keeps two 200 amp-hour batteries, and ample deep stowage behind, with cedar shelves, and if that wasn't enough to knock your eyes out, he even put in a piece of teak trim to hide a piece of fibreglass bonding inside the cupboard. But he isn't done yet. There are grabrails all along the overhead, right up to the bow, but for Cecil that's not enough, he has made grabrails, that is he routed 4 inch long handholds with 2 inches between, out of each and every 3 inch high searail, bookholder and dripboard in the boat. Now you say that doesn't take much time and you're right, it's nothing you and I couldn't do in a week or two.

There is space for a little heating stove between the mast and the forward bulkhead, and a good thing too, for you can easily sail in northwest waters all year round, just so long as you have a cosy cabin to retreat to when things get nippy out.

The salon layout can, of course, be altered to taste, with or without the pilot berth. If the boat is normally to make passages with a crew of no more than three, then the pilot berth can be left out in favour of more stowage, since you end up with three good sea berths anyway.

The head has been made small by the fact that the bulkhead is a foot or so forward of the mast, but it is functional enough. What the boat does lack is a wet locker and there is only a medium sized hanging locker across from the head — the rest of the stowage being shelves. Perhaps the stowage across from the head could be made into two hanging lockers, one wet and one dry, and although this is a long way from the companionway, and you'd drip all over the cabin, it's still better than nothing.

The forepeak has much volume and light, especially in Cecil's own boat, in which the berth was so low that there was a full 3 foot clearance between the berth-top and the foredeck, and with a filler it could be made into a 6 foot wide berth and it could be very well lit with four portlights (two in the forward face of the cabin) and two deck prisms in the foredeck, an ideal place for those who like to see beauty as well as touch it.

This lowness of the berth does cut down on stowage below it but let us in all honesty put priorities in proper sequence; man was a passionate animal long before he became a pack rat.

Outboard and above the berths run two 7 foot long shelves, varying in width from 3 inches to 6 inches, with nice 3 inch high searails, and you guessed it brother, they are all routed out for handholds. You never let up do you, Cecil?

I tried to leave quickly before some other bit of craftsmanship jumped me, and I was already out of the companionway but I turned around to pop in the dropboard and there it was: insult to injury, salt on the wound — the droplids in the galley counter. As I mentioned, the galley counter was ¾ inch edge-grain maple and the droplids were also edge-grain maple, but Cecil didn't want the ends of the strips and their plywood backing showing when you lifted out the lids to get out some dirty old pot or other, so he actually *trimmed out* the lid and the hole, in teak!

Okay, Cecil, I give up, I'll say it: You're a master boatbuilder and I'm a good-for-nothing chicken-gutter! . . . There. You happy now?

The ultimate yacht interior built by Cecil & Bob Lange. The hulls of the Cape George yachts are heavy fibreglass while the deck and house are wood. The Langes, of Port Townsend, Washington, are master craftsmen.

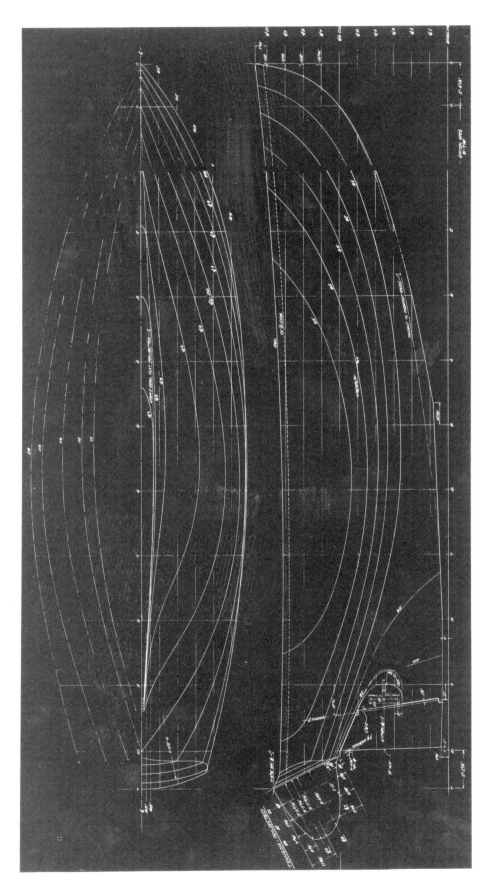

The unforced lines of the Cape George 40 show Bill Atkin's firm belief in a balanced hull, yet in this broad-transom version he provided very good power in the quarters. The rudder area as drawn by Mr. Nolan shows much care regarding performance under both sail and power for both the rudder and the deadwood fairing have been made as fine as possible. The curved wine glass transom is a pleasure to behold.

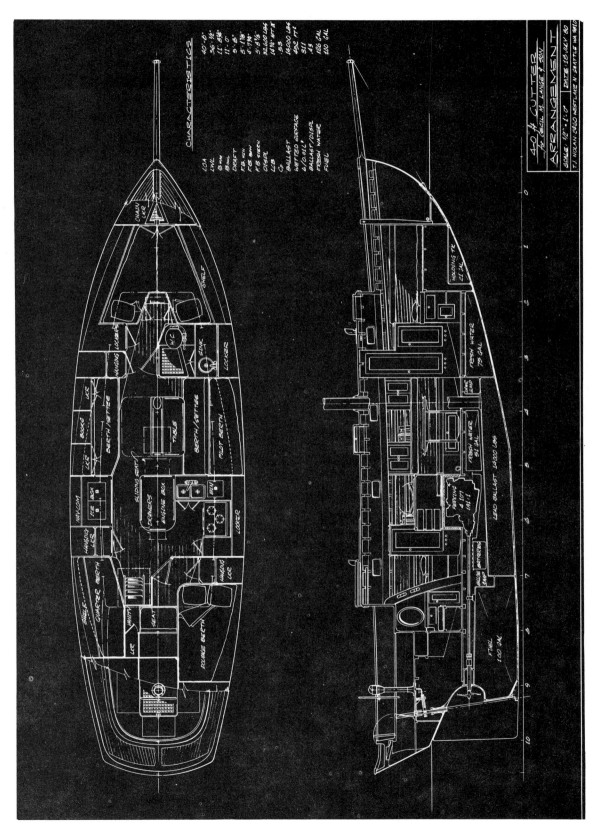

The Cape George 40, a true no-nonsense heavy displacement ocean cruiser with excellent seaberths in both the quarterberth and the pilot berth, good stowage everywhere, and ample tankage of 126 gallons of water and 100 gallons of fuel both kept down in the keel for added stability. The aft stateroom is spacious with a hanging locker and a seat, and all that is made possible by setting the companionway off-centre and putting the engine amidships under the galley counter.

That night I stayed in James House on the hill, a finely kept Victorian bed-and-breakfast place high above the harbour. To drown my sorrows and catch up on my notes, I went to eat at a place well south of town in a little bay, an unpretentious place that was called Ajax, where they had pictures of old American movie stars, and Afghan drapes, and Greek music, and one-dollar bills stuck to the ceiling with forks and knives and fishhooks, and they gave you warm brown bread and a huge fresh salad and a jug of wine and a mountain of the freshest steamed clams God ever made, and I ate and drank my sorrows away, all for $9.50.

A laminated knee in the Cape George 36. The workmanship is so awesome it makes you want to throw away your own tools forever. Oh yes, notice that even the bookshelves have handrails.

Construction

The next morning I followed Cecil's improbable map out to a cape called George, on a road that wound out of town through forests and farm fields, and there, out in the middle of nowhere, was a wood sign with a painted sailboat and above it "Cecil M. Lange & Son, Boatbuilders." Here in a small compound of sheds and barns were gleaming hulls, and there was sawdust and woodchips everywhere and I felt as if I had stepped back half a century.

To make a long story short, Cecil and Bob Lange do build wood boats, but to eliminate the problems of upkeep and rot and expense of a wood hull, they mould the hulls out of fibreglass and build the rest of the boat with wood beams and wood decks and a wood house, just like Cecil and his dad used to back in New Zealand. This might be the best way to build a beautiful yacht today, using a perfectly practical and strong hull built of fibreglass, and finishing it out with pleasant to work, easy to build wood. A glass hull with a wood house and wood deck is of course more expensive than a laminated fibreglass deck, probably to the tune of 60% or 70%, but one should realize two factors which can bring that difference down substantially. One — with the wood deck, its fine beams and solid house-sides, you can consider that portion of the interior as finished, save for painting and/or varnishing. If you were to try to finish the inside of a fibreglass deck and house to a similar degree of beauty and craftsmanship, you would probably be looking at four weeks of solid amateur labour. Of course if you are going to cover your overhead with naugahyde or formaldehyde or something of similar visual nauseousness, then your labour output will be greatly reduced but some cost will still be incurred. Two — the degree to which the wood deck is to be finished out at the boat yard is usually negotiable; that is to say, the owner can take over at any point whence he feels able to continue on his own, and thereby save money. Whether this is at the bare hull part, or after the deck beams have been laid, has to be a choice of the individual, based on his confidence and willingness, and to a lesser degree his ability. For Bob Lange to build a wood deck for a 36 foot Cape George, would normally take about seven weeks, but he works like a demon and has been doing it for some time, so it's rather hard to tell how long it would take an average incompetent like yours truly. Anyway, the labour for such a deck and house would run you about $6,000.00 so you can figure your savings out accordingly.

So, if you are contemplating a wood deck, keep the above in mind, and if you are seriously contemplating building your own, read and study a book like Chapell's *Boat Building*, or better still offer to sweep out or paint Cecil's boat sheds in exchange for a crash-course in deck-building. He does cooperate totally with owners, and the owner can work with him on a boat unless Cecil deems him to be a total disaster and whooshes him off the premises.

The boats are built well over Lloyd's of London

The framing for the all wood deck of the Cape George boats. The underside of the deck beams and carlings are bull-nosed for an elegant interior finish.

specs and there are some very fine ideas worked into their construction. The hull laminates go like this: First — one mat, one cloth. Second — one mat, two rovings put in longitudinally up to 6 inches above the water line. Third — one mat, two rovings (run athwartships). Fourth — one mat, two rovings (run athwartships). Fifth — one mat, three rovings (run athwartships). This business of running the roving athwartships (usually in 3 foot widths) is an interesting one that adds a lot of strength to the keel area, for each run goes past the centerline and up the other side about a foot.

Now, since each consecutive layer is overlapped, you end up with a hull that is totally unified or dovetailed, as well as being 1 inch thick in the keel and stem areas. As if this didn't result in a strong enough hull, the Langes add in a couple of 2 inch by 8 inch bilge stringers of Alaska yellow cedar 18 inches either side of the centerline, and bond over it, laminating it to the hull with three runs of roving. Then, of course, the floor timbers are bonded over these, so that the hull should be one of the stiffest anywhere. For about $1,300.00 the Langes will totally insulate the hull for you (after the bulkheads are in) with ½ inch balsa or Klegicell, and cover it over with a mat and a roving, after bonding the insulative core to the hull with a layer of mat. This will not only insulate the hull, but stiffen it a good deal too, and if you want to cover the ceilings (the sides of the hull) with strips of cedar or whatever afterward, you can screw the strips *(with very short screws, Elmer, so you don't go into the hull!)* right into the glass cover over the insulation. This will save a lot of the normal messing around, which involves bonding ribs to the hull to which the strips can be screwed or nailed.

The bulkheads are not only bonded to the hull in the true yacht fashion, with two runs of roving and a mat, but they are sandwiched between two floor timbers and through-bolted, and also sandwiched between two deck beams and throughbolted, to tie the whole thing together. But before we go too deeply into discussing the deck, I want to say one more thing about the hull. The Lange's glass work and lay-up is as meticulous as their finishing joinery, and that's the way it must be, for what good is it having a dazzling finish when there is nothing but neglected mush beneath.

Now on to the deck. For those who are in-

terested in basic deck construction, I'll give you a minimal sketch; for those who aren't, you can look at the pictures. The hull and deck are united by means of a *shelf* (same as a wood boat) which is about 5 inches high and is laminated up of five 1 inch thick pieces of Alaska yellow cedar, and bonded to the hull with one layer of mat and three layers of roving. The deck beams, 1½ inches by 3 inches on 12 inch centres, are set on this shelf and are bolted to it with countersunk 5/16 inch bronze carriage bolts. Around the openings, such as hatches, or where the forward deck ends and the raised house begins, the beams become 3 inches thick, i.e., double the thickness of normal beams. All joints are let into each other and glued. The let-in joints not only increase the integrity of the deck by restricting movement, but they also increase the amount of surface that can be joined with glue.

A note about sequence. The bulkheads are the first things put into the hull after the foredeck and the aft-deck are in place, so their location and shape is critical. The location of the bulkheads is vital for obvious reasons, and their shape is critical, *especially* the angle of the slope of the part that goes below the side-decks, because the carling (the inboard framing member of the side-decks running parallel to the hull) will be set onto these. The foredeck and aft-decks are built before the side-decks because they run from gunwale to gunwale, and once they are in, the carlings can be set into them. Next come the side-deck beams, which are set on the shelves and into the carlings. Then comes the plywood decking, glued and nailed down with copper nails. Then comes the house. If you think this is an over-simplification, then you are absolutely right.

All plywood in the boat is Bruynzeel, which is a marine plywood approved by Lloyd's and is guaranteed for ten years against delamination, and is guaranteed to have no voids, and costs twice as much as regular mahogany plywood. The housesides are solid 1⅜ inch by 8 inch Port Orford or yellow cedar, and the teak decks are ⅝ inch thick. The house top is two layers of ¼ inch Bruynzeel plywood covered over with a layer of mat and cloth. The mat and the cloth both cover over the seams of the house-side and the house top. Tankage is 135 gallons of water and 92 gallons of fuel, both of which bespeak a long-distance cruiser.

The bulwarks are laminated out of two layers

of ¾ inch Alaskan yellow cedar, epoxied to the hull and bolted to it on 18 inch centres with 5/16 inch bolts.

As I said before, all Cape George yachts are true yachts of the finest quality and if you can afford to, by all means let Cecil and Bob Lange build you a finished boat. You will be finding little jewels of craftsmanship forever.

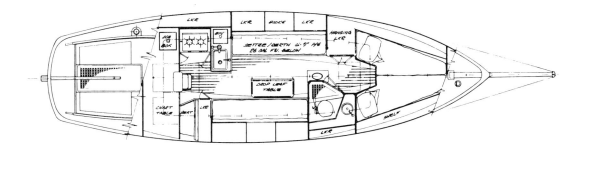

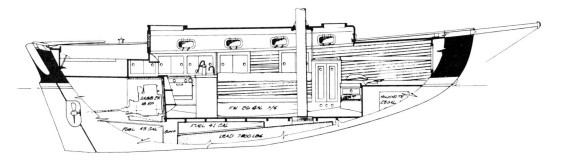

The beautiful little Cape George 31 has the loveliest transom of the Cape George yachts. She carries a lot of sail, giving her a sail-area-to-displacement ratio of 17.46 which means she'll move very well in light airs, and to make up for her lack of beam-provided stability, she carries about 50 per cent ballast and some cleverly located tankage to boot. Her galley and chart table are first class but her head could be narrowed to bring the salon into symmetry. A perfect little cruiser for two, beautifully built with all wood decking by Cecil and Bob Lange.

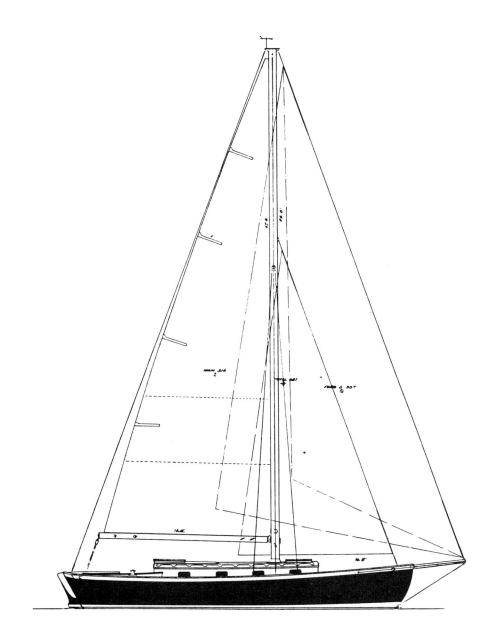

Cape George 31 — Wm. Atkin/T. J. Nolan
LOA—31'0"   LWL—27'6"   Beam—9'6½"   Draft—4'8"   Displ.—15,835 lbs.   Ballast—7,000 lbs.   Sail Area—681 sq. ft.

Just a little something the Langes thought up; a winch-base of heavy stainless steel finished like a piece of jewelry.

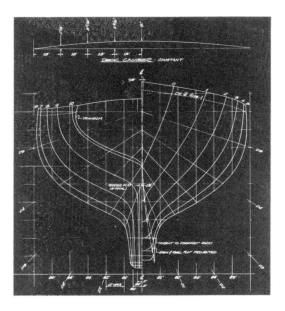

The lines of the Cape George 40 show a marked resemblance to other well-balanced and gently shaped Atkin hulls like the Ingrid.

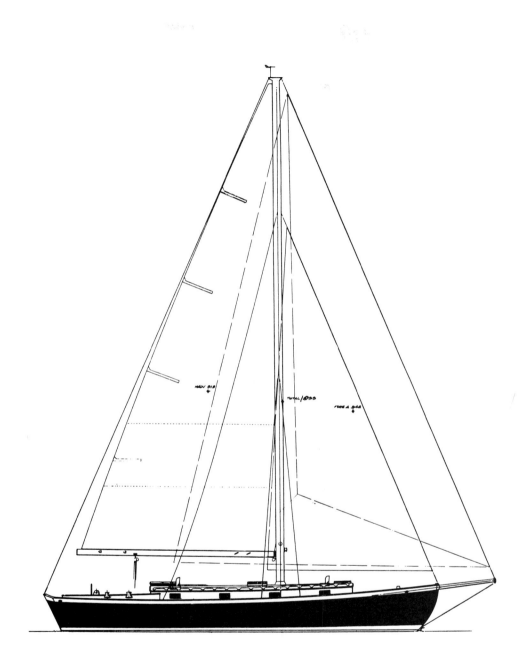

Cape George 40 — Wm. Atkin/T. J. Nolan
LOA—40'6" LWL—36'1½" Beam—11'8" Draft—5'8" Displ.—32,600 lbs. Ballast—14,000 lbs. Sail Area—1,055 sq. ft.

18

Gentleman Bill
Crealock 37

Beauty may be fickle and hard to define, but ugliness seems to have a universal recipe, for how else could someone in the Isle of Wight build a boat that is just as ugly as one built in Miami or another in Taiwan.

Many designers huff and puff when you criticize their work and tell you that beauty is not their main concern, they are after a better rating or more speed or more accommodation or headroom in the lazarette; and when you hear that you had better run because you are talking to a plumber, not an artist. For what good is it getting into port first or having a little tennis court below, if you have to wear the paper bag of shame over your head every time you step onto the dock because your boat is so ugly. It's ugly if its lines don't flow, it's ugly if the proportions are wrong, it's ugly if the deck house doesn't complement the hull, it's ugly if it's drawn by a dishonest man who doesn't draw from the heart but from greed, and last but most importantly, it's ugly if it's ugly. A beautiful boat will rise from a total vision, an ugly boat will be pieced together from a handful of "great" ideas; a beautiful boat will have a soul and purity, and an ugly boat will be an imitator and a

fraud; and a beautiful boat will be like a portrait of a serene woman, while an ugly boat will be a wanted poster tacked together from multiple choice noses and eyes.

I would almost rather see a poorly built ugly boat than a well built ugly one, because the poorly built one at least has the decency to break up and sink in short time, but a well built ugly boat will be around to torment our eyes forever. And it's really all our fault. If we refused to buy ugly boats there wouldn't be any. Maybe it's time for an ugly tax.

The Crealock 37 wouldn't have to pay.

Bill Crealock is a rare breed indeed, intelligent and pensive — he exudes enough thoughtful warmth to raise your confidence to a level where you are ready to go cheerfully to sea in a paper cup. If anyone ever has a role for a thoroughbred gentleman naval architect, Bill Crealock is the man to call.

His 37 foot cruiser is the first of his many designs to bear his name, and what a fine place to start. The boat is elegant and sleek with a very sweet sheer, a fine bow made graceful with slight spooning and a generous overhang, and a light canoe stern that manages to retain much reserve

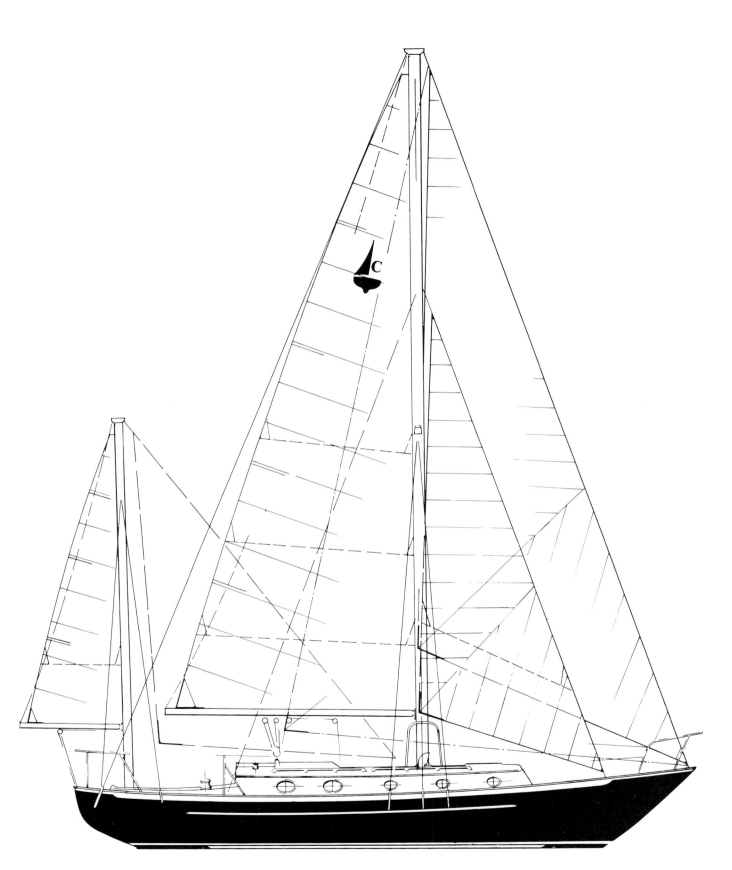

Crealock 37 — W. I. B. Crealock

LOA—36'11"   LWL—27'7"   Beam—10'10"   Draft—4'4''/5'5''   Displ.—16,000 lbs.   Ballast—6,000 lbs.   Sail Area—Cutter:758 Yawl:666

buoyancy without suffering from the droopy elephant-butt look that many canoe sterns have. The latter is accomplished by again allowing a generous overhang and most importantly, by *not* reversing the stern but letting it flow easily to the sheer. Replicators of Bimbo's mama take heed.

This achieving of gracefulness through long overhangs — almost ten feet in all, compared to 5.9 feet of a Valiant 40 and 7 feet for a Swan 37 — may be considered a self indulgence in this day of high cost boat construction and moorage, but the results are so beautiful that the price is well worth paying. Unfortunately few people dare, notable exceptions being Bill Luders and German Frers, whose F and C 44 must surely have the most beautiful lines of any boat drawn in recent years. I must confess an incurable weakness for Frers' designs, to the point where I get excited just at the prospect of seeing one of his boats, so my ravings should probably be taken with a grain of salt.

Back to the daring Mr. Crealock. The grace of the profile of his 37 is harder to compare with modern cruisers than with such classics as Al Mason's 31 foot boat designed twenty-one years before. Indeed the bow of the 37 is even finer. She has none of the hostile looks of modern racer cruisers, nor the stodgy pudginess of cutey-sweety gingerbread cruisers of today. Her fine entry matches her stern and I think it appropriate and illuminating to include here Mr. Crealock's thoughts on his design:

"When setting out to design the Crealock 37 I had the luxury of doing it for myself, without obligation to builder or dealer. I did not have to pay homage to interiors festooned with bunks, or revered classic features, or long waterlines or short or distorted ends. Shakespeare, I recall, said, 'There is a destiny which shapes our ends,' while the Crealock 37's ends could be shaped by her destiny, and if drawing them out a little, gives her a little more grace and a longer sailing length, I was free to do so."

Let's face it, every builder of cruising boats claims that his product approaches the speed of light underway, sails straight into the wind, is built to smash ice, has a penthouse within it, and is sold by a non-profit organization.

In the school of open waters, however, one must be a little more realistic in one's requirements. I wanted speed, as we all do to some extent, but only if it could be achieved without the handling problems which beset many boats with a relatively short keel and skeg underbody. A great deal of time was therefore spent on the design of the keel, skeg and rudder, and judging by the reports of owners who have been caught out in heavy weather, it seems to have done the trick — even under surfing conditions.

It should also be remembered that you might well regard the stern of your boat as a potential bow, for when the weather is truly bad, it is the stern rather than the bow which will bear most of its venom.

The 37, then, is an attempt to provide the weekender and the cruising man with a boat which will travel fast between ports under complete control and which will yet remind him that the passage itself should be one of the pleasures of the cruise."

Mr. Crealock's attempts seem to have succeeded. Earl Hines of *Sea Magazine* said of a trial run that started in moderate breezes and gained as the day went on, "The sailing polar shows that we were attaining 6.5 knots of boat speed, which is a healthy 92% of hull speed. The speed held up well when on a dead run, even though we did not use a whisker pole for wing and wing running.

The heel of angle of the boat was moderate during both sets of sailing tests, reaching a maximum of 20 degrees. Returning to the harbour we experienced heavier winds on a long beat to weather and we were able to put the rail down in the water as we drove along close-hauled at 6 knots plus, with 22 knots of wind over the deck. Such sailing is a realm of the racer and had we been farther from the jetty entrance we surely would have put a reef in the main to ease the heel angle [and probably increase her speed—F.M.]. Nevertheless, the Crealock, with wheel steering, was easily controlled."

Hal Roth did put a reef in and said, "The boat moved quite well under reefed main and the number three jib in twenty knots of wind. She steered easily, heeled only slightly and was responsive and quick. I was surprised at her speed to windward. Certainly the hull design is fast. In smooth water we tacked through 70 to 75 degrees."

And better still, Dave White finished second aboard a 37 in the single-handed Transpac race, logging 2,482 miles at a 6.76 knot average. That's

Dave White, the possessed solo sailor, aboard his Intention *at the start of the single-handed Transpac. The yawl version of the Crealock 37 breaks the 666 square foot sail area down to easily manageable small sails.*

A more serene shot of the Crealock, this time a cutter, with total sail area of 758 square feet.

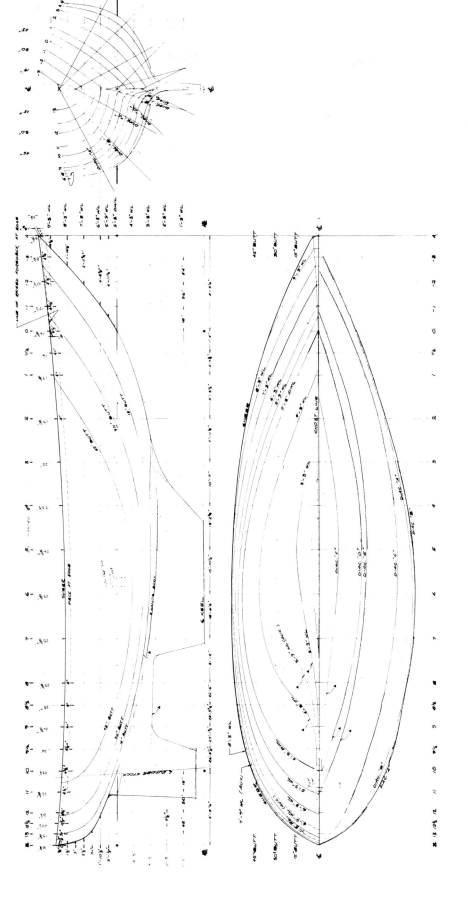

Gentleman Bill Crealock's 37 footer, shows a split underbody with substantial skeg and highly effective rudder. She has a moderate entry and much buoyancy aft without the saggy elephant-butt look that many designers think irresistible. This may be one of the best performance-comfort balanced boats in this book.

pretty fair single-handed sailing. It's nice to hear the comments about windward performance for a cruising boat, especially one with an outboard rig. Her displacement-to-waterline-length ratio is 264, meaning medium in every way, and her 6,000 pounds of lead is externally bolted on.

To continue on with the underbody, the line of entry is very clean, without the hint of a knuckle so frequent on modern boats, and the relatively long thin keel is connected to the large skeg with plenty of bridging, both of which will greatly help in directional stabilility and handling. The bottom of the keel is long and stable, which would make the boat easy to ground and tie to pilings for bottom cleaning or repairs in distant ports, without jeopardy of tipping forward or aft, although a forward brace should be used anyway. The bottom of the skeg is slightly higher than the keel to protect it during both intended and non-intended grounding, while the rudder is in turn slightly higher still, to lessen chances of damage to it.

The propeller is accommodated in an aperture in the skeg. Many designers object to this and justifiably so, because it does create some turbulence and directly over the rudder at that, but to locate a free prop on a shaft punched through the bottom would mean giving up the bridging between the keel and skeg, thereby weakening the skeg and sacrificing a bit of directional stability, and would also necessitate the use of a "V" drive, (unless the engine were somehow relocated well forward, which can be very restrictive with an aft cockpit and a 10 foot 10 inch beam). This would make for an extra coupling to have problems with off the totally abandoned coast of Papua, New Guinea, where a friend of ours grows the best damned tea you ever tasted (and they have nice stamps too).

Let's come up for air. The topsides have been mentioned enough, so let's proceed on deck. Bill Crealock's careful eye is evident in the design of the stern pulpit. Note how in profile the line of the stern is carried right through to the top of the pulpit, with minor adjustments made to the lower horizontal, probably for the backstay. You can note in the work of many other designers, pulpits that thrust skyward at the most inappropriate angles, either through lack of attention or misjudgement. For the most eye pleasing and graceful effect Mr. Crealock's method is the one to follow.

The lazarette is enormous with plenty of space for two propane bottles or plenty of depth for two CNG (compressed natural gas) bottles, whose shapes resemble a diver's tank more than the pudgy propane jugs . . . which reminds me . . . but never mind, this is a book about boats. The cockpit coaming is beautifully drawn and the slope of the coamings and their height affords one of the most comfortable backrests I have yet sat in. But here lies one of my few complaints about the boat, and that is the height of the coamings as they join the deck house. In the profile drawing this line flows elegantly and is perfectly matched to the flow of the sheer in the bow, but in reality the coaming here seems rather high and adds a bulkiness to an otherwise delicate cabin line. Now if you shrug your shoulders and say, "So what," then I'll know you're the guy I saw looking through the joke shop window, wearing checkered lime pants with a red striped jacket and yellow polka dot shirt, stuffing his face with nitro-glyceride filled Twinkies, and I knew right then that Dostoyevsky was right to roar out in anguish, "Why does such a man live!?"

The footwell in the cockpit again shows Bill Crealock's thoughtfulness, for it flares in the aft section to give the standing helmsman a wider space to brace his feet, when on a heel. But there is a problem here with the hinges of the two seat lockers aft and God save you if you like sailing in your birthday suit beneath the hot tropical sun, for if you ever tire of standing at the helm and sit down absentmindedly on the seat behind you, you will be sporting the *Four Flying Hinges* brand forever emblazoned on your tender cheeks. Oh Billy, Billy, you're a cruel, cruel man! And he knows it too, because he didn't dare show the other little bonus feature on his deck layout drawing, which is a 4 inch diameter bronze cap hiding the emergency tiller hookup located *right in the centre of the four hinges*. Now if that doesn't bring tears to your eyes I don't know what will.

The rest of the cockpit seats are built for those much lower on th S & M preference scale. The steering pedestal houses instruments as well as a compass, and what a fine place to have them where no crew can block the helmsman's view of them. The cockpit has tremendous volume, but then it has good coamings all around, and the boat does have much reserve buoyancy in the stern, so getting deluged is not as imminent a problem as on

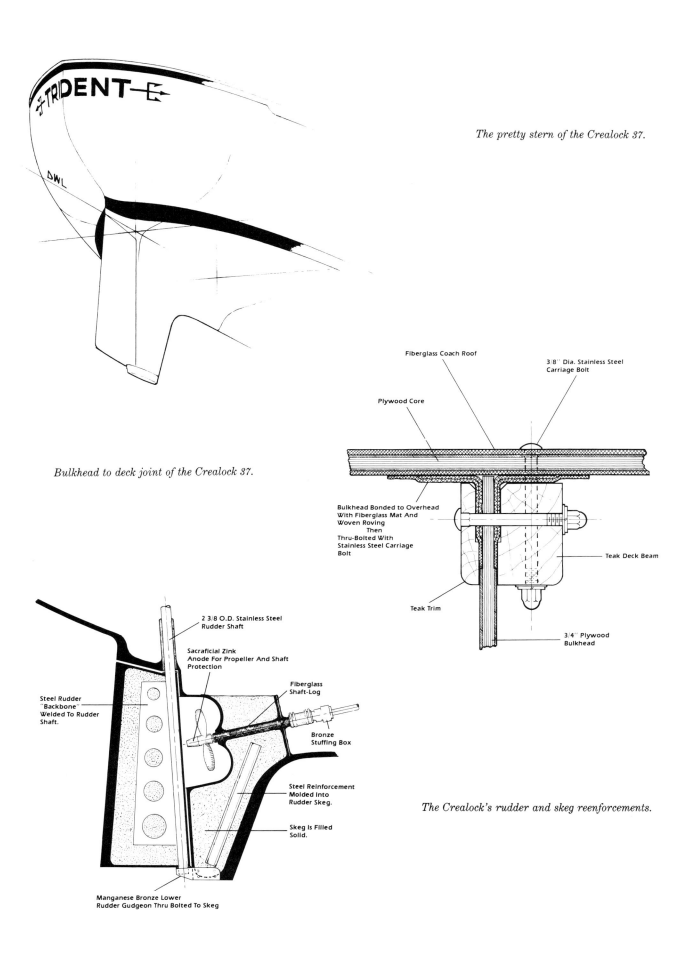

TRIDENT

DWL

The pretty stern of the Crealock 37.

Bulkhead to deck joint of the Crealock 37.

Fiberglass Coach Roof

3/8'' Dia. Stainless Steel Carriage Bolt

Plywood Core

Bulkhead Bonded to Overhead With Fiberglass Mat And Woven Roving Then Thru-Bolted With Stainless Steel Carriage Bolt

Teak Deck Beam

Teak Trim

3/4'' Plywood Bulkhead

2 3/8 O.D. Stainless Steel Rudder Shaft

Sacraficial Zink Anode For Propeller And Shaft Protection

Fiberglass Shaft-Log

Steel Rudder ''Backbone'' Welded To Rudder Shaft.

Bronze Stuffing Box

Steel Reinforcement Molded Into Rudder Skeg.

Skeg Is Filled Solid.

The Crealock's rudder and skeg reenforcements.

Manganese Bronze Lower Rudder Gudgeon Thru Bolted To Skeg

some other designs.

The side locker in the cockpit opens into an enormous space down to the hull, which would be wonderful sail storage and access to the back of bilge pumps if only the battery charger and cold plate compressor were located elsewhere. Not only is this a chancy choice because of corrosive action of sea water wandering in here, but delicate electrical and pipe fittings should not be combined with sail bags, whose drawstrings will catch on anything. The sheet winches are very well located for single handing, but the cleats are not, unless the turning blocks on the aft end of the coaming are a necessity for all headsails, which I doubt. All halyards are led aft from blocks at the mast base which are snapped or shackled onto a perforated sided stainless plate upon which the mast is stepped. This idea has been used by the Nautor built Swans for some years, except that Nautor uses an aluminum plate which is bound to wear away with the stainless block fittings gnawing at it.

The side-decks are of a moderate width, made more secure by a generous height bulwark, which at its minimum is 4 inches high. The portlights are large and bronze and opening, and in combination with the two transparent Bomar hatches — one in the salon and one in the forepeak — they light and ventilate the boat well. Grabrails run all along the cabin top, as they should. The mainsheet traveller is over the companionway, where it is well out of the way. The teak hatch has its own very low profile hatch cover, which combined with high coaming makes for one of the most waterproof main hatches I have seen. The foredeck is spacious, unencumbered by a man-eating jib boom — praise the Lord.

The Crealock 37 seems to be begging for a teak deck, the laying of which would involve some difficulties only from the point where the cockpit coamings begin their journey aft. Here some crafty nibbing would have to be thought up, but maybe Bill has it all thought out, like everything else on the boat — the Four Flying Hinges notwithstanding.

Very fine cast bronze hawse pipes are used with a nicely tooled anchor roller fitting on the bow, where the anchor can be stored in place. The deck has a very good (very rough) moulded in non-skid surface; the forward view from the cockpit is

first rate; and the vertical opening of the companionway has been wisely kept down to a safe size, the bottom of the hole starting at the top of the seats. In plan view the cockpit shape is simply beautiful.

The rig of the Crealock 37 is very flexible. A sloop version is standard but a mizzen can be added to make it a yawl with 47 additional square feet of sail and much flexibility with downwind staysails, or a staysail stay can be installed as home to a 92 square foot staysail to fill the slot and probably add a good third of a knot to windward. As far as I can tell the standard single spreader rig remains the same, with the same manageable 272 square foot main, but running backstays are added for the cutter and yawl, with the latter requiring the split backstay as well. The 37's sail-area-to-displacement ratio is 15.47, which again emphasizes Bill Crealock's approach to moderation.

A touch of elegance is added topsides with a teak main hatch, caprails, eyebrows, and a covering plate over the cockpit coamings.

Belowdecks

The accommodation plan, although in a traditional vein, shows some very thoughtful refinements. The starboard galley is spacious with upper cabinets designed for maximum utility, and include a wine rack. The icebox remains large even with the cold plate in place; the stove has a restraining bar in front of it; the sinks are deep, although their location is a bit too far off centre, forced there by a cutaway in the lower cabinets which is necessary to allow one to get past the companionway into the galley proper. Engine access is gained by removal of the companionway and a lid.

The chart table is very large and has a lift-lid with deep storage below. The electrical panel is out of weather and harm's way, outboard of the chart table. The table has its own seat which could be a comfortable little place (backrest against hull) just to sit and read with a bit of privacy from the salon. The quarterberth is a large and airy double providing good accommodation, although some leeboard system — or full sailbags — would be required to make it a safe single at sea.

Storage is everywhere, below berths, below seats and on the aft face of the trunk cabin. The salon is spacious indeed with an "L"-shaped dinette and a marvel of a table that can serve five different functions. 1) It can be opened into a double-leafed table seating four, 2) It can be folded into a single-leaf table serving two, 3) It can be dropped down in its double-leaf position to create (with the help of the backrest cushions) a double berth, 4) It can be folded up flush against the galley cabinet to be completely out of the way when Fred Astaire comes aboard, or 5) It can be torn out and thrown overboard to be used as a belly-board in the surf.

The mast reenforcing 4 inch by 4 inch post is attached to the end of the starboard main bulkhead. The area forward of this bulkhead shows much creativity, for Mr. Crealock has engaged the service of some very helpful angles to maximize the usefulness of the spaces. The head is set at 45 degrees off the centreline, allowing its forward bulkhead to be angled, which in turns allows creation of a very spacious double berth forward, complete with a cozy seat for reading or private contemplation. Shelves and bins are everywhere. Bill Crealock spent eight years cruising, so his appreciation is well honed for the need of small, accessible storage compartments aboard a cruising boat. Sure the construction is costly and time consuming, but it certainly beats attaching your

The warm interior of the Crealock 37, catching a glimpse of the large chart table and broad quarter-berth. The galley area has been well utilized with numerous small cabinets high and low.

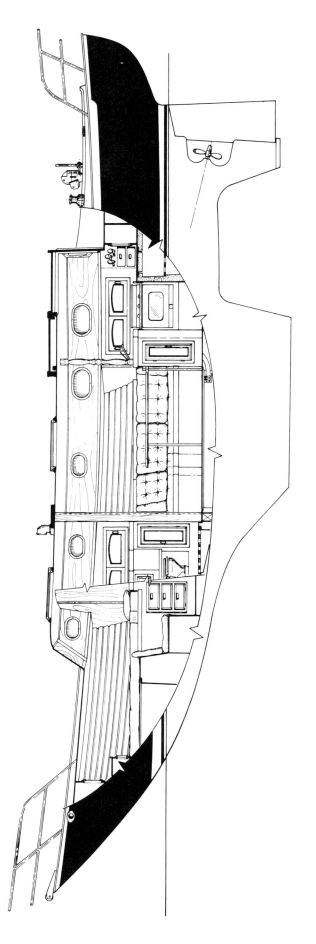

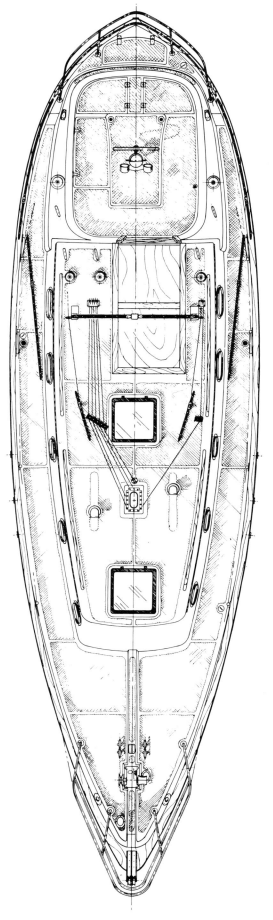

The lines are led aft on the Crealock 37 from a stainless mast base into which blocks can be snapped. The beautifully drawn cockpit has its aft footwell area flared to give the helmsman better footing on a heel. On the helmsman's seat are the infamous brass hinges for the seat-lids (see text).

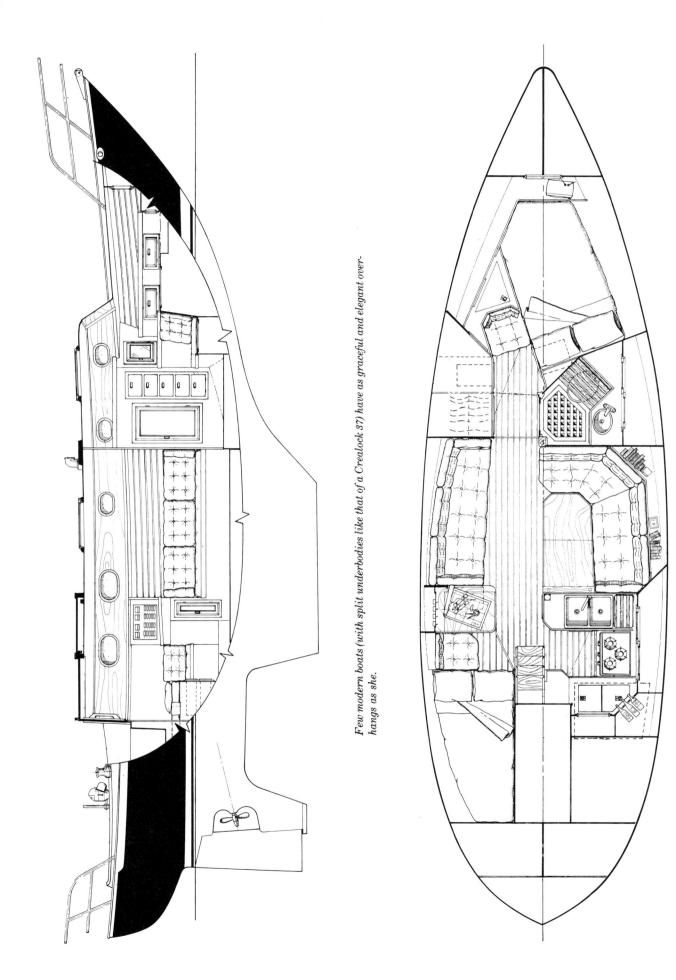

Few modern boats (with split underbodies like that of a Crealock 37) have as graceful and elegant overhangs as she.

Bill Crealock's beautifully drawn interior uses chopped corners and angles to maximize interior space. The forward cabin is just that—a spacious cabin. An excellent live-aboard but she has only two good seaberths.

underwear to the bulkhead with shockcords.

Across from the head is a voluminous hanging locker and five drawers. Despite its open spaciousness the Crealock 37 is blessed with more imaginative storage space than most other boats its size, and it is this attention to details of comfort and livability that will add to the pleasure and indeed, chance of success for most cruises, infinitely more than sweating over reducing the prismatic coefficient of the bustled rimrack by .007 crugents.

Construction

The Crealock 37 is built by Pacific Seacraft in Santa Ana, and for their background see Flicka. The hull is one piece hand-laid-up with the following average thicknesses: ⅜ inch minimum at the sheer, ⅝ inch at the turn of the bilge, 1¼ inch at the reenforced bow and stem, 1½ inch where the keel is bolted and bonded in place, and the hull is also reenforced at the chainplates. The laminates are: mat, cloth, four units of mat and roving plus two extra units of mat and roving down the centerline, one unit 36 inches wide and the next unit 60 inches wide. The skeg is laid up in two halves to enable perfect lay-up of the skin, otherwise it would be impossible to reach down into such a long and narrow mould and do a good job. The skeg is then joined and bonded together, then the unit is internally bonded with laminates to the hull. A 3 inch wide steel channel is imbedded in the skeg to provide stiffness and prevent flexing. The whole skeg is then filled up with chopped fibre and resin mush. The lay-ups of the hulls I saw at the factory were well squeegeed, guaranteeing high fibre content, hence good strength.

The lead keel is bolted into place with ten 1 inch diameter stainless steel bolts that are set in two staggered rows in the casting. Epoxy is used to bed the keel in place and 4 inch diameter washers are used on each bolt. The external versus internal ballast controversy is, of course, still going on, with the internal advocates claiming unavoidable leaks, and this is perhaps so if a very vicious grounding occurs, although I have seen many lead keels with monstrous gouges in them (we live right next door to a small boat repair yard where many sailboats are hauled out each week, so I get to see more than my share of boat ailments), indicating very hard impact with rocks, and yet very few of the keels had to be removed, although

most of them had to be resealed. On the other hand, I have had the inimitable pleasure of driving *Warm Rain* on the rocks, sailing at 5½ knots. As we hauled out I was ready to set my eyes on gaping holes and delamination, but found only two short scrapes barely ⅟₁₆ inch deep, which are readily fillable with epoxy. We ground away around the scrape just to check and there was zero delamination. So I don't know. Both systems have their good points and bad, and both depend on proper installation, the bolt-on keel being the more tricky and demanding for proper seal. If it is well done—well tooled, fitted, epoxied and bolted and backed up in a well reenforced hull — I think I would choose the external ballast. I keep thinking of it as a good shin guard.

The deck is reenforced with ½ inch plywood and the hull to deck joint is the by now standard hull flange and through-bolt. I shudder to think that only a few years ago most builders used pop-rivets to hold their hulls and decks together, and sadly enough some still do. The bolts used in the 37 are ⅜ inch stainless steel on 8 inch centres which I would be happy to see reduced to 4 or 6 inch centres. Polyurethane adhesive (very sticky and remains pliable) is used as a seal between the flanges.

As mentioned, the hull is reenforced in the chainplate area and a one piece backup plate ⅛ inch by 2 inches is used instead of individual washers. This is the best system of reenforcing bolted plates, for all pressure is spread evenly on all the bolts all of the time. The chainplates themselves are ¼ inch thick by 2 inches wide, and the bolts used are ½ inch stainless steel. The bulkheads are bonded to hull and cabin top on both sides, plus they are through-bolted to the deck beam which in turn is through-bolted to the deck (see drawing). This should certainly stop the bulkhead from coming adrift, in spite of all the loading that is present here because of the mast and rigging.

The rudder has a 2⅜ outside diameter stainless steel rudder shaft. To this is welded a ⅜ inch thick perforated backbone, then the whole thing is encased in a glass fibre shell. The shaft sits in a skookum manganese bronze shoe that is through-bolted into the base of the skeg.

The mast is heavy gauge 5½ inch by 8¼ inch untapered extrusion. The water tanks are integral fibreglass, and a thoughtful touch is added with the plumbing and wiring installation in that where the hoses and wires pass through bulkheads, the holes are drilled oversize and the hoses and wires are inserted in a 4 inch long rubber tube to prevent chafing and wear. Very nice.

A few thoughts for the home builder. The question will arise again whether or not to buy the interior fibreglass liner. Unfortunately, in the case of the 37 the liner is all one piece right from the forepeak aft, up to and including the engine pan, so it's an all or nothing situation. I must say, as I have said before, that for the cost of a liner you can have a decent shipwright put in a rough interior for you exactly the way you want it, and all pieces can then be bonded to the hull for ultimate longevity. Or if you choose you can do the whole thing yourself, for building the cabinetry is the simplest and fastest part of boat building. It's a pity that the engine pan doesn't come separately, because designing a bedlog system may involve a bit of engineering, but then maybe you can coerce Henry into helping you out one way or another.

I can see only two tricky things involved in finishing the Crealock 37, one is the engine alignment and the other the caprails. The engine alignment is a bit more critical on this boat than on some others, because the fibreglass stern-tube is of such great length (see drawing). The best way to do this is to set the engine in place, connect up all fittings to make sure everything is aligned and that there is no side loading on the shaft, *then* go ahead and fill up the cavity with mish-mash around the fibreglass tube.

The only other toughy will be the caprail, but if you are really unsure of yourself you can get the patterns from Pacific Seacraft, or have them precut the pieces for you; they do try to help as best they can. To quote from a letter sent to Henry by Crealock 37 owners Diana and Rudy Severns, "We believe you're trying very conscientiously to build a first-class offshore cruiser . . . and you are succeeding." Hear, hear.

19

Halleluja
Alajuela 38

Well, I just don't know for sure. I pant and flutter around marinas and yacht clubs like a fuzzy-cheeked kid in the parlour of his first sporting house, looking at all the glistening and dazzling wonders, ultra-lights and ultra-thins, and I must admit I am fascinated and immediately want one of each. But then I behold the fine sweet curves of some old-fashioned beauty, built for comfort and moderate speed, and all the jitters and flitters disappear, and I calm instantly down, and something very deep inside me says, "She's the one."

And all that in the face of common knowledge and personal experience that fast is fun, and lighter boats with smaller sails and quick response are much more exciting to handle, but deep down inside I'm just a lazy loafer who loves the motion and comfort of a nice big momma who can lull me to sleep.

The Alajuela 38 is a boat of comforting, reassuring beauty, designed following the lines of William Atkin's *Ingrid* and built with almost paranoidal pride by Betty and Don Chapman of Alajuela Yachts in Huntington Beach, California.

It all began like the story of so many other cruising boats, with someone who wanted to build a safe, comfortable cruiser, but could afford it only if he built a good number of them and sold all but one. Such was the case of Mike Riding in the early '70's who had dreams of cruising with his lady whom he had met in the little Costa Rican town of Alajuela. With help they built and filled and ground away at a plug for over three years, until they were satisfied that it was as good as they could get, at which point they pulled a mould, and voila, Alajuela was born.

Now three years for a hull may not sound like too much to you, but many companies tool up a hull and a deck in three months. Mike and his friends lived and worked in a dusty lot, while up the street in a clean and airy building, Westsail — who had started not much before — was the star of *Time* magazine and was popping out boats at the rate of fifteen a month in different stages of completion.

Meanwhile, Alajuela caught fire too. They decided no more fooling around, rolled up their sleeves and finished tooling up the deck in twenty-two months. Then they puttered and fidgeted, making their own bronze castings for gudgeons and pintles and portlights — that don't store even one drop of water — into pieces that would make a

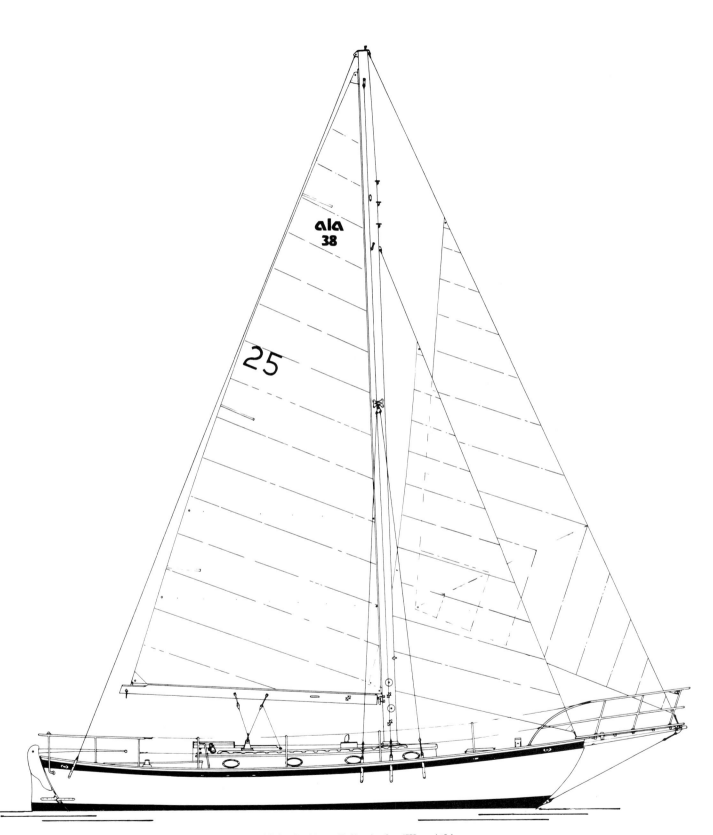

Alajuela 38 — Colin Archer/Wm. Atkin
LOA—38'0" LWL—32'7" Beam—11'6" Draft—5'7" Displ.—27,000 lbs. Ballast—10,000 lbs. Sail Area—880 sq. ft.

jeweler proud.

Westsail was turning out good boats indeed, built like icebreakers and finished in such workmanship that everyone in the industry tried to emulate them, but not Mike Riding. If Westsail did it well, Mike did it better; if Westsail put in five layers of roving, he put in six; if Westsail used 1 inch teak caprails, Mike used inch and a half; and if Westsails could withstand twenty-one consecutive typhoons, Mike's could withstand twenty-two. The pursuit of quality was almost pathological and the results were impeccable. Most things were invisible or at least not noticeable to the uninitiated, for the Alajuela 38 was so clean, simple and unpretentious she was almost dull, but the quality and engineering of such things as the hull-to-deck joints, bulkhead installation, and shaft log assembly were truly unquestionable.

So they crept along, putting out but a few works of art a year and selling some hulls and decks to a few local crazies like Betty and Don Chapman, until after almost six years of operation they had turned out an astronomical fifteen boats.

Betty and Don Chapman bought hull #6 and deck #2 — such was the way of Alajuela — and set out full time in another dusty lot to finish off their boat. There existed no interior kits or exterior kits, or drawer kits or floor kits, or even a single sketch for an interior layout, so they went and ad-libbed all along the way. Betty says it was one of the most enjoyable times of their lives; until the grey paint. They wanted a traditional looking yacht, which, in spite of common belief, means white painted interior with varnished teak trim, so they began sanding and painting, sanding and painting, everything with grey undercoat. They painted the bulkheads and the overhead and the lockers and the furniture and the bilges, until the whole interior looked like one endless grey twilight. It was twilight for weeks as coat after coat went on. Betty began to see grey, taste grey and smell grey, and almost abandoned the whole project when finally one day they started painting white. That was much better — at first. Then for weeks on end the interior looked like a blinding blizzard. Such is the way of boat building.

They lived aboard and sailed the boat for over a year, then when Mike Riding wanted out of the Alajuela company Betty and Don decided to get involved. And with all their sanding and painting experience, why not? But they are still a small company with only a handful of employees, who have over the years upped the total of Alajuela 38's produced to seventy. During the same time Westsail put out seven hundred of its boats and if you say the proof is in the pudding, then you are right, but in the case of Westsail the pudding is long gone, eaten up by creditors and foreclosures, while Alajuela moves along with the patience and perseverance of a marathon turtle.

But the 38 herself is anything but slow. Although her keel is about as full as they come (and with the sweeping line from stem to stern, one of the most beautiful as well) in the 1976 Newport to Ensenada race, an outing notorious for light and fickle winds, the Alajuela 38 *Wathena* was a second place trophy winner, placing well ahead of cruising boats her size and displacement, and finishing thirty-second overall on corrected time. Not bad in a fleet of five hundred boats.

Her entry has been fined down from the Atkin hull for better performance in light airs, and her lines are fine indeed in stern and bow, the latter of which makes her less buoyant aft than, say, a Valiant 40, but makes her a lot prettier as well. In the stern she does carry her sheer-beam well down to the waterline so there is no need to panic, there is plenty of reserve buoyancy.

The sheer is perky, lively and graceful and one of the prettiest around with very moderate freeboard dimensions — 4 foot 1 inch forward, 3 foot 6 inches amidships, and just under 4 feet aft — which is a very good thing in the bow for when working to windward it minimizes the surface that can be pushed at by the wind. A long bowsprit perfectly following the sheerline helps to draw out and gracify the lines (as if they needed it) and enable the Alajuela to carry 880 square feet of working sail, which even at her 27,000 pound displacement (well over the weight of one and a half Santa Cruz 50's) gives her a sail-area-to-displacement ratio of 15.7. In comparison, a Valiant 40 is 16.8, hardly a

The Alajuela 38, as happy as a pig in a puddle storming along in a good blow. A new powerful rig drives an old seakindly Ingrid hull. A first class boat for serious cruisers.

marked difference.

The Alajuela's single spreader rig is tall, 54 feet from the waterline, so watch those bridges. The main is getting into the *grande* category at 366 square feet, so you had best stay in good shape. Even though many people will consider 500 square feet to be the safe upper limit for a mainsail, I at my decrepit 155 pounds find anything over 400 square feet to be quite a handful come reefing or stowing time.

Just as I finished this line of wisdom I flipped over a blueprint of a sail plan drawn by Ray Richards, Naval Architect, for the Alajuela 38 Mark II, which shows an even larger main of 409 square feet. Thanks a lot, Raymond. I tried to reach him by phone but to no avail, so after close study of his new plan I have to draw my own con- clusions. He has made the following changes: Jib minus 32 square feet, staysail plus 21 square feet, main plus 47 square feet; for a net gain of 40 square feet to a new total area of 920 square feet. This does two things: It increases the sail-area-to- displacement ratio from my previously calculated 15.7 to 16.42. Very respectable indeed. With the apparent shifting of the net gain toward the stern one would be led to think that the Alajuela must have experienced previous lee helm which creates an unpleasant mushy feel, and the sail area was shifted aft to correct that. And indeed I found an old photograph of the boat going windward in medium airs with the tiller pushed over to the lee side.

Anyway, back to the handling of a large main when reefing in a blow. The whole operation hinges on the helmsman, for if he can keep the flail- ing boom well under control by working the helm and the mainsheet with dutiful care, life will become, if not much easier, at least extended. Since the mainsheet traveller on the Alajuela is over the companionway instead of on the bridge- deck, this exercise of control by the helmsman will be made slightly more difficult, but with a little stretching it will not be impossible. Yet if given a choice, and what home builder isn't, it may prove prudent to relocate the traveller to the bridgedeck where, although it may be a hindrance to traffic in

and out of the companionway, it would certainly be more accessible to the helmsman and require about 20 per cent less power to operate, since the lever arm from the fulcrum — the gooseneck fitting at the mast — will be lengthened by about 4 feet or the length of the main boom of 17 feet 6 inches. To alleviate the usual amount of tripping involved with having the main sheet track on the bridge- deck, the track should be set on the fibreglass deck below the level of the teak decking. If you are for some unfortunate reason, like cost, sworn against teak decking on the seats, then at least a fairing piece of teak, say a ¾ inch thick by 1¼ inch wide, placed directly aft of the track should be a consid- erable help.

The rest of the deck layout of the Alajuela is a sailor's and builder's dream. The cockpit is spacious, with the two side seats having a length of 7 feet 2 inches, which is ideal for sleeping in the tropics with a very simple mosquito net tent suspended from the twin backstay and the boom. The side-decks are 22 inches wide and have parallel sides, which would make the laying of teak decks very simple and most felicitous to the point of ir- resistibility. The foredeck is thoughtfully clean ex- cept for the large hatch which transmits much light to the forepeak and makes the transport of large headsails almost dull compared to the usual push- kick-curse-shove of bear wrestling, usually in- volved in such an operation.

The bulwarks are integral parts of deck and hull and average about six inches in height and give a feeling of security to the broad decks, while help- ing to visually lower the side of the deck house. The house itself is ended blissfully short forward, avoiding the common pratfall of carrying the line too long for the sake of a bit of volume below, thereby creating a coffinesque box of most depressing proportions.

While on the foredeck I should mention the massive, 5 inch square samson post which, with its mass and structure, would be just the thing to use as a tow bit in case the *Queen Mary* ever ran aground.

Ray Richards has redesigned the house and deck incorporating into the mould such functional

The 38 splitting the ocean and leaving a great streak of frothing calm in her wake. Few things are as fine for the heart as being at the helm while reaching in good winds in a seaway.

things as hatch coamings, a dodger base, winch pads, and some very fine bases for a teak Dorade box forward of the main hatch, and a Dorade box-cum-line and winch handle box just aft of the mast. Oh yes, also two cowl vent fittings on the aft deck to vent the engine room. These, along with eight opening ports and three hatches, should make an extremely comfortable boat in the tropics where every hole is worth its weight in gold — whatever that means.

The rudder, as easily seen, is aft hung on three jewelly gudgeons and pintles and coaxed by a tiller of truly eyebrow raising length. This is without doubt the most foolproof steerage man has ever devised and although it complicates access to the lazarette and clutters the cockpit somewhat, it is ideal for hooking up to a windvane steering system and is universally acknowledged by even the most ardent wheel advocates as never failing. And if you don't believe me, then show me a boat that comes with a standard tiller whose naval architect felt unsure enough about the system to install provisions for an emergency steering wheel.

The rig is tall but the bilges are moderately stiff and her 10,000 pounds of lead give her a ballast-displacement ratio of almost 40 per cent, and apart from that all tankage — fuel, 65 gallons; water, 100 gallons — and even the holding tank for extra water, are well below the waterline. So is the engine, which adds the extra characteristic of enabling use of a nearly horizontal shaft, which in turn allows the propeller to work at maximum efficiency, unlike some shafts which angle well down and force the propeller to spin away relentlessly as if trying to propel the boat to the moon.

The mast is gracefully tapered over the last ten feet to cut weight and windage aloft. There are two backstays chainplated directly to the hull, a solution which eliminates the need for a boomkin, which with its whisker stays and fittings has to be considered a weak link. Having two backstays going all the way to the masthead does, however, seem a little reactionary, causing expense and weight aloft, when a single backstay split a dozen feet from the deck would achieve the same purpose.

The rig is outboard, which means you won't be able to flatten the genny as much as you would like, so you will give up a few points to windward. The distance between the forestay and the headstay is over 6 feet at the bottom — where it counts most since this is where the bulk of the genoa will be passing through — and this should make tacking manageable, although not nearly as fast as if a quick release system were put on the forestay, so it could be stowed back by the lower shrouds somewhere when the genoa was in use.

Belowdecks

The most striking feature of the layout of the Alajuela is how unstriking it really is. It is indeed the ultimate conventional layout that upon close inspection reveals the most important aspect of the Alajuela, which is scale. By this I don't mean unused volume — quite the contrary — it's the size of the furniture in it that makes the boat a standout, and a very rare offshore cruiser indeed. The chart table is just the right size for open charts at 43 inches by 28 inches. Perhaps I have a frighteningly sievish memory, but I'll be damned if I can flip a folded chart back and forth and remember exactly what was on the other side. Stepping off distances with dividers on a small table is sheer agony, and trying to draw in a compass course with parallel rules with the compass rose folded into four bitty pieces is worse than Chinese water torture. There is one problem with the chart table however, in that there is no chart stowage designed into it. The large area below the chart table is accessible through doors and three adjoining drawers, which at about 14 inches in width are just too narrow for charts. A wider set of drawers cannot be used because the companionway ladder would interfere with their opening. The problem could be remedied simply, by installing one wide top drawer, as wide as the companionway ladder will allow. If you are a fan of wide, shallow drawers as I am, and you dislike narrow oilskin lockers as I do, then a bit of simple redesigning will give you both the wide drawers and the wide oilskin locker. This would involve moving the bulkhead between the chart table and settee farther forward, so it will align with its mate on the starboard side — about 12 inches. There are no interior liners of any kind — hallelujah — in the Alajuela; even the cabin sole is plywood on solid floors, so this change involves no trickery at all. The oilskin locker bulkhead can be moved the same amount, resulting in a generous sized locker, where wet gear can dry easily, especially if a few holes are drilled into the engine room

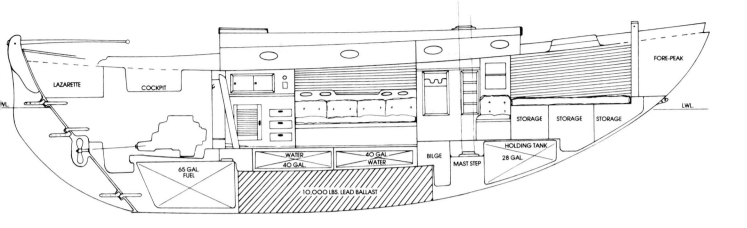

LAZARETTE   COCKPIT   FORE-PEAK

WL.   LWL.

STORAGE   STORAGE   STORAGE

65 GAL.
FUEL

WATER
40 GAL.   40 GAL.
WATER   BILGE   MAST STEP

HOLDING TANK
28 GAL.

10,000 LBS. LEAD BALLAST

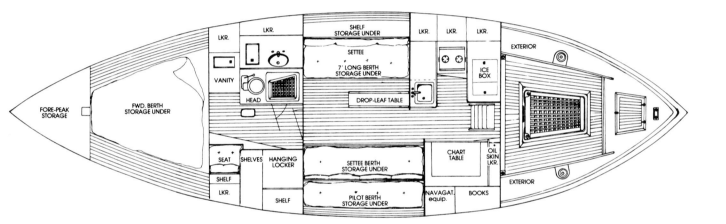

FORE-PEAK
STORAGE

LKR.   LKR.   SHELF
STORAGE UNDER   LKR.   LKR.   LKR.

EXTERIOR

VANITY

SETTEE
7' LONG BERTH
STORAGE UNDER

ICE
BOX

FWD. BERTH
STORAGE UNDER

HEAD

DROP-LEAF TABLE

SEAT   SHELVES   HANGING
LOCKER

SHELF

LKR.

SHELF

SETTEE BERTH
STORAGE UNDER

PILOT BERTH
STORAGE UNDER

CHART
TABLE

OIL
SKIN
LKR.

EXTERIOR

NAVAGAT.
equip.   BOOKS

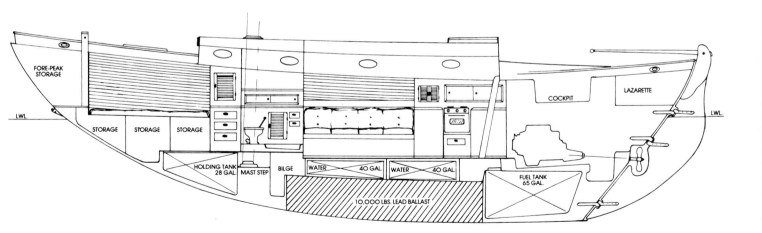

FORE-PEAK
STORAGE

COCKPIT   LAZARETTE

LWL.   LWL.

STORAGE   STORAGE   STORAGE

HOLDING TANK
28 GAL.   MAST STEP   BILGE   WATER   40 GAL.   WATER   40 GAL.

FUEL TANK
65 GAL.

10,000 LBS. LEAD BALLAST

The Alajuela 38 (Ingrid) interior with its enormous owner's cabin forward. The berth is so large here you'll have trouble finding your mate. The rest of the boat reveals an ideal offshore cruiser. Note that with ample keel all tankage can be located low down to add to the already increased ballast. But then her sail area has been much enlarged since Bill Atkin drew her plans many moons ago.

to facilitate ventilation.

So. Now that you have moved the bulkhead you have also rendered the two forward berths useless, but you can redeem yourself by, a) poking a hole in the main bulkhead for a foot-well for the settee berth, just like the starboard settee has under the galley counter, and b) building a similar foot-box for the pilot berth. It is true that you lose space in the forepeak hanging locker this way, but that locker is the largest in captivity anyway, and you are actually gaining an equal amount of hanging space in the oilskin locker.

Now that we have massacred this fine ship let's go on. The galley is laid out just like it says in the book, with a large top-loading icebox 30 inches by 15 inches, gimballed stove with oven, and single sink — a double is unattainable here because of the berth foot-well. Storage is good outboard of the stove and under the sink but I think I would venture through the engine room bulkhead above the icebox to gain more storage there — in a galley you can't have too much. An even simpler solution would be to construct a flying dish rack (see the cover and page 46 of Volume I of *The Finely Fitted Yacht*.)

The salon berths are a good size, 22 inches to 26 inches in width, the dropleaf table is by the book, and the light through the four ports and the skylight (not in drawing) is very sufficient indeed.

Now comes the unusual part. Through the opening in the main bulkhead you pass into what can only be described as a stateroom. Space and light and storage is everywhere. The huge double berth measures over 90 inches at its widest part and has a large opening hatch above it for ventilation — and a little variety now and then. A seat to port makes for a very private reading place, or if your interests are more narcissistic, you can sit and stare at yourself in the mirror above the vanity across the way. It isn't called a vanity for nothing, you know. The head is a good size with a shower pan.

Some people might feel that having the main stateroom up forward is less than ideal because of motion forward, but you must consider that, a) the motion is only bad here going to weather, and b) the berth will be used as a double primarily in port anyway. The gains made by locating the stateroom here allow for the most private, self-contained and spacious stateroom on a boat of her size and lines,

and almost more importantly, leaves the port quartersection alone for the chart table. With that quarter left untouched, the engine room — and it can certainly be called that — gives excellent access to all parts of the engine through a very large single leaf door. I emphasize single leaf because on much too many boats, access to the engine is gained only after the dismembering of cabinets and steps and bulkheads. Not so here. One ladder hinges up and one door hinges out, *es todo*.

Construction

The basic engineering and construction of the Alajuela is extremely good. The hull is laid up by hand in a one-piece mould with 4 units of alternate layers of mat and roving, with a minimum thickness of ½ inch at the sheer thickening to ¾ inch in the bilge except where the bonds over the ballast overlap in the turn of the keel, and here the thickness becomes a monstrous 1½ inches. The ballast is all lead — 10,000 pounds. The rudder has a steel core that is embedded in foam and glassed over. The bronze pintles we've already discussed.

The deck is sandwiched plywood and the hull-to-deck joint is one of the best in the industry. This is not to take anything away from a well bolted joint, for combined with the modern bedding compounds the thing will never move the width of an eyelash, but Alajuela does produce what is ultimately a monolithic hull and deck. As you will remember, the deck is surrounded by bulwarks of an average height of 5 inches. There is no flange on the hull. The deck laminates are turned upward to create the bulwarks. There is very little clearance between the two (see drawing) and this is the basis of the structure. The areas where the hull and deck touch are coated with mish-mash (resin thickened with fibres) then the deck is set in place and with lightening speed — because the resin is going off — a hundred wood clamps are set in place to hold the joint tight until the resin sets. This is not a simple task. Don and Betty activate every able body in the boatyard for each deck placement, to mish-mash, place, hold and clamp, for once the resin goes off Charlie, that's it. What you see is what you get.

Once the bond is set the clamps come off and the hull is laminated to the deck with alternate layers of mat and roving from down below. *Then* the two mahogany clamps at the top of the bulwarks are bedded and screwed together, then

Looking aft in the Alajuela. To one side is the enormous chart table, to the other the spacious galley. The portlights were designed with much thought by Alajuela. The bottom of the sleeve is sloped outward so all water drains out, instead of gushing into the cabin upon opening.

the caprail is screwed to them, and *then* each stanchion with its four bolts is through-bolted to the bulwarks. Sounds like it will stay together for a week or two.

The bulkheads are of ¾ inch and routed where the bonding will be to remove the oily teak or mahogany layer, and make for a nearly flush finish. As mentioned, there are no liners, everything inside is plywood and this — because it goes together one fitted piece at a time — is without doubt the most precise way to fabricate the interior. There is no foam between the hull and bulkhead, but I am sure if you stamp your feet and throw yourself on the floor Don will go ahead and have it done for you. Just don't tell him I told you so. Every piece of plywood in the boat is bonded to the hull, and this will make for a boat with a very long life.

The joiner work is precise and they even

bullnose (around the corners) the seating cleats and drop-lids under the berth cushions. Not even Candace does that.

The stanchions will come out only if you take the bulwarks with them, and the bowsprit on the new boats is no longer a flimsy 8 inch by 8 inch tree trunk, but a welded stainless steel A-frame, which was developed by Bill Crealock for the Westsail 42. No chance of dry rot here. The rudder cheeks are 1½ inch ash, which will rot if not maintained, so maintain it. The mast is keel stepped.

In all, she is a beautiful yacht. She might not get you to weather like a fin keeler, and it might take a bit to get her going in light airs, but once she is moving, look out. And the way she's built she'll still be sailing merrily along, long after you've sold your soul to the devil for a piece of solid ground to die on.

A hint of the owner's cabin of the Alajuela 38. Here there is excellent stowage and even a seat for reading or quiet contemplation or for changing your socks.

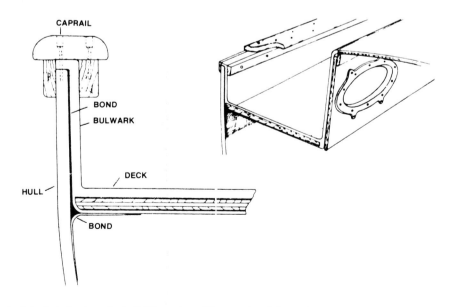

Alajuela's deck fits into the hull like a glove. They are bonded together with mish-mash, then clamped with a jillion clamps, then they're bonded below with layers of mat and roving, then they're held together at the top by the caprail reenforcement. If that's not trying your best, I don't know what is.

Finely tooled bronze gudgeons and pintles and rot-proof bowsprit/bow platform, of the Alajuela 38.

20

The Man Who Would Be Happy
Ingrid

I once met a man who knew all about happiness. He knew exactly where to find it, its latitude, its longitude, the shape of the mountains around it, the colour of its sky, the texture of the sand on its beaches, and the direction the palm fronds bowed during the day when the winds were cool, and during the night when they were warm and gentle. He knew the sounds of its stony piazza, the number of marble steps that led down to the bay, the shape of its women and the look in their eyes. He knew the flowers of the tidy gardens, the windows of the little houses, and he kept talking about the perfection and the beauty and the care that was there — care for everything and everyone. He knew the place where happiness was, better than anyone else, and yet he had never been there, only in his dreams, but he would be there soon, just as soon as he could manage, just as soon as he could shrug off all the misery around him that he had always known and would know a little longer, until the moment he began his journey to happiness. But until then, he would go on as he had all his life, indifferent toward the place he lived, or the shabby houses he built or the lives he affected, waiting and working for the first day of happiness

just a few more years away. But he had added wrong or multiplied wrong, because before his day of happiness, came the day of his funeral when a beam of one of his shabby houses gave way. Which prompted an old Hungarian friend of my mother's to say, "Those who live by the shabby beam, die by the shabby beam."

Jerry Husted can plan his life without worrying about his beams, because 10 years ago he decided to build the safest, strongest cruising boat he knew how, and he has been doing his best ever since. He also made an interesting choice, and a wise one it seems, for he decided to stick to constructing only the basic structural components of hulls and decks, and installing only major parts such as ballast, bulkheads, rudders, engines, chainplates and rough cabinetry, and doing it all with the greatest of care, but stopping there, and not diluting his attention and that of his boatyard with details of finishing, for he felt that that could be best left to owners and finishers, who could decide for themselves how important details of completion were to them.

Yet he by no means abandons the owners, for he provides complete drawings for the finishing,

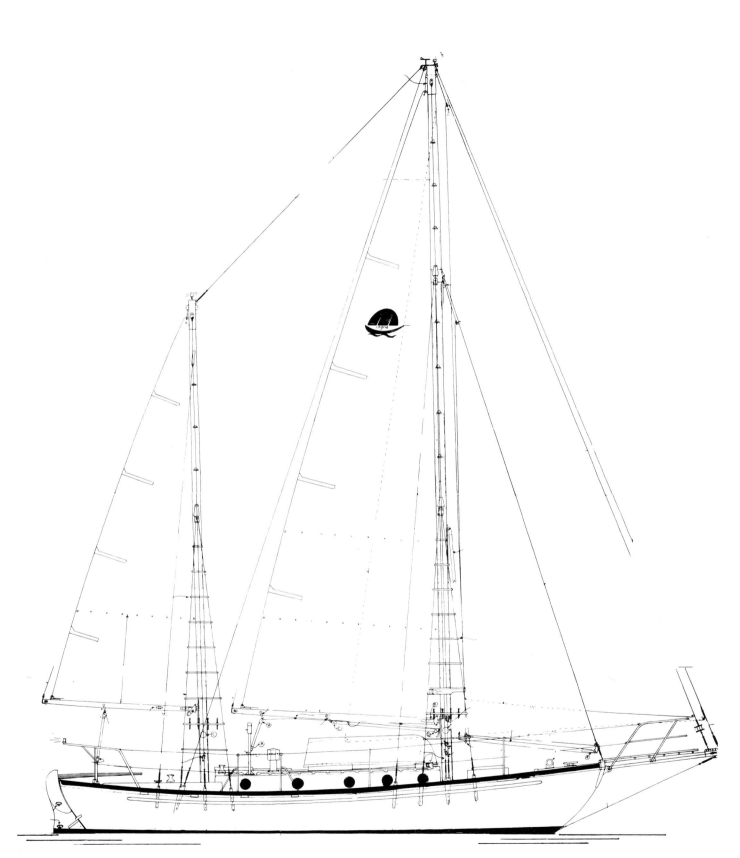

Ingrid 38 — Colin Archer/Wm. Atkin
LOA—37'8"   LWL—32'0"   Beam—11'4"   Draft—5'8"   Displ.—26,000 lbs.   Ballast—8,000 lbs.   Sail Area—848 sq. ft.

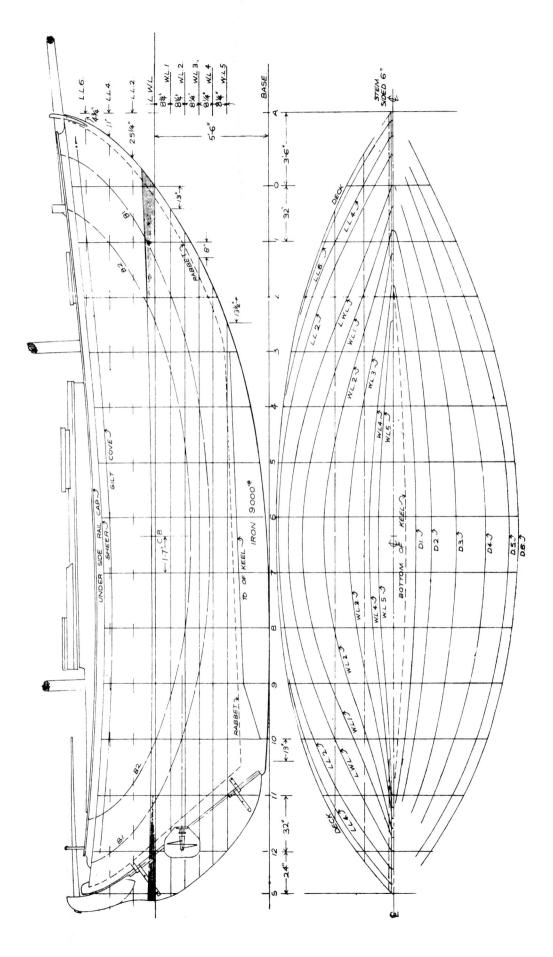

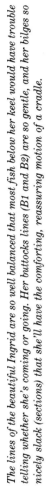

The lines of the beautiful Ingrid are so well balanced that most fish below her keel would have trouble telling whether she's coming or going. Her buttocks lines (B1 and B2) are so gentle, and her bilges so nicely slack (sections) that she'll have the comforting, reassuring motion of a cradle.

and he supplies wood parts and all the custom stainless steel hardware of the best grade, even down to the mast fittings necessary for a wooden mast if that is what you choose.

To build a solid, safe boat, he chose the design that was the basis of most of William Atkin's long line of double enders, the 38 foot Ingrid, originally designed by Colin Archer. This is an identical hull to that built by Alajuela so I will skip the identical details and talk about the differences. The Blue Water Ingrid lays its emphasis more greatly on authenticity and variety, by using a split house (see *The Bristol Channel Cutter* for pros and cons), a ketch rig, wood spars, and a great choice of interior layouts. That, one can be heard saying, is hardly enough to make the Ingrid worth repeating in one book but what makes it worth repeating is the fact that Jerry's construction is rather outstanding.

Since we have talked about hull shape and general performance of the Ingrid already, let us move on to the rig, for some interesting things have happened since the original Atkin rig was modified from a ¾ to a masthead rig, which was done to give the boat better light air performance. This she did get, up to a total sail area of 848 square feet, which gives her a sail-area-to-displacement ratio of almost 16 and that will make her a pretty decent light air sailer. What has happened though with the increased sail area, is that the boat is now rather tender, to the point where the main has to be reefed very early or eased right off until it is neither quite pulling nor thrashing

about, (see photo). This latter method is quite acceptable for a short time, but it is unthinkable on a long voyage and certainly not the best fun in a gusting blow, where you can be sailing with the rail close to being down and the main so loose that it is just along for the ride, when a gust hits and affects not only the sails that were pulling before, but also fills the main and pushes the boat over and slows her down very noticeably, giving the helmsman one hell of a powerful dose of weather helm to boot. So as I say, this is a fine way to sail for a short time, because it is a good lazy man's reef, but overall the main should be reefed, or as Jerry suggests, even dropped. They have sailed *Ingrid Princess* with the latter configuration of jib, staysail and mizzen only, and the boat moved at 6 knots with no tortuous weather helm. Most people will realize at once that this is less than a spectacular performance for a boat with 32 feet of waterline (*Warm Rain* will do a steady 6 with a small genoa, staysail and reefed main and she has a waterline that is 4½ feet shorter, so a better solution should be found), but when you think of it, this mainless sailing could be a very nice way to sail if you are not in a hurry, for you will have only one good sized sail to handle — the big jib at 322 square feet — for the staysail is only 127 and the mizzen but 135. For those who don't like this arrangement I suggest they try her to see how it works and if you still don't like it you can always get her as a cutter. Yet I think there is another solution for those who love ketches and the key to it lies in the following observations.

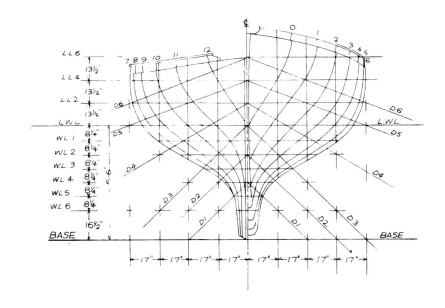

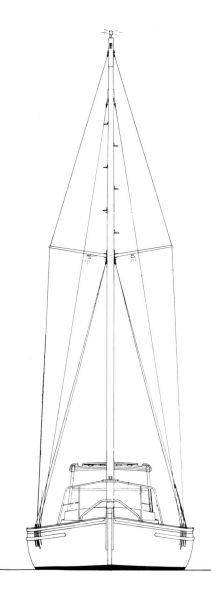

The stable beamy Ingrid with both travellers raised off the deck. The mainsheet traveller is incorporated into the boom gallows on the deck house.

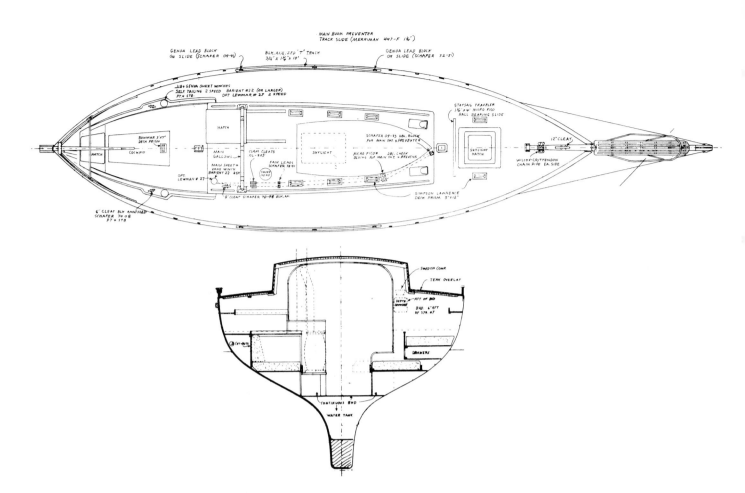

The deck layout shows Ingrid's broad, safe side-decks and her large foredeck. If you want to install all nine deck prisms shown, you'd better find yourself one rich widow.

The major difference between Blue Water and Alajuela Ingrids is in the amount of ballast used and I think herein lies the Blue Water's problem of being overpowered with what appears to be too much sail. Alajuela uses 10,000 pounds of ballast and Blue Water 8,000, and to top it off Alajuela uses all lead and Blue Water uses steel, which brings the total mass higher. So even if you consider that the sail area of Blue Water's Ingrid is smaller by about five per cent, that still doesn't justify carrying twenty per cent less ballast. Old Atkin drawings call for a total of 9,000 pounds of ballast and as you recall that boat carried even less sail.

Alajuelas have shown that they can sail very well into strong winds, and I did see a long series of aerial photos of one in what was said to be 30 knots and the seas certainly look it, and she had all sails flying and no reef taken, and although she was never shown totally close-hauled she seemed

tight enough on a couple of occasions and still she was sailing merrily on. I bring this up not to praise Alajuela or to degrade Blue Water, but only to point out Ingrid's potential with a higher ballast ratio.

In light airs Blue Water Ingrid is said to move at half of wind speed up to 8 knots of wind, which is nice enough for average cruising but will not impress sailors of ultra-lights who most often attain, and at times surpass, true wind speed.

Belowdecks a number of layouts have been worked out. This flexibility is made possible by an off-centre companionway, allowing for a larger area in the starboard quarter.

I pondered for some time the five plans Jerry gave me, and found that three seemed interesting, and although most of you will know at once that I'll prefer the good old staid layout with the symmetrical salon and pilot berth and large chart table aft, I will go through the other two, for it is always

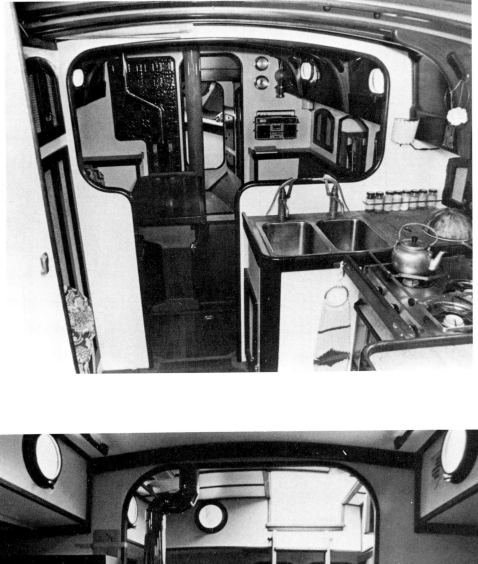

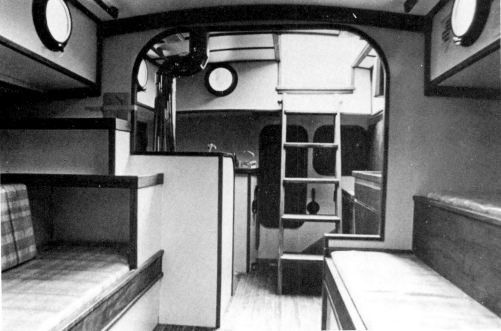

Few sailboats have the feel of a real ship, but this Ingrid is certainly one of them.

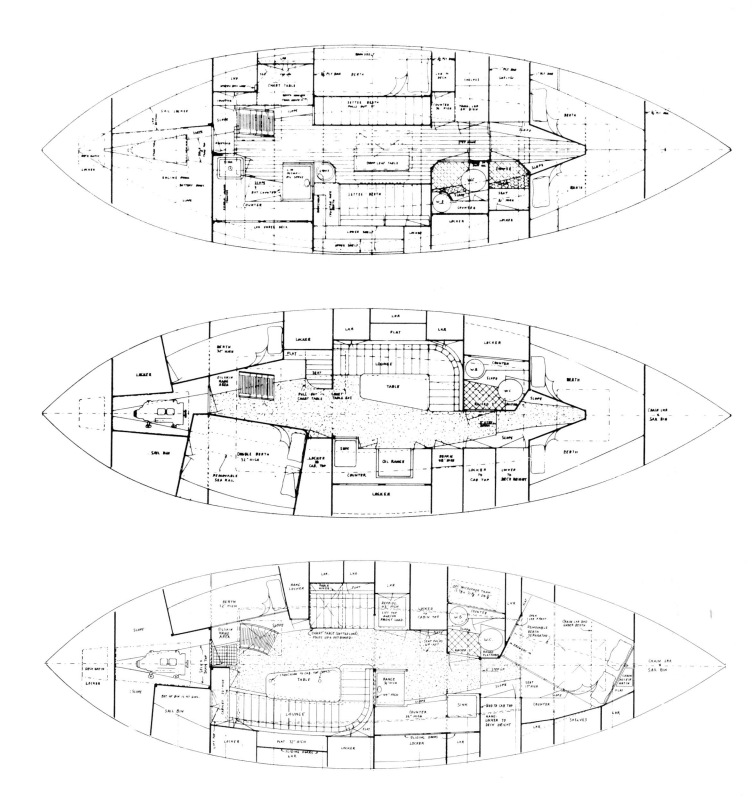

Three layouts for the Ingrid. The top one is the most conventional and most conservative with three good seaberths, a large galley and chart table area, ample stowage in various lockers and a very large forward cabin. The second plan swings the galley across from a dinette area opening up a large area in the starboard quarter for a double berth which is fine for local cruising or island hopping with two couples but it's a bit short on seaberths. The third layout with the salon aft is interesting in its own way, but I'm surprised no attempt has been made to stick the head aft into the starboard quarter, opening up the rest of the boat to all sorts of interesting possibilities.

nice to see some innovative thinking, especially when it is inside such a fine traditional boat.

The one with the large double berth aft seems like an interesting plan for two couples cruising together, as it allows for, what can be, two very private sleeping areas. You will have to do some leeboarding and hot-bunking when voyaging, because the plan is scarce on seaberths, and I have never much liked the idea of the galley occupying the same area as the salon, but it is a possible solution.

The other plan with the grand salon aft has a

nice feel to it, reminiscent of yachts of old whose galley was up forward in a place where the owner never ventured. This layout does provide for an enormous galley by having the icebox to port with counter space beside it, but it is very stingy on seaberths so the salon settee would have to be made convertible to a berth. But for a couple or a single hander this might be an interesting arrangement, especially if a skylight is used to provide both light and much needed ventilation in the galley.

The true yacht interior of an owner-completed Ingrid puts to shame the ridiculous excuse some builders have for not selling unfinished boats because they don't want owner-finished boats giving their factory boats a bad name. Cecil Lange, who is without doubt one of the finest shipwrights on the continent, (and has sold many of his Cape George yachts unfinished) looked me straight in the eye and said about owner-builders, "You know, some of those buggers do a better job than me." Amen.

Construction

This is the most interesting part of the boat, for this is where Jerry has really done his homework, especially in the area of laminates.

Now it is a generally known fact that the mat, in the alternate mat/roving method, serves basically as a filler between the irregularities of the rather coarse roving layers, which, one would logically assume, would otherwise be filled with unreenforced resin. The resined mat does add some strength, but its random short fibres cannot compare to the tightly woven, heavily concentrated strands of a roving. Since the glass fibres of mat are not concentrated as are those of roving, a greater proportion of resin will build up in the mat compared to the roving, and we all know that it is the laminate with the highest fibreglass to resin ratio that is the strongest. Thus it makes sense that, given that you could have less resin buildup between two layers of roving than you could with a layer of mat between them — through some extremely careful squeegeeing which could in effect work the lumps of one layer of roving into the dimples of the other — then *layer for layer* an all roving hull will be much stronger than a hull which has alternate layers of mat and roving. In other words, a hull built up of six layers of roving only will be stronger than a hull having three layers of roving and three layers of mat. According to a study done by Gibbs and Cox, a very highly respected engineering firm in the field of fibreglass, an all roving hull will be fifty per cent stronger in flexural and tensile strength than a mat/roving hull, and that makes sense for you will be greatly increasing the overall fibre content. Even in compressive strength you will gain about eighteen per cent with the all roving lay-up. Again you must remember that this strength is gained through *substituting* roving for mat, and not by just *leaving out* mat.

If you haven't nodded off yet, there is more. Although it will result in a much stronger boat, you must remember that strength costs money, for roving per square foot is much more expensive than mat per square foot, and squeegeeing a hull by hand using a rubber squeegee is much slower, thus more expensive, than rolling it with a serrated brass roller with long handles. But per weight you will get a stronger hull and although it is virtually

impossible to tell how strong is really strong enough, it makes sense that a stronger hull will have better longevity through normal cruising use, and probably even a more noticeable longevity under extreme situations of over-strain, such as violently confused seas when much distorted force is placed on the hull, or in great winds when the rigging is threatening to abandon ship.

So if it is a very strong cruising boat you want, all things being equal, the Ingrid is one of the best, for her lamination schedule will leave even the most pessimistic among us shaking their heads. The lay-up goes like this: Gel, ¾ ounce mat, 7½ ounce cloth, ¾ ounce mat, then seven, count them, *seven* layers of 24 ounce roving topsides, two more layers of roving starting 1 foot above the waterline and down, with the last six layers doubled over the centre seam, and *six* extra layers down the stem and stern.

After the ballast is installed it is bonded over with a layer of mat and six layers of roving creating in effect a double bottomed boat. The deck and house are laid up with 1½ ounce mat, 7 ounce cloth, 24 ounce roving, 1½ ounce mat, ¾ inch balsa core, 1½ ounce mat, and three layers of 24 ounce roving. And that should be enough to hold up the Statue of Liberty.

The bulkheads used are a full 1 inch A.A. marine plywood (and these are almost heavy enough to substitute for the ballast) and they are *triple* bonded with roving to both the hull and deck with 12 inch wide strips, which is about thirty per cent wider and fifty per cent more than most people use. There is of course foam stripping between the bulkhead and the hull to avoid any hard spots, not that there would be any on this armour plate of a hull, but you might as well have it just in case. The joint of the hull and deck is made as waterproof as possible by bonding them together belowdecks with a layer of mat and *three* runs of roving. There is no "lip" on the hull — it continues almost straight up and instead the deck is turned up to form the bulwarks. The minimal space between them is filled with resin, then comes the bonding below, then the two hardwood bulwark boards are added, one outboard, one inboard, and these are bolted to each other, clamping tight the hull and deck in the process. So in effect you have two very good joining systems at work here; one using the mechanical fasteners, the other the chemical adhesion of the bonding. A note of caution if you are going to undertake the hull and deck joint bonding yourself: Bonding upside down has replaced Chinese water torture as the ultimate brain musher, so make sure you are totally at peace with yourself before you begin — practice yoga or take a bottle — and most certainly take a little brass roller to get all the air pockets out. Squeegeeing upside down is not recommended, resin will cascade quickly down your arms and set up in your pits. I'll say no more.

Overall, the Ingrid is a fine vessel indeed and certainly one of the best built boats in this book. There are over two hundred fibreglass Ingrids sailing from Alajuela and Blue Water combined, and countless lovely wooden ones. With the general integrity shown by Jerry Husted and the specs you saw above, his boats should stay together in even the most exuberant seas. When you are betting your life on something, you might as well stack your deck the best you can.

The annual gathering of Ingrid owners to exchange ideas, ogle and vent frustrations.

21

A Friend in the Dark Alley
Gillmer 31 & 39

It is interesting to look through the work of a designer whose career has spanned over four decades and find that although the designs vary enormously in detail, and certainly follow new steps in technology, something basically identifiable flows through them all, a unity or a style, what may best be described as a particular vision of what a yacht should look like. Thomas C. Gillmer, whose designs must by now number well over six hundred, must constantly have a vision of beautiful yachts before him, because every design of his that I have seen is a joy to behold.

I have never understood what it is about sheerlines that affect a viewer so, and I am not speaking of the obvious, that it is the single strongest visual element in a yacht, what I mean is, what earthly difference can it make to me whether the sheer is flat or springy, smooth or broken, balanced or rising, but it does and it's a lot of difference. There is something about a smoothly curved sheer with a goodly spring, something that reaches out to my eye and even deeper inside and says quietly, "friend." But show me a boat that has a long flat sheer and a straight stem to boot and I will show you a boat that says to me loudly, "I'm mean, go away." I am not just talking about

modern racers either, whose style befits their single task of speed, I am talking about those many sadly drawn cruisers whose lifeless lines make them look dead in the water.

Mr. Gillmer's yachts never do. You can spot his designs anywhere, like you can the mad bold strokes of Van Gogh, or the cautious smudges of Renoir, and when you spot one it says to you, "Step aboard, boy, we're gonna see the world." And if his designs stand out in a crowd, well, so does Tom Gillmer. In looking through a book of pictures of designers you will come across the pensive eyes of L. Francis, the kind grandfather face of Howard Chapelle, the boyish smile of friendly Billy Atkin, then you flip the pages and see Tom Gillmer there, and you yell out, "That's the guy. When I go into a dark alley at night, that's the guy I'm taking with me."

That Tom Gillmer draws tough, as well as beautiful, yachts has not gone unnoticed, for he has been chairman of both the Naval Engineering and the Naval Architecture departments at the U.S. Naval Academy. One of his early yachts, *Calypso*, designed almost forty years ago, was a portent of things to come from his drawing boards, for she was both hefty looking and sturdily built at 10 tons,

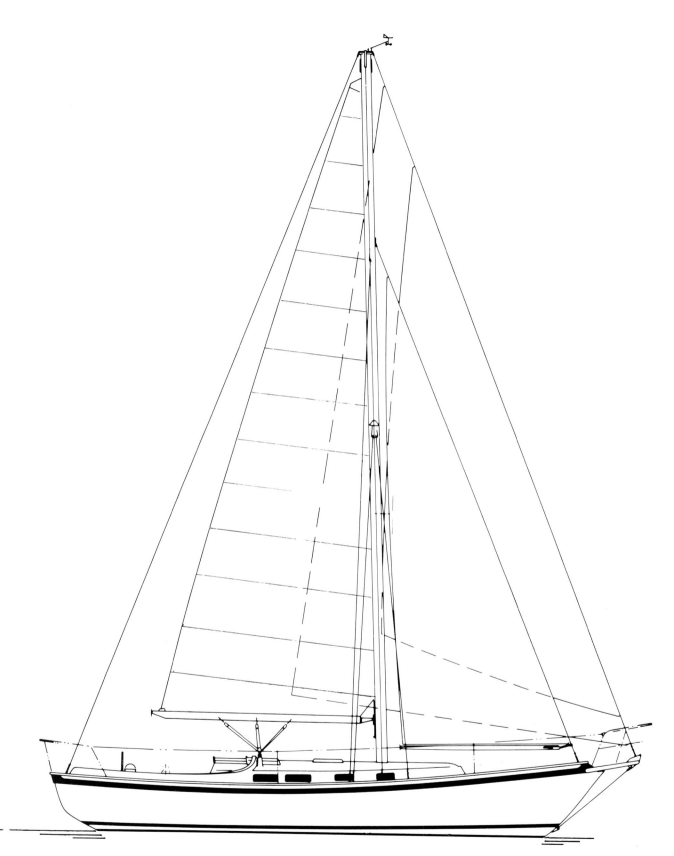

Gillmer 39 — Thomas Gillmer

LOA—38'7''   LWL—31'0''   Beam—12'1''   Draft—5'4''   Displ.—21,000 lbs.   Ballast—7,676 lbs.   Sail Area—835 sq. ft.

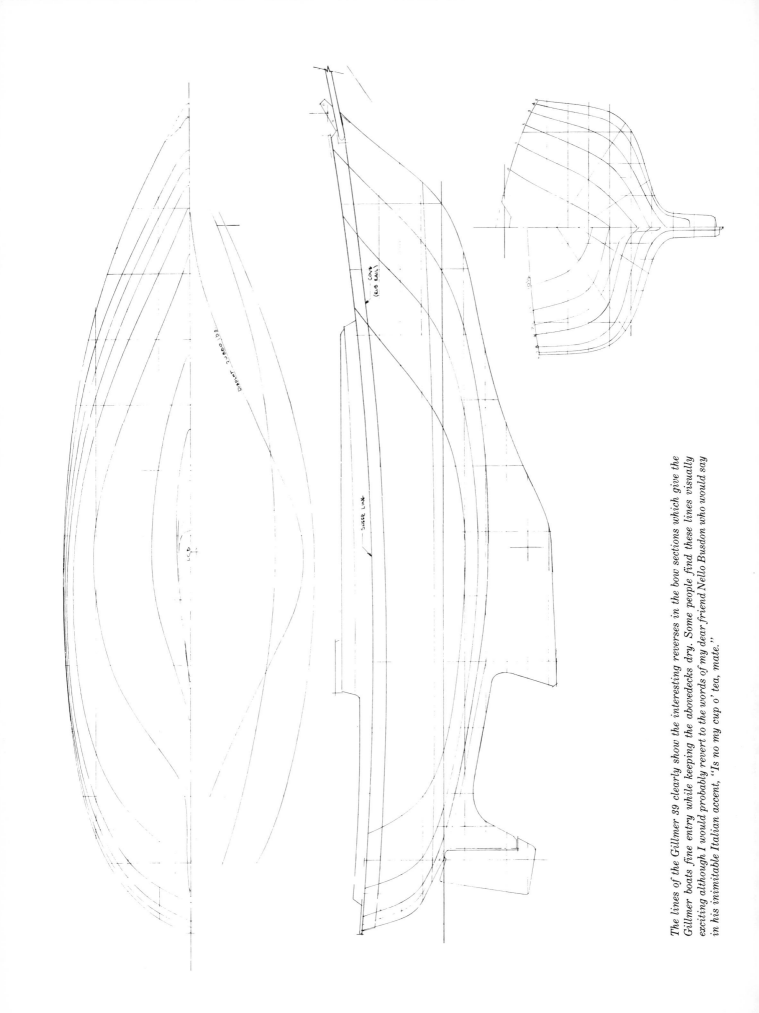

The lines of the Gillmer 39 clearly show the interesting reverses in the bow sections which give the Gillmer boats fine entry while keeping the abovedecks dry. Some people find these lines visually exciting although I would probably revert to the words of my dear friend Nello Busdon who would say in his inimitable Italian accent, "Is no my cup o' tea, mate."

with pesky lines, a fine sheer and high bow, but a bow that was slightly hollowed above the waterline for cutting through waves, and a rig that was big enough to move her well. Interestingly enough, close comparisons can be made between that beautiful *Calypso* designed in 1945 and the Gillmer 39 of some thirty-five years later. *Calypso's* critical dimensions were: waterline length — 31 feet, 3 inches; displacement — 10 tons; sail area — 827 square feet. The new Gillmer 39 has a waterline length of 31 feet, displacement of 10.5 tons and sail area of 835 square feet. This reminds me of something I wrote some years ago, "Many things have changed since the old days; but not the sea." And don't for a moment think that this makes Tom Gillmer old-fashioned or conservative, for both boats have a displacement-to-waterline-length ratio of about 320, which is considered medium-heavy even by today's standard, and a sail-area-to-displacement ratio of 17.3, — compare that to Ron Holland's Swan 371 at 15.6 and tell me who is conservative.

As a vote of utter confidence for the speed and reliability of Gillmer's designs, his Gillmer 39 (the Southern Cross 39 in real life) was chosen by Professor Marvin C. Creamer for a circumnavigation of the North Atlantic in a boat that would have absolutely no instruments aboard, to attempt to determine how the ancient navigators, the Norsemen and the Phoenicians found their way. When I say no instruments, I mean no instruments: no sextant, no compass, no radio, not even a watch. Professor Creamer used rough measurements of star distances for his navigation, hence the boat was aptly named *Navstar*.

Now Mr. Creamer was no novice adventurer, having had five previous transatlantic crossings, all done at a good clip, for he believes that "the safest passage is the fastest passage." He has had previous experience with Tom Gillmer's designs, having crossed the Atlantic a few times in *Scotia*, an Allied Seawind ketch designed by Mr. Gillmer, so he knew what he was getting into. That the passage of *Navstar* was a success is now a matter of history, as is its contribution to the world of navigation, and it is certainly another well-earned

feather in Tom Gillmer's cap.

Those wishing a semi-custom yacht of the essential Gillmer, are very much in luck indeed, for no fewer than four of his designs are currently being built by C. E. Ryder of Bristol, Rhode Island, and that's a good neighbourhood indeed, for they are just down the road from Shannon Yachts, who along with Hinckley are the known leaders in production boat building. But back to Tom Gillmer. The boats built by Ryder are all vintage Gillmer, lovely double-enders, ranging from 28 feet to 39 feet, with a 31 and 35 in between, and they come with a variety of sterns, from a moderate ended aft hung ruddered 31 to the full-buttocked 35 which is the newest of the line. The bows vary as well, with moderate spoons on the 28 and 31, and pinched flared bows with slight reverses in the upper part of the stem of the 35 and 39. The choice of under-bodies should please everyone too, for the 28, 35 and 39 have variations of moderately long fin keels and skeg rudders, while the oldest, the 31, has a full keel with a modestly cut away forefoot.

One thing that remains fairly basic, however, is the rig. All four boats are cutters, two having plentiful, one modest, and one hurricane-gulch-only sail areas, yet the largest mainsail of the bunch on the 39 is a very manageable 337 square feet. The new boats, the 35 and 39, have high aspect ratio mains, while the 31 is fairly long of foot, and the 28 falls somewhere in between. The 35 and 39 both have sail-area-to-displacement ratios of 17, which means they will move very well in light airs, while the 28 has a modest 14.5 ratio and only the 31 has a desperately low 12.7. This seems much too meagre for coastal cruising, although probably sufficient if one is to do nothing but sail in the Trades, for you should be able to nicely cruise there without reefing, on all but the most blustery of days, although with a ballast ratio of only 32 per cent you might be doing a lot of that sailing on your ear. As for the point of its being under-rigged, I just ran the numbers through on the Hiscocks' *Wanderer III* and came up with a sail-area-to-displacement ratio of 11.25, amazingly low I agree, but then I hear they did manage a few weekend trips of some length totalling a few hun-

The little Gillmer 31 with the typical Tom Gillmer wrap-around cockpit coaming. Her seakindly ends and long keel make her a joy at sea.

dred thousand miles, so maybe 12.7 isn't so low after all. But if you insist, I am sure the rig can be heightened even if a bit more ballast is needed to balance it. The newer boats of 35 and 39 have 40 per cent and 36 per cent ballast ratios respectively, with firm bilges and generally similar hull shapes.

Before I go too far with all this confusing data of mixing and matching four different boats, I suppose I might as well commit myself and pare the number down to two to make matters easier, and that being the case I pick the 31 and the 39 as my favourites and here is why. The 28 seemed just a little small in accommodation with a rather chopped up salon and little space for a chart table, while the 31 has enough volume to overcome these problems, and accommodate a much greater weight of stores. I much prefer the outboard rudder, for then the tiller is far aft, giving you good cockpit space, and the rudder is easily repairable and quite frankly, less likely to need repair with a deep keel in front of it for protection, especially since Tom Gillmer raised the 31's rudder well above the heel of the keel. All this reasonable stuff aside I must confess that I am a sucker for aft hung rudders. Apart from the above I very much like the extra 5 feet of waterline length that the 31 has over the 28, which gives her about 25 per cent greater hull speed. I would increase the rig on the 31, but that is no big deal since all concerned, Tom Gillmer, C. E. Ryder, and Metalmast Marine, who build the very good masts for these boats, are all flexible and creative people indeed.

As to the choice of the 39 over the 35, I have to say that the major influence has to be the accommodation potential, for the 39 has been modified to contain a private and workable aft cabin which gives us, as the saying goes, a brand new ball game.

Perhaps I tend to over-react to private cabins with unusual zeal, and if I do, I apologize broadly, but it was not until the fifteenth year of my life that I had a real room of my own, spending my first five thousand nights on front room sofas, so perhaps I exaggerate the importance of private places, but boy, there is nothing like a nook of your own where you can shut out the world and stare out the window and dream. I wouldn't trade all the pleasures of Sodom and Gomorrah for those times, although I must say that perhaps a fifty-fifty compromise would be the ultimately sensible approach.

As for the 35, I must say I do like the all in-

board rig she carries, for bowsprits are inherently impractical with extra fittings to wear and fail, and I did spend some time on a 35 and found it a very finely conceived and spacious yacht with a layout generally the same as that of the 31, with infinitely more room to move and to stow and to do all those things that most people like.

My one hesitation about the 39 is regarding the V-drive. Now I know it has worked well for many years, but again it is just one extra mechanical thing to go wrong, and no one will ever convince me that it is as foolproof as a hunk of a coupling with a few bolts. But then one can also argue that a transmission is more complex than a shaft coupling, yet I still depend on it, and to that all I can say is, "True, but why make a bad thing worse?"

The 31 I really like. This little boat, known as a Southern Cross 31 when finished by Ryder, seems to be the ideal cruising boat for a couple, whether it be local or extended cruising, and I somehow feel that Tom Gillmer would agree, for the 31 possesses that sense of beauty, simplicity and single-mindedness of function which Arthur Beiser, in his book *Proper Yacht*, called in reference to another Gillmer design, "That primary attribute of a ship — the ability to get from one place to another safely and efficiently." And I hope you won't think me presumptuous if I expand that to mean "without frightening the breakfast or the bejeesus out of the crew," which many boats have a habit of doing through thoughtless design, engineering and construction.

Now down to brass tacks. In case you've forgotten or have gotten lost in that mess of numbers in the beginning, the 31 has a 25 foot waterline, a beam of 9 foot 6 inches, a draft of 4 foot 7 inches, displacement of 13,600 pounds, ballast of 4,400 pounds and sail area of 447 square feet. As you can see from the drawings, the 31 has been thoroughly thought out; the keel is long for good directional stability and for careening in odd places; the cockpit well is small so that it holds little water; fresh water tanks and fuel tanks are of good size and are kept down low to aid the boat's stability; the rudder has ample surface, again down low where it is most likely to be out of turbulent water; the backstay has been split just above the boom so it can be based on the hull without the need for a boomkin; and even the weak sister of the rig, the bowsprit, has been made less vulnerable by being kept short and strong without the need of

A closer view of the 39 shows the enormously comfortable cockpit with all lines led well aft; the quarter wave is doing its best not to be left behind. The broad decks and high bulwarks make for a safe working platform at sea.

whisker stays being set port and starboard.

There can be no doubt that the rig of the 31 is designed to go voyaging. Tom Gillmer's drawing shows a single spreader rig with permanent intermediate stays to counter the pull of the staysails, and for a bit more reassurance, especially when beating hard, there are running backstays as well. Again a quick reminder for those who may have forgotten: a running backstay is called "running" because it is part of the running rigging and not the standing rigging. It is not used while the boat is running before the wind — quite the contrary — it is set up as mentioned on an extended hard beat when a staysail is putting much strain on the usually unsupported section of the mast. Most cruisers with cutter rigs have a substantial enough mast

section that the running backstays need not be set up during normal coastal cruising, but they do become necessary when the seas are running hard and the mast pumps heavily. That is when the most subversive strain is on the mast, and that is when it needs all the help it can get.

The traveller is cleverly set forward of the companionway hatch where it is out of everyone's way and leaves the bridgedeck free and clear, and most importantly it acts as a partial vang controlling the boom. This is not to suggest that a proper vang should be totally left out, especially on the run in heavy seas, for the best control can only be gotten by a vang that limits boom movement totally, which means a vang outboard of the boom, usually clipped to the toerail where the vang is pull-

Gillmer 31 — Thomas Gillmer

LOA—31'0"   LWL—25'0"   Beam—9'6"   Draft—4'7"   Displ.—13,600 lbs.   Ballast—4,400 lbs.   Sail Area—447 sq. ft.

ing against the mainsheet, rendering the boom immobile. On the other hand, the disadvantage of the traveller forward is twofold: minorly, it has only a short lever arm (say half the main boom) to work with, meaning it will put a hell of a load on the gear and the track and the house, and even more significantly a hell of a load on the person trying to tighten the mainsheet in a blow. But then the main is quite moderate on the 31, so perhaps it will work out all right. The major disadvantage of this location comes into play for single handers, who'll find they will have to leave the helm to adjust the sheet. Leading the sheet aft through a block system is possible but it will add much unnecessary friction to an already loaded system.

On a cruising boat the best reason to put the traveller up forward here (and with the coaming over the house it would appear that this is what Tom Gillmer had in mind) is to facilitate setting up a dodger over the house. If a permanent dodger of any width and height is required, setting the traveller on the bridgedeck is an impossibility. I did see one beautiful dodger engineered with tolerances the width of a gnat's facial hair; unfortunately something went amiss on the trial run and someone forgot to move the car over before they let the main fly and instead of the main it was the dodger that flew. Anyway, those are the pros and cons and I am afraid the choice is yours.

One piece of gear which will reap unquestionable approval is the split backstay, for it can be set up with a very simple tensioner giving you better control over the shape of the mainsail, and you can load your forestay by tightening your backstay, which will help keep the luff of your genoa tight and give it a better leading edge and make you sail just a bit faster.

On deck the 31 is simple and clean with a beautifully drawn cockpit coaming that continues over the house, and as mentioned, acts as a fine dodger base, as well as keeping stormy waters from coming back into the cockpit, setting lines and cushions adrift.

The cabin house has the mandatory full run of grabrails, and plenty of holes by the way of opening ports and three hatches — one over the salon — for good ventilation and lots of light below.

Belowdecks

The galley is generously laid out with double sink and large icebox and enough room for the cook to stay out of the traffic. Storage is plentiful, especially with the thoughtful placement of a drawer and a door on the inboard end of the sink island. Were these placed on the aft face of that island they would be very hard, if not impossible, to open once the boat was on a heel and the gimballed stove had swung into the way. I am convinced that it is this kind of thoughtful detailing that shows attention to every position of the boat, that separates a true architect of yachts from a designer of mobile homes, whose boats work fine on a stable parking lot, but get them out to sea, brother, and it's Katie bar the door.

The rest of the layout is not to my liking, and of course this is the beauty of a semi-custom yacht, that you can do what you please as long as you stay within a few structural limits. First, there is something that I find not so pleasant about an asymmetrical layout; it seems to create a feeling of unsettledness, which is the last thing I need on a boat. Interestingly enough, in this case what causes the asymmetry, also causes a structural aberration, and here I refer to the dog's leg bulkhead which stabilizes the mast support. I say mast support because the mast is stepped on the house and the loading is transferred to the keel by the compression post or mast support. That this post not wander away is critical, and although I don't really believe the one as shown has much more wanderlust than a single solid athwartships bulkhead, I would still think that it is easier to separate two stones than one stone. So let's move first stones first and slip the main bulkhead back where the good Lord intended it and turn the head athwartships into a narrow little booth, for which you will have enough room if you knock a couple of inches off that 77 inch berth. The head sink will have to take a walk, either across the passage to where the hanging locker now is, or it can be made into a slide-out type of affair which can live outboard of the head when stowed and slide out above the head when needed. The starboard settee can then be moved up to the main bulkhead, opening up the area across from the sinks for a proper chart

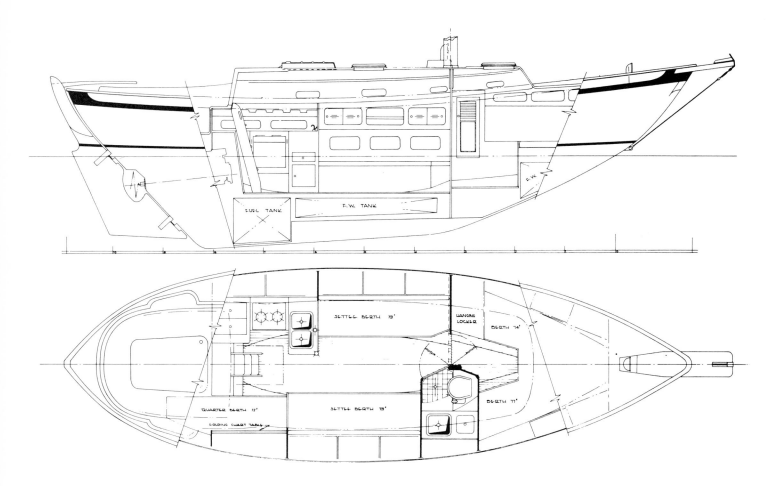

The Gillmer 31 is a first class basic cruiser with an outboard rudder, long keel, clean low house and protected cockpit. The interior would gain by splitting the head athwartships, moving the starboard salon berth up and making room for a permanent chart table at the head of the quarterberth. All tankage has been kept blissfully low.

table of either the sit-down or stand-up variety. Now that we have chainsawed Mr. Gillmer's interior, let me close by saying that the engine room is well laid out with good access around the engine, and most importantly, *above* the engine, which lets you crawl aft and do your dirty deeds.

The Gillmer 39

To begin at the beginning, the 39 has a waterline of 31 feet, a beam of 12 feet 11 inches, a draft of 5 feet 4 inches, displacement of 21,000 pounds, ballast of 7,676 pounds and sail area of 836 square feet, which translates into sail-area-to-displacement ratio of over 17, and a displacement-to-waterline-length ratio of 320 which should give you a lovely comfortable motion. The rig we have talked about, and it is much the same as the 31's, with an intermediate stay to balance the staysail (which here is clubfooted), and a short bowsprit.

The backstay is now one piece and this is made possible by the fact that the rudder has been moved under the counter instead of being outboard.

The underbody of the 39 is vastly different from that of the 31, with a long fin keel, a fairly high aspect ratio rudder, and a strong generous skeg. Combined with lines that are hollowed forward and have good fullness in the buttocks, she will be a powerful and weatherly boat. With the tall rig, her mast is stepped on the keel.

On deck the layout of the 39 is beautiful. The decks are broad, protected by high bulwarks, and the cockpit is spacious, protected by coamings that do create a rather large well. She does have an enormously buoyant stern as you can see in the photo, nevertheless sure is sure, and if serious voyaging is to be contemplated, perhaps it would not be a sign of overcautiousness if a couple of 1½ inch drains were installed in the seats themselves

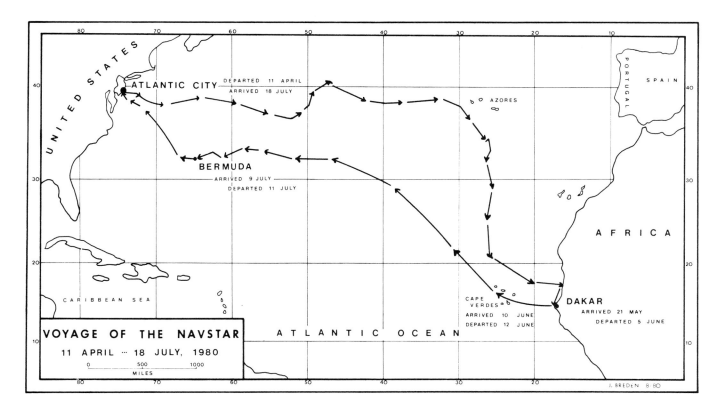

The voyage of the Navstar, a Gillmer 39, without sextant, compass or even a watch, was made to try to confirm theories of how ancient navigators like the Vikings and Phoenicians managed accurate and successful sea-journeys.

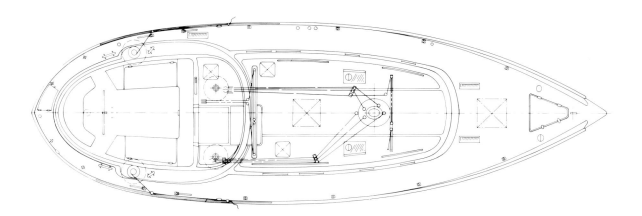

The Gillmer 39 deck plan shows a beautifully drawn cockpit with the sheet winches accessible to the single-hander, and comfortable space for a goodly crew. Tom Gillmer believes in plenty of light and air belowdecks; note skylight hatch in main cabin with three additional small transparent hatches over aft-cabin, head and galley. The side and foredecks have three additional deck prisms and the two Dorade boxes on the house show transparent tops.

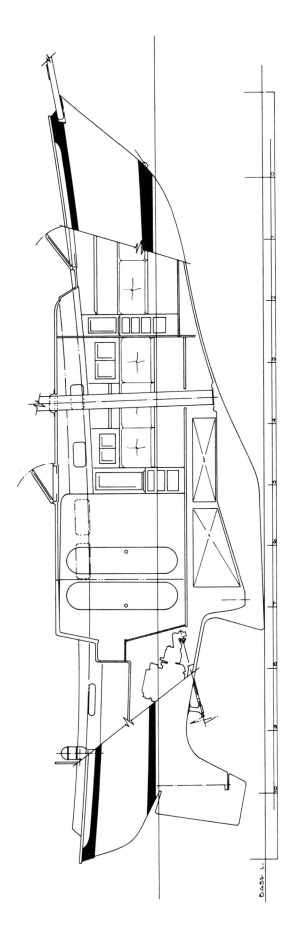

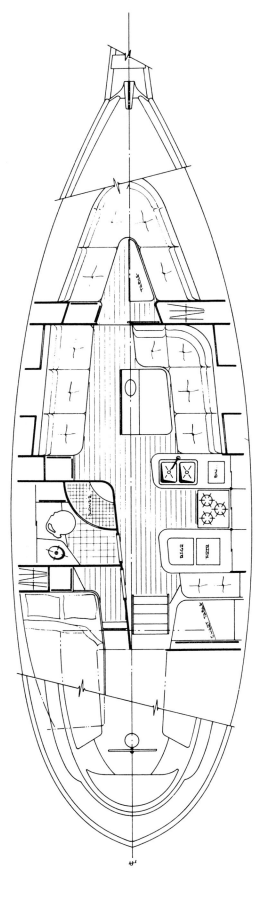

The efficient split underbody of the Gillmer 39 belies her classic exterior. The interior is one of the best realized ones I have seen in any boat under 40 feet with a usable aft cabin, ideal chart table, safe U-shaped galley and large open salon. The forepeak has its own little table for when you want to hide away and read or write.

in addition to the cockpit drains. These could drain via through-hulls well above the waterline so they would be no structural threat to the boat. To balance this off I must say that I have steered a Westsail 32 in ten to fifteen foot seas on a dead run for over twenty-four hours and got no major water over the stern, which is much less buoyant than that of the 39, and has a few inches less freeboard and no cockpit coaming to boot. So, who knows?

The 39 has a beautifully drawn house, good ventilation and light, and if it sounds like I am in a rush to get below, then you are right because belowdecks she is really something to behold.

Belowdecks

The most striking feature as you step belowdecks is the oak interior, made up of magically curved corners and oval bulkhead openings. It is without doubt one of the most innovative interiors on the continent, utilizing the warmth of wood and some space-age technology called "vacuum moulding," which somehow takes a steamed piece of plywood, opens its great big mouth, and sucks the plywood into a curve, something like the way you used to stretch a hunk of balloon over your mouth and suck a little baby ball into it. Now is that a lucid, scientific explanation, or what?

Before I forget, I should mention that the interior was conceived by Peter Van Lancker, who graduated from the Rhode Island School of Design. The work is first class and certainly feels yachty in its own way. As you can see from the photos, the galley is a cookie's dream with even an elegant dish rack hanging above the icebox.

The aft cabin to port has a good sized berth with enough room to get in and close the door, and it even has a hanging locker. The head is straightforward and spacious, and the chart table aft is large enough for a model train set. The aft cabin is of course massaged into the boat by having the companionway slightly off-centre.

The salon has an L-shaped dinette — which makes into a double berth — and the very nicely conceived centre table has a portside leaf that reaches all the way to the port settee so a great number of people can be seated for dinner. The forepeak has a very large double berth with a massive chest of drawers to port and a large locker or a seat, or whatever you prefer, starboard.

With the tanks in the bilges, there is ample stowage below the settees, and as you can see there are very fine small lockers everywhere, including the whole end of the sink island which opens up to reveal a first class liquor cabinet. This cabinet is mounted on a long piano hinge so that you can go ahead and load it up and it won't come crashing down. I almost forgot. The whole starboard quarter of the boat is available for stowage, giving excellent room for sails, fenders, etc. The access to the engine is good through double doors behind the companionway ladder.

One small note before we leave. Aside from the obvious eyeful that the interior is, it is the small things that make it first class, like the good high searails and table fiddles, the overhead grabrails in the salon, the stainless steel rod in front of the stove, the handholds routed into the sides of the companionway ladder, and the handgrips flanking the companionway opening. In all, she is a fine combination of a most seaworthy yacht with excellent performance characteristics and an interior that is so beautiful you will hardly ever want to go topsides.

Construction

It has been known broadly through the industry that Ryder has been doing excellent glass work for many years. They have had good experience in custom boat building, which has allowed them opportunity for experimentation, a diversion not available to most production boatyards, who, once they lock onto a system, cling to it for dear life to keep the line going.

There is nothing spectacular about the construction of Ryder's yachts except that they are very good industry standard (see Luders 34) with one-piece hull moulds and hand-laid-up laminations, good squeegeeing and beautifully faired underbody appendages. The internally cast ballast is well filled all around with a resin based filler so there can be no movement. The bulkheads are well bonded in, although I did see one whose top was not bonded to the deck — why, I don't know — for what you will actually do if you bond everything, is build an almost indestructible honeycomb, whereas the other thing will — if not tomorrow or the day after, then one day — shake itself loose.

The hull can be had with the foam core if you prefer, but whichever way you get it, you get foam between your bulkheads and the hull, to guard

The rounded plywood cabinets of the Gillmer 39, made possible by an advanced engineering technique called vacuum moulding, which, as close as I can figure, is akin to stretching a hunk of balloon over your lips and sucking until you're blue in the face.

Looking aft in the 39 over all the moulded oak cabinetry. The first oval door aft leads to the head, the second to the large aft cabin.

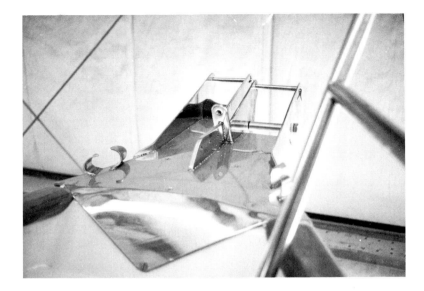

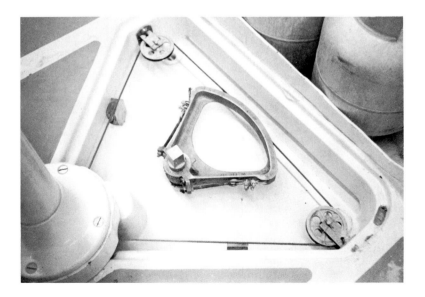

The fine engineering of the Ryder yachts as shown by the tightly tooled anchor well, double stainless steel anchor rollers and a removable lid over the steering apparatus for easy maintenance and repair.

against potential hard spots, and that is the way it should be.

The hull is reenforced with extra runs of mat and two rovings in the chainplate areas, a 4 foot wide run that goes from sheer to sheer.

The hull-to-deck joint is done in an interesting fashion in that the hull flange is turned out, not in, so that nuts and washers are put on the bolts (which are ¼ inch on 8 inch centres, but 4 or 6 would be better) on the outside, and remain accessible for adjustment later on. The teak caprail fits over the head of the bolts and the lip turns down from the deck, which not only hides the nuts in profile but also helps to keep the decks drier in a seaway. The decks are hand-laid-up as well, and balsa-cored everywhere except the foredeck, which is mostly plywood where the windlass bolts through.

The tanks are externally built fibreglass, all gelcoated inside and bonded into place.

As I mentioned, the interior finish is excellent, even down to the tops of bunks which are hidden by cushions; even here very good mahogany plywood is used. Small touches, like the large piano-hinged double lids over the sail locker bin, (under the double berth in the forepeak) make it much easier to use than a free-floating lid. To ensure longevity a big 3 inch by 3 inch reenforcing beam runs down the centre of the hole on which the lid's free ends sit. And everything that is accessible is bonded in. Bronze seacocks and through-hulls are the norm, with teflon slides on berths for easy and long lasting operation. The floor timbers are solid mahogany, the engine pans are very heavily built and it even has pockets for tools and spares. The plumbing and wiring are neatly laid out and well secured. The counters on the boats with oak interiors have a kick space beneath them so you won't destroy the oak plywood, and all cabinetry is finely finished inside, as well as out. The only liner in the boat is a very nicely tooled one for the head compartment, with well engineered shelves.

The bow has a monstrous sized and very well crafted double anchor roller on the 35 and 39; the rigging is ½ inch Navtec rod, and, as mentioned, the masts are works of art by Metalmast Marine. The masts sport a collar around them at deck level for blocks to lead halyards aft to the cockpit. Ryder has developed a very nice anchor-well mould which sits vertically in the deck, leaving the deck structurally more sound with such a small cutout. The well snugly houses a good sized Danforth anchor.

The low profile hatches are very nicely tooled, with an equally low profile main hatch dodger, and I almost forgot that the coaming on the house for the spray dodger has little slots tooled into it to allow the halyards to be fed aft without interrupting the pretty line of the teak capping over it or disrupting the dodger itself.

So there you have it. Take your pick, and as best as I can tell, you will have a beautiful and solid craft for a long, long time.

22

Way Down Yonder
Frers 40

For someone who loves sailboats there is probably no better place in the world to be than Antigua in April, for boats come here from all ends of the earth (old schooners and new cat ketches, and old sleek yawls and new flat racers) and they are stern-tied to the stone quay beside the cannons that Lord Nelson left behind, and you can walk and stare and feast your eyes or you can sit on the deck of the old hotel and sip Pina Coladas and feast your eyes from there.

As I walked among all this colour and opulence and carnival a few years back a small white yawl caught my eye. She was modest and graceful, with broad teak decks and a refined low house, and all her brightwork glowing, and I fell in love with her on the spot. The owner must have seen that on my face for he invited me aboard, and I ogled at the fine bits of thought and the loving bits of craftsmanship, and upon leaving he told me the designer's name: German Frers.

That was of course German Frers Sr., but the name has grown to mythical proportions in my brain, and when a few years later I saw a beautiful black racer designed by his son, the memories of that English Harbour lady came back to me at once.

German Frers Jr. learned to draw beautiful boats by watching his father draw beautiful boats, and he watched him as a young boy in Argentina and learned from him as a young man. He went to New York at the age of twenty-five to work with Sparkman and Stephens, and there he learned some more, and three years later he went out on his own and opened up an office on the floor of his one room apartment, where he lived and worked with his expectant wife, and when things went badly they went home to Argentina where things didn't go much better for a while, until he got to design a boat for a Brazilian architect, which was seen under construction at the Palmer Johnson yard by a Michigan curtain rod maker who decided that he had to have one too, and that boat was *Scaramouche*, and then things started rolling, and now ten years later there are three designers whose boats dominate the Grand Prix sailing circuits of the world and one is Ron Holland, the other Doug Peterson and the third is German Frers Jr.

German Frers Jr.'s boats are not always the fastest, but they are usually the most beautiful, and once you have understood beauty, whether you end up drawing racing boats or wheelbarrows the beauty will still come through.

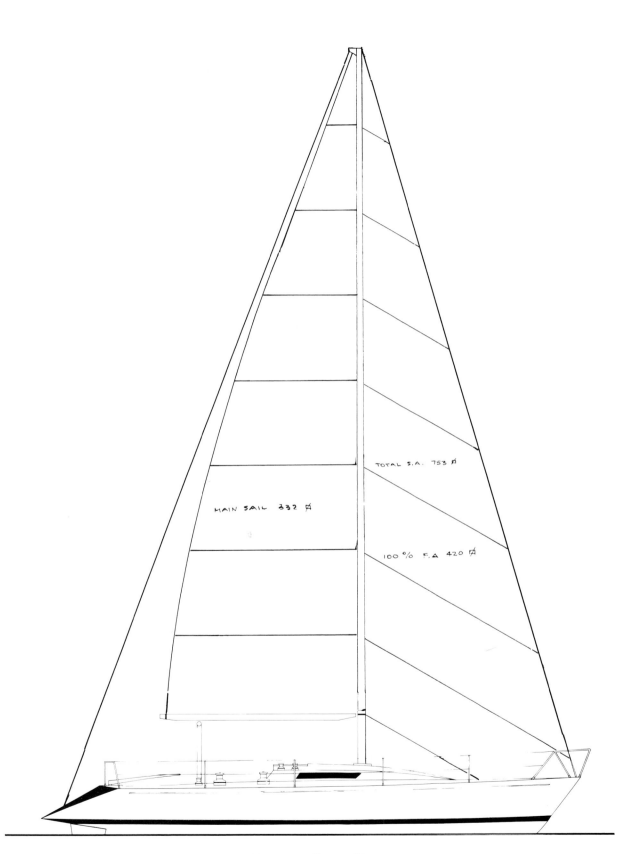

TOTAL S.A. 753 ☐

MAIN SAIL 332 ☐

100 % F.A 420 ☐

Frers 40 — German Frers

LOA—40'0"   LWL—34'0"   Beam—12'6"   Draft—7'6"   Displ.—15,000 lbs.   Sail Area—753 sq. ft.

With today's racers looking as distorted as they do, one would have to reach pretty deep before a word like beautiful would surface, but racing boats should be looked at in a world of their own, and they should be looked upon with some respect, for they do work most efficiently with the wind and the sea, and the advanced ideas and notions they pioneer do one day come to benefit all sailors.

The Frers 40 is an example of an advanced design, not just in terms of performance but in structural innovations as well. The first of this design was the much contested *Acadia* who came in second overall and first in class in the Admiral's Cup (only to have that result changed to third overall, but still first in class, after a protest and measurement) and although she reveals nothing particularly revolutionary in looks, what with the long devil's-tongue stern and high aspect ratio fin and rudder and a dead flat bottom (see section drawing), her engineering is certainly exemplary, and more of that later.

That the Frers 40 is designed as a pure racer there is no doubt — topsides her creature comforts are nil and her belowdeck accommodations make even a Spartan long for the luxury of his home — but as a single purpose machine she is absolutely perfect. Her bow will knife through the water, while her flat bottom will keep her atop it as much as possible and in ideal circumstances bring her near planing, as well as allow maximum profile height for the keel to help her claw to windward.

On deck the Frers 40 is wonderfully simple. After having written about backrest heights, and seat depths and coaming angles and such, one feels like an idiot looking at the Frers, for everything has been pared away and designed down to its utmost functional simplest.

The house is but a short sliver providing excellent broad clear decks for working, and the cockpit is but a foot-well without any obstructions over which the crew could trip. Apart from the tracks and winches, there is simply nothing else aboard. Excuse my oversight for I almost forgot the six bits of kindling strewn aft in some moment of frivolity. You can see these on the deck layout plan as long pyramid-shaped things. There are two either side of the tiller and two more in the crew-pit sole. These are braces for the crew (in the pit) and for the helmsman (by the tiller) helping them

remain in place and helping their feet find a firm hold. If you are a little puzzled by the helmsman's slats, then remember that this is a racing boat and all the weight of the crew should be on the high side as much as possible, so it is important to get and keep the helmsman way outboard as well.

While we are back here we might as well discuss the tiller. You may be surprised to find a tiller on a boat this size but remember that a tiller has even more advantages for a racer than for a cruiser. First, of course, there is always the matter of cost, although on a racer a couple of thousand dollars is a drop in a large bucket, but much more important is the simple fail-proof steering that the tiller provides. Both of the above are important factors for the cruiser, but for the racer there is even more, having to do with weight, for not only does a tiller weigh much less than a wheel with its assorted apparatus, but weight will also be saved in construction, for there will be no need to reenforce the deck for pedestals, blocks, etc. Furthermore the weight of the helmsman can be manipulated as ballast for he too can hike out to the high side with the rest of the crew by using a tiller extension, a performance rather difficult on a boat with a wheel unless the helmsman has had a goodly amount of practice steering with his toes braided around the steel rim. And lastly, and this is nearly as important for cruisers as for racers, your visibility both forward and to windward, is much better if you are up high and outboard by the lifelines, instead of down low sitting behind a wheel. If you're still not convinced, I give up.

The Frers 40 is no ultra-light at 15,000 pounds displacement (it weighs in around 13,700 pounds) on a 34 foot waterline, which gives her a displacement-to-waterline-length ratio of 172, considerably heavier than a Santa Cruz 50 at 67. Her sail area is 753 square feet with a 332 square foot main and a 420 square foot 100 per cent fore triangle. Her sail-area-to-displacement ratio is within a hair of 20 which ought to make her a very good light air sailer, again no ultra-light type skimmer, but then ultra-lights don't go as well to windward and are not designed to rules or ratings.

The rig of the 40 is a state of the art triple spreader Stearn rig, and Stearn seems to be a top mast maker on the East Coast much as Sparcraft is on the West. With the triple spreaders, the 40 has double running backstays for optimum mast

control and of course she has the standard hydraulic gear for backstay, vang and babystay.

Belowdecks

This should take about a sentence and a half. As you can see there are some strong beliefs at work on this interior. According to Frers, he was the first to really give much thought to weight distribution. He said in the interview with *Nautical Quarterly*, "I tried to keep the crew in the same position fore and aft, whether on deck or below . . . This was the first boat with bunks aft and the galley forward. That's a rating advantage as well as a performance advantage, because you measure the boat in bow down trim, and then you get the boat back and trim with people." Thus the head and galley are up front with light pipe berths aft of them. The rest of the interior appointments include an engine, companionway-ladder and a chart table and that is all — everything you need to make a boat go and no more. There is no icebox aboard but there is a provision in front of the engine for a portable type of ice-chest. The ladder is aluminum for lightness and the interior finish is raw fibreglass — or if you want to be pampered — paint.

There is one point worthy of discussion here and that is the use of pipe berths. These are of course extremely light weight, just tubing and canvas, and set up so that they can be set either flat or at 20 or 30 degrees, depending on your angle of heel, so that in effect you can sleep comfortably on a flat surface regardless of the boat's plane. This beats the hell out of sleeping wedged into a trough against the hull or dangling from canvas leeboards. It's a more restful way to sleep, for your muscles will spend less effort bracing and shoring. The disadvantage to a cruising boat, using pipe berths instead of fixed berths, will be that the hull-reinforcement which a built-in berth provides will be lost, but this can be replaced by either partial bulkheads or reenforcing beams which are coming right up under *Construction*.

Construction

For those interested in how a state of the art racing boat is put together, the following few pages will be a treat, for others it might be a total bore; you stand warned.

The Frers 40 is built by Tom Dreyfus in New Orleans at his boatyard appropriately named New Orleans Marine. He has built a great number of one-off racers and cruisers, and now builds the racers designed by Frers and Doug Peterson. Tom's basic thoughts about boat building in general and about his own boats in particular are revealed a bit later in the conversation I had with him, so for now let me just tell you what I saw aboard one of his almost complete Frers 40's.

The first impression you get as you go below and see all the exposed structure is, "My God, someone sure knows how to build boats." Basically a Tom Dreyfus boat is a thin shell built of extremely strong unidirectional roving (not woven in two directions like standard roving) and reenforced with a monstrous network of longitudinal and transverse fibreglass beams. These beams are bonded directly to the hull along their entire length so that the skin or hull itself becomes a part of the structure. Now when I say beams I mean beams, for these things are 5 inches wide at the base (the part that fits flush against the hull) and they are 3 inches in thickness. Their tops taper to 2 inches in width. Some of these are not unlike stringers in wood boats, but there are a lot more of them (six in the sides of the hull alone) — one every 18 inches longitudinally, and one every 12 inches running transversely in the keel-chainplate areas where much of the stress is found. But even forward of the ¾ inch thick main bulkhead there is a profusion of transverse beams, run in conjunction with the three partial bulkheads (which are left full through the crown) located forward of the main bulkhead. These ½ inch bulkheads are no more than 44 inches apart, and they are not relied on for support in the conventional way only (which would mean bonding them directly to the hull and leaving a potential hard edge) but instead they are all set atop and bonded to transverse beams of the same 5 inch by 3 inch monster dimensions. Now that is good boat building.

Aside from the six longitudinals on the hull sides, there are two 12 inch high plywood longitudinals, totally bonded over, running the entire length of the boat. These are about 4 feet apart and between them are two more megabeams also running the full length of the boat. These two

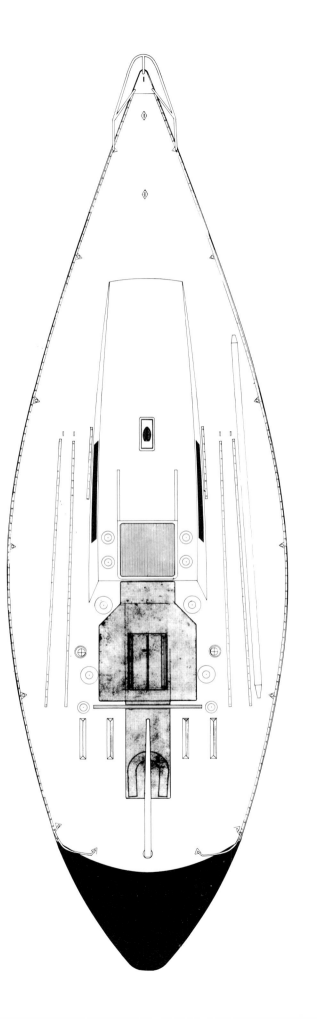

German Frers at his best and simplest with a forward deck so clean there's nothing for even a gnat to trip over. The helmsman sits in the cockpit-well only downwind, while at other times with the help of a tiller extension and the little teak foot braces he can hike out to the high side with the rest of the crew. The Frers 40 could just be one of the most beautifully drawn racers around.

beams are 14 inches apart and flare a little wider in the stern where they become the bedlogs for the engine to sit on. Tom tells us later just how strong this system has proven to be. As if this wasn't enough, Tom reenforces the keel bolts, not with ordinary single washers but with a series of 2¼ inch by 10 inch plates ¼ inch thick, each of which couples two bolts together.

The main bulkhead is the base for the chainplate. It is made of ¾ inch plywood that is reenforced on both sides, almost in its entirety, with multiple layers of unidirectional roving (that run well onto the hull and onto the overhead) that are built up to a thickness of 3/16 either side — as thick as the hull. To this monolith you attach the chainplates made of a ⅝ inch thick piece of stainless steel, backed up by a similar shape of 3/16 inch stainless. The plates are bolted to each other through the bulkhead with ten stainless steel bolts ⅝ inches in diameter. Tom comments later on how well these have held.

The house sides are solid ¼ inch fibreglass, and the decks and house top are reenforced with balsa. The hull-to-deck joint is the now familiar, through-bolted flange, using the aluminum toerail as backup.

The tube that houses the rudder shaft is well laid-up fibreglass, laminated solidly to the hull below and the deck above, and a nice reenforcing touch is added with sets of gussets (knees) on both top and bottom to help the tube stay in place. Outside, the good engineering continues, from the massive but light aluminum tiller, to the stern and bow fittings. To keep down weight, these are made of aluminum, but to keep them from wearing where the stainless hardware attaches to them, they are sleeved (the holes are lined) with stainless steel inserts.

I've talked with Tom Dreyfus about his boats, and I include part of a conversation here. I left it intact because to leave out his own words with their wonderful Southern energy would be cheating the reader.

F: Well, I went through the Frers 40 and I was very impressed with the construction ideas.

T: Thank you. I must say that we have done all our own engineering on all the boats we have done.

F: Tom, what comes to you from Frers or Peterson? What do you actually get as far as con-struction goes, what kind of instructions?

T: Well, they kind of trust me now, so I say to them, just give me my lines and offsets and tell me what you want the boat to weigh — what would you like the hull and deck to weigh basically. Normally they will say "as light as you can make it." Well, as you could see by that boat, it is not the lightest boat in the world. I do not want to be known as the lightest boat builder in the world, I want to be known as the best boat builder in the world. I figure there is a happy medium between being light and being strong. The sister ship to Jack's boat went on Northwest Rock going to Bermuda this year.

F: *Acadia?*

T: That's right. Now called *Rolling Tide.* And I was talking to Dave Pegas up in Newport last week. They calculate that that boat was reaching at between 8¼ and 8½ knots and had a number two up and reefed main...Blowing about 28 - 30 over the deck, and they went from 8½ to a dead stop in six inches. I mean it broke ribs, fractured skulls, all that kind of crap.

F: People's ribs?

T: Oh yes. When they finally got it off, *no* structural damage at all. Didn't leak, didn't spring the keel, didn't spring the rudder, it finally got off the rocks, and of course it tore up about the first three feet of the keel and then it got hung on the rudder and tore off the last foot and a half...the rudder...bent it at a 75 degree angle, the propeller strut and the shaft got all mangled, but Pegas said he could not find one evidence of structural foul up. So I must say that they are not the lightest boats in the world. But the pedigree... obviously they win races, I mean *Acadia, Crude,* you name them, *Swampfire, Gonnagetcha,* all the boats we've built have all won good races, but I don't really feel that you have to go that light to get the desired results. The thing we have been pushing for a long time, not so much to the industry, I mean I've never written any letters on the subject, except to the customers, I keep telling them — look, these cored boats and all this stuff you are buying are not going to be around in ten years.

F: Did you ever build cored boats?

T: One.

F: And, what happened?

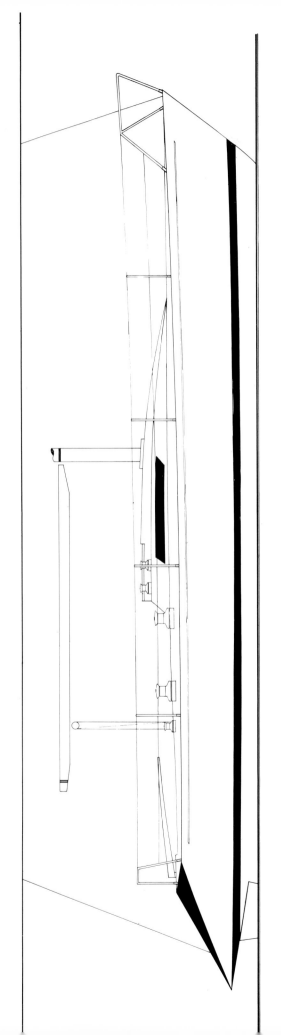

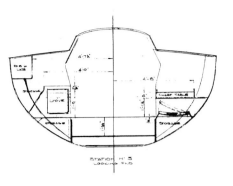

T: That was the worst, I felt . . . we have done —
which is not an empirical study by any means,
just a reference. We use that string test. A
relative test. The worst boats I have tested
were the cored boats.

F: You mean the string over the deck test?

T: Right. I tie the string to the pulpit and to the
back, make a mark on the mast, pump up to
6,000 pounds on the hydraulics and see how
much the hull deflects. That's a relative test.
The worst boats I've ever gotten were the
cored boats. I mean, I was so proud of ³⁄₁₆ inch
deflection that we built a Britton Chance one
tonner, oh, very esoteric too, carbon fibre and
Kevlar, all that bull, and it bent a full ¾ inch.
Look at *Evergreen*. It was supposed to be the
state of the art core boat. I just put a string test
on her this weekend up in Newport; she's bending 1¼ inches with 6,000 pounds. On the other
hand *Kahula*, which is a sister ship to both
Acadia and Jack's boat, at 6,000 pounds only
deflected ⅜. The boat that came off the rocks. . .
did a test to it up there — what's this guy's
name, has a shipyard up there in Rhode Island
— I forget his name, he's a new big brain up
there. Anyway, he put the test on it. It only
deflected ⅜. He put a test on it and he's a boatbuilder and very critical . . . Reeves Potts is his
name. He used to be a 12 metre guy on
Freedom, one of the winch grinders, and now
he's working with some guy in a shipyard up
there in Rhode Island some place.

F: Tom, when did you start building boats?

T: Back in 1971. As I understand it, New Orleans
Marine is the oldest custom glass builder in the
United States. We don't do any repair work, we
are not on the water, we don't have a haul out
service, we don't have winter storage, all we do
is build custom boats . . . Only done custom
boats for eleven years.

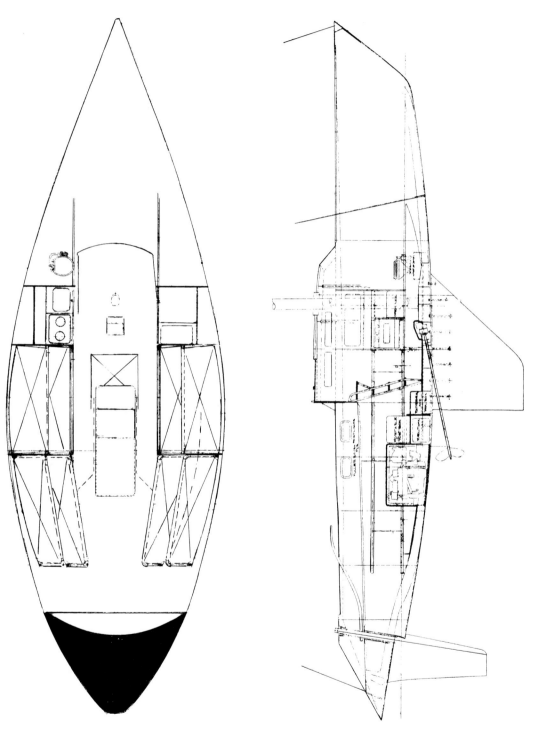

The lean underbody of the Frers 40 with a long overhang for rating combined with good water separation. The hydraulic drive shown has been replaced by a V-drive, but the light eight pipe berth interior with minimal galley and navigation areas have been left intact.

F: Mostly racing boats?

T: Mostly. We've done some cruisers of course, and we've done a lot of tooling, like for the Hunter 54 and for the New York 40. And we did the original Peterson 34. We've done a lot of tooling for people.

F: You said that some people use a lot of esoteric stuff. Do you use Kevlar or carbon fibre?

T: *Louisiana Crude* was built with Kevlar and carbon fibre.

F: Did someone come to you and say, 'We want to use Kevlar and carbon fibre?'

T: Well, I keep my ears to the ground too, you know. The first of the guys to come out with all this stuff was Britton Chance. Brit started trying all this stuff. I tried it with Brit, and then we decided we didn't think Kevlar was any good. I still don't think Kevlar has an application yet. Carbon fibre yes, I think carbon fibre in decks . . .

F: What's wrong with Kevlar?

T: Where would you want to use Kevlar? I mean, what would be the reason for using Kevlar?

F: What did Chance say to use it for?

T: Well, he thought it was strong and was going to be lighter, but it wasn't.

F: What about the Holland boat built for . . . the big realtor out west in Los Angeles?

T: Kilroy.

F: His new *Kialoa* has a lot of Kevlar.

T: So he made a mistake. I mean, it's not my fault . . . It'll jack up the price of the boat. I don't think it's necessary. It has a very high impact resistance. But look at it this way — you get back to how strong is strong.

F: Well, a Santa Cruz went on the rocks here. They were doing about 9 knots, plus the current was running, so it was about 12 - 14 knots — and they broke her back. Yet somebody ran a string test on her too and she only bent half an inch at 4,000 pounds.

T: Oh, I'd bet it was much more than that.

F: This is a local guy that did the string test.

T: Much more than that. I guarantee with 5 - 6,000 pounds, you can't hold headspace straight in those . . . I'm not knocking the design. The design is good for what it's meant to be, but you can't go upwind, and it's a very bendy boat.

F: Getting back to you, what is your concept of boat building?

T: My concept is single skin, longitudinally framed with various intercostal transverse frames. That would be our concept of building boats. We want to keep the boat as simple and as inexpensive as we can, yet maintain, you know, the Grand Prix esoteric type of winning thing that everybody's after.

F: Is the hull mostly UDR?

T: Mostly UDR.

F: Is the mat skin on the outside?. . .

T: No mat.

F: What do you use for skin?

T: We just use UDR.

F: How many layers do you use on the average?

T: It varies. Something we always use is unidirectional roving. We use a certain percentage longitudinally and a certain percentage athwartships. You have to design the scantlings to whatever boat you are building.

F: Say in the 40 foot range, how many layers of UDR would you use?

T: Again I can't answer, because it depends on what weight UDR we are using. We've got 15 ounce, 13 ounce, 11, 12 ounce. What we do is, we try to develop a skin of roughly $\frac{3}{16}$ thick. We know a certain thickness is so strong and that's what we go for. Certain areas require more and then we never go much less than $\frac{3}{16}$.

F: When you are running UDR do you usually run it like 45-45-45?

T: No, we use zero-90.

F: Are those foam logs inside those big longitudinals and transverse beams?

T: Just non-structural urethane foam inside, and it's all UDR all over those as well. In our decks we use balsa core and Klegicell. Klegicell is probably the most popular these days.

F: What does that do that balsa doesn't?

T: Well, Klegicell is a lot lighter than balsa, and has a lot less absorption rate. It's got some structural strength, but . . . all it is, is the web of a beam separating the two skins.

F: Just reading little things in my notes, like the rudder, how you have around the shaft . . .

T: . . . four gussets, yes. People just don't think of that and it's such a little thing to do, but it's those little things that probably make the thing stay together longer. As far as we know we have never had a structural failure in the hull of a boat since we've been in business.

F: You're kidding. Not one?

T: Not one ever came back. We've had a rudder or two break, but I've always thought that was kind of a problem with the designer. But as far as our structural hulls are concerned, unless somebody has modified them, we have never had a structural failure in the hull.

F: You mean chainplates haven't torn out or anything?

T: We've never had a chainplate pull out. Never ever in the history of our company has anybody ever pulled a chainplate out of a boat.

F: I liked your stern and stem fittings too . . . aluminum with a stainless sleeving. Was that all your idea?

T: . . . That's our idea, yes. I go out, take pictures, take ideas here, ideas there.

F: For puncture proofing, how strong is a $\frac{3}{16}$ inch UDR hull? How many layers of well done woven roving would you have to go to compare, do you know?

T: Roving, oh hell, you'll need about 30% more weight with woven roving to have the same strength. We've got 4 or 5 or 6 layers of UDR, so you would need from 5 to 8 layers of woven roving of the same weight to equal that.

F: What else can you tell me that you think is important that you do that other people don't do?

T: We build what we call a monocoque construction. A monocoque is where the skin takes the loading as well as the engineered framework on the inside, like an aeroplane or a race car. Everything takes its share of the load. As far as I know, we are the only ones that do that.

F: How did you figure all this out?

T: Just working on it.

F: Common sense?

T: I kind of like to call it that, yes. I just don't like to jump overboard, and I mean there's so much bull in this industry, about who does what. Well, you know the thing we do that no one else in the industry does? We have a book that's eleven years old, and we've weighed every hull, deck, keel and rudder that has ever been built in this factory. Alongside it we have what it was made out of, how big, etc. We've got records for eleven years of exactly what things weigh and what it takes to get strength and how much this weighed, and we run it through Tulane University Physics lab and they make all the tests. Their Physics lab runs all our laminate schedules for us. We have also submitted our laminate schedules to the ABS — American Bureau of Shipping. They have accepted them and they think they are very good, in fact, in some of their books they have used our scantlings as examples.

F: That's impressive, but still the most important thing of course is, as you know, the wear of the boats.

T: That's what I call pedigree and we have a very good pedigree as far as what our boats have done in the world, how long they have lasted. Also, we build inexpensively — we are not, again, a very expensive builder.

F: Give me a little bit of a record of the Peterson 43 *Acadia*, would you? What races has she won?

T: . . . won the SORC.

F: What year was that?

T: That was in 1980. It was a member of the United States Sardinia Cup team. We won the Sardinia. It was the only boat to win its class in the Bermuda race in 1981 in both PHRF and MHF — not '81 — I take it back. That was in 1980. Won the circuit in '80 and also, Bermuda — it was the only boat to win its class both MHF and IOR and then it went on to Sardinia and was a member of the Sardinia winning team for the United States.

F: Do you know how many boats you have built all these years?

T: Oh, I think about 300. We run at about 30 a year. Our biggest year I think was, like, 42 boats.

F: What have you got moulds for now?

T: Right now we've got moulds for a Peterson 43, Frers 38 and a Frers 40, and a Frers 42. The 38 is the newest one.

F: Do you cover the keel with laminates?

T: No. The keel is just straight solid lead.

F: And nothing happened to the boat that hit the rocks?

T: No.

F: How many bolts were there on that?

T: I think we are using about eleven ¾ inch keel bolts.

F: Is there anything special that you do in the keel area?

T: One of the things we do is pretty good. We carve the top of the keel, the lead, so that it fits the bottom of the boat perfectly as opposed to some people who have a flat top to the keel and they put a little mish-mash on top to make it form to the bottom of the boat. We actually carve with a torch, carve the keel from a template that fits the exact bottom of the boat.

F: That fairing seacock that Jack was telling me about, was that your own design?

T: The seacock? No, that's just a regular off-the-shelf seacock.

F: What make is it, do you know?

T: Scott.

F: That's the only seacock there is in the boat?

T: Right.

F: Okay, the deck. The deck is UDR as well, and there's no roving or mat in there?

T: That's correct. We put a sacrificial half ounce mat on the outside of all this stuff to give it something to grind and fair to, but in the mould we use no mat at all; we just use gelcoat and start laying UDR.

F: You bolt the deck?

T: Right. We have a big flange that comes in off the hull, you know. It turns in and the deck lays on that and we put a bunch of 5,200, and with the toerail track bolted together, it's a pretty good bond.

F: That's on 4 inch centres, then with 5/16 bolts. But you never bond underneath?

T: Right. No.

F: Tom, if you were to say that there is a weak spot in the hull, where would that be? Would that be in the backbone?

T: I think the weakest part of most boats is in the chainplate/maststep area.

F: Is there something you have done to the maststep?

T: We just made that structure a little bit bigger.

F: How thick do the beam walls get?

T: No more again than 3/16 probably.

F: What kind of a general weight do you keep a 40 foot boat to, or what does the designer come to you with?

T: Oh, like a 40 foot, they want to keep the weight down to about 2,000 pounds for the hull.

F: What about the deck?

T: They want about a 600 pound deck.

F: Well, Mr. Dreyfus, that sounds very good.

T: I hope I've been some help.

F: You sure have.

23

The Boat that Broke the Rock
The Spencer 1330

There is basically nothing wrong with being dead. Some of my best friends are dead, and one of them cited just the other night the wonderful freedom from the evils of this world you gain, like not having to get up on rainy days, or cross the street to avoid someone you hate, or nod and grin stupidly for fifteen minutes each time Mrs. Lukovitch corners you at the bottom of the stairs with her enormous body, and for the nineteenth time itemizes for you, examples that confirm the incurable audacity of her daughter-in-law, who didn't really go to Oshkosh for a seminar at all, but snuck off to New Jersey for a nose job and came home looking like Bob Hope.

No, Death can be okay, providing it comes at a prearranged rendezvous, after all deeds have been done and races all been run, and not sneaking up from behind on a cold stormy night when you are untangling wet lines — with your dinner gone cold, and your shirtsleeve soaked in honey — and unloading the masts on top of your head, as if you didn't have enough troubles already. And that is just because some horse's patooty decided to save a few dollars on your hull construction, or on the bolts that hold your chainplates where they should.

That won't happen to you if you own a Spencer. Spencers are built with care and integrity and, what's just as important, much thought and know-how. Pat Brandlmayr (née Patricia Spencer) and her naval architect husband John, started Spencer Boatworks almost thirty years ago. John designed the boats and Les McBerney built them, and John Brandlmayr has since passed away but Les is still there building them and Pat Brandlmayr and her son Grant are looking after engineering and design.

Spencer has become famous in boating circles because of the quality of their construction, the flexibility of their yard in accommodating the needs and desires of the owners, and not to any small extent because of Margaret and Hal Roth, who launched their Spencer 35 *Whisper* in February of 1966 and in the sixteen years since, have sailed her around the Pacific and around Cape Horn, and *into* the hard rocky coast of Tierra del Fuego — over fifty thousand miles in all, and they still have *Whisper* and are happy as can be, off on some new adventure to God knows where. To keep and *use* a boat that long, bespeaks their satisfaction with the design, and for a boat to stay

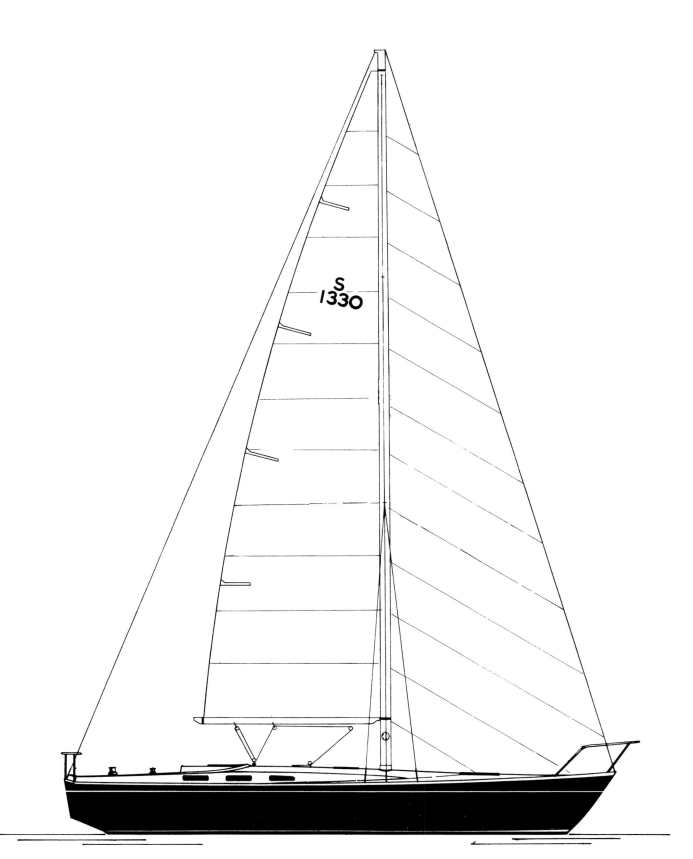

Spencer 1330 — John Brandlmayr

LOA—43'8" LWL—35'0" Beam—13'0" Draft—7'0" Displ.—23,000 lbs. Ballast—10,000 lbs. Sail Area—882 sq. ft.

together through all that bespeaks *Whisper's* excellent construction. At Tierra del Fuego, *Whisper* was slammed against the shore for over twenty-four hours until part of her hull finally wore away. Such an encounter would have left most production boats drifting in hanky-sized chunks over the seven seas, but *Whisper* stayed together and was rescued by the Chilean navy, and under Hal Roth's frustrated supervision (for they wouldn't let him work on the boat himself), she was repaired in good time and has been well ever since. And maybe I'll digress here for a note of interest.

In case of major repairs to a fibreglass hull, it is next to impossible to do a good job over a large area without use of a mould. The standard method of repair is to cut away all of the damaged and delaminated pieces, and even pieces suspected of delamination, then lay up, in a mould, a new piece to fill the hole. This piece is faired in and bonded into place from the inside, leaving as little filling and fairing as possible on the outside, where the finish will be most visible. But since in all likelihood there will not be a hull mould available for your Leadbelly 40, in Ricky Ticky, New Hebrides, you will have to be ingenious and take patterns and make templates from the undamaged side of the hull. You have to roll each pattern 180 degrees (one piece at a time), then join them and make up a plug from which to take your mould. The plug can be made up of fairly thin strips of wood stapled to the hull templates and filled and faired with fibreglass resin and filler.

As you can guess, I have left out some steps and a few hard days of work, but I have given you the gist of it so that if the time ever comes you will be ready.

Back to Spencers. Another thorough testing of the integrity of construction of a Spencer was done by my friend Peter Marshall, who one night unknowingly decided to take a shortcut through the middle of Lasqueti Island. The only problem was that there was no shortcut, so he flew at nine knots running wing and wing, unhampered and uncushioned into a perfectly vertical granite cliff. Now that is enough to make a grown man weep. And *then* since the wind was behind them, the boat kept bouncing back and ramming the cliff again and again, until Peter ran up top and got things under control. He had to get a new stemhead fitting and replace six inches of the tip of the bow, but

that's not bad for trying to split an island in half with a twelve ton boat. So much for the pedigree of Spencers.

The Spencer 1330 was designed by John Brandlmayr in 1973 and her deck layout was completed by Grant some months later, based on his father's fundamental vision. The result is a boat with very pleasant lines of elegant simplicity. The bow has a very slight spoon making her less unfriendly looking than her straight-stemmed relatives, and the stern is of the older school, resulting in a little smaller transom that is very pleasing to the eye, although it does cut down on the advertising space that racers seem to cherish. If you are dead set on a reverse transom however, Spencer will accommodate you. They have the willingness and ability to do many changes; they have lengthened deck houses and raised deck houses and shortened deck houses, all with very fine results, and their ability to temporarily modify moulds is truly uncanny.

For the connoisseurs of underbodies the 1330 is a delight of flowing lines. Missing, happily, are the hard knuckled bows and pinched buttocks of modern racers, replaced by lines of fluidity and grace, like the smoothly flowing profile line from stemhead to the heel of the keel. Both the keel and the skeg are, what I believe are called "scimitar" shapes in design circles, and aside from the fact that they make for good shapes to limit induced drag (a force created by the disruption of water flow caused by the keel), they are also of advantage when grounding occurs, in that the rounded shapes cause the boat to ride up on the seabed or reef, distributing and cushioning the impact by absorbing it over a period (very short) of time. This will most certainly limit the amount of damage that will be incurred. Another strong point of the keel configuration with respect to groundings, is the shape of the keel stub — the piece to which the lead keel is bolted. Because the stub's bottom is angled up toward the bow, any impact caused by grounding of the rounded lead will be transmitted partially *into* the hull. Were the stub not so angled, as is the case with most modern racers, and were the keel of the more vertical edged variety, most of the force absorbed would act to shear off the keel bolts without any absorption help from the hull. The resultant damage is of course very infrequently a complete loss of the keel, but rather bending of the

keel bolts and loosening of the fit, which even minimally will bring about annoying leaks that are impossible to repair without haul-outs. If you intend only local racing or cruising, this is no big deal — providing money is your middle name — but the Spencer is built as a fast and able cruiser, and there is no telling in what corner of the world she may end up.

The deck lines of the 1330 are as beautiful as her hull lines, and although this may bring shrieks of disbelief from those of you who love the serenity of trunk cabins, you would have to admit that the simplicity of the lines is kept to an elegant best. The deck and house look much like those of the very beautiful Swans from the drawing boards of Sparkman and Stephens and Ron Holland, except that the Spencer even comes out ahead, in that the profile line of the deck tapers off all the way from the mainsheet traveller aft, whereas most of the Swans continue aft horizontally from their highest point, resulting in a rather boxy look, especially where the coamings get hacked off at the stern. So much for Swan-bashing; but I still wouldn't kick one out of my berth.

The resultant deck is very spacious indeed. The top of the house, the side-decks and the foredeck as well, make for very good and safe working surfaces. If you are the kind of person who insists on large aft cabins, then you can choose the centre cockpit version of the Spencer. Its house structure is designed much lower than most, but the freeboard on it is about six inches higher than that of the aft cockpit boat, and the house structure is not nearly as well realized. In all, the aft cockpit is by the far the more beautiful boat. I do have one objection to the deck and it is a minor one, having to do with the design of the forward hatch. As you can see, the hatch is large as it should be for the passage of sails, but my objection is to its height. One can, with a bit of tricky engineering, build a very good, flusher looking hatch, and although it will mean having to install a set of drain holes, etc., I think the gain aesthetically would be well worth the trouble. And of course a flusher hatch would also mean fewer trippings.

If you can afford the teak decks by all means get them, for on a flush deck boat like this they have an extremely beautiful effect. If you have a chance to look at a Spencer, take note of the large diameter circles in the deck areas and the rectangular ones in the forward hatch. These are the world's most leak-proof and trip-proof skylights. In these areas the gelcoat is clear and a balsa core has been left out of the cored deck. The tapering off and fairing in of the edges is time consuming, but they will never break or leak and they transmit vast amounts of light belowdecks. Of course you should be moderately certain of your interior layout before you decide their location, lest one ends up directly over a bulkhead.

The cockpit is simple and on the largish side as far as volume is concerned, so large in fact that my friend Peter had four 2 inch drains installed just to be sure. The companionway is off to one side to make room for the double berth stateroom below, but it has a very small opening and is well protected, in case of a knockdown, by the high cockpit coaming. There is a raised helmsman seat to make for pleasant steering and the cockpit seats are comfortable and the wide bridgedeck makes in and out traffic very safe.

Performance

At 44.4 feet of overall length the 35 feet of waterline length may seem a bit short, yet her displacement of 24,000 pounds gives her a displacement-to-waterline-length of 254, which shows her to be toward the lower end of medium, meaning she will be easily driven but still have a very lovely motion, especially with her long (compared to smaller boats) waterline.

The sail area is 882 square feet, which gives you a sail-area-to-displacement ratio of almost 17, showing her to be a good performer in light airs, and all of Mr. Brandlmayr's designs have done well in local northwest club races. The shrouds are only moderately inboard about 9 inches, so the boat will be outpointed by some, but she is a banshee off the wind. Peter Marshall, who has sailed his *Kacheena* over 8,000 miles, gave me the following working numbers: In 15 knots of apparent wind she will reach at 8½ to 9 knots. In the same wind conditions she will beat at 7½ to 8 knots, depending on sea conditions, and will hold this speed in up to 20 knots of wind, at which point she will be in need of a reef. On a dead run he has had *Kacheena* doing 12 knots in 40 knot winds with a Number Two Genoa and the main wing and wing, and at 45 knots she

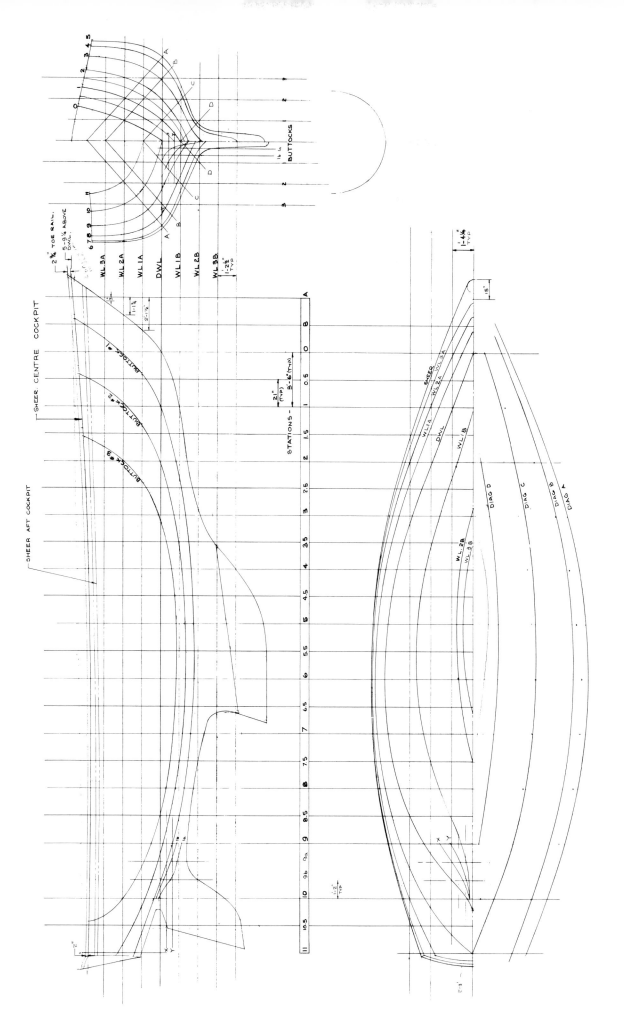

Powerful buttocks show in the Spencer 1330 lines, along with a very fine entry and moderate sheer. Note how sheer of aft cockpit version is 6 inches lower than aft cabin one, making for a much sleeker looking hull.

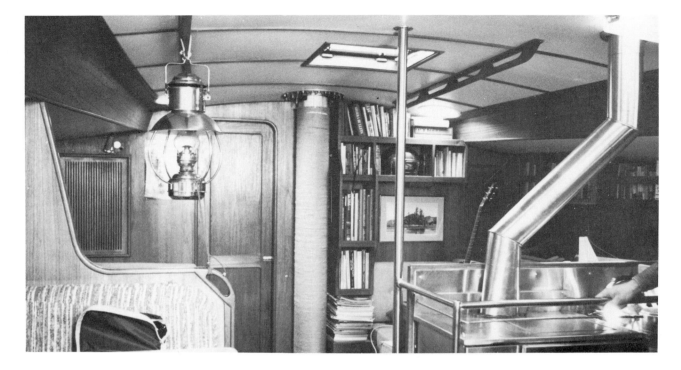

A typical photo by yours truly with the foreground out of focus and a hand in the background. Beyond all that is the spacious salon of the Spencer 1330.

did 6 knots under bare poles. With large self-tailing winches (about Barient 30's) two people can handle her well. The main is a manageable 360 square feet, but a 150 Genoa will be close to 800 square feet, so don't get carried away when you are flying downwind or you'll have a time and a half getting the sail aboard after you yell "Uncle."

One point about ground tackle. A craft this size will need lots of chain for cruising, so every effort should be made to bring that weight (most likely well over 400 pounds) as far aft as possible, so the bow won't tend to bury itself and impede the boat's progress.

Down Below

Spencer is such a flexible boat builder that to present a layout here and call it standard would be much too limiting. Almost every boat they have built has a slightly varied interior to suit the owner's wishes, although all basically revolve around the two interiors shown. At first glance the interiors look not at all unusual, but you have to remember that all areas are unusually large. This boat has a 13 foot beam carried well forward and aft, thus she has enormous volume. The closed off

double berth aft is 53 inches wide. The chart table to port, with a fold-up leaf that converts the whole thing into a usable surface, is the only table I have seen on a boat this size that allows you to use an Admiralty chart completely open and flat. The area just forward of it has been converted by a number of owners into a dinette, with athwartship seats which have good room for four adults, although they may seem a little redundant when the salon and table can be but a few feet away. I have seen both interiors in real life and they both do work very well, so it's really a matter of whether you want another giant hanging locker and drawers (there is one forward that you can literally walk into) or the dinette. The Brandylmayrs show a diesel heating stove just inboard of the storage, a stove that will give you great flexibility in which ends of the world you can cruise.

The galley again has to be looked at with fresh eyes since the area is so great. To give you an example, the aft countertop — from the port edge to the face of the cupboards starboard — is over 6 feet long, meaning that two people can work nicely in the galley without getting too much in each other's way. As you can see, there is plenty of space for a

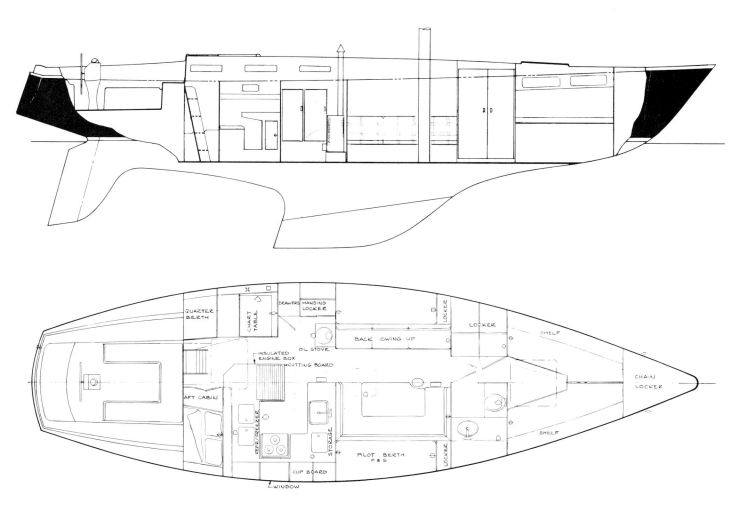

The profile of the voluminous Spencer 1330 reveals her scimitar-shaped keel and skeg. The tooling on these boats is truly fine. The space belowdecks is so great that it's almost futile to discuss any interior save for the fact that I very much like the one in the plans. The 44 foot Spencer would be a comfortable and fast passage-maker indeed.

separate freezer and fridge and good accessible space to the cockpit (the engine is under the galley counter) for compressors, battery chargers, etc. Stowage is plentiful.

The main salon is, again, roomy, with 6 foot 6 inch berths, but one of my favourite things in the boat is a pilot berth to starboard. As you can see it is very roomy, but the best part of it is that it is recessed below the back of the settee so much that the top of the berth cushion is actually 8 inches below the back of the settee. Not since my cradle days have I seen such a cozy and secure sleeping place. You can huddle in there at the peak of a raging storm, clutch your great soft pillow, plug your ears and sleep like a baby. The portside settee is drawn a little narrow, but its back can be pushed outboard, as it has been done on Peter's boat,

resulting in a most comfortable settee 22 inches deep, with bookshelves outboard of it. The area forward of the main bulkhead is very flexible, again with acres of room. *Kacheena's* main bulkhead was moved aft, even with the mast, which enabled her to have a small bathtub installed. You may think this an absurd luxury, but then the Pardeys, after eight years of cruising, are building one into their new 30 foot Seraffyn, into the area where the engine would be. Lin Pardey very ably described the reason for her choice in an article for *Sail* magazine:

"One of the biggest cruising hassles is getting clean. It's a real nuisance gathering clothes, towels, and toilet kits, for the dinghy ride into the yacht club or marina. Staying at these places can be expensive too, so onboard bathing facilities will be an efficient luxury. We didn't opt for the normal enclosed shower arrangement in a head compartment because it has always annoyed us; each time you shower, the whole head gets wet and steamy, and just when you are feeling the cleanest you have to get on your hands and knees to mop up the mess. Our sit-down shower tub will contain the spray and be placed in an airy space enclosed only by a curtain. Since it will be next to the companionway it will be a good place for drippy wet weather gear, and even in a seaway we will be able to bathe safely because we will be sitting down."

No matter how you lay out the Spencer, the forepeak will end up as a veritable playpen. Enjoy.

Tankage on a Spencer bespeaks a long range cruiser, with 90 gallons of fuel and 160 gallons of water tank potential. The tanks are premoulded by hand lay-up to the shape of the hull and glassed in place. There are inspection plates of stainless steel on top of each tank and the fittings for the tanks are attached to this plate, making for very easy repair or tightening. An engine of about 45 horsepower will drive the Spencer at 7.5 knots at 2,000 R.P.M.

Construction

As I said earlier, Spencer excels in both structural and finishing construction. The hull is laid up in one piece, using Airex PVC foam core. The foaming starts a few inches below the sheer and continues down to the turn of the bilge. From here on down it's all solid fibreglass to allow for the fitting of the keel and the through-hull fittings.

The hull and deck lay-up are as follows: Topsides get 2 layers of one ounce mat followed by a layer of roving and another unit of mat and roving. Then one ounce mat is laid in and wetted and on top of it goes ¾ inch Airex foam, followed by two more units of mat and 24 ounce roving, and a final layer of mat. Below the water, starting at the waterline, they add in three extra units of mat and roving, and starting about 15 inches below this point they add in two more units of mat and roving, so that in the keel section there is a total of fourteen layers of mat and ten layers of roving.

The deck has a total of four units of mat and roving, plus two extra units of mat. Sandwiched between two outside and two inside units is ¾ inch balsa everywhere, even on cockpit sides and cabin sides, to provide a stiff and well insulated deck.

The balsa is replaced in areas where hatch-slides and winches are to be placed, by ¾ inch plywood, to prevent the collapsing of balsa when the bolts are tightened hard. The lay-up with the ¾ inch core will make for a very stiff and seaworthy hull.

The hull and deck joint unites the two, into a single monolithic unit that should remain as leakproof as any. The deck is fitted onto the hull while the latter is still in the mould, so that the two can be united perfectly without any deformation in the hull which could result in a boat with two asymmetrical sides. John Brandlmayr insisted that this is the way that it has to be done, and eight years after his death it's being done exactly so. Very few boat builders follow this procedure because they want to free up the moulds to put them into use for the next hull. Anyway, at Spencer once a deck is in place, alternate strips of mat and roving are used, a total of five units in all, getting wider and wider with each layer, until a width of 14 inches is achieved. This is a great improvement over the few layers of mat they originally used on Hal Roth's boat, which after a few days of pounding into head seas in the Pacific, opened up a seam of over two feet in length at the stemhead. If Peter's boat suffered as little damage as it did during the assault on the cliff, then you can be sure that the hull and deck joint will hold.

What is astounding at Spencer is to see the patience with which they fill and fair and gelcoat the outside hull and deckjoint seam until it is cosmetically perfect.

The bulkheads are ¾ inch thick, and are bonded to both hull and deck with two units of mat and roving each side. To get a fair finish they pre-rout the place of the bonds. There is no need here for foam between the hull and bulkhead since a ¾ inch layer of Airex foam is already built into the hull.

The last piece of vital bit is the installation of the chainplates. Spencer's system is a little like the Scepter 36 in that there are no solid vertical plates below the deck level, but instead, Spencer uses an upside down "T" that fits below the deck with a leg of the "T" protruding. This is welded up of ⅜ inch stainless steel with a 3 inch by 4 inch bottom plate distributing the load over the deck. To limit any flexing or movement of the deck, a set of gussets is made up for each plate which carries the load of the shrouds down to the hull. These gussets are hand-laid-up of fibreglass with a resultant thickness of ¼ inch. They reach 18 inches down the hull and are about 10 inches deep. If you don't think this is strong enough, then let me tell you that they lift the boats out of the mould by using only two (one on each side) of these plates. You may shrug at that because a 1330's lead keel is bolted on after she's out of the mould, but in the case of the Spencer 35, 5,000 pounds of internal ballast is already bonded in place at the time of this lifting. They have been doing their building this way for ten years and they haven't pulled a chainplate loose yet.

In closing, I have to say that to talk to Pat Brandlmayr is to talk to a lady of the highest integrity and principles. Listening to her taught me an interesting thing — if you are really not sure whether somebody means to build a good boat or not, just look into their eyes and listen to their voices. . . not even the words, just their voices, and you will know.

24

Thanks for the Memories
Cherubini 44 & 48

Frit Cherubini is sixty-two years old. He builds boats that are works of art, but he hates to talk about them. He will drift away quietly into the background and let his son Lee do the explaining and he'll reappear only now and then with a few soft-spoken words. But the work that you see as you wander around speaks incessantly and eloquently. The lines Frit's brother John drew up for the Cherubini 44 and 48 are very close to those of L. Francis Herreshoff's *Ticonderoga,* a ship whose fame has now reached mythical proportions. All lines flow gently and gracefully — the long elegant shear, the fine clipper entry and the counter that, with its beautiful combination of curves and sweeps, must be one of the most eye-catching achievements in the history of yacht design.

The affection of the Cherubinis for the designs of Herreshoff are openly talked about and John did contact L. Francis on a number of occasions; but the greatest tribute one can pay to an artist is perhaps emulation, and when the emulation comes with as much understanding, both aesthetically and technically as John Cherubini possesses, then the result will usually mean an improvement.

If any budding designers reply to this, saying that copying is easy, then think again, because we're not talking about copying here, we are talking about application of knowledge by two men with similar sensibilities. And furthermore, and this is in no way meant to be denigrating to L. Francis, most designers will agree that it's a considerably easier task to make a larger boat *(Ticonderoga* was 71 feet overall) look graceful and fine than a smaller one, which will have to provide sufficient cockpit, side-decks, house height, as well as interior accommodations while maintaining the look of regalness and grace. Indeed the sad truth is that you don't have to look very far to find boats whose well-meaning designers tried, with sadly little success, to blend a group of wonderful ideas from magnificent ships of the past, and came up with little more than a tidy little yacht of horrors.

But John Cherubini has succeeded very well where others have failed, and has added some beautiful and functional touches of his own. Most noticeably, the house has been extended past the mast for better accommodations, the clipper bow has become even more graceful, more tumblehome has been added to the hull, the forefoot has a better slice taken out of it for improved maneuvering, and

Cherubini 44 — John E. Cherubini
LOA—44'0" LWL—40'0" Beam—12'0" Draft—4'10" Displ.—28,000 lbs. Ballast—12,000 lbs. Sail Area—1,133 sq. ft.

one of the most pleasant touches, although many would consider it insignificant — the beautiful cockpit which John drew is, in plan, a lovely long stemmed mushroom. He must have his heart in the right place.

Although the Cherubini 44 is traditional at first sight, it has concepts that are much cherished by designers today, and this shows too, for on her first outing she won the P.H.R.F. division of the Sea Bright Cup, one of the biggest events for ocean racers in New Jersey, well attended by proven ocean racers and many stock cruiser-racers. And to top that she took first overall in the seventh annual Fort Lauderdale to Key West race, a well attended 160 mile event with such well-known boats as *The Dealer,* which owns a number of speed records, the 60 foot *Running Tide,* and Bill Martin's 39 foot Nelson Marek designed *Stars and Stripes* which was the top American boat in the previous year's Admiral's Cup. No Wednesday night "Beercan Race" this.

Her performance stems from a combination of factors, one of which is her enormous waterline length which, at 40 feet, is only 4 feet less than her overall length and, as you can see, that allows less than 10% overhangs, which is a sign of very modern thinking indeed, with the exception that most modern boats with those dimensions tend to look chopped and ungainly, while the Cherubini maintains all the elegance of a swan. Most boats of Herreshoff's day had long overhangs; as a comparison, *Cock Robin,* designed by John Alden only three years before *Ticonderoga,* was 57 feet on deck and 39 feet on the waterline, which gives you 18 feet of overhang, or 30% of the overall length. Apart from the high hull-speed for overall length gained through short overhangs, or put more intelligently — through long waterline, is the generous accommodations of her belowdecks, but more of that later. Still in the realm of performance is her very fine entry which will give her good through-the-water abilities, but the bow flairs to the topsides, so she should be a dry boat as well. Her beam is carried well aft, which will let her stand up better by providing more buoyancy and letting her carry her sails longer, and hence, make her go like stink.

The Cherubini is no light boat. She's all of 28,000 pounds, which makes her 5,000 pounds

heavier than the Spencer 43, but her enormous waterline length gives her a displacement-to-waterline ratio of an amazingly low 195 which puts her at the lower end of that spectrum, indeed putting her in line with the best of racer-cruisers, ultralights notwithstanding, of course. What this means is she'll be easily driven by her sails, but what it might also mean is that she won't have quite the gentle motion of slightly heavier boats that have a ratio of between 250 and 350. In her case, however, her long waterline should help dampen motion as well as give her a hull speed of close to nine knots, which is exhilarating just to consider, never mind achieve, especially if you have been topping off at seven knots, like I have, most of your life. The Cherubinis are as generous with their sails (1,100 square feet) as they are with the amount of excellent workmanship they put into their boats, and hence the boat has a sail-area-to-displacement ratio of 19.67, which is very high indeed, meaning she'll go like a bat out of hell in light airs, but she'll also have to be reefed, the sooner the better. This of course is the best compromise for most coastal cruising, but it will probably mean a permanent reef in your main if you do windward work in the Caribbean or other areas ruled over by Trade winds.

A most important cruising feature of the boat is that her draft has been kept under 5 feet without the use of a centreboard, which if well constructed is no great menace, but it is nice to have a shoal draft without any moving parts like blocks, cables, pins, etc. The shoalness is achieved by use of a patented keel designed some years back by Henry Scheel. In theory, the Scheel keel does two things: a) It places all the ballast in the lower, bulbous end of the keel and thereby lowers the centre of gravity, compared to that of a conventional keel, making the boat a little stiffer, b) The curve in the Scheel keel "holds" the water on the high pressure (leeward) side of the keel, not allowing the water to slide past under it as easily, thereby increasing the boat's resistance to leeward. To use a simple analogy, think of a swimmer's cupped hand and what it does to *resist* its movement through the water compared to a flat hand, which is the equivalent of a flat conventional keel. If you're not totally confused yet, let me cloud things further by mentioning tests done by one of the continent's

Cherubini 48 — John E. Cherubini
LOA—48'9'' LWL—44'0'' Beam—13'0'' Draft—5'0'' Displ.—37,000 lbs. Ballast—16,900 lbs. Sail Area—1,227 sq. ft.

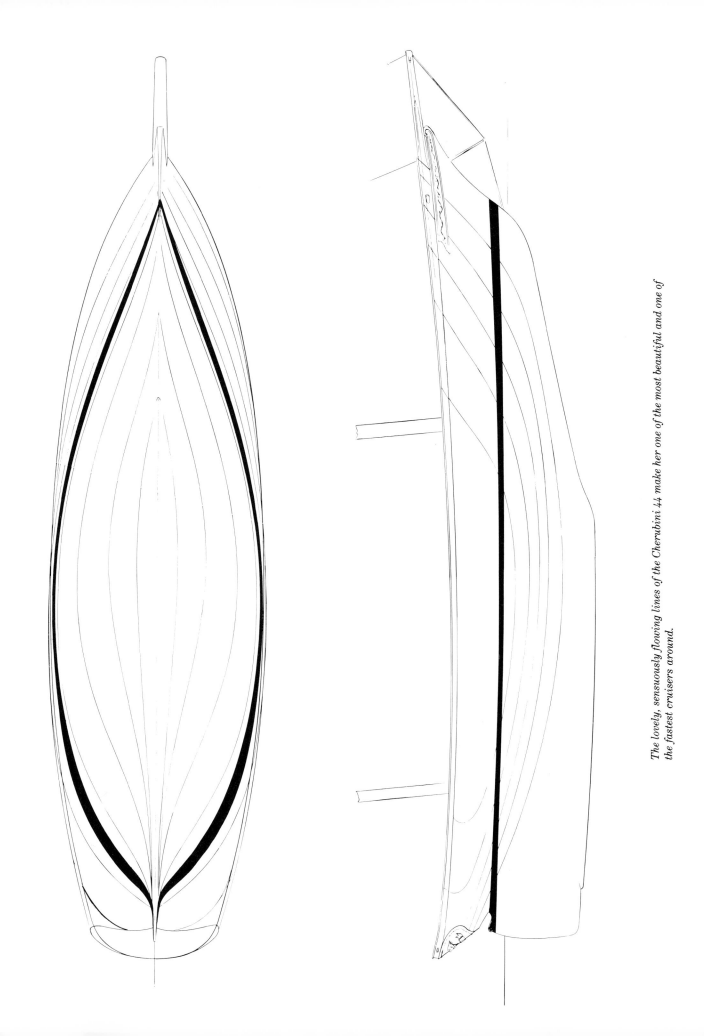

The lovely, sensuously flowing lines of the Cherubini 44 make her one of the most beautiful and one of the fastest cruisers around.

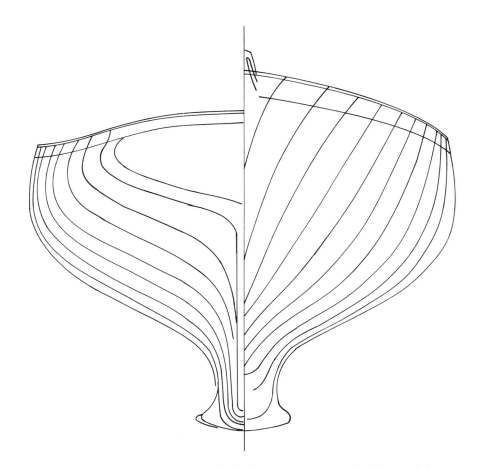

This is not a fanciful work of art. This is the sections drawing of the Cherubini 44.

most knowledgeable designers, Ted Brewer, who says regarding the Scheel keel that:

"In tank tests of the Morgan 38 at the Stephen's Institute, we found it made more leeway and had more frontal resistance than an 11 degree wide NACA fin only 2 inches deeper. In fact, during testing extensively in tanks of 5.5 metres in the sixties, we found that no bulb keel worked as well as the standard streamlined shape and that no keel wider than the minimum worked as well either. The added stability given by carrying the ballast lower in the wide keels simply did not offset the greater resistance." Such is the wonderful world of yachts.

Even with the well cut back forefoot, the 44 has plenty of length to her keel for safe careening in out of the way places, and she has a large rudder with plenty of meat down low out of aerated waters.

In all, her hull is a beautiful creation that, with its slackish bilges and ballast relatively high up will give a very gentle rolling motion in beam seas, without the up-chuck snap that a flat-bottomed boat that conforms to the angle of wave surface

tends to have. Her slack bilges, cutaway forefoot, and shallow keel should give her a surprisingly low wetted surface area which again reenforces that she's a performer indeed. This should of course come as no surprise, for her ancestor, the great *Ticonderoga* ruled Class A of ocean racing for over forty years, with uncounted firsts and nearly as many records. Although she was built in 1936, her greatest feat came in the 1965 Trans-Pac race where she finished first overall and set a record averaging over ten knots over the 2,400 mile run. That was the famous duel she had with *Stormvogel* who crossed the line just minutes behind her. As an added tribute to her, the record she broke was ten years old, set by the much larger *Morning Star* which was 98 feet overall.

And yet although she sails so well, the Cherubini's greatest appeal is still to the eye and the heart, and the photos here speak so well for her that all I am able to do is reenforce what is obvious to the observer, which is that she's as beautiful in real life as she looks on these pages.

Aside from her beauty, she is most functional as well. Her cockpit is safe and spacious with a nice private area for the helmsman where he can comfortably brace himself in any seas, and a well-radiussed helmsman's seat which is equally comfortable and easy to brace oneself in, no matter what angle of heel the boat is on. With the curved back, the helmsman is also assured of being within easy reach of the helm at all times. The two little peninsulas that separate the helmsman from the rest of the cockpit make for excellent bracing in a seaway, as well as act as bases for the primary winches. This is a decided advantage when single-handing or if your crew is made up of wall-to-wall ninnies who are sitting immobile in their 24 inch wide cockpit seats. My notes tell me that there are tons of storage below the seats, so it must be so. The whole cockpit is a fibreglass mould, so all the beautiful lines can be had at a decent price, and also the complex curves and angles can be permanently sealed without fear of leaks. The seatlids are notched at the lower edge so they act as vents into the engine room.

Everywhere you look, the Cherubini shows thought, care and intelligence. The companionway opening is kept to a safe 16 inches in height (with a 2 foot wide bridgedeck for safe commuting or sleeping), and what's even more intelligent — the drop-boards have a 10 degree *reverse* slope so they can be taken out even in the rain, and with the hatch in place, no water will fall belowdecks.

The decks are broad and safe, aided by a bulwarks for you to stand on when the wind is blowing in your teeth. Heavy teak grabrails run the full length of the house and that's the way it must be, not just for handholds but also for footholds, for where else do you stand on a heeled deckhouse when you're tying reef points in the main. Of course, you could head up, to have a nice level surface, and let the sail beat you to death, but somehow I much prefer a good grabrail to stand on. Working of the headsails should pose no problem, for although there is no bowsprit platform per se, the bowsprit itself is 12 inches wide with raised toerails on the aft half of its length and with a fine pulpit as well, so you should encounter no difficulties.

The exterior is beautifully trimmed in teak, with teak hatches with heavy Lexan inlays for ample light belowdecks, a solid teak hatch cover over the hatch that in itself is a work of art, and a large skylight over the salon that is engineered not to leak, and can be lifted up and turned right around to catch the most wind.

Here I should voice a complaint. It probably is the only one I have so I'd better voice it before I forget it and end up sounding like a paid commercial. The design of the skylight is not in keeping with the rest of the boat, which is brilliantly sleek in all its aspects, including the hatch cover. To saddle such grace with such a bulbous skylight seems a mistake, and to complicate it with all the various methods of opening is unnecessary and inviting leaks and maintenance problems. The ideal skylight I believe would be a very low profile one that resembles the old skylights, with a raised spine for strength and brass rods for safety, but there's no reason why it can't open like a regular forward hatch with hinges both fore and aft to capture winds no matter what their direction. There... now I feel better, so I can get on to more raving. Before I leave the deck I must mention the monstrous Kentucky white oak samson post, with chain lockers either side of it, with their own fibreglass liners, beautifully fabricated of course.

Before we run away belowdecks, let's mention the rig. To start out at the bottom, the bobstay is a humungous ¾ inch solid stainless steel rod. The sail area for the ketch is over 1,100 square feet, which is a lot, but you have to have it if you want to move fast in light airs. The boat does come with a cutter rig if you like, which will unquestionably be a better windward performer with its larger foretriangle, but the main will be getting into a size that will take some toothgritting to handle. On the other hand, the ketch is a nuisance, what with the extra mast, extra sail, extra rig and extra handling. What the solution is I don't know. The best thing to do is to sail the boat, or even better, do a few days' sailing in boats with comparable rigs and see how you feel about them. One solution is of course to follow the example of a Mr. Merrick Pratt who finished his own Cherubini from a hull and deck, with some mind-bogglingly beautiful craftsmanship, and also totally mechanized it with Hood stowaway furling mainsail, two roller furling headsails, operated by electric winches, to the point where you could almost stay home and just tell the boat where you want her to sail, and she'll sail there and drop you a postcard. But then Merrick Pratt is a mechanical engineer and he revels in this stuff, whereas mechanical things frighten the

The long, powerful hull of the Cherubini 44 has no trouble shouldering her way along. Note the beautiful helmsman's cockpit. For quality of design and workmanship as well as performance (she has won some major ocean races) she may just be the best large yacht around.

hell out of me, and I'd rather work my back into a brace than rely on anything electrical at sea. But this is a personal phobia, and if you want to electrificate your yacht, by all means go ahead but take a long paddle for when all the machines jam to a grinding halt. While I'm languishing in my paranoia, let me pass on one more fair warning. As miraculous as the stowaway mains are (the ones that disappear at the blink of an eye into the mast) they do have two shortcomings. They can jam in the mast, requiring a ton of T.N.T. to get them out, but worse than that, at anchor with the sail tucked

away, the long slit in the mast will give the eery howl of a thousand banshees that will make a breeze sound like a typhoon. If you have good nerves or you can turn down the old hearing aid, then there is no problem, but if not, be sure you spend a night with howling Heathcliff before you decide.

Now where on earth was I? Oh yes, the rig. The ketch is of course very handy downwind, for a great mizzen staysail can be set, and boy do these look pretty and help the boat move out as well. The raked ketch rig is unquestionably more in keeping

The elegant Cherubini reminiscent of the great lady Ticonderoga. *Her hull is excellently laid up fibreglass, but her deck and house are wood.*

with the boat's character, but don't forget that with the ketch the mainsail traveller has to be well forward, over the main hatch, which is a long way from the helm, whereas with the cutter the traveller can be on the bridgedeck. I did see a photo of a ketch where the sheets lead aft to the traveller, but this puts the sheet at quite an angle, obstructing all sorts of cockpit traffic. Anyway, that's all I'll say on the matter; make up your own mind.

Belowdecks

The workmanship and thought belowdecks is equal to that of the topsides. Light is everywhere through the Lexan-centred hatches and ten large portlights, and here I might as well tread water and talk about the portlights for a minute, for they are the most intelligently creative touch on the yacht.

Let me start by saying the portlights were nothing like I have ever seen before and at first view I said to myself, "These people have completely lost their marbles." But as Lee demonstrated the operation of the embarrassingly simple thing, I had to agree that their marble bag was full up to the brim.

The portlights have no hinges, no dogs, and what's best of all, no leaks. The bizarre looking white thing in the photo is a single piece aluminum casting that the Cherubinis dreamed up and had cast themselves. Its lower trough, that is the space outside the base of the "U" drains directly out, with no points or seams in between. Now, there is a ring part of the casting (still in one piece) which goes right around the hole and this ring part has a rubber bead around it *and* (get ready for this) a piece of tempered glass with bevelled edges and radiussed corners *sits* — no trim, no bolts, nothing — the little nipper just *sits* there in the U-shaped trough. If you want the portlight closed, you stand the piece of glass up against the rubber bead ring, and slide the two wooden bungs between the glass and the aluminum "U," and voila — wedged in there, snug as you please. Now if you want a little ventilation, you pull out the bungs and let them hang on their lanyards in port or slide them in front of the glass so the glass doesn't bounce around under way, and the top 2 inch wide slit above the "U" is now open. If you shrug and say, "So what, you can open other portlights just a little," then just stop and think about it, Elmer, because this means that you can leave your portlights open in pouring rain and not get a drop inside the boat. Now I don't know about your portlights, but if I did that to mine I'd be screaming at Candace to man the pumps in no time flat. Furthermore, if you want the portlights completely open you just slip the glass out of its little "U" trough and put it somewhere. Don't ask me where, just find a place.

Back to basics. The layout of the Cherubini can be varied according to the owner's needs, and there is substantial volume in the boat even though you wouldn't think so with all those broad decks. But the broad decks are good and high above the settees so you can sit and lie very comfortably below them. The plan in the drawing seems to be the most in demand. The Cherubinis only build about four boats a year and have been at it just over six years so a pattern is hard to set, but this plan does seem to be the one most sought after. It's

a fair layout, as layouts go, with a good galley, a nice-sized afthead and a functional and cozy salon, but there are a few things I do dislike. In general, one has to decide what one is trying to achieve with a given interior, especially in boats around 40 feet, for one can do his utmost to achieve two-cabin total privacy, and chop up the interior accordingly, or one can admit defeat and say there is no such thing as privacy on a small boat and go from there.

If we take the first option and try for the two private cabins, then the layout of the 44 as shown is not bad, but you have to realize its severe limitations. First of all, you are taking up precious space duplicating things, namely a companionway and a head. Now, the need for a second head may be mandatory for some, but access to the aft head can be made very private to start with from either fore or aft, and secondly you'll have a hell of a time convincing me to drill an extra set of holes in my hull, and install an additional nerve-teaser just so somebody can use a head 9 feet farther away than they would have in the first place. If you say that that is not a spatial but rather a timing problem, then I say do some nip-ups and tone your muscle control. Good.

Now that we've gotten rid of the forward head and installed a splendid seat inboard and a huge locker outboard, let's get on with the rest, the rest being the second companionway. A much nicer solution than a second companionway cluttering up the salon, is the optional hatch house forward of the main mast which has been used on some Cherubinis. With this little house there is a sliding hatch and dropboards and a slim companionway, which could be used in port or, as convenience dictates, without taking up valuable space in the salon. So now that we've gotten rid of the companionway in the salon and installed a first class wood burning salon-stove and a locker in its place, we've got ourselves a pretty good layout, except for the navigation area, which unfortunately is tucked under the companionway aft. This looks very workable on paper, but in real life this space is hard to work for lack of elbow room, not to mention the amount of water dripping down onto your charts and gadgets from the companionway ladder. If it were my boat, and I'm wishing as hard as I can that it will be, I would put the companionway back on the centreline, divide the double berth off with a sliding door or shippy curtain, to create a

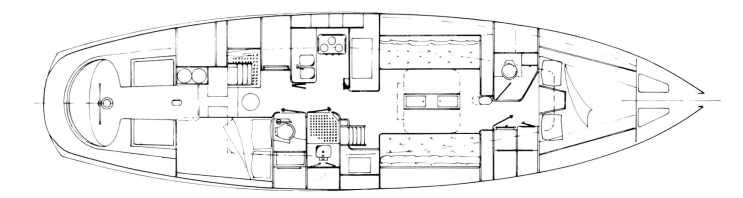

The Cherubini 44, one of the very finest and most beautiful yachts on the continent, with her magic-mushroom shaped cockpit, beam carried well aft and forward, shoal draft and much, much speed, and enough accommodations belowdeck to satisfy even the most restless among us. The layout shown is only one of many and certainly not the best with one too many companionways and one too many heads, but with this much volume you can have a wonderful time drawing up your own interior. No Lazy-Boys or wet-bars please.

sleeping booth, and install a vast chart table port of the ladder. That's what I would do, and that's why Cherubini is a custom yard, so owners can exercise their dreams of being yacht designers.

Aside from the above, the boat is beautiful and perfect below. You'll have to use bunkboards to create good seaberths, but if it's seaberths you're after, you can put in two singles aft, port and starboard. There are ominous amounts of stowage below the cockpit, very good access to the engine with a bit of panel swinging, and general signs of intelligent thinking everywhere below, with shelves, searails, and things to grab on to anywhere you reach. The wet locker is the first I've seen in a while with a generous 16 inches of width. The head has an ingenious layout, with six individual identical cubby holes for six sets of crew's toilet gear, and again, there is storage and things to hold on to in every conceivable place.

The galley is truly huge, with good floor space and vast storage space and fine cane doors that seem to have blossomed on every good yacht since Candace revitalized old metal cane doors for *Warm Rain* and put them in *From a Bare Hull.* The icebox is a whopping 6.5 cubic feet, which is enough to hold a small calf.

There's evidence of elegant thought and workmanship everywhere you look: in the brass lamps, with brass Cherubini nameplates on them, in the positive soldering that all wiring is attached

with, in the electrical panel that's built to aeronautical specs of endurance (John Cherubini worked at Boeing for some years) and even in the forepeak, where the filler between the berths has two settings — one up high to create a double berth and another down low to create a small seat. The lockers are lined with ½ inch foam with a tasteful fabric over to eliminate hull sweating and mildew, and there are knees and dividers to break up all large and wide areas into small useful ones. One of the boats I saw in the Cherubini yard had left out the forward head, and had another set of hanging lockers and drawers installed to match those starboard, and that should be enough clothes storage even for Liberace.

Even above each berth in the forepeak there are sizeable lockers running under the foredeck, not obstructing the berths at all, but certainly handy to them. In the salon, the main bulkhead is reenforced with a secondary short bulkhead, and between is more good stowage space.

There's elegant, rounded trimming and radiussed corners everywhere, and under the portlights is a drip trough (just in case) which acts as a grabrail as well, that is made out of a most beautiful piece of 5½ inch wide by 1⅛ inch Honduras mahogany you've ever seen, and it's varnished to a gleaming finish.

Digging through my notes I found the following odd bits: There's a nice hatch over the galley for ventilation; a fine wine locker forward (I can't remember where, but someplace); the tanks are aluminum,coated with epoxy just to save corrosion, and that is first class; the tanks hold 165 gallons of water and 75 gallons of fuel and those are good numbers for four on a long cruise, and the fuel is more than sufficient when you consider how good a ghoster she is; one of the salon berths (must be the port) can open into a huge airy double; and the engine is insulated with a 1 inch thick amalgam of lead sheeting and de-coupling foam, which has something to do with the breaking up of sound.

Construction

Frit Cherubini started building boats with his dad Leon, and Lee has been building boats since he was five years old, so they have a pretty good jump on the system. The overall basic construction is first class and I'll try to rattle off the main points as elliptically as I can for I have six pages of notes left and we'll all die of exhaustion by the time I'm done if I don't start skimping on the words.

The hull is all hand-laid-up 24 ounce Fabmat, and aside from the double mat against the gel, at the shear there are four units in the flange area, for a thickness of a full ½ inch and that's almost bullet proof. The flange is set 4 inches below the shear and it is made up of four units of 24 ounce Fabmat and has a finished width of 6 inches. The hull thickness and the number of laminates increase until it's 1¼ inches at the turn of the bilge and 1½ inches in the keel where there are as many as twenty Fabmat layers back to back. The hull is reenforced with uni-directional roving in high stress areas like the chainplates, where UDR runs from one shear down through the bilge and up to the other shear. Two layers of UDR are put here, in 5 foot wide strips, so the hull becomes a full 1 inch thick where the ¼ inch thick piece of stainless steel angle goes under the flange to act as a chainplate reenforcement.

The cabin sole and bulkheads are fitted and bonded in place while the hull is still curing in the mould (about two full weeks) so that when it's removed from the mould, there is no chance of distortion or deformation.

The bulkhead bonding is done with two layers of 24 ounce Fabmat over mat tabbing, to produce 3 inch wide bonds on both the hull and the major piece being bonded in. The horizontal bulkheads,

like counter tops, berth tops, etc., get one layer of Fabmat over a single mat tabbing. Everything in the boat is bonded according to the loading it takes. The main bulkhead is ¾ inch thick.

The ballast is internal or external depending on choice. With the shoal draft Scheel keel, very good stiffness has been observed. Lee told me that he sailed a 44 against the 61 foot Sparkman and Stephens *Stormy Weather* (which has 8 feet of draft) in big swells off the Virgin Islands, and going to windward he lined up the two boats and found the masts to be aligned on the same angle of heel. The external ballast is bolted into place with the astounding number of eighteen stainless steel bolts, ¾ inches in diameter, and a couple of boats that have run aground (one was on a reef for a day before being yanked off by a tug, the other bounced for three hours in the Bahamas) have suffered no structural damage.

The internal version of the ballast is put in as lead pigs with molten lead poured over. This is done with a *sacrificial* layer of mat in place, and they have run tests before attempting it, and found that the stuff cools so fast that the hull doesn't even get as hot as if it had sat out in the sun. They originally laid up a mock hull and set in a fifty/fifty batch (fifty per cent hard lead and fifty per cent molten lead, which is much higher than normal molten proportion), then they cut it apart and found that the heat had not affected the laminates at all.

The main mast is stepped on the ballast. The tanks in the bilges are bonded into place for the most positive holding you can get, and there are inspection plates on top of all tanks, and all fittings are set into these plates, so if you ever have to change or replace a fitting, you just unscrew the plate and do your deed.

Now for the good part. The house and deck are all wood. The 1⅜ inch deck beams on 12 inch centres are bedded in 5,200 polysulphide, and double-screwed to the flange. A double layer of decking of ⅜ inch and ½ inch fir plywood is epoxied and screwed down to the ribs. To further avoid delamination and movement, ⅛ inch diamter by ⅛ inch deep holes are drilled one per square inch into the plywood to give the epoxy something positive to grip. Next, a ⅞ inch thick bulwark is epoxied on, and epoxy coves are built up at deck-to-bulwark

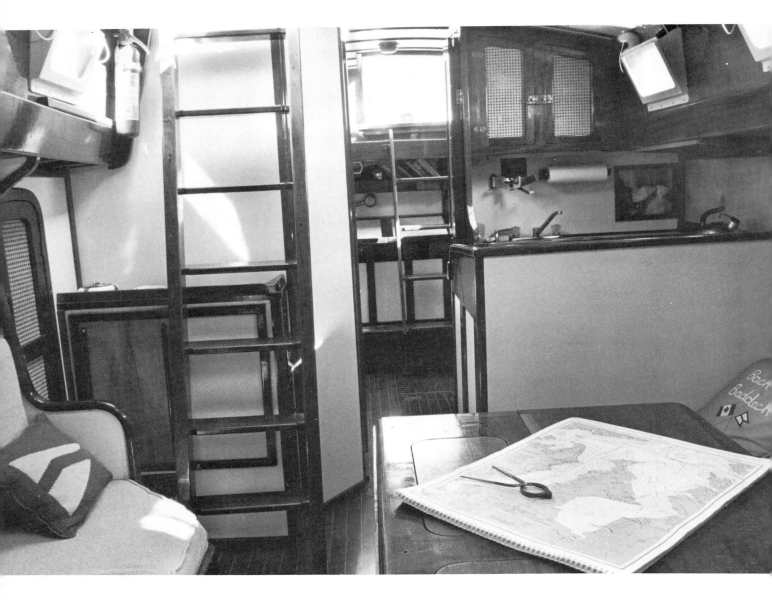

Looking aft in the Cherubini into her commodious galley and broad salon. The chart table under the aft companionway is, however, rather cramped.

and deck-to-house joints, to give more strength and less vulnerability to the glass that is laid over. The deck is coated with two layers of epoxy, then one layer of 10 ounce cloth is laid in epoxy, followed by two more coats of epoxy. The oldest deck is now nearly seven years old and has had no problems with leaks or separations.

The house sides are solid 1⅜ inch mahogany (or teak if you're very rich) and they are held to the deck with twenty-two pieces of ¼ inch stainless steel all-thread that goes vertically through the whole house side and comes out the bottom of the carling, which is a piece of ⅞ by 2⅜ inch Honduras

mahogany. As if this wasn't enough, the house side is held down by 4½ inch long #14 wood screws on 5 inch centres. At all bulkheads, knees are screwed through the bulkhead and also through the cabin-side from outside to tie everything together. Oh yes, then the corners of the deckhouse come right through to the bottom of the deck beams to do more tying.

The coach roof is three layers of ¼ inch fir ply epoxied together in a forming jig (cold moulded really) to get the proper crown. Full sheets are staggered, generally every 2 feet, to spread the seams. Belowdecks, this is then ribbed and covered with a formica finish to hide nuts and wires, but I think it would be nicer if the plywood were sanded out and painted and wires rerouted elsewhere, like under the decks, and the cap nuts of handrails etc. allowed to show on the overhead.

The hull is insulated by kerfing (almost cutting right through) strips of ¾ inch fir plywood to allow it to conform to the hull shape, and bonding in place. Then ¾ inch sheets of urethane foam are laid between the ribs, and a white-pine ceiling, in the form of strips, is nailed to these with scutcheon pins. These hold well enough in most situations, but if you ever have to repair the hull in a hurry you can just yank the little scutcheon-pin-held strips right off.

The engine room shows meticulous wiring and plumbing, with even a spare PVC tube in the bilge for leading wires or hoses forward at a later time. The engine has a fibreglass-pan liner, which has a ⅞ inch hardwood core, so it's almost an inch and a half thick where the mounts are attached. Then the engine pan is sound-insulated. Now that's class.

The installation of the stuffing box is something to be emulated by other builders. The

The Cherubini's main salon with a beautiful fireplace. These were the old portlights before the Cherubinis invented their wedge specials. The ceiling strips are attached lightly to the ribs to facilitate quick removal in case of damage to the hull.

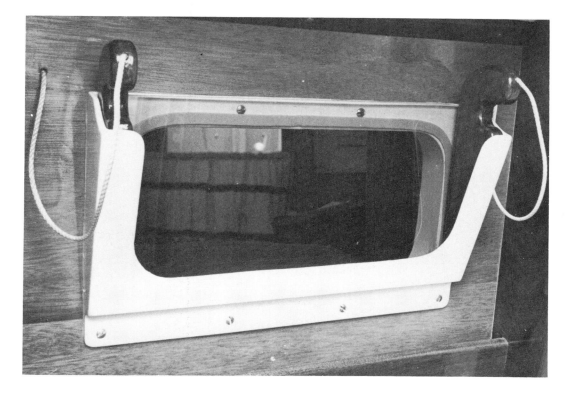

The magic portlight of the Cherubini 44. For a description of how it works see text.

amount of potential wear on the cutlass bearing — that strange looking brass tube with the variegated rubber inserts that holds the shaft where it passes through the hull — has been cut to the minimum. First to clarify: the rubber bearing is kept from wearing away at a rapid rate by the water that moves through the variegations and lubricates the rubber. Sadly enough this process is impeded on many boats by too much dead wood in front of the propeller aperture, which causes much turbulence, and obstructs the smooth flow of water. To ensure a permanent flow, a fitting should be added *inside* the boat which takes water off the engine cooling system (where it's pressurized by the water pump), and literally shoots it through the bearing — in its forward end, and out its aft end into the sea. This is precisely what Cherubini has done and it is precisely what too many people don't do. I've seen boats that have had to have this bearing replaced after about 400 hours of engine operation, costing the owners almost $300.00, for it takes an experienced man about eight hours, and special tools, and presses, and of course parts. If you continually have to replace your cutlass bearing at that rate, you can

easily figure that you're paying as much for wear on your cutlass bearing as you are for your diesel fuel, hardly a pleasant thought, and even a worse thought if you undertake a long cruise, where there are no presses and no parts. If a badly worn bearing is not replaced, much vibration can set up, causing wear and fatigue in mounts, couplings and fittings. To cut down even more on vibration and allow the cutlass bearing to last many many years, the Cherubinis have added a length of heavy fibreglass stern tube in which the shaft runs its last bit inside the boat. The aft end of this tube is bonded of course in the hull, and the forward, free-standing end has been stabilized by wrapping it with a few runs of uni-directional roving which is then run up and bonded to the hull. It is these little touches that will make a well-built yacht last a long, long time, while a badly built one will shake, wear, and beat itself to bits within a few years. Another example of good engineering is the rudder shaft. It is a known fact that welds are the weakest part of a structure, and welds under salt water are more vulnerable yet, so to fend off any possible failure way down the road, the Cherubinis avoid welds below the waterline. To reenforce the rud-

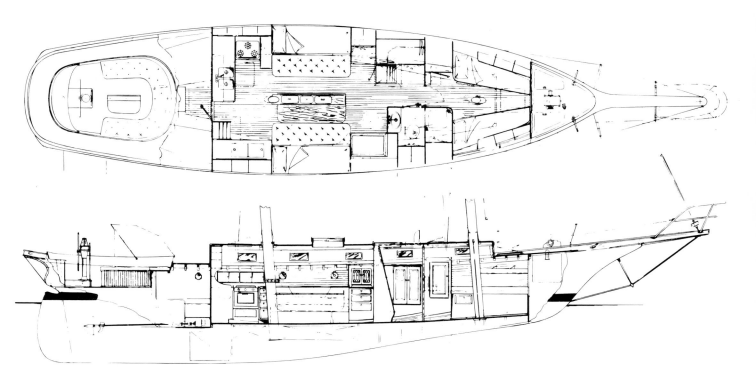

The regal accommodations of the Cherubini 48 show a cockpit fit for the most formal tropical dinners and an interior with a large aft cabin that runs the whole breadth of the ship, a huge salon with a wine locker and much open space and a truly spacious forepeak with lots of floor space and much stowage. A lovely schooner with excellent lines and an unbelievable draft of only 5 feet.

der, they simply have the rudder shaft bent and have it continue down the centre of the rudder. To spread its effect and to enable a fine fairing of the rudder, they have the shaft pinched in a massive press. Many will look at this with utter disinterest, and to them all I can say is, "Please accept my condolences, for if you care as little about the rest of the chain as you do about this one link, then you are truly not in the best of shapes."
shapes."

Another stroke of genius is the cockpit drain system, where a solid PVC pipe is glassed generously over, with the joints wrapped four times with fibreglass cloth, so there is never a danger of hose clamps coming loose, or hoses puncturing, or seacocks leaking.

The hatches have all their pieces splined, so the joints can't open up, and the slides are of ultra high molecular weight polyethylene which makes the hatches slide as if they were on ball bearings. And

last but not least, the genoa tracks are set on the caprails with the wood bulwark reenforcement below. Here, holes are drilled on 4 inch centres, for 3 inch long ⁵⁄₁₆ inch bolts. But the hole is drilled over-size to ⅜ of an inch, then filled with epoxy, and at maximum saturation time (when it has soaked well into the wood but not yet gone hard) the bolts are slipped into the epoxy and let set. I shook my head in doubt about this system, but Lee just laughed and told me that they had made up a dummy and sent it off to an engineering outfit for testing, and it broke the machine. Amen.

So that's it. The story's told, the details laid out and my writing hand's gone to sleep. If you have the dollars, this is the yacht to get, or if you have more dollars, Frit and Lee are finishing the first 48 foot schooner of the same lines, which could just be *the* ultimate yacht. Thank you *Ticonderoga*, and thank you L. Francis, and thank you, Cherubinis.

25

And Then Along Came Bill
Santa Cruz 40 & 50

Bill Lee is the ultimate conservationist. He uses so few words you'd think he had a quota, and he uses so little material in his boats that if all boat builders followed suit the price of resin and marine plywood would be driven into the ground, and he greatly conserves the time of sailors who own his boats because they get to where they are going twice as fast as other boats do.

Bill Lee pioneered a trend that is fast spreading all over the continent, and he started out with a phenomenon called *Merlin*, which has an overall length of 66.5 feet, a waterline length of 62 feet, and a beam of 12 feet 2 inches and displaces all of 21,000 pounds, which is not much more than our boat, except that our boat's length is less than half of *Merlin's*.

People laughed when *Merlin* hit the water looking long and flat like a size 15 running shoe, and they said things like, "You can't build a 66 foot Laser and have it stay together," and, "It will pound so bad it will crumble like an ice cream cone." But *Merlin* did not, instead she took off and started surfing at 28 knots and everyone held his breath, until *Merlin* did a mad dash to Hawaii in the 1977 Transpac, averaging 11 knots over 2,250

miles, and set a record that still has not been broken. Then everybody shook his head and said, "Maybe there *is* something to this guy after all." So just to prove he was no one time flash, Bill scaled down *Merlin* to 50 feet with a 46.5 foot waterline and 12 foot beam, and because he likes simplicity he made the displacement 16,000 pounds even, cut that in half and stuck in 8,000 pounds of ballast, and hung on 1,050 square feet of sail and off went the Santa Cruz 50's to embarrass the rest of the sailing world once again. When the first ten boats stormed across the finish line in the 1981 Transpac — which saw *Merlin* miss breaking her four year old record by 46 seconds — the Ala Wai docks looked like the Bill Lee boat show, for beside *Merlin* were lined up seven Santa Cruz 50's, the only other boats there being the 62 foot *Ragtime* and the 84 foot *Christine*.

One journalist who talked to the crews wrote, "The Santa Cruz 50 sailors all spoke enthusiastically about their rides, and several boats mentioned that drivers fought for the helm, hungry for kicks . . . The Santa Cruz 50's have two speeds: subsonic is around 9 or 10 knots where the steering is a little tricky; supersonic is over 13

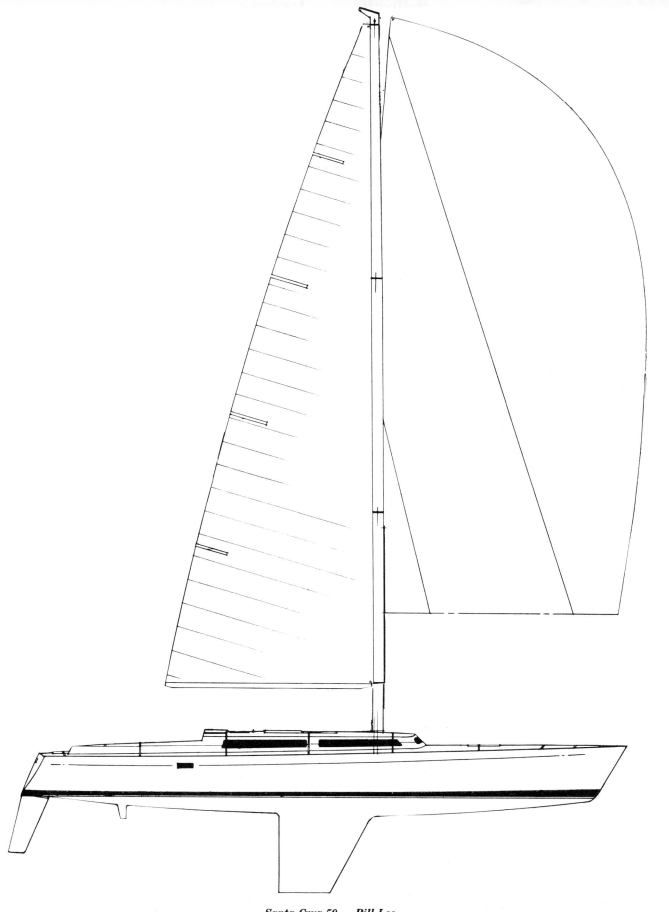

Santa Cruz 50 — Bill Lee

LOA—50'0''   LWL—46'5''   Beam—12'0''   Draft—8'0''   Displ.—16,000 lbs.   Ballast—8,000 lbs.   Sail Area—1,050 sq. ft.

knots where the steering becomes a dream." Rich Kania, who owns a 50 called *Audaz*, and who has sailed on other 50's in a number of long races, backs that up saying that on 12 to 14 knot spinnaker runs you have to muscle the boat about, but with her long waterline she holds her course well. A word of warning: Rich Kania has a handshake like a vise, so when he says muscle he means muscle. But he, as most others who sail the 50's, concur that her sailing abilities are awesome. In a story in *Pacific Yachting* Gerry Kidd wrote, "I wasn't prepared for the uncanny lack of fuss — the washless, whispering hiss as the boat moved effortlessly *over* the water at more than 10 knots. Because there is so little underwater and because it takes so little breeze on her powerful rig to get the hull to "break loose" and plane, the quarterwave is almost invisible, and the wake is virtually flat at 10 knots. I had also expected the steering to be heavy, given the rush of water around the spade rudder at these exotic speeds, but it was incredibly light — the boat is instantly responsive with two fingers on the wheel."

Windward the boat will pound, flat bottomed and light as she is, but she will keep sailing as long as the sheet is eased off a bit. She will excel windward in flat seas, easily hitting 7 knots in 5 knots of true wind, but she will have to be reefed around 10 knots and with a sail-area-to-displacement ratio of 27.63 and a narrow beam it is no wonder. To say that she is ultra-light is an understatement, for her displacement-to-waterline-length ratio is an unbelievable 67, which is half that of the little Naja, who is built of ½ inch plywood and has an almost empty interior.

But Bill Lee's boats stand up well to the seas. Rich Kania, who has had the boat beating hard in 30 knot winds and 3 foot seas, saw no oil-canning, or rippling of the hull, and best of all, heard not a sound of anything moving or cracking. One 50 did self-destruct after hitting a reef at about 14 knots, breaking the back of the boat and causing severe delamination (although the keel stayed on), when the bottom 3 inches of her keel caught a rock. One finds it hard to determine how much damage a sailboat like this should sustain under these circumstances, mostly because few boats move at 14 knots, and one must keep in mind that the 50 has an 8 foot draft, which makes for one hell of a long lever arm with which to do damage around the keel

stub. More than anything, the above brings out, not the vulnerability of a Santa Cruz 50 but perhaps the weakness of balsa foam cored hulls, for a large amount of the damage which resulted in the above boat, came about when the boat sat in the water for some days and the balsa core osmosed itself full of water. This problem is impossible to correct without virtually tearing the whole hull apart from the inside.

Many people dislike cored boats and one of them, Hugo Du Plessis, who is an associate of the Royal Institute of Naval Architects and a senior member of the Society of Plastic Engineers, makes a forceful statement in his book *Fibreglass Boats*. "A sandwich hull should be only for a short-life racing machine carefully stored ashore," yet the world's most reputable boat yard, Nautor of Finland, builders of the Swans, uses coring in their hulls. So what to do? First, if you have a cored hull, make certain that all penetrations are well sealed off. The way to be sure of this is to do what Bill Lee does, that is, put solid glass in all areas where a through-hull is to be fitted. Second, take great pains not to damage the boat and if you do, get it out of the water immediately before the core can start to absorb and saturate itself. Third, it is best to avoid dark colours in cored hulls if you live in hot areas, for while a single skin hull seldom delaminates under thermal stress — since it acts and reacts as a single unit — a sandwich hull with its insulative coring can set up conditions where the outer skin is very much hotter than the inner skin, thereby causing differential expansion and possible sheering of the outer skin from the core. Du Plessis states that, "On a wide surface, such as the deck of a catamaran, the expansion of the outer skin can be as much as ¼ inch *more* than that of the shaded area beneath." And he feels that this is too much for a rigid or brittle core, and a severe strain even on a semi-flexible foam. Last, and most important, with a balsa core much of the worry can be eliminated if the core is properly saturated with resin, which can be done by vacuum bagging (this is what Bill Lee does), which "draws" the fluid resin from the outer skin deep into the core, thereby not only sealing it and inhibiting water travel, but also making the core a more integral part of the outer skin, cutting down on potential sheering and delamination.

Back to the Santa Cruz 50. Since she is a sound

boat with great speed, some people criticize her because she must be reefed so early when on the wind. This, to some degree, is valid, for many a boat is so designed that it can be run as an "automatic," that is; the sails can be hoisted up in light airs and not touched until the wind blows 20 knots. This is all fine and well, but those people do not mention the beating you will have to take trying to reef down such a large main in a blow or change down from a large headsail to a small one. Once these concerns are taken into account the Santa Cruz does not seem like such a bad thing for she forces you to reef early, because her round bilges and narrow beam do not give her much initial stability, and her high ballast ratio and deep fin do not really come into full effect and stiffen her up until she is on her ear with the rail down. But even reefed down she does well, and many a time I've seen a 50 reefed and loosened off a bit beating up Howe Sound in the winter races, with a good blow coming out of the snow fields, and for a while she was pointing so low that she seemed to be in another race, but her speed stayed so high she didn't lose much distance, and downwind she easily ran away from the fleet. There is, however, one danger associated with her downwind flight, which is that skippers tend to leave their big spinnakers up much too long, and understandably so, for as Gerry Kidd points out, if the wind is blowing 30 knots true, the boat will handily maintain 15 to 20 knots of speed, making the apparent wind a gentle 10 to 15 knot breeze, and in those conditions why not let her go. This is all fine until something goes wrong and the boat slows and the full 30 knots catches you with all your laundry out, for then it will be knock down time of the highest order.

But perhaps this is an unnecessary point to dwell on, for those who indulge in a boat of this kind do so — or at least *should* do so — with an understanding of the sacrifices they will have to make and the chances they will have to take, for the thrill of occasionally outsailing an ocean liner. I am not necessarily implying that the Santa Cruz 50 is strictly a racer, and indeed there are those, Rich Kania among them, who intend to use their boats solely for cruising, and short-handed or even single-handed at that. This can be achieved with relative ease with a furling gear for the headsail (although Rich has talked himself into a foil which does not require unhanking and hanking) and all lines, including reef lines, can be led back to the cockpit. There is a drawback with a boat like the 50 for single-handers, which is that she will usually sail so fast that the wind will be more often than not abaft of the beam, requiring extensive use of a reaching pole, which no doubt is the meanest critter on any boat and probably more so on boats of such light displacement, for especially those with a shorter waterline length than the 50, will tend to move about considerably. The 50's waterline, however, is its saving grace, and indeed I have seen it move through the water in all kinds of conditions and she floats as flat and steady as a raft.

On deck the 50 is plain Jane at her plainest — no fuss, no hoopla — a flat house, clear decks, grabrails, cockpit coamings and hatches, and that is it. There are no anchor-wells or dodger-bases, or boxes for vents, and you just know that the boat was designed so there will be nothing in the fast moving crew's way, and even more importantly, there isn't a pound of extra weight anywhere. The foredeck has a huge 31 inch by 31 inch Bowmar hatch which will accommodate any sails the 50 needs to use. Bill Lee did allow himself one indulgence: the cockpit coamings have eight moulded-in beer can holders, which subtly tells you the number of crew the 50 needs to be properly raced. One skipper in the 1981 Transpac did attempt to cut down the total weight by jettisoning a couple of the crew (before the race began), and fortunately they had moderate winds, for the 50 does need a crew of eight to handle her in rough going and to generally let her sail to her potential.

But everything has been kept "ultra-light" on the 50; there is no curved or raised helmsman's seat, not even an aft coaming, just a structural horizontal piece of the aft deck and that is it. But then once she starts really moving — which is almost as soon as the water ripples — you will be standing at the wheel anyway to get the full feel of the ride. There are small pockets for winch handles, etc., in the back of the seats, which in turn are almost a foot high and very comfortable; but, save for a lazarette hatch, there is nothing to add bulk or weight to the boat. The house top does have a second sliding hatch which maintains a low profile when open, unlike a hinged hatch which stands up, and this is a must on the 50 for the house has no opening ports and as I said, no vents; and air has to be gotten below somehow, and this is about as positive a way of getting it as any. There are a couple of ports cut in the cockpit well, and another pair in the transom to help pull the air through the boat. The rig has double spreaders, a tapered mast and Navtec rod rigging, with Navtec hydraulics for the backstay and vang. The sail area of 1,050 square feet has 468 square feet in the main and 582 square feet in the fore triangle. Critical measurements put the I at 61 feet, J at 19 feet, P at 55 feet and E at 17 feet, which gives you a main of better than 3 to 1 and a stick whose top is 66 feet above the water, so watch those bridges.

The acres of clean foredeck space of the Santa Cruz 50.

Belowdecks

If you are accustomed to well trimmed and over detailed yachts like I am, the first thing that will come to your mind upon entering any ultra-light like an Olson or Santa Cruz is, "where is the rest of it?" These interiors are usually completely open save for the head and there are generally no doors, no drawers, no bookshelves, no weighty trim and very little to cover up the hull, which is usually painted and left. The soles are often thin plywood or as in the case of the 50, spaced teak slats set over the floors. Not only does this cut down enormously on the weight, but also almost proportionately on the cost of labour to install it. There are no frills to contend with, like carpets on the hull or a saggy overhead, for 90 per cent of what is there is structural, save for a few searails and a slat or two of teak as ceilings on the hull beside the berths. Yet the 50 does not look cold per se, for the overhead and cabinsides are all Bruynzeel marine mahogany plywood — all structural members of the house. Don't for a second say, "Yuch, mahogany," for this is no rotary door material, but beautifully grained wood, reminiscent of rosewood, except for the colour.

There is plenty of light belowdecks, for as you can see from the photo, the 50 has "wrap-around" windows, plus a series of Lexan deadlights in the house, which are flush above, for their frames are recessed in the mould.

After the plainness and the light, you will next notice a "structure" in the middle of the boat which raises the sole close to a foot and reduces the 6 foot headroom to below 5 feet. Bill is a master at turning a negative into a positive and he will tell you that this is the "famous" *Merlin* settee arrangement and it comes "standard," and the floor is raised to allow for storage and the crew's beer icebox, and it lets you sit eye level to the cabin windows. This all sounds just peachy, but the raised sole also *lets you* crawl forward bent in half, and lets you play kissy face with your table partners as you try to get by them. But what it actually does more than anything else is let the boat stay in one piece, because all the mast reenforcement and most of the chainplate reenforcement is provided by some hefty beams running every which way inside this box, but more about this later in *Construction*.

The box can be home to watertanks (the boat carries 150 gallons in total) or things like batteries, of which Rich put in two, of the type used for electric golf carts. Not only do these have 205 amp-hour capacities, but they are designed to be *dragged down* and charged up again, something most sailboat batteries regularly undergo. Above the box are comfortable settees with plywood backrests which are removable to allow the settees to be turned into double berths. The only accessible stowage found forward of the galley is under these settees, but as I mentioned there are no locker doors so you will have to live out of your duffel bag.

Forward of the raised salon is an area for sails and other gear, but this is a totally open and "undeveloped" space and you will have to make it workable yourself, with nets or bags or whatever you can think of. Forward of this area is a double berth with some shallow stowage in compartments below.

The galley is totally workable with a three burner with oven stove, an icebox, etc., and best of all, a large opening hatch overhead to provide lots of fresh air and ventilation for the galley.

The chart table to port has its own seat, although a better solution might be what Rich did in *Audaz*, which was to eliminate the seat, and fill the whole area with a huge stand-up table with ample stowage for charts beneath.

Sensibly, Bill installed but one head, (can you imagine a designer of ultra-lights putting two of these monsters aboard?) aft of which is another double with a seat, and across the way another double still with a seat, and low and behold even a hanging locker. The engine is between the doubles with good access, and aft of it is a huge space, accessible from the lazarette, where many things can be stowed, although the space should be divided and closed off so things cannot roll around. A 75 gallon fuel tank is behind the engine and with the way this boat sails in even the lightest airs, that much diesel should last you about twenty years.

If you look at the photos you can discern such details as a table around the mast hung between two posts with two gimballed racks above it, and another nice touch, a secondary set of steps leading up the forward end of the galley island. I am not sure what practical value this has since the owner's cabin has a door on it for privacy anyway, but it does look good and adds a bit of fun to the

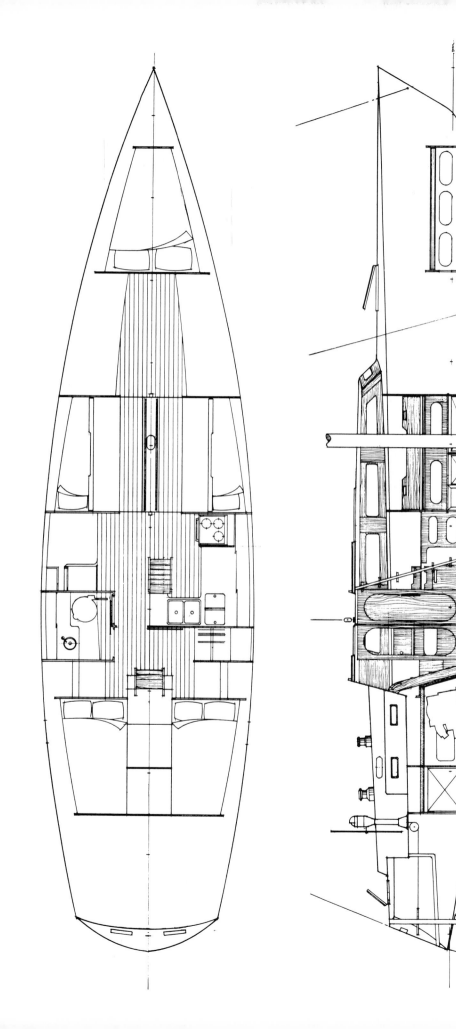

The Santa Cruz 50 with two large doubles aft, a workable galley and a vast area for sails forward of the mast. In the profile you can see the mast sitting on the big aluminum I-beam. The solid vertical line just aft of the mast is a plate that ties the bilges together and acts as chainplate reenforcement, transferring all the load down to the I-beam.

Bill Lee's minimalist concepts, at their cozy best with varnished wood, everywhere. The hull is just painted and left and if you look close in the photo you'll see just how even the glasswork is.

place.

And that is it — short and sweet, except that I will mention that the handholds that you see in the corners of the bulkhead do work very well, for the plywood is Bruynzeel, which makes the handles so strong that you can yank the thing with all your might and it still stays put.

Construction

Well again, as so often in this book, this is the best part, and whatever else you may think of Bill Lee and his designs, you must give him the great credit due, for it is innovators like him that keep sailing and boat building a vital and fascinating field that grows by leaps and bounds, and fuels the imagination as it examines and pushes one approach to the limit. And that is the way his work should be looked upon; not as the ultimate approach but *one* approach, although his application

of some conventional materials can be looked upon as perhaps the *best* approach.

Specifically worth mentioning is the head liner and cabinsides, which are also of Bruynzeel plywood, and are vacuum packed so that they become a structural part of the cabin top. This has very pretty results, and is a very clever method, putting to structural use something most builders apply as weighty and costly decoration. Vacuum packing is no magical process; in its simplest form it involves coating with resin the surfaces to be bonded, laying the piece in place, then covering it with plastic, sealing off the edges and removing the air by creating a vacuum. Once this occurs, atmospheric pressure will act as a weight or giant vise to hold the pieces together until the resin sets. And if you don't think that this creates enough pressure, then try taking a large suction cup off a piece of glass.

But let us start at the beginning with the hull construction. As I said, Bill Lee is not a man of many words, indeed when you are wanting facts you have to pull some out of him with pliers. Our conversation about the 50's lay-up schedule went something like this:

"Okay Bill, can you give me the hull laminates starting from the gelcoat in?"

"Why is that important?"

"Because there are some people who like to know what they are getting for the $150,000.00 they shell out."

"But why should I tell you?"

"Because if you don't I'm leaving you out of the book."

"Two layers of ¾ ounce mat, 24 ounce roving, ¾ ounce mat, 24 ounce roving, 1½ ounce mat, ¾ inch balsa, ¾ ounce mat, 24 ounce roving, ¾ ounce

mat, 24 ounce roving."

"Thanks."

The above shows that there is no skimping on hull material, but I suspect they do reduce the overall hull weight by some very excellent squeegeeing, for the glasswork I saw was truly first rate with no signs of thick resin lumps anywhere, just a smooth, very even surface.

As you can see in the profile drawing, the keel is not bolted directly to a flat bottom, but to a keel stub which is part of the hull. This allows the ballast to go a little deeper for added stiffness, but more importantly it leaves some more room inside for the reenforcing glass floor-beams that you see drawn as tall double lines. These thick-walled hollow beams are on 12 inch centres, and run all the way from station 2 to station 7. They are 1½ inches in width in most places, but with extra

The ultra-light and very-bright interior of the Santa Cruz 50. Bulkheads and cabinetry are built of 5⁄16 Bruynzeel marine plywood—the best stuff there is—and everything is kept to its most basic and simplest possible. The overhead wood liner not only looks good but is a structural part of the boat. No wonder Bill Lee could keep this 50 footer down to 16,000 pounds.

layers to make them 3 inches wide about 1 foot each side of the centreline. The entire backbone of the boat is reenforced with unidirectional roving for extra stiffness. The extra UDR runs 12 inches either side of the centreline. A hull so built was tested by one owner by cranking the hydraulics to 4,000 pounds and running a line from bow to stern and marking the string's position on the mast before and after the hydraulics were applied. The actual measured warpage was found to be around ½ inch, and that is unbelievably good for a 50 foot ultra-light boat. It makes you want to run a string test yourself. If you worry about these kinds of tests and think, my God, how much flex can fibreglass take, then let me assure you it can take a lot more than a ½ inch bend over 50 feet, for I have photographed Candace's sailplane coming in for a finish at 120 miles an hour with the wingtips of her 45 foot wingspan curved up almost a foot past their normal lines. If you are still not convinced, give your fishing rod a couple of good whips.

The hull-to-deck joint is done using the standard hull flange, with polyester adhesive between it and the deck, and ¼ inch stainless steel through-bolts (which hold down the aluminum toerail as well) on 4 inch centres, holding the hull and deck together.

All chainplate areas are reenforced with extra runs of fibreglass, but most of the loading is led down to the mast step I-beams as follows. The chainplates are the Navtec U-bolt through the deck type, which become two ½ inch rods belowdecks running down to a 12 inch long horizontal bar, which in turn is glassed into the reenforced hull. Just inches below where this occurs, is a ½ inch thick by 6 inch high aluminum plate which runs on edge athwartships, from hull to hull just below the raised area of the cabin sole. If you look at the cutaway profile you will see a vertical line just aft of the mast; that's the plate.

Running perpendicular to and below this plate is a hefty 5 foot long, 4 inch by 8 inch aluminum I-beam, upon which the mast is stepped. The beam and the aluminum plate are joined by a hefty aluminum knee. The I-beam in turn sits on the hollow glass floor beams and is bolted to them. With this structure most of the loading is taken away from the sides of the hull and transferred right back to the mast so in effect you can almost say that the mast is holding itself up.

The rudder shaft is almost a full 4 inches. They start building it with a 1½ inch heavy walled aluminum tube core, and wrap it with UDR until it is built up to over 1 inch thickness all the way around. The tooling on both the rudder and the keel is extremely well done with very fine trailing edges, and this is no easy task on the keel, for after the lead has been bolted on with fourteen 1 inch diameter bolts (this is the most I have seen for a fin keel), the lead is covered with glass which runs right up to the keel stub and fairs into the hull. Not only does this add some strength, but it also helps to totally seal off the keel joint which is always a trouble spot of leaks.

The deck is reenforced with ½ inch balsa except in areas of stress (winches, etc.) where plywood inserts are used. The construction of the stanchion bases is worth mentioning, for they are set into moulded-in pockets about 4 inches deep (somewhat akin to the beer can holders), so in fact there is no penetration of the deck with heavily loaded fasteners, meaning again fewer potential leaks.

As you can see from the profile cutaway, the cockpit drains through the transom above the waterline, cutting down on the number of below-water holes, meaning less friction through turbulence, less weight (no seacocks) and fewer leaks. To ensure against rainwater leaks into the boat, Bill uses rigid PVC pipe and glasses it to the hull, cutting down on potential failure of soft hoses and mechanical clamps.

The best I have left for last. The entire interior reenforcement of the hull comes from 12 millimetre (⁵⁄₁₆ inch) Bruynzeel plywood bulkheads, which is just over half the thickness of most comparable sailboat bulkheads, which usually run from ½ inch up. And yet the 50's seem to manage very well for six basic reasons not found in most other boats save for ultra-lights. The first is that the shrouds are tied into the aluminum beam system as explained, so the bulkheads don't have to literally keep the shrouds from pulling the hull-sides in. Second, the ¾ inch balsa adds much stiffness to the hull; and third, the entire raised midship's box, with the assorted pieces above it, creates a monocoque beam amidships where all the forces of keel and rigging exert much of their power. Fourth, the plywood used is Bruynzeel and I cannot overstress how excellent this material is, with

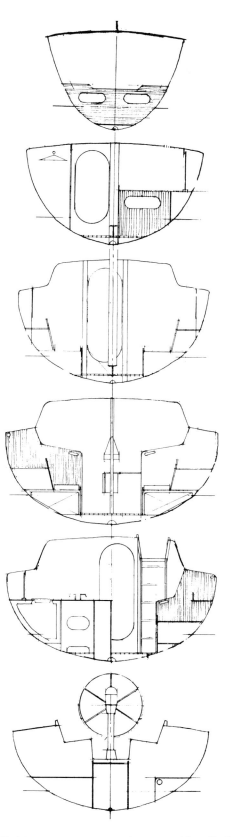

The Santa Cruz 50 reassembled from stem to stern to give you an idea of hull shape. For an idea of the interior you have to pretend you're standing amidships, i.e., looking forward through the three bow sections and looking aft for the three stern ones. If that's not enough to boggle the average mind I don't know what is.

no voids or flaws; and fifth, there are no liners in the boat and everything in the boat is bonded in. Now you may laugh and say, "Yes, but there is not much there to bond in," but the pieces that *are* here are *all* bonded both sides, tops of bulkheads included, which is a lot more than you can say for the "floating" liners used in many production boats.

The engine is a Volkswagen conversion Pathfinder 4 cylinder diesel, which puts out about 42 horsepower, but the problem is that it puts that out at 4,000 R.P.M. meaning that, all things being equal, the engine may wear out considerably faster than something like a Volvo or Perkins, which attain their peak power at just over half that many R.P.M.'s. The advantages of the Pathfinder are its low weight (a couple of hundred pounds less than most other engines) and its considerably lower price. Check into both in detail before you decide.

I have left one of the most important ingredients for last, and that is that Bill has managed to instill a sense of family pride in his small crew, in his hillside yard near Santa Cruz overlooking the Pacific Ocean, and whether he has done this by running an open yard where the workers are welcome after hours and weekends to use the yard's tools or the company truck, or just by having such fierce pride in the quality of his boats himself, or a combination thereof, is hard to say, but whatever it is, the workers' attitude is that they don't dare do sloppy work for everyone else in the yard will come down on them.

So, you may disagree with Bill Lee's concepts but you must admire his daring, and even more you must admire that his heart and soul are in his work, and that is why without any doubt his are some of the best boats on this continent.

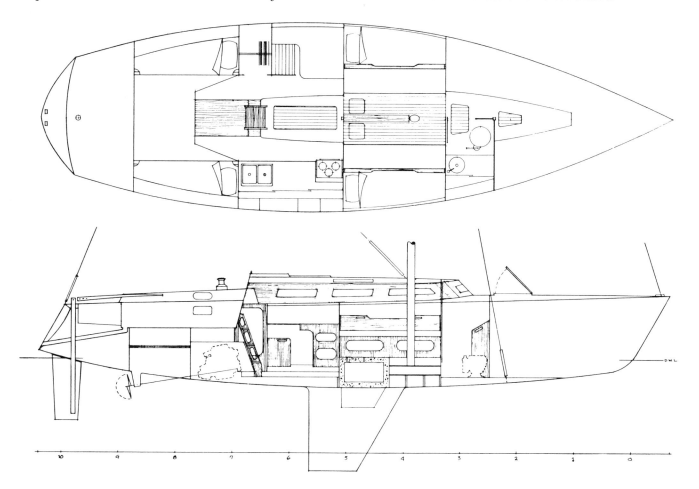

The little sister to the ultra-fast Santa Cruz 50, the Santa Cruz 40 has a much more proportionate beam and harder bilges for added stability. The interior is sensible with four first class seaberths and a good-sized chart table, although the fore-and-aft galley will require some fancy footwork when clawing to windward on a starboard tack.

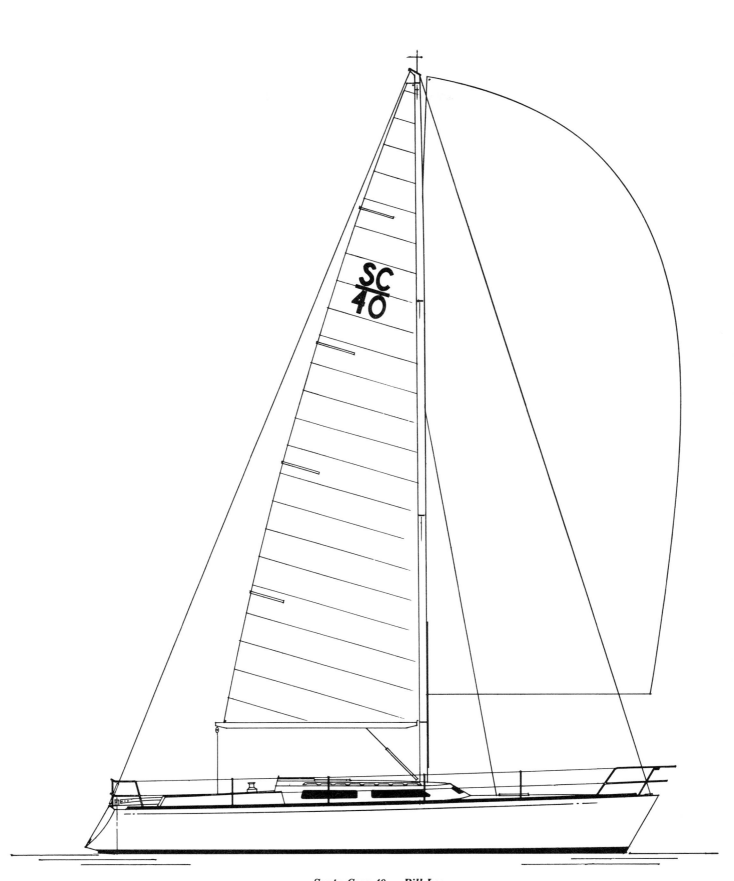

Santa Cruz 40 — Bill Lee

LOA—40'0'' LWL—36'0'' Beam—12'0'' Draft—7'0'' Displ.—10,500 lbs. Ballast—5,500 lbs. I = 50 J = 15.5 P = 44.5 E = 13.6

26

Up the Lazy River
The Nordic Tug

I worked on an old tugboat in my younger days, the hours were brutal and long — thirteen a day — and the pay was just enough to pay the moorage on my listing houseboat and put food in me regularly and that's all, but the skippers I worked under were some of the best men I've ever met and I just kept going back for more. Anyway, when you work thirteen hours a day your're never really awake enough to quit.

You worked in miserable weather, in cold winter rains on icy decks, crawling around great scows in the dark, or tiptoeing over log booms that were just dying to have you fall among them so they could close over your head for good. And you worked in damnable seas with spray covering you over, and knocking you about as you tried your best to lasso a runaway scow, and you would almost have the line over the great steel bit, when the sea would give you a great kick in the ass and you'd let go the line as fast as your hands could open and grab out at the dark for something firm to hold.

But when you climbed back into the tug with her oil stove blazing and kettle steaming, you felt so good and snug you wouldn't have traded places with the King of Siam.

A little tugboat is a fine, fine workboat and a good fishing boat and, if you want her to be, even a fine yacht. She will glide silently at 5 knots, and use but a quart of diesel an hour, or she will cruise at 6½ and use 2, and leave a wake so small it would make a sailboat proud.

Now we all have acquaintances who have somehow lost their way, stumbled off the path of good sense into the violent venom filled jungle of power boats, that scream and snort and screech and roar and hurl themselves at the calm green sea like mad dogs. These sad lost friends need help, for they will never leave their jungle and take to sail, deeming themselves too slow of body or mind to make the change, so if they insist, let them stay with a boat without a sail, but at least get them to throw away their laughable monstrosities, and take to the sea in something that can do a good day's work, something built with reason and thought and heart, and not something designed solely to show the other pathetic next door, "Hey Schmo, look at mine, it's bigger than yours."

Tugboats, like fishboats, are bits of history in the Northwest; the Cates family has been tugboating here for over a hundred years, so to us they are as much a part of the sea as sailboats and lighthouses, and when I came upon a little tug at Jerry Husted's yard, where the beautiful Ingrids are built, I couldn't believe my eyes. And when Jerry asked if Candace and I would like to take her for a little cruise, we were out the door and off to the dock before he'd finished his sentence.

Now normally power boats scare the hell out of me; I can't believe that people go to sea relying on wretched gas engines alone to move them, but this was a tug with a proper little diesel, so off we went. It was toward evening and the wind was easing, and Jerry's brother Jim had told us when he pushed us off to be sure to take her up a pretty little river called Sammamich, so we pulled out the chart, looked at it silently as we putt-putted along, then Candace stared out the window at the muddy river mouth covered with reeds, and said, "The guy's nuts." And according to the chart he was. The chart showed 6 feet at this end of the lake, which was bad enough for someone who for the past six years has been on the water with a 5 foot keel below him, but the cartographer's generosity ebbed even more at the river mouth, to 3 feet, then

2, then 1, and then zero. "Maybe it's okay," I said. "Maybe this is high tide." And Candace looked at me with pity in her eyes, smiled sadly and said, "This is a small lake, Hunky, not the Pacific Ocean."

I eased the throttle forward and the little tug slid silently toward the marshes and a glint of the river in the forests beyond. At half throttle you could hardly hear the engine and we moved through the water without a wake. *6, 6, 6,* the fathometer flashed, and I held my breath and on we went. When it flashed *5* I closed one eye, when it flashed *4* my heart stopped, and when it flashed *3* I started to say goodbye to Candace, but she smiled and said, "Lots of room. You've got six more inches." The sounder stayed at *3* for a while, then jumped to *4* and I sighed with relief, and it was a hardly audible little sigh but the bastard gadget must have heard it for it jumped back to *3* again and started to dim, as if I were burying its bloody transducer in the mud.

The marsh closed in and the reeds rubbed the hull and a mallard lit and quacked loudly, then we were in the river and the wind of the lake was gone, and there was just the silence of the evening

The Nordic Tug coasting quietly in silent shallow rivers.

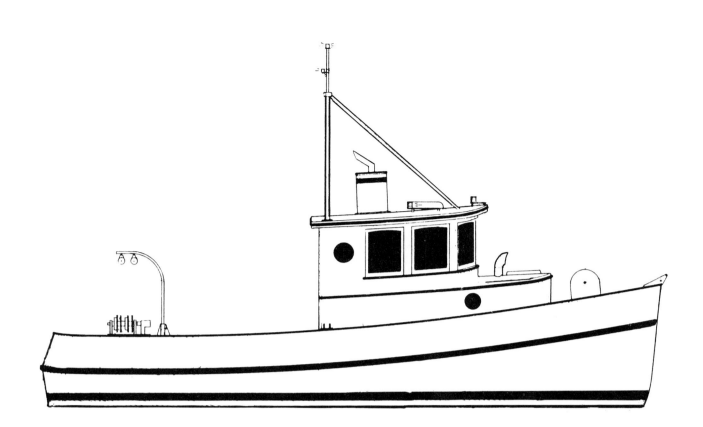

The Nordic Tug short-house version gives you ample deck space aft for a safe working area, while providing a couple of good berths, enclosed head, trim galley and a fine table for two belowdecks. An ideal workboat or fishboat for skipper and mate. The Perkins diesel engine will push her quietly at 5 knots and use less than ½ gallon an hour.

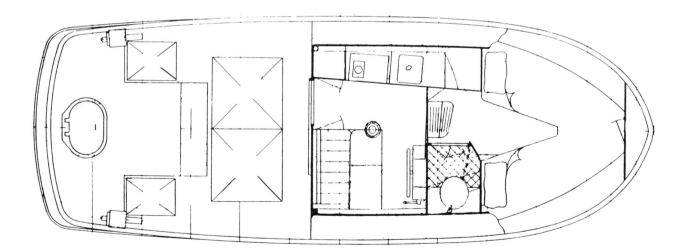

Nordic Tug — Lynn Senour
LOA—26'4"   Beam—9'6"   Draft—2'8"   Displ.—6,000 lbs.

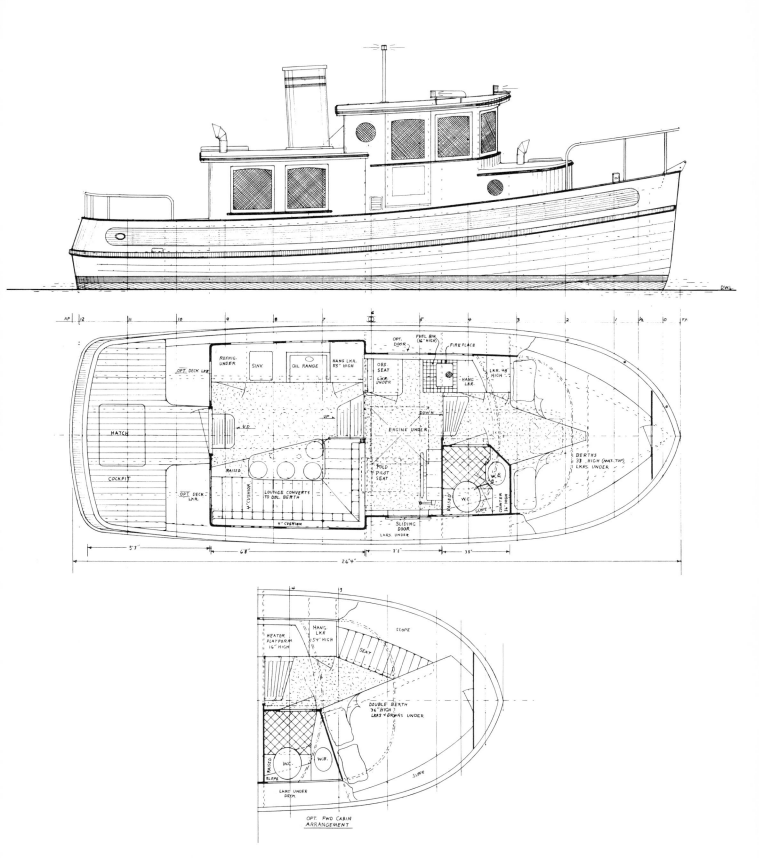

The long-house version of the Nordic Tug has a larger head, two seats in the pilot house and a fireplace. The deck house has a fine dinette and good galley, in all an excellent craft for discovering shoal
areas and remote inlets. But whatever you do, do not install a generator that you may be tempted to
run in a silent anchorage, for if I'm nearby I'm going to shatter your eardrums with the most vile
string of words you've ever heard. Remember, Hungarians are world swearing champions, who
laughingly mix curses, carnal acts, bestiality and saints. One old Hungarian was known to swear for
a steady half hour without repeating a single word. Beware!

and the trees leaning in from the narrow banks. The tug moved upriver as if pushed by a ghost. The sun was going down and its light came through the trees and fell on the river in patches. The water was dark-green everywhere but where the sun fell on it it was brown, and the tug moved quietly from spot to spot as if tiptoeing over flat stones.

3, 3, 3, the sounder flashed and a shrill bird call came with it, three, three, three. The trees leaned in so close we were almost in a tunnel, and you could hardly see the sky when Candace yelled out softly, "Dammit, reverse." The tug stopped. Just a few feet ahead the foliage looked solid overhead, strangely solid, and strangely flat along the bottom as if someone had pruned it in a straight line.

"It's a log bridge," Candace said, "too bad."

That's what it was, just overhead in the trees, a couple of great logs slung from bank to bank, and ordinarily that would be the end of a voyage, but not when you have a veteran tugboater aboard.

"Go up top," I said calmly, "put your eye at the level of the top of the funnel and I will ease her ahead. If you don't think we can make it, yell and I will stop."

Candace looked surprised, "You must think I'm a simpleton," she said. "What if you don't stop, then off comes my face, right?"

"Not if you duck," I said.

"Oh," she said and went out.

Past the bridge of logs the river got wider and the bends longer and the sky darker, so you could just see the glimmering water up ahead. Then a brighter glimmer, a red glimmer, began glowing before us and it pulsated softly among the shimmering boughs. "Look," Candace whispered, *"The Heart of Darkness."*

The Nordic Tug, built by Jerry Husted and his brother Jim and a fine lady called Gail Davis, who does some of the lay-up work herself, is built and laid-up by hand of three alternate layers of mat and cloth, and its decks are balsa cored, and all glass content is kept high, around 47 per cent, and there are reenforcing laminates in the bow and stern and the whole bottom, over the heavy stringers. It is built to stay together in anything inland waters have to offer, and that is a lot when you count the Strait of Juan de Fuca and Johnstone Strait and the Gulf of Alaska, where a number are now used as fishboats and workboats. She is not just a work tug in looks and basic construction, but also in her finish, with heavy cast hawsepipes, monster cleats, and a cast watertight hatch in the aft deck. She has a semi-displacement hull with a long keel and we found she rode nicely in chop and tracked well, and has such a responsive rudder that she spun like a big rowboat. She has a single screw but it is all you need if you have half a brain, for there is nothing to spinning a true tug without moving her more than a foot or so, fore and aft, by giving her reverse until she starts to move, then giving her hard forward with the rudder over hard, then when she moves forward give her reverse again, and so on. Canadace learned it in no time on *Warm Rain*, and she turned the Nordic tug around just fine in the river that was but a few feet wider than the tug's length. A little brain work will often replace a lot of claptrap.

The Nordic tug is 26 foot 4 inches overall, 9 foot 6 inches in the beam and she has 32 inches of draft. She can go practically anywhere a duck can, and she will be stable because of her beam, and with her V'd forefoot she won't pound much.

On deck you have two choices: a short trawler house which leaves you with a vast aft deck for work or for cargo, or a long tugboat house which shortens the deck considerably but still leaves it large enough for fishing or just sitting, and you will still be able to mount permanent trolling gear on each side.

The trawler house has a galley to port, big enough for a small Dickerson oil stove and a sink, and a big enough counter to chop up fish and vegetables for your chowder. A two seat table is right behind the steering station, and there is a large hatch leading to the engine room where you will find plenty of space for proper maintenance. You take two steps down to the fo'c's'le where there is the hanging locker, the head, and two comfortable berths — a nice setup for a man and his wife to fish a season, with 118 cubic feet of room in the hold to carry 6,500 pounds of fish and ice, and there are permanent bait boxes on deck. The access hatches to the hold are over 30 inches square, and there are two side by side just as there should be. The side-decks are 12 inches wide and this should be enough, for you will end up walking on the caprails half the time anyway, holding the top of the house for support.

For those who love nature and want to explore distant shallow bays and hidden rivers, and require more space and storage for their books and what-nots, the long house would be a better choice. This has a large galley aft with a generous eating area to port for when you have the good luck to find new friends in distant places, and there is plenty of storage for food and gear and even a refrigerator. Two steps aft will take you to the aft deck, where there are two boxes for storage of fenders, lines, inflatables, and the like. For sunny climates a sun top would be a good idea out here.

The pilot house itself is ideal for a nature loving couple, with a seat to port right beside the wood stove, which will keep you cozy on those spring and autumn days that are nippy enough to keep you indoors but not cold enough to have the oil range going. Visibility is good in all directions, although the long house does reduce the aft window of the pilot house to a degree. The wheel itself is a little farther aft on the long house version, and this makes the pilot house a little smaller, but it also increases the area of the head in the fo'c's'le, enough for a sink and a shower and some stowage. Do not mistake the fo'c's'le in either boat for a Black Hole of Calcutta, for there is good livable space here with headroom and lots of air.

One of the best parts is that with either version you get a genuine smoke stack, but the sad part is that you have to pay a lot of money to get a genuine Kahlenberg air-whistle mounted on your stack to give a wonderful throaty 'toot, toot.'

The sturdy Nordic Tug with the long-house chugging along in Lake Washington's winter mist.

More Boats

Falmouth Cutter — Lyle C. Hess
LOA - 22'0" LWL - 20'10" Beam - 8'0" Draft - 3'6" Displ.-7,400 lbs. Bal.-2,500 lbs. Sail Area -357 sq.ft.

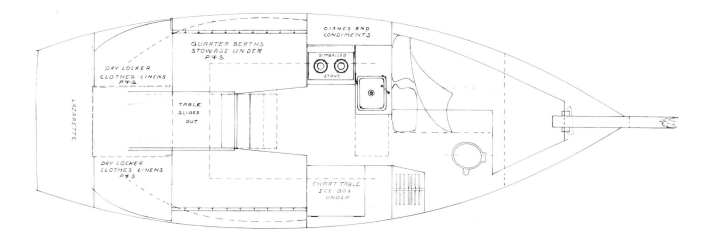

Falmouth Cutter

Builder's Comments

Nineteenth century England produced many fine cutter models, some of the best of which were working boats from the west of England such as those of Itchen Ferry, Falmouth and the Bristol Channel. These were heavy displacement vessels with good beam and firm bilges, enabling them to sail well with cargo and to stand up to wind and sea in heavy weather. Some models were especially notable for their performances in off season racing and many came to be built solely for that purpose.

Designer Lyle Hess has long admired these remarkable craft and he determined to incorporate their qualities into a more modern design yet retain the beauty of the originals.

Renegade was the first of a series of Cutter models which has brought Mr. Hess great distinction in his field. Renegade was a beautiful gaff rigged yacht and was fast — surprising ocean racers in the 1950's by winning twice in the Newport to Ensenada race.

A young man named Larry Pardey admired Renegade and asked Mr. Hess to design a marconi rigged sistership. He did, and Lin and Larry built *Seraffyn* and sailed her around the world. With their message of "go small, go simple, but go now," they have kindled a tremendous interest in small boat cruising.

Inspired by the success of his ideas, Mr. Hess went again to his drawing board and designed a smaller 22 foot version to be his own personal boat, the boat he would build for himself some day. We build the Falmouth Cutter as we do the Bristol Channel Cutter — for going to sea. Both vessels were designed as true cruising yachts with the heavy displacement necessary to provide capacity for the stores and equipment required for a long voyage. Displacement is not only weight — it is cubic space, inside the hull, below the waterline where you need it most. Displacement and waterline length are the two best criteria of a yacht's size.

Our boats are not mass produced — there is no assembly line — we build to customer order only, and since we sell direct, we do develop a close working relationship with each buyer. Every boat which leaves our yard bears the personal stamp of its owner in the custom modifications we have made to suit his needs. We build very carefully so we can truthfully say "this is a proper yacht for ocean cruising" — she is very strong; we have conformed to the highest standards of construction. She is an honest boat and you can place your trust in her. These boats are not for eveyone — they are more expensive because it simply costs more to build this way. But, if you really want an ocean cruiser, isn't it wise to have her built like this?

Absolutely true. [F.M.] For details see Bristol Channel Cutter in the main section.

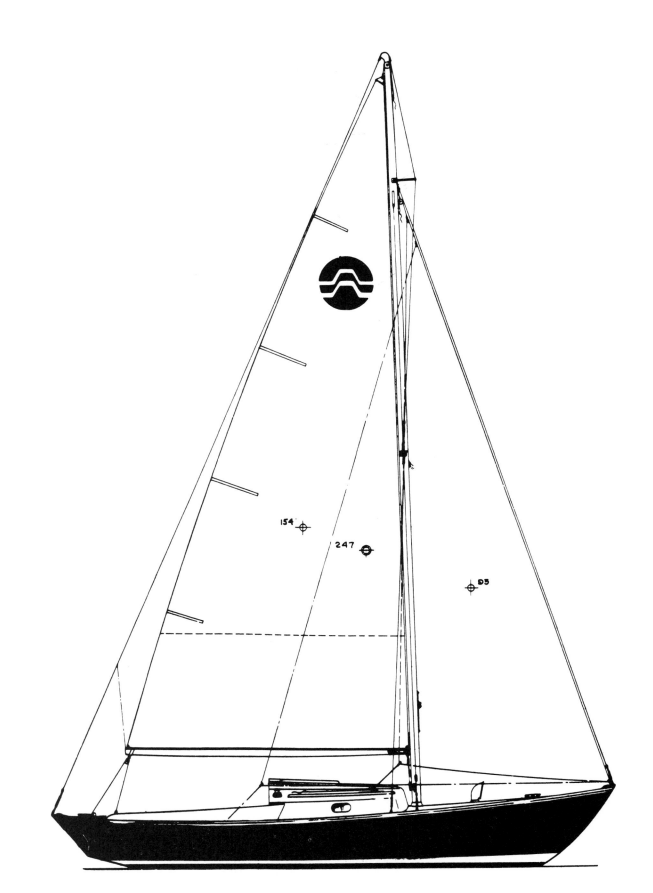

Alberg 23 — Carl Alberg
LOA - 22'6'' LWL - 16'3'' Beam - 7'0'' Draft - 3'0'' Displ-3,350 lbs. Bal. - 1,400 lbs. Sail Area-247 sq. ft.

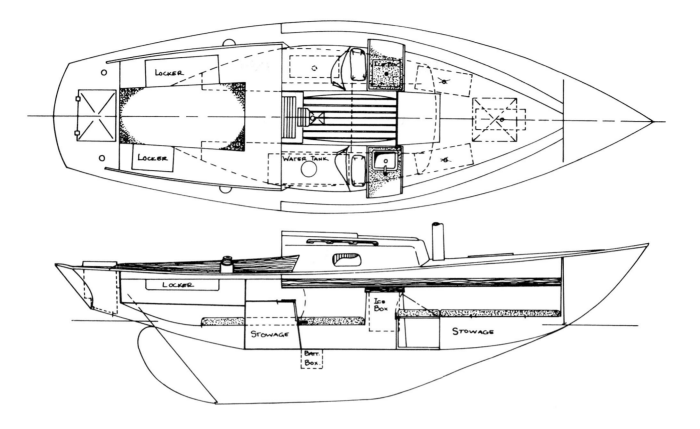

Alberg 23

The Alberg 23 is not what you'd call hot off the press. She was designed 25 years ago by Carl Alberg, and she has an elegant wine-glass shaped hull and a full keel. She is built by Ryder Yachts (see *Friend in the Dark Alley)* along with another fine little weekend cruiser, the beautiful canoe-sterned Ted Brewer designed Quickstep 24. Her underbody is typical of Ted Brewer's work with broadly cut-back forefoot and a big bite taken from the aft section of the keel. Both of these cut-aways help to reduce wetted surface, thereby increasing performance, as well as enabling the boat to come-about more readily under either sail or power.

Oysterman 23 — H. I. Chapelle
LOA - 22'6" LWL - 21'1" Beam - 8'0" Draft - 1'8" Displ.-2,600 lbs. Bal. - 700 lbs. Sail Area- 355 sq. ft.

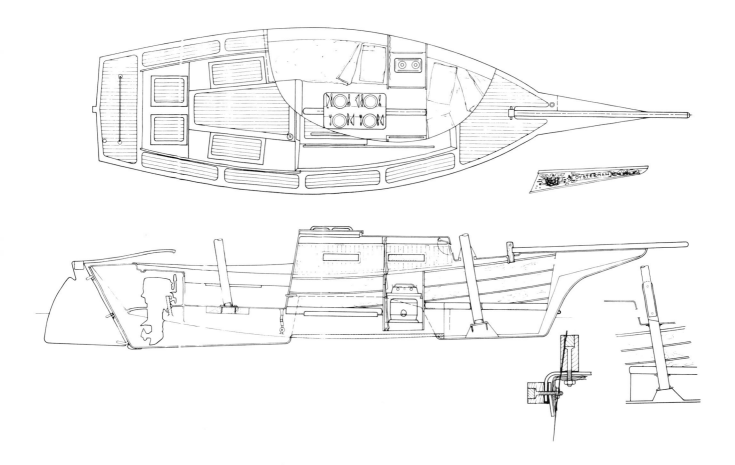

Oysterman 23

A Letter from the Builder,
Mr. William M. Menger

The original hull lines of our Skipjack are by H. I. Chappelle and are on file in the Smithsonian Institute, Washington, D.C. We have slightly modernized the sail plan and added a ketch option, increased length and size of cabin and made the cockpit self bailing. There are boats sailing in the Keys and in New Hampshire. Last fall, we took the demonstrator to Skipjack races off Sandy Point park near Annapolis and did quite well.

When we first introduced kits, we worried about someone assembling an Oysterman improperly and giving the boat a bad name. We have not had this happen, as almost all kits have been very well put together. (We do all glass work on kits, including glassing hull to deck. Since most kit builders are inexperienced in glasswork, this has assured us that the boat is structurally sound). As you will note in our specifications, there are five

pages on fasteners alone. I don't think other builders go into this detail. It has paid off in the quality of the kit-built boats. I can spot differences from our factory productions, but generally the kit boats are almost indistinguishable.

The designer, H. I. Chappelle was curator of ships at the Smithsonian for many years, and took his lines off a lot of skipjacks. He knew what made them go. In 1955 he designed a wooden boat which we have copied in FRP except for slight changes (ketch, cabin, rig).

I myself have been building boats since 13 years of age. I am a graduate Civil Engineer, 47 years old, with 16 years' experience in reenforced plastics, first as a production manager and for the last 6 years running my own fibreglass reenforced plastics business.

There are over 40 "Oysterman" scattered around the Eastern Seaboard. Most are ketches.

Luders 27 — Bill Luders
LOA - 27'11" LWL - 20'0" Beam-8'10" Draft-4'3" Displ.-7,600 lbs. Bal.-3,000 lbs. Sail Area-340 sq. ft.

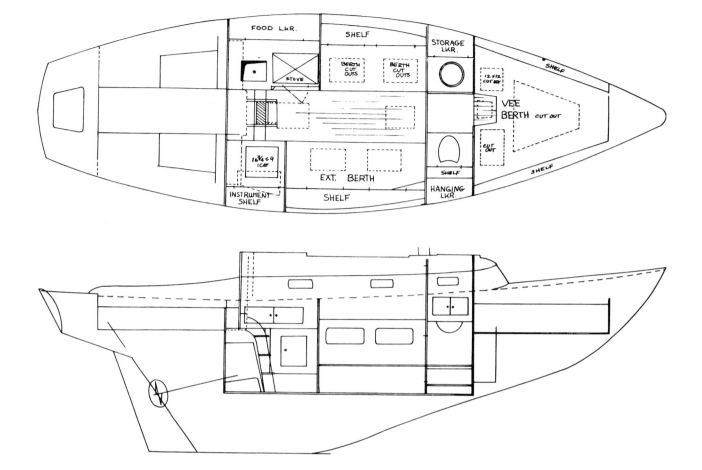

Luders 27

The Luders 27 is another pretty boat from Bill Luders, whose keynotes are moderation and excellent proportions. Her displacement to waterline length shows her to be a very seakindly craft with good motion and her sail-area to displacement ratio of just under 15 means she won't have to be reefed too early. Even though the numbers show her to be anything but a light-air speedster, Bill Luders' boats have a tendency to somehow defy numbers as well as logic, and quite predictably outperform themselves. The 27 is built by Ryder Custom Yachts, and for more information on them and on Bill Luders, see chapter titled *One for the Heart*.

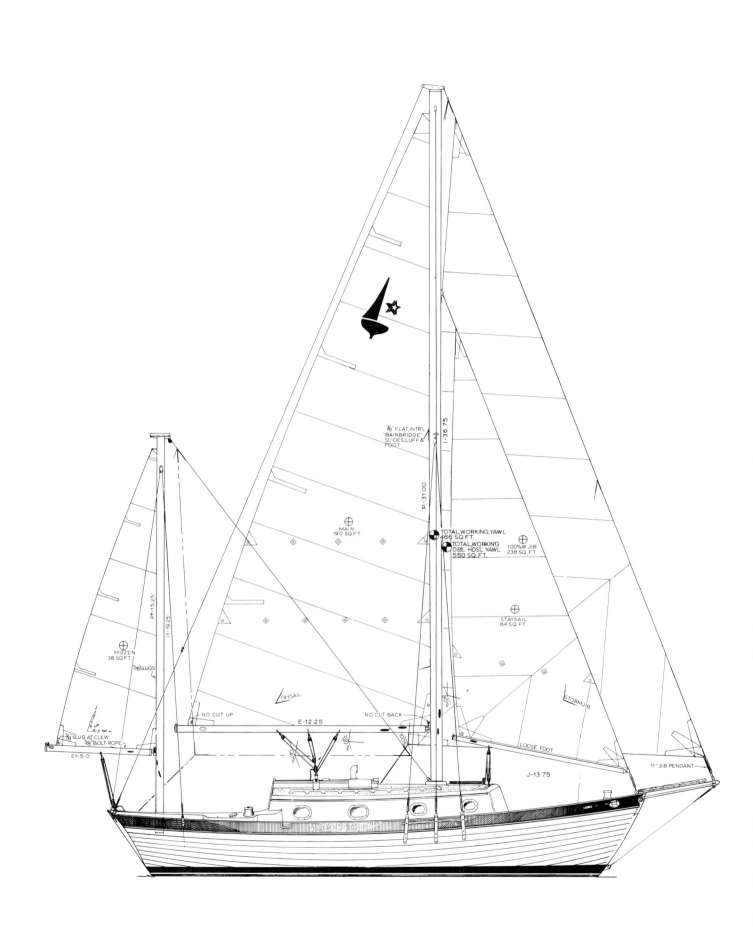

7/8" FLAT, INTR'L "BAINBRIDGE" SLIDES, LUFF & FOOT

I-36.75

P-31.00

MAIN
190 SQ.FT.

TOTAL, WORKING, YAWL
466 SQ.FT.
TOTAL, WORKING
DBL. HDS'L YAWL
550 SQ.FT.

100% W JIB
238 SQ FT

PY-15.25

IY-19.25

STAYSAIL
84 SQ.FT.

MIZZEN
38 SQ FT

3/8 SLUGS

TRYSAIL

NO CUT UP

E-12.25

NO CUT BACK

STORM JIB

3/8 SLUG AT CLEW
3/8 BOLT ROPE

LOOSE FOOT

EY-5.0

J-13.75

11" JIB PENDANT

Orion 27

Designer's Comments

Orion is designed for long distance cruising. Her full keel provides directional stability and rudder protection.

Ground tackle aboard the Orion is sturdy. Two solid oak Sampson Posts secure the anchor rode. They are protected from abrasion and exposure to weather by polished bronze caps. In addition, bronze hawse pipes protect the rode and the teak capped rail from abrasion. Orion's custom cast bronze hardware also includes hasps, hinges, cleats, deck drains and ports.

Dorade vents aboard Orion are designed to assure ventilation below decks. They are molded into the cabin roof with teak boxes fitted over them. No chance for unwanted water below decks, nor problems of water condensation and mildew.

If you push the main hatch forward, you'll find the sea hood. This keeps water from getting below through the hatch runners by utilizing a series of baffles and drains to remove it. Orion's lifeline stanchions are mounted through raised deck pads. This not only provides greater strength to the stanchions, but also prevents errant drops of water from finding their way through bolt holes on deck.

Her hull and deck are hand laid up, then squeegeed out, assuring the greatest strength to weight ratio. The hull to deck connection is engineered with a double flange completely bedded in polyurethane compound and then through bolted with 18 - 8 stainless steel bolts. Chain plates are $\frac{3}{16}$ inch thick and $1\frac{3}{4}$ inch wide type 304 S.S., through fastened to the outside of the hull, with S.S. bolts and full back-up plates. All chain plate fastenings are fully accessible from inside the hull, and are less likely to leak than deck mounted chain plates.

She is equipped with a sloop rig as standard, but is also available with optional cutter or yawl. Because of her wide 9'3" beam and unique modular construction, the new Orion 27 is spacious. She has comfortable berths for six, including double berth forward, a wraparound lounge which converts to a Queen size berth, and a wide quarterberth. The sit down chart table is completely independent of any berth.

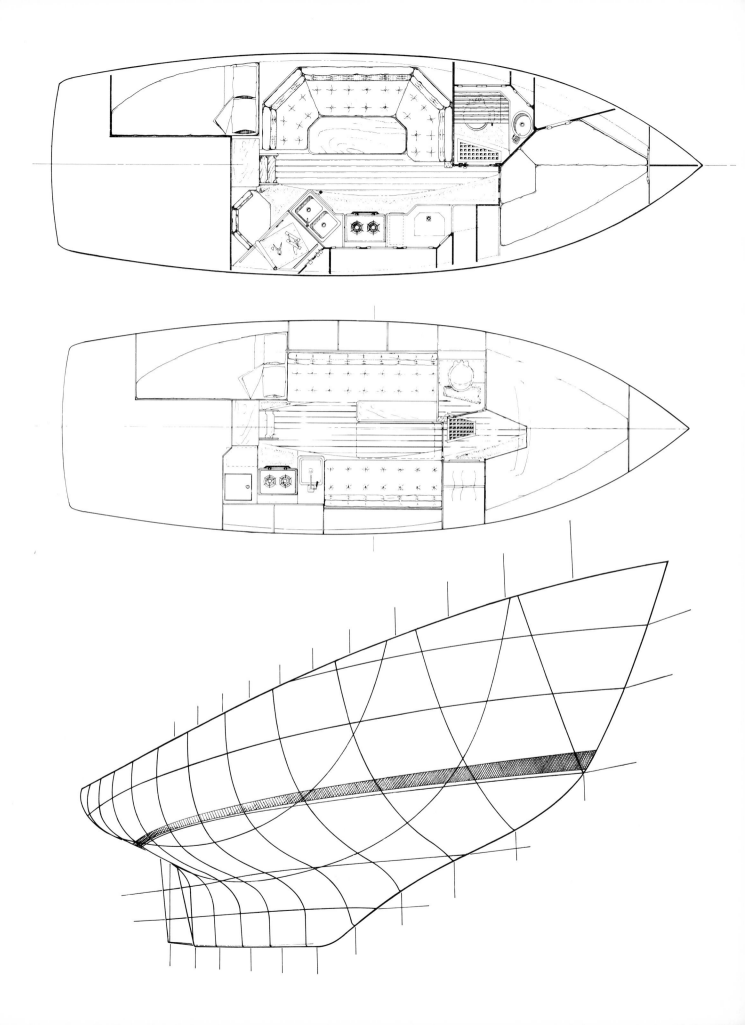

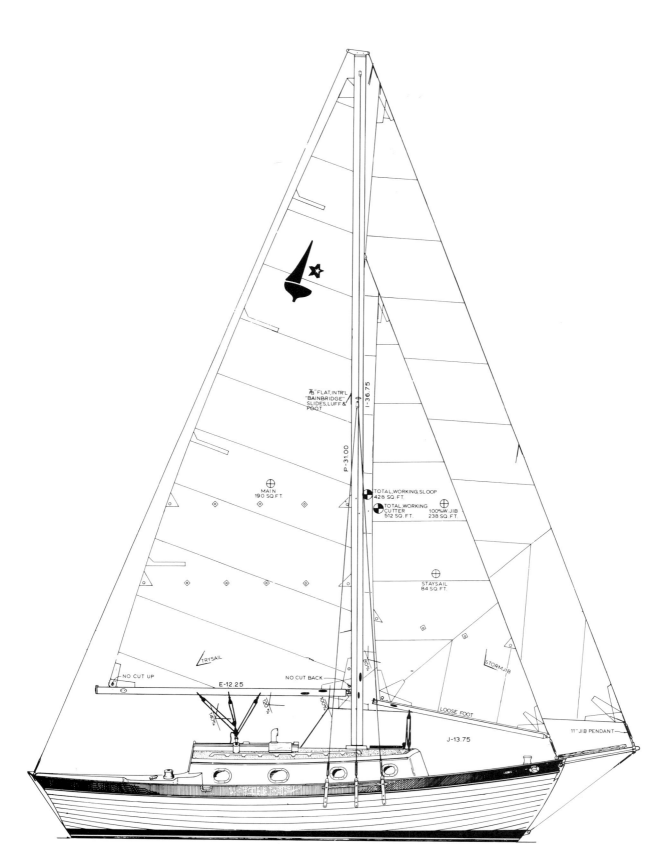

Orion 27 — Henry Mohrschladt
LOA — 27'4" LWL - 22'2" Beam - 9'3" Draft - 4'0" Displ.-10,000 lbs. Bal.-3,200 lbs. Sail Area-421 sq. ft.

Vancouver 27 — Rober B. Harris

LOA - 27'0" LWL - 22'11" Beam - 8'8" Draft - 4'0" Displ. 9,200 lbs. Bal. - 4,000 lbs. Sail Area - 379 sq. ft.

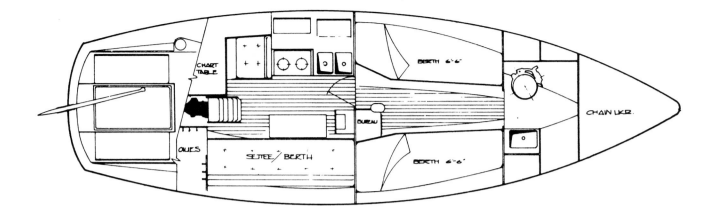

Vancouver 27

Builder's Comments

Vancouver 27s have crossed oceans and have successfully negotiated gales in the English Channel and North Sea. Owners reporting on their passages confirm the effectiveness of the long keel of the Vancouver 27 to render a very stable helm and excellent balance on all points of sailing, a necessity for successful wind vane steering. To this we can add that with the rudder and propeller well protected from coral reefs and nets by the keel, skeg and sternpost arrangement, there is little chance of damage to the underbody. Protection from boarding seas is assured by a generous freeboard both at the bow and at the stern and by a small but comfortable cockpit which will not endanger the boat if filled by pooping.

In spite of all the protection gained by the underbody configuration, the sailing speeds as reported by owners are surprisingly good. Reaching and running, Vancouver 27s have ex-ceeded theoretical hullspeed many times. With her especially designed V shaped keel she hangs onto weather remarkably well.

The rig for the Vancouver 27 is generous but with the mast set nearly amidships, the mainsail is reasonably small and easy to handle, while the foretriangle is large but split into a double head rig with a roller furling jib topsail reefing down is simple. All reefing lines for the jib topsail and the mainsail can lead to the cockpit for single handed operations.

Hull layup specifications: Gel coat, 15 to 20 thous. — skinout - mat — hardened — 1½ oz. mat and 18 oz. roving — hardened — 1½ oz. mat and 24 oz. roving — 1½ oz. mat and 24 oz. roving — 1½ oz. mat and 24 oz. roving to 6 inches above waterline — 1½ oz. mat and 24 oz. roving keel cavity to 2 feet up the hull sides — Airex foam core — available as an extra.

Evetts 31 — John Evetts
LOA - 30'8" LWL - 24'0" Beam-11'2" Draft-5'7" Displ.-6,800 lbs. Bal.-3,000 lbs. Sail Area-410 sq. ft.

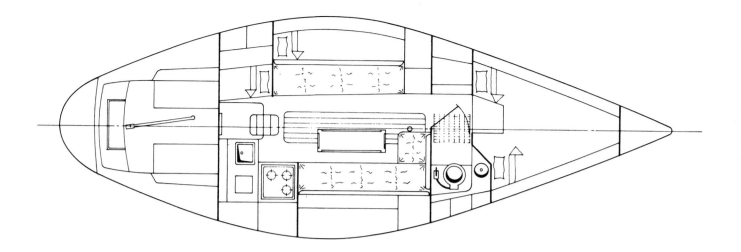

Evetts 31

Builder's Comments

Her beamy hull (11'2") and long waterline give both the internal space and performance of a larger boat, whilst her fairly light displacement and tall rig give her excellent light air speed, helping to make her a good boat for cruising in any area in North America.

The builders, Alvis Marine Ltd., known in the Vancouver area for their quality marine repair work, have designed and engineered the Evetts 31 to be a 'State of the Art' fibreglass yacht. The cored construction in both hull and deck with special cruciform bottom stiffeners, solid glass backbone and bonded-in structural bulkheads ensure a rigid, warm and dry boat that will continue to perform year after year.

The deck layout is designed to be both comfortable and efficient for cruising and racing. Particular attention has been given to making her easy to sail short handed.

Good visibility over the low coach roof, wide side decks and T-shaped cockpit (wheel steering can be specified) help.

Ease of handling is helped by conveniently mounted large 2-speed sheet winches, bridge deck roller traveller and in-board genoa track.

The interior is large and airy with 6'1"
headroom. To starboard there is a 6'4" L-shaped settee which makes into a double berth. Outboard and forward is an additional locker with door, aft a shelf with cupboards behind. A single flap teak table, with storage, can seat 5 in comfort. On the port side there is a 6'4" pilot berth outboard with a settee berth below. Forward there is a cabinet with drawers, a counter above and behind a further stowage area.

The beamy hull (11'2") allowed the designing of a spacious L-shaped galley set aft on the starboard side but out of the main traffic area. There is a deep sink, with foot pump, large insulated (2" minimum) ice box, gimballed 3 burner propane stove with oven. Plenty of storage bins, dish and crockery racks are provided.

There is a 6'4" Vee Berth with filler cushion and storage underneath. There is a full fibreglass liner, and a full length shelf over each berth. A large alloy framed hatch gives light and ventilation.

Her mast has streamlined single spreaders, 1 x 19 stainless standing rigging with single lowers and 'Baby' stay, internal halyards with 2-speed Genoa halyard winch. A fixed gooseneck is attached to a boom with internal out haul, and two sets of Jiffy Reefing.

Clark 31 — Herreshoff/Clark
LOA - 30'2" LWL - 26'3" Beam-9'3" Draft-5'0" Displ.-11,800 lbs. Bal.-4,300 lbs. Sail Area-579 sq. ft.

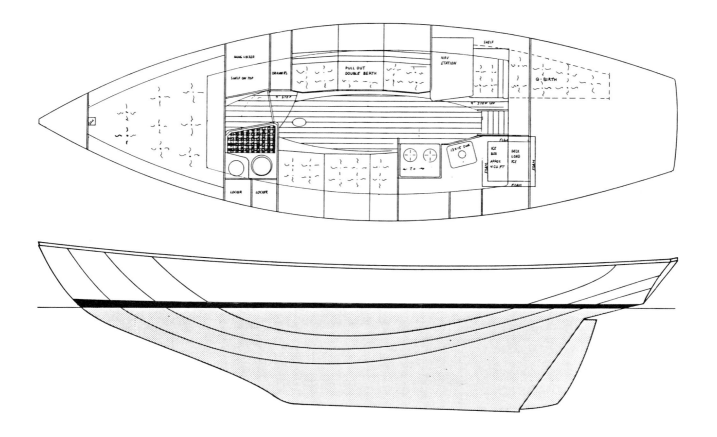

Clark 31

A Letter from Bill Clark

The Clark 31 is a modification of L. Francis Herreshoffs' H-28, the obvious changes being the counter transom and deeper draft. Other modifications are greater beam (from 8'9" to 9'4") and from 2,800 lbs. to 4,300 lbs. for the ballast. The original H-28 was a fine sailing boat but small inside for her length for today's needs. The modifications gave the boat much more usable interior space and greatly improved her ability to go to weather in light and heavy conditions.

Before the boat was put into production, my wife and I sailed the prototype to Hawaii and return. Out of this came only one change; raising the cockpit floor three inches. The boat has a very easy motion due to its deep V hull sections and is very dry for a low freeboard boat. Our best day's run was 150 miles in 24 hours under working sails.

The prototype was launched as a stemhead sloop, then was rigged as a cutter and finally as a yawl with bowsprit and boomkin.

One of the big problems for the home builder (or professional builder for that matter) of a traditional boat of this type is finding the proper hardware. Consequently, some years ago I began to develop our own bronze hardware line, which includes a complete hardware kit for the Clark 31.

The layup schedule is as follows: Mat, cloth, mat, cloth, mat, cloth, mat, roving, mat, roving. One extra mat, roving at sheer. Three more mat, roving on stem, keel and stern.

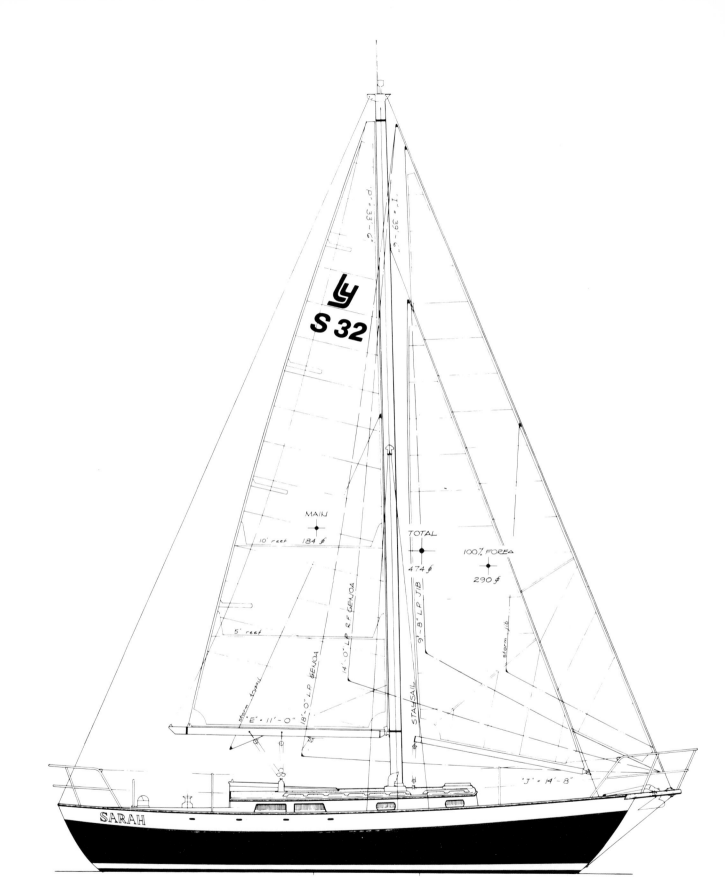

Sarah 32 — Chuck Paine

LOA - 31'5'' LWL - 25'10'' Beam-10'4'' Draft-4'9'' Displ.-11,100 lbs. Bal.- 5,100 lbs. Sail Area-473 sq. ft.

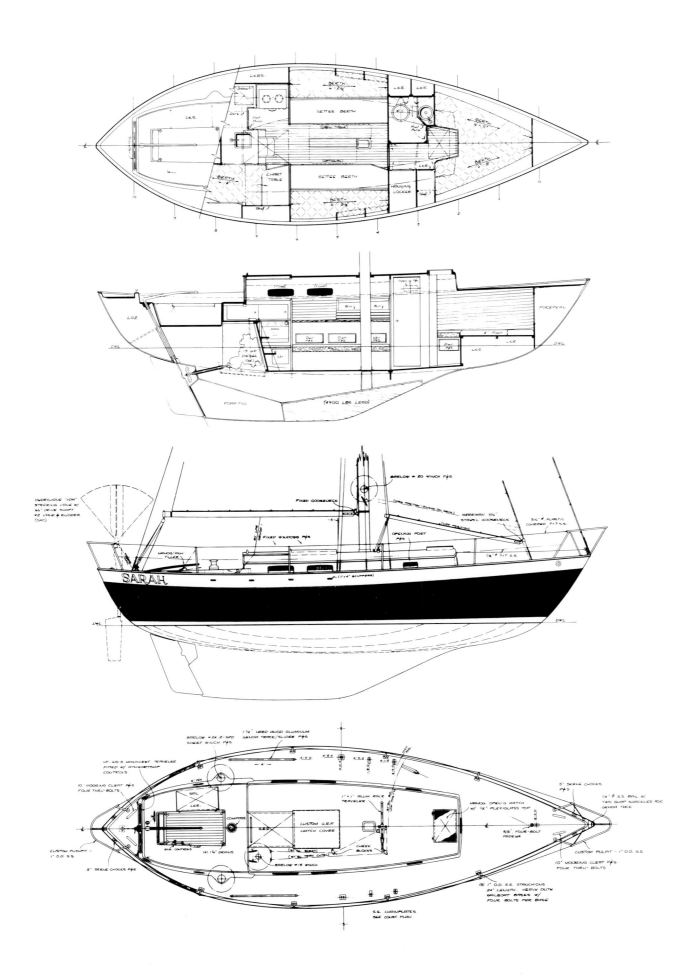

Sarah 32

Builder's Comments

Sarah is a fast, handsome, full-keel, double ended cutter designed by C. W. Paine. She is being produced in fibreglass on a semi-custom basis by Loomis Yachts of South Dartmouth, MA, and should be well received by those cruising yachtsmen desiring a responsive yet thoroughly capable offshore passagemaker.

Sarah is a very stable boat with her 46 per cent ballast/displacement ratio, and can carry her sail well in a breeze. Her displacement/length ratio: 287 and sail area/displacement ratio 15.2. Sarah's cutaway forefoot enables her to maneuver nimbly in tight quarters, but her full keel provides excellent tracking qualities. Notably, the keel joins the hull in a tight fairing radius which causes a marked advantage in pointing ability by increasing the area of more effective lift generating surface.

Her construction is sound: solid, hand-laid hull, external lead ballast, all teak interior with bulkheads bonded to both the hull and deck.

Construction details include things rarely, if ever, seen on today's production boats — a solid teak companionway hatch, a real tongue and groove teak and holly cabin sole, and even true tongue and groove paneled locker doors rather than the more common plywood backed framed doors.

Sarah's standard accommodation plan shows 7 berths. A revised interior presently in production has a permanent double berth offset to starboard in place of 'V' berths forward, a larger head, and a larger navigation area. The transom berth to starboard becomes shortened to a 5 foot seat (or child's berth) with a shelf outboard.

Since Loomis is a small yard which prefers to build fewer vessels of unusual quality, interior modifications can be readily accommodated.

Hull: Solid, hand layed fibreglass, tapering from 9 alternating laminates of 24 ounce woven roving and 1.5 ounce mat at the sheer to fifteen laminates on centreline. Deck: Hand layed with seven alternating laminates, incorporating ½ inch balsa core for stiffness (replaced by marine plywood or solid fibreglass wherever fittings are located), molded in non-skid. Ballast: One piece casting, externally mounted with nine ¾ inch SS keel bolts. Spars and Rigging: Cutter rig with bowsprit standard. Mast, boom, and staysail club of anodized aluminum by Metalmast Marine, with SS tangs and fittings. Jiffy reefing with winch on boom. Stays and shrouds of ¼ inch 1 x 19 SS wire with Merriman ½ inch integral toggle turnbuckles. Running rigging of Samson prestretched dacron. Bonding: Stays, shrouds, thruhulls, engine, and electrical system are grounded to keel for lightning and electrolysis protection. Interior: All hardwood, with extensive use of either teak or Honduras mahogany trim. Tongue and groove teak and holly cabin sole.

Spencer 34

Builder's Comments

The S-34 was designed with two goals in mind -to provide a racing machine on the exterior and comfortable accommodation and appointments for family cruising on the interior. The 11'2" beam and wide stern contribute to the interior roominess.

A fine entry is used for a smooth ride into a chop. The high freeboard provides for a dry sail and for good headroom in the interior. The solid lead fin keel and high aspect ratio spade rudder contribute to the excellent tracking, maneuverability, stability and control. The high ratio of ballast to displacement and very wide beam provide stiffness, especially after 18 to 20 degrees angle of heel. The keel has a 12 percent cord to length ratio with the maximum cord at 35 per cent of L to give maximum lift in all conditions. The reverse curve to the transom counter helps separation of water flow away from the hull to achieve minimum linar flow thickness for given waterline length.

The hull is hand laid-up as a one-piece unit using "Airex" PVC foam sandwich construction for maximum stiffness and for insulation of both sound and temperature. Bulkheads of plywood are glassed to the hull to contribute to transverse stiffness and to hull integrity. Longitudinal stiffness is achieved by glassing the various structural interior components to the hull. To minimize pitching in a seaway, the mass moments of inertia are reduced by keeping weight to a minimum at both ends of the boat.

The deck, cabin and cockpit are also hand laid-up alternating glass and woven roving and using a sandwich core of light-weight, end-grain Balsa for maximum stiffness and insulation. The hull/deck joint is achieved by means of successive layers of internal fibreglass bonds.

Ballast keel for the S-34 is solid lead which reduces the wetted surface and establishes a relatively low centre of gravity. It is a high aspect ratio external fin keel weighing approximately 4,750 pounds. Antimony is added to the lead to provide hardness and strength and to prevent 'creep.' The keel is attached to the hull with a close run of stainless steel bolts.

A balanced, reinforced fibreglass rudder with a high aspect ratio is integrated with a stainless steel rudder stock on Delrin bushings. The rudder has a 60 degree turning angle. The tiller is made of laminated mahogany and yellow cedar.

The mast is an elliptical aluminum alloy extrusion with an integral groove and stainless steel mast tangs. Standard rig has double spreaders. Standing rigging is stainless steel wire rope and turnbuckles; rod rigging optional. The boom is an aluminum alloy extrusion with integral groove.

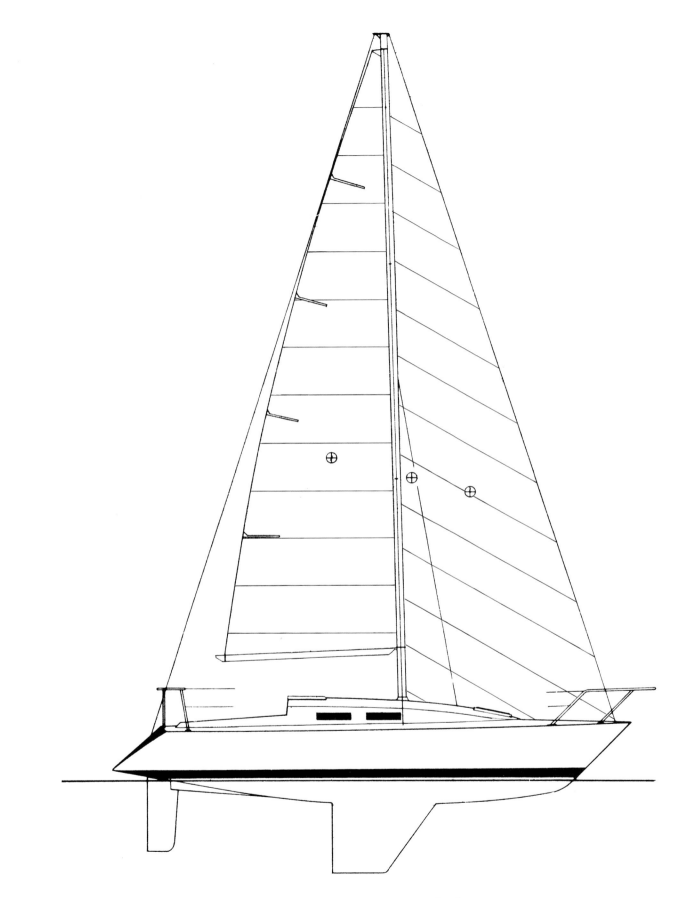

Spencer 34 — Vladimir Plavsic
LOA - 33'9'' LWL - 27'0'' Beam-11'2'' Draft-6'0'' Displ.-10,000 lbs. Bal.4,600 lbs. I-44.1 J-13.5

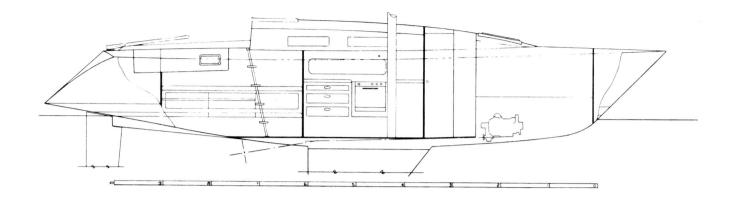

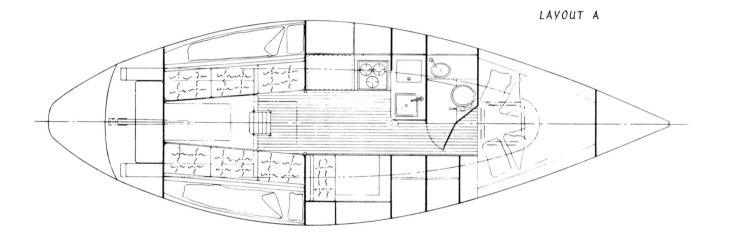

LAYOUT A

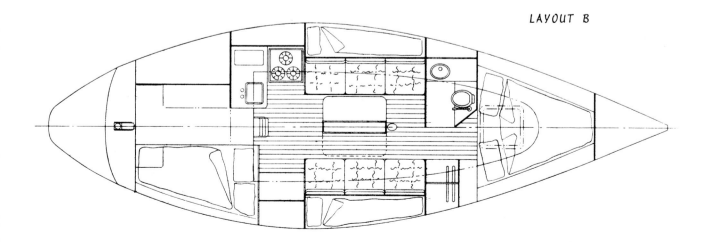

LAYOUT B

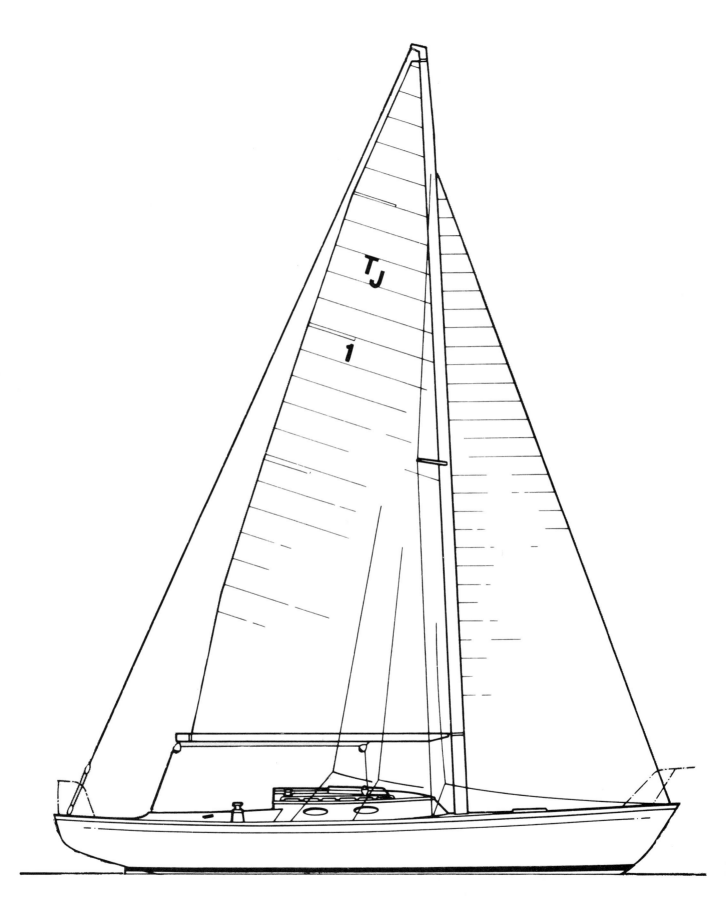

Tiffany Jayne — Paul Kotzebue
LOA - 33'10'' LWL - 25'0'' Beam - 8'0'' Draft-5'6'' Displ.-5,790 lbs. Bal.-2,900 lbs. Sail Area-451 sq. ft.

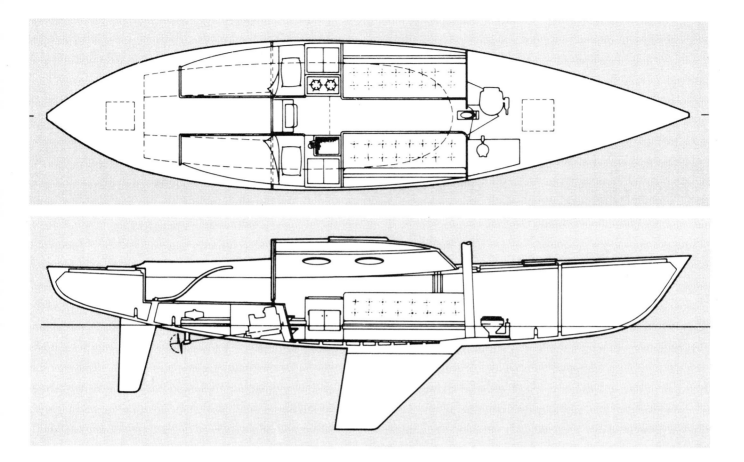

Tiffany Jayne

C & B Marine is now building Paul R. Kotzebue's *Tiffany Jayne* design in fibreglass and is offering bare fibreglass hulls and decks to those wishing to complete the boat themselves.

The owner of the first Tiffany Jayne has compiled a successful racing record on San Francisco Bay.

Home builders can buy keels, rudders and masts from C & B as well as hulls and decks. Each customer is entitled to a full set of plans and Paul Kotzebue is available to answer any questions concerning the construction of *Tiffany Jayne*.

Mr. Kotzebue is a graduate of Yacht Design Institute and has worked in the offices of Bruce Bingham, Bruce King, Dick Carter, Gary Mull and Arthur DeFever. Currently he is designing high performance cruising sailboats, traditional cruising sailboats, and also custom motor yachts, in association with Knight & Carver Marine Construction.

Passage 34 Pilot — Grahame H. Shannon
LOA - 34'3" LWL - 28'4" Beam - 11'6" Draft-5'6" Displ.-15,750 lbs. Bal.-6,500 lbs. Sail Area-623 sq. ft.

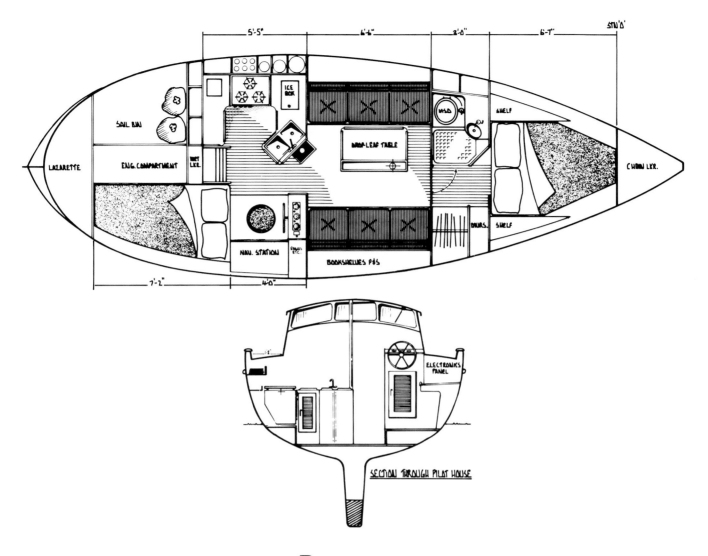

Passage 34

Builder's Comments

She was conceived as a cruising sailboat for a family of two to four people. The size was chosen with an eye to cost and easy handling. The hull combines the appearance of a traditional Scottish fishing vessel with a state-of-the-art modern underbody. The displacement is moderate and the sail area of the all inboard rig is ample for good performance in all wind conditions. Designed by Grahame H. Shannon, the underwater lines show a long NACA foil section keel carefully chosen for windward performance. The large rudder is mounted right aft on a substantial skeg which results in a very steady helm. Buttocks aft are kept as flat as possible to enhance downwind and reaching performance. The wide beam combined with a good ballast ratio results in a boat which stands up to her sail, even in a blow.

The designer's specifications are carefully followed to the letter. Heavy 24 oz. woven roving and 1.5 oz. mat are used throughout. The glass to resin ratio is strictly controlled and guaranteed to exceed 40 per cent. Hull thickness is ⅜ inch minimum, about ½ inch at the waterline and 1½ inches at the centre line. Additional reenforcing is applied in the keel and skeg areas as well as chainplate areas.

The rig is an easily handled cutter rig. The tall double spreader mast with inboard shrouds allows close sheeting to enhance windward performance. The Passage 34 will tack in 85⁰ or less.

The Passage 34 Pilot is the pilot house version of the Passage 34 plus the comfort of inside steering. The difference in weight and windage is minimal.

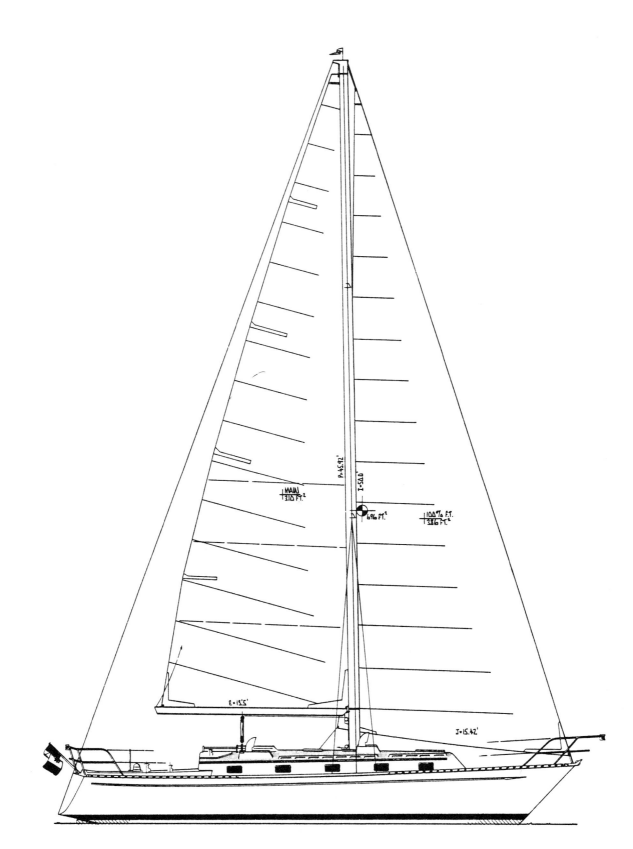

Reliance 37 — Robert H. Perry

LOA - 37'1" LWL - 30'0" Beam-11'4" Draft-6'3" Displ.-17,200 lbs. Bal.-5,500 lbs. Sail Area-696 sq. ft.

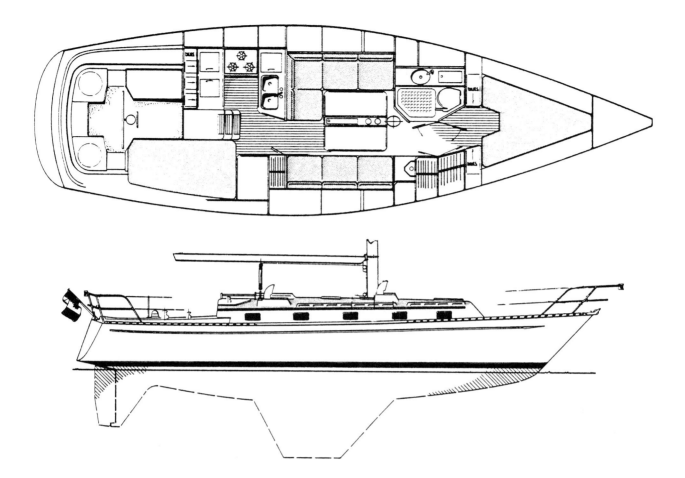

Reliance 37

Designer's Comments

From the beginning, it was apparent that my clients for the Reliance knew exactly what they wanted. This is, of course, the most advantageous way to begin a new design. It can save a lot of hours discussing design possibilities if the client has some experience with the type of boat he is looking for and primarily if the client has sailing experience and not simply "sale-ing" experience. The Reliance group is made up of two partners, one with extensive and recent offshore work to his credit and the other with both distance and closed course racing background. This to me is a magic combination and the Reliance 37 is a blend of off-shore features and performance features that reflects the varied sailing styles of the clients.

The hull shape of the Reliance is very up to date and features a low wetted surface shape with moderate beam. The beam is carried well aft for power and stability and the entry is quite fine and coupled with a low prismatic forward for speed on the wind. I purposefully restricted the beam on this design relative to many exaggerated modern designs for several reasons. Helm balance and "feel" can be controlled better with less beam and, of course, speed is enhanced. The bilges are firm for initial form stability and the ballast is carried low and on the outside to further add to the stability. I have used a slight bustle aft on the Reliance to help boost the speed off wind. Note I have used a large skeg and rudder combination with a proportionately small rudder. This will result in a boat with stable and positive steering characteristics and yet good maneuverability due to the location of the appendage.

The displacement to length ratio of this design is 281 with the boat in a full, loaded for cruising condition with a displacement of 17,200 pounds.

With offshore sailing in mind, several features of the interior were required. The quarter berth provides an excellent sea berth and it would be a simple option to add one or more pilot berths to the main cabin area, outboard of the settees. The galley is in the familiar U-shape and there are three separate hanging lockers. It is a misconception that the wind always blows "hard" offshore. In fact, the predominant breezes in areas other than the "trades" are usually below fifteen knots.

This was one of the key points on which I based my initial work with performance cruiser types. The Reliance 37 is designed to take advantage of light air and has a relatively tall rig with an (I) dimension of 50 feet and a (J) dimension of 15.42 feet. The mast is stayed with double spreaders and there are fore and aft lower shrouds. The sail area to displacement ratio for this rig is 16.59.

Construction of the Reliance will be to conservative offshore standards with safety factors large enough to insure peace of mind. The ballast is lead and outside the monocoque hull. While there is always debate relative to the merits and demerits of outside lead, you will never hear them in my office. We are very convinced that high quality cruising boats should have outside ballast. It is more expensive to fabricate and the attachment is labour intensive as each lead piece has to be faired to the molded hull, but it is the finest grounding shoe you can have, not to mention the advantages of a lower centre of gravity. Work on the hull plug and appendages show the Reliance to be built to very close tolerances and we look forward to seeing an excellent example of yacht construction.

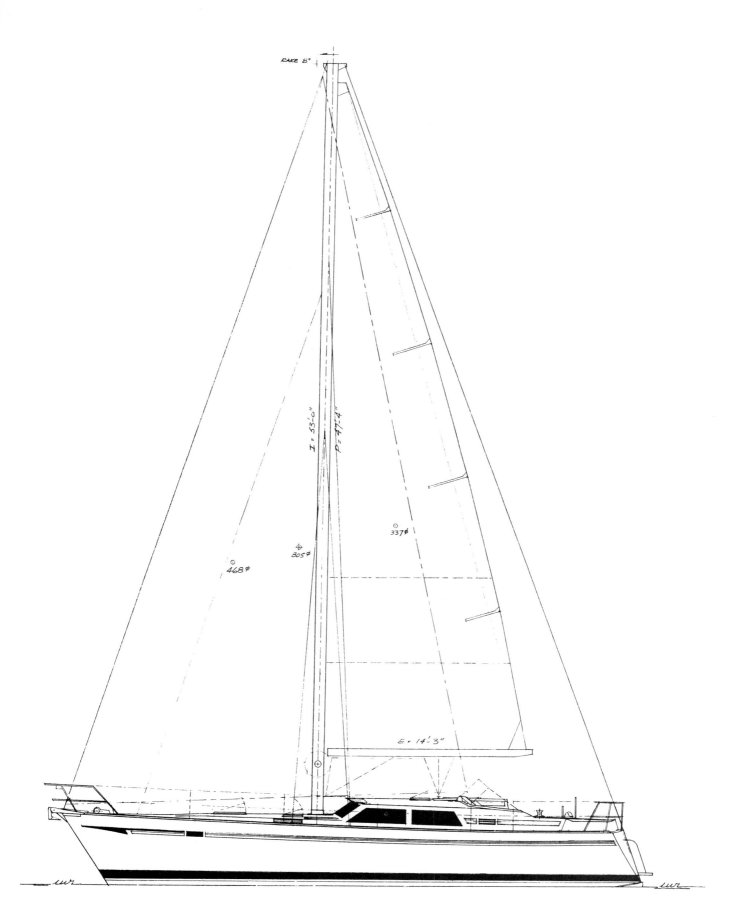

RAKE 8"

I = 53'-0"

P = 47'-4"

468#

305#

337#

E = 14'-3"

LWL

LWL

Sceptre 41 — Hein Driehuyzen
LOA - 41'0" LWL - 36'0" Beam - 12'8" Draft - 5'8" Displ.-21,495 Bal.-8,000 lbs. Sail Area-805 sq. ft.

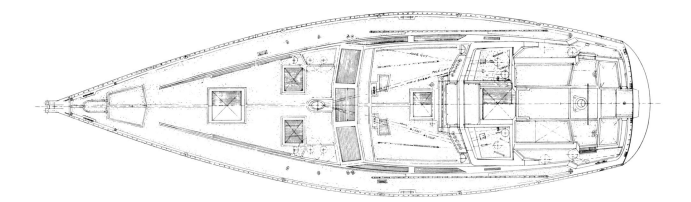

Sceptre 41

Designer's Comments

The design concept of the Sceptre 41 called for a boat with dual helm stations in which up to three couples can cruise comfortably even when wind and weather are not cooperating. Good performance under sail or power, easy handling characteristics and convenient access to a swimgrid for dinghy boarding, scuba diving and swimming complete the concept of the Sceptre 41.

The requirement for an inside helm station usually leads to a variation on the pilot-house theme, with inherently inadequate visibility from the cockpit (and not infrequently, from the inside helm station as well). As our concept of safe, enjoyable sailing does not include having to stand up at the helm to get a clear view forward, we designed the Sceptre 41 so that cockpit occupants would be afforded a clear view over the house while comfortably seated.

Good forward visibility from the inside helm station in the Sceptre 41 was achieved by providing an essentially flush foredeck, flat sheer, and positioning the interior helmsman close to the windshield. One of the major challenges in designing the Sceptre 41 involved finding aesthetically acceptable solutions to freeboard, cabin and cockpit relationships which in turn were complicated by the need to provide a coaming for a fixed safety glass dodger.

The interior arrangement provides privacy for two couples in widely separated fore and aft cabins. A third sleeping area between forward and main cabin offers reasonably private berths for two without infringing on activities in the main cabin.

The raised dining area with windows and ports all around the trunk cabin eliminates any feeling of being cut off from the outside. Although the temptation to put the galley forward near the mast was great, we decided to keep it aft adjacent to the companionway. Here the boat's motion in a seaway is least, the cook can communicate visually and vocally with cockpit and main cabin occupants, and libations en route to the cockpit are least likely to end up on the cabin floor.

To make access from cockpit to main cabin as easy as possible, we eliminated the bridgedeck. With only three steps between cockpit and cabin floor levels, access up or down is convenient, even with a grocery bag in each arm.

Enclosed quarterberth cabins tend to be somewhat claustrophobic. Due to the raised cockpit and provision for plenty of light and ventilation, this cabin in the Sceptre 41 feels spacious and airy.

On deck, the almost flush foredeck provides plenty of sunbathing space and allows obstruction-free movement for foredeck work.

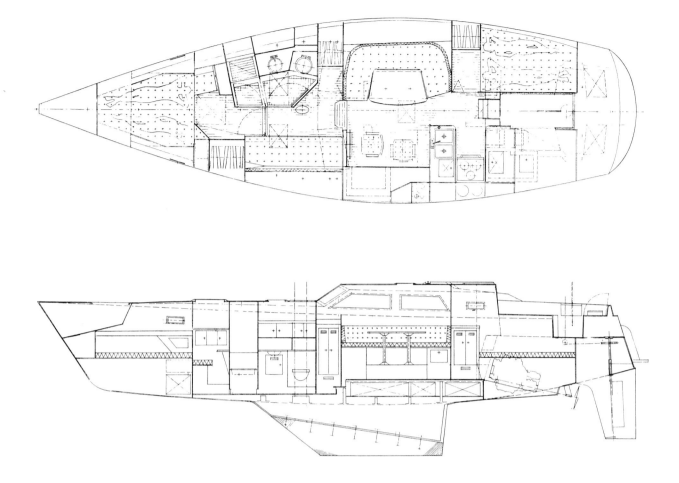

The T-shaped cockpit has an opening transom gate, giving access to swim ladder or swimgrid without having to climb over the transom combing.

The hull design combines a long waterline with moderate beam carried well aft, short overhangs, fine bow entry and flat run aft. The long waterline and moderate displacement results in a low (for cruising boats) displacement to length ratio of 203, indicative of an easily driven hull with good potential to exceed the theoretical hull speed of 8.1 knots.

To provide access to shallow waters, we designed the Sceptre 41 with a relatively shallow draft keel. The external lead keels aids stability due to its low centre of gravity and helps to protect against expensive repairs in case of accidental grounding. The generous keel plan is complimented by a relatively deep forefoot, ensuring good windward performance.

A skeg-hung rudder mounted well aft, in combination with balanced displacement distribution, provides excellent tracking and handling characteristics.

In keeping with the requirements for easy handling, we have kept the standard sail plan on the moderate side. As the hull is easily driven, this rig should give excellent performance in all but very light air.

The 50 h.p. diesel with 2:1 reduction swinging a 20'' x 13'' propeller provides ample power to cruise economically in the 7.5 knot range. Special attention was given to provide quiet, vibration-free motoring.

One of our fundamental design concepts is to provide easy access to all vital systems for routine maintenance or repair. Much consideration was given to make the engine, fuel, water, plumbing and electrical systems in the Sceptre 41 readily accessible.

Tyler 44 Corsair
LOA - 44'4" LWL - 31'1" Beam-12'11" Draft- 7'0" Displ.-21,000 lbs. Bal.-9,455 lbs. Sail Area-779 sq. ft.

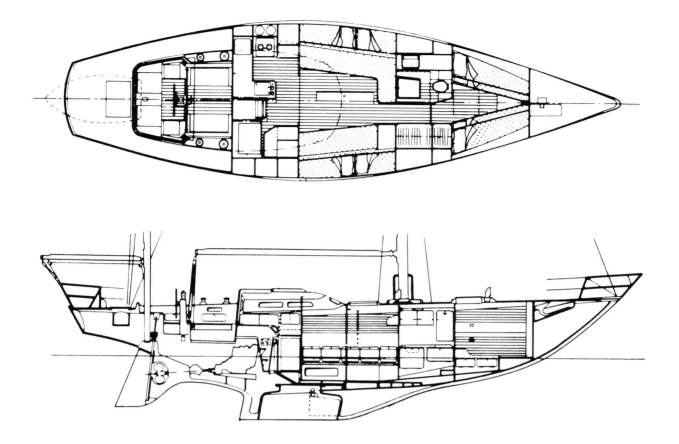

Tyler 44 Corsair

Builder's Comments

She is notable for her speed and easy handling characteristics. The aft cockpit permits a long clear uncluttered foredeck and allows the boat to be sailed by the minimum of crew. The spacious accommodation in the standard arrangement shown provides nine comfortable berths although many owners wish to incorporate their own ideas within this capacious hull.

All mouldings are produced from the highest quality glass reenforcement using an E-type chopped strand mat and woven rovings laminated with a marine grade polyester resin. As a precaution against the effects of osmosis and to facilitate inspection during manufacture, Tylers use only a clear gelcoat as a surface on the underwater area of the hull. Permanent colour to the remainder is achieved by adding pigment to the clear gelcoat resin.

Providing mouldings to our high specification greatly simplifies fitting out for the home builder or the professional yard.

Specification

G.R.P. hull with white pigmented gelcoat above the waterline and clear gelcoat below the waterline, with a white deck, coachroof and cockpit moulding securely bonded to the hull. The deck moulding which includes an anchor well hatch, incorporates general stiffening and reenforcement for genoa track, main sheet track and winches. Copper cockpit drain spigots are fitted. The mouldings include chain plate boxes. Eight half bulkheads of Lloyds approved marine ply are securely bonded to the hull and deck. Approximately 4,290 kg (9,455 pounds) cast iron ballast is fully encapsulated within the hull.

Flashings on the hull are ground off, gelled, rubbed down, polished and surface cosmetic work is carried out.

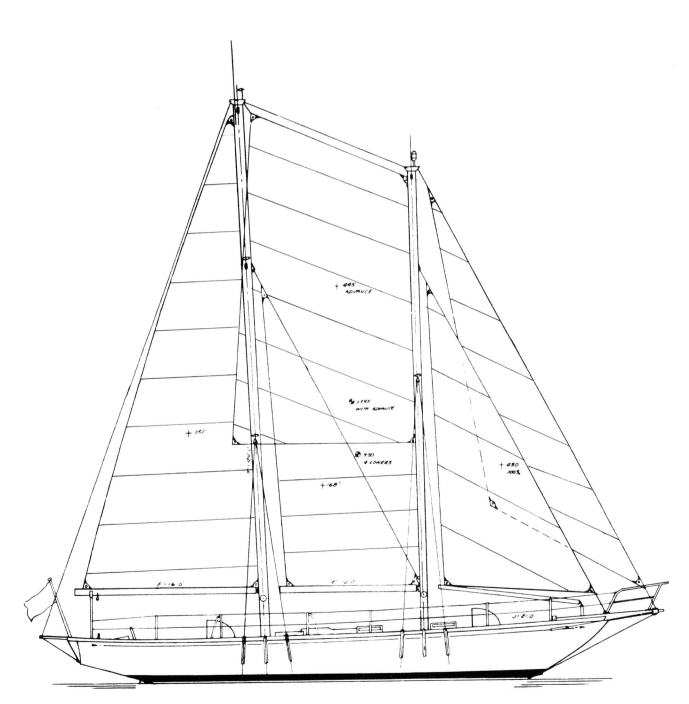

Worldcruiser 50 — Worldcruiser Yacht Co.
LOA - 50'0" LWL - 34'4" Beam-12'1" Draft-6'8" Displ.-32,000 lbs. Bal.-13,000 lbs. Sail Area-1,395 sq.ft.

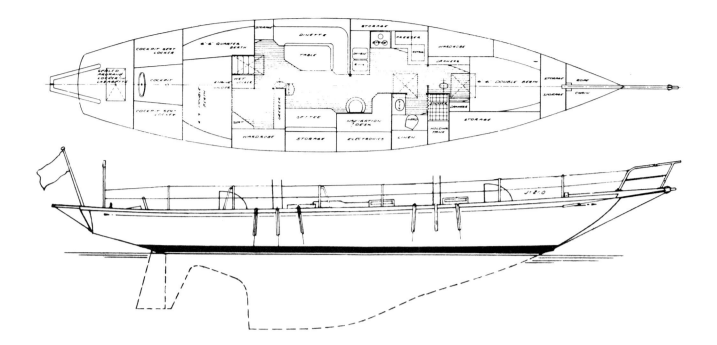

Worldcruiser 50

Builder's comments

For those sailors who have longed for the deck space only available from a flush deck sailboat, and for those who appreciate the convenience of a divided rig, Worldruiser is offering a 50 foot Schooner. This 50 foot has sweeping sheer, long overhangs, low freeboard, and a modern underbody; with wide, spacious decks broken only by skylights and scuttle hatches, and a small cockpit aft. Over half of the interior length has full headroom almost all the way out to the full beam of the boat as a bonus of the flush decks, resulting in the possibilities of a very spacious interior arrangement.

The modern staysail schooner rig offers all of the advantages of a split rig. She can be shortened down to an all inboard, self-tending rig of less than 600 square feet, or in light weather, with a large genoa or reacher and a gollywobbler between the masts that reaches to the deck, she carries over 2,000 square feet. With the balanced rig of a schooner, no appreciable weather helm is noticed, regardless of the sail combinations or wind strengths.

Trimming all of the sails on a schooner is vital to top performance, particularly when hard on the wind. It just takes a little practice to get the hang of it, and since all of the working sails are relatively small, they are easily trimmed.

Index

Builders

P. & M. Wordwide Yacht Builders P.O. Box 10281 Costa Mesa, CA 92627	Westsail 32 Aleutka 25	C.E. Ryder Corporation 47 Gooding Ave., Bristol, R.I. 02809 (Ryder Custom Yachts)	Quickstep 24 Alberg 23 Luders 27, 34 Gillmer 28, 31, 35, 39
Jarvis Newman Inc. Southwest Harbour Maine 04679	Pemaquid 25 Dictator 31	Sam L. Morse Co. 1626 Placentia Ave. Costa Mesa, CA 92627	Falmouth Cutter Bristol Channel Cutter
Cherubini Boat Co. 222 Wood St. Burlington, NJ 08016	Cherubini 44 Cherubini 48	Bill Lee Yachts Inc. 3700 B Hilltop Rd. Soquel, CA 95073	Santa Cruz 40 Santa Cruz 50
Able Marine Southwest Harbour Maine 04679	Whistler	Nordic Tugs P.O. Box 314 Woodinville, WA 98072	The Nordic Tug
Spencer Boats Ltd. 12391 Twigg Road Richmond, B. C. Canada V6V 1M5	Spencer 31 Spencer 34 Spencer 35 Spencer 1330	Marshall Marine Corp. Box P-266 Shipyard Lane South Dartmouth, MASS. 02748	Sandpiper Sanderling Marshall 22 Marshall 26
Sceptre Yachts Ltd. 1720 Cowley Cres. Richmond, B.C.	Sceptre 36 Sceptre 41	Apprenticeshop Maine Maritime Museum 375 Front Street Bath, Maine 04530	Assorted wooden rowing and sailing boats
Headway Woodworks & Marine Services No. 5 - 8100 River Rd. Richmond, B.C. V6X 3A3	Buzzards Bay 14	Duck Trap Woodworking R.F.D. 2, Cannon Road Lincolnville Beach Maine 04849	Assorted wooden rowing boats
Blue Water Boats P.O. Box 625 Woodinville, WA 98072	Ingrid	Vashon Boat Works P.O. Box Q Vashon, WA 98070	Quartermaster 8 Quartermaster 10
Whisstocks Woodbridge, Suffolk 1912 IBW, England	Naja	Raider Yachts Box 365 - A1. RD1 Medford, N.J. 08055	Raider 33
Alajuela Yacht Corp. 5181 Argosy Dr. Huntington Beach, CA 92649	Alajuela 33 Alajuela 38	Martin Yachts 8091 Capstan Way Richmond, B.C. Canada	Peterson 35 Martin 32
Pacific Seacraft Corp. 3301 South Susan St. Santa Ana, Calif. 92704	Flicka Crealock 37 Orion	Miller Marine 7659 N.E. Day Rd. Bainbridge Island, WA 98110	Jason
Morris Yachts Custom Boat Builders Clark Point Rd. Southwest Harbour, ME 04679	Frances Annie Leigh	A. & T. Marine P.O. Box 1423 Tacoma, WA 98401	Naja

Cecil M. Lange & Son Rt. 3, Box 202 Port Townsend, WA 98368	Cape George 31 Cape George 36 Cape George 40	Clark Custom Boats 3665 Hancock St. San Diego, CA 92110	Clark 31
Bristol Channel Cutter P.O. Box 91387 West Vancouver, B.C. V7V 3P1, Canada	Bristol Channel Cutter	Loomis Yachts Box 575 South Dartmouth, MA 02748	Sarah 31
New Orleans Marine, Inc. 3027 Tchoupitoulas St. New Orleans, LA 70115	Frers 40	Soverel Marine 2225 Idlewilde Rd. North Palm Beach, Fla 33410	Soverel 30 Soverel 36

Tyler Boats 730 Poke St. San Francisco, CA 94109	Corsair 44

Alvis Marine No. 5 - 12331 Bridgeport Rd. Richmond, B.C. V6V 1J4 Canada	Evetts 31

Other Boats

Hidden Harbour Boat Works 2029 Whitfield Park Ave. Sarasota, Fla 33580	Vancouver 36
Worldcruiser Yacht Co. 1300 Logan St. Costa Mesa, CA 92626	Worldcruiser 50
Jomarco 322 E. Dyer Rd. Santa Ana, CA 92707	Jomar 55 Westsail 28 Westsail 42
Coast Yacht Design Inc. No. 7 - 1285 Harwood St. Vancouver, B.C. V6E 1S5 Canada	Passage 34
Liberty Yacht Corp. Rt. 2, Box 548 Leland, N.C. 28451	Pied Piper 28
Menger Enterprises 77 Cedar St. P.O. Box 141 Babylon, N.Y. 11702	Oysterman 23
Nor'sea Yachts Laguna Hills, CA	Nor'sea 27
Seair Ltd. 20 Bewicke Ave. North Vancouver, B.C. V7M 3B5	vancouver 27
The Old Boathouse 2770 Westlake N. Seattle, WA. 98109	14' Whitebear Skiff
Rawson, Inc. 9001 151st Ave. S.E. P.O. Box 83 Redmond, WA 98052	Rawson 30
Reliance Yacht Corp. P.O. Box 46527, Stn. G. Vancouver, B.C. V6R 4G8 Canada	Reliance 37
Seamaster Yachts 3381 S.W. 11th Ave. Fort Lauderdale, Fla 33315	Seamaster 45
C & B Marine 1053 Seventeenth Ave. Santa Cruz, CA 95062	Tiffany Jayne
Yacht Constructors, Inc. 7030 N.E. 42nd Ave. Portland, Ore. 97218	Cascade 23, 27, 29 36 and 42

Photo Credits